THE SCOLE REPORT

An Account of an Investigation into the Genuineness of a range of Physical Phenomena associated with a Mediumistic Group in Norfolk, England

by

Montague Keen,

Arthur Ellison

and

David Fontana

Previously published as
Proceedings of the Society for Psychical Research
Volume 58 Part 220 November 1999

London
SOCIETY FOR PSYCHICAL RESEARCH
49 MARLOES ROAD W8 6LA

1st Edition 1999   ISBN 0 900677 06 6
2nd Edition 2011   ISBN 978 1 908421 00 5

Published by
Saturday Night Press Publications
England

www.snppbooks.com

Printed by
Lightning Source
www.lightningsource.com

*The photographs on the front and back cover are the original
colour versions of some of the plates included in the book.*

Appreciation

The Society for Psychical Research would like to express its appreciation to David J Ellis, of West Chiltington, West Sussex for all his typesetting work and the production of the First Edition and for supplying the files for the electronic production of the 2nd Edition.

The Society for Psychical Research would like to express its appreciation for the production of the 2nd Edition, including the new cover, by Ann Harrison of Saturday Night Press Publications, England.

CONTENTS

SYNOPSIS OF CHAPTERS

INTRODUCTION

Background and nature of present investigation – inauspicious precedents for inquiries into physical phenomena – significant differences attaching to Scole investigation – interlocking nature of evidence.

CHAPTER I: THE CONTEXT OF THE INVESTIGATION

The Scole Group and their background – Noah's Ark Society founded by Robin Foy – apparent integrity of Group members – origin and circumstances of investigation – hostile attitude of NAS to psychical research – role of PRISM – involvement of investigators – nature of evidence claimed – purported role of 'Spirit Team' – emphasis on physical phenomena – reported objectives of communicators – conditions in which sittings conducted – extensive ranges of reported phenomena – apports – films – abandonment of cameras – involvement with Polaroid products – experience of stage magician – experimental conditions – description of séance room – record-keeping: shorthand notes and tape transcripts – background of principal investigators.

CHAPTER II: THE SITTINGS

Duration and conduct of sittings – type of controls – procedure. First sitting (October 1995) – description of phenomena – personalities of main communicators – behaviour of lights – apparent intelligent animation – levitational behaviour of ping-pong ball – proposals for future sittings. Second sitting (December 1995) – experiment in raising lighting levels – infra-red photography: investigators' suggestions – communicators' reluctance to alter programme – sittings abroad.

CHAPTER III: THE PHENOMENA: LIGHTS AND TOUCHES

Catalogue of light phenomena – forms, shapes and touches – apparent semi-materialisation of multiple entities – physical effect on sitters – 'texture' of touched lights – accuracy of directional touches – apparent irrelevance of séance room location.

CHAPTER IV: THE PHENOMENA: PUZZLES AND HINTS

(Musical) inversion of melody noted – Lord Rayleigh drops in – the GOM reference – The Albemarle Club – F. W. H. Myers's sealed letter – Brother Ernest and Homer – Mrs Holland's recollection of *ProcSPR 21*, p.213 – Founders' Day, January 1882 – Selwyn Gardens and the Selwyn College Archway error – celestial mechanics and Professor Roy – technical responses to questions on mechanism of tape recordings. Discussion: how evidential?

CHAPTER XI: THE IBIZA EXPERIMENTAL EVIDENCE

Circumstances and location of sittings – details of séance room and observers – MK's role in Polaroid experiments – description of protocol – precautions against fraud – successful outcome – modifications in second sitting – link between oral and written message – tape recording experiments – checks to ensure microphone removed from machine – timing synchronised with comprehensive recorder – messages on tape – poor quality but evidential.

CHAPTER XII: THE RACHMANINOFF RECORDING

Final sitting – procedure for experiment – two synchronised tapes – DF's control over microphoneless tape – musical message promised for MK – Rachmaninoff's 2nd Piano Concerto recognised – voiceover unclear – no recording apparent of any other sounds cf. Foy's synchronised tape.

CHAPTER XIII: THE VIDEO FILM

Group's closure of investigatory sittings pending new experiments – investigators' appeal for replication – concentration on psychomanteum-type experiments with video film in light – Hans Schaer's report of successful outcome.

CHAPTER XIV: AUTHENTICITY: PRELIMINARY DOUBTS EXAMINED

Genuineness of communicators – investigators' failure to insist on book tests, etc. – why no permanent paranormal object? – why no maths problem solutions? – why such trivial pursuits? – absence of infra-red equipment suspect – why no body searches? – why no physical constraints? – were mediums really entranced? – why no professional illusionists as investigators? – why no uniformity of procedure for films?

CHAPTER XV: THE POSSIBILITIES OF FRAUD

Unique features examined – implications of fraud hypothesis – value and weaknesses of testimony – differentiation from ectoplasmic phenomena – limitations imposed on investigators – history of criticism regardless of extent of precautions – all or nothing option for fake hypothesis – absence of apparent motivation for fraud – extensive implications of fraud theory – wide range of expertise required – deception vs. authenticity: general considerations – weakness of criticisms based on neglect of entirety of evidence.

CONCLUSION

Evidence pointing to survival: inconclusive – Ruth film: in public domain – the 'Alan' box controversy – why no replication efforts? – would spirit scientists disregard standard protocol? – why were investigators' proposals unacceptable? – residual puzzles – absence of motive for deception – positive features suggesting integrity – formidable array of qualities needed for deception – risks of discovery – physical feats required for some phenomena – presumptions of determined critic.

LIST OF PLATES

(at pages 109 to 124)

PREFACE TO THE NEW EDITION

This new edition of *The Scole Report* is a complete and unabridged copy of the *Proceedings* originally issued by the Society for Psychical Research in 1999. The decision to re-publish the report is a response to the continuing interest in the events described, but should not be considered as an endorsement of any collective view as to whether the observed phenomena recorded were genuine or otherwise. Since its foundation in 1882, the Society has held no corporate opinion as to whether phenomena termed psychical or paranormal occur. Rather the Society seeks to encourage and promote the scientific investigation of such phenomena, with a view to understanding their nature and mechanism, howsoever they may be caused, including the possibility of paranormal causation. *The Scole Report* is an important example of practical research in this field and illustrates the difficulty and complexity involved in assessing claims of paranormality, as well as demonstrating the degree of dedication and commitment required by investigators.

The Scole Report sets out the research and conclusions of the three authors, Professor David Fontana, Professor Arthur Ellison and Montague Keen arising from their direct investigation into claims of paranormal phenomena occurring at séances held by a group of spiritualists meeting in a private house at the village of Scole in Norfolk. Besides the authors themselves, a number of other members of the Society for Psychical Research attended these sittings and witnessed what were claimed to be examples of mediumistic phenomena including the appearance of strange lights, the movement and materialisation of objects, anomalous images appearing on film and the transmission of messages claimed as emanating from deceased individuals.

Members of the Scole group attributed these phenomena to the intervention of discarnate intelligences, perhaps the spirits of deceased individuals. Claims of such phenomena have been made and investigated many times before, but what was unusual about the Scole phenomena is that unlike on many occasions in the past, a number of observers present came away impressed by what they had witnessed and satisfied that no normal explanation could be offered for what had occurred. In short, many believed they had witnessed events which were genuinely inexplicable and which must be paranormal in nature. The three authors of the *Report* worked more closely with the group and were present at more sittings than anyone else. Each was an experienced investigator of claims of the paranormal in his own right. Individually and jointly, they were satisfied that paranormal effects arising from the survival of human personalities after death were the most likely explanation for what they had observed.

Hardly surprisingly, such claims and their expression were met with scepticism and indeed disbelief from many quarters, including from some within psychical research. One of the main reasons for this scepticism was the history of spiritualism itself and the suspicion that many, if not all effects had been achieved by fraud and misperception or occurred only in conditions where fraud could not be conclusively eliminated. Whilst many researchers have been open to the possibility of psi, many have shared the opinion of a former President of the Society for Psychical Research Professor C.D. Broad who remarked that the fact that séance room phenomena cannot occur in the presence of equipment "may or may not be a significant fact, but it is certainly an unfortunate one" (Broad, 1937). This has resulted in many researchers abandoning any hope of establishing definitive proof of the reality of such phenomena. Scepticism concerning physical mediumship increased after 1945, with the apparent disappearance of many dramatic séance room effects produced by earlier generations of mediums, coinciding with refinements in infra-red photography that better enabled the detection of trickery in the dark.

Just why such spectacular effects as materialisation of apparitions, the production of ectoplasm from the bodies of mediums and the levitation of objects should decline just as the means to detect and record them improved is unclear, but many investigators took this as evidence that such effects had been fraudulently produced all along, and that mediums could no longer perpetrate frauds without risking detection and exposure. Others believed complex psychological mechanisms might be at work but did not exclude the possibility of psi-effects (Brookes -Smith, 1974).

As a result, although particular researchers might from time to time encounter apparently inexplicable incidents in the context of individual sittings with mediums, there was a general feeling that the great days of physical phenomena at séances were well and truly over and that the subject had become principally one for the historian. Such claims of physical phenomena as were still being reported were often mired in controversy even amongst spiritualists themselves (Lustig, 1978). This apparent decline in phenomena even led some to speculate that certain psi phenomena might occur only for a certain period of time and then decay, and that many aspects of physical mediumship including the materialisations of spirit forms or physical objects, known as 'apports' fell into that category.

It was against this background that the Scole phenomena emerged and were investigated so far as conditions permitted. The three authors of this report set out their extensive observations on sessions held with the group. Others who attended were equally impressed. Observers also included skilled conjurors, whom some critics have argued are the best persons to be deployed in investigating alleged paranormal effects. Indeed, at least one, James Webster, came away convinced that he had witnessed phenomena for which he had no explanation (Fontana & Keen, 2006). But sceptics remained, and for that reason, various reservations and criticisms of the investigation and its conclusions, including contributions written by Professor Donald West, Dr Alan Gauld, the late Tony Cornell, Dr John Beloff and others with experience in investigating cases outside laboratory conditions were incorporated in the original *Scole Report* and are reproduced here. The responses of the three principal authors to these critiques are also included.

Few people reading the records of these experiments and observations for the first time – especially the complete original accounts can feel other than a sense of bewilderment. In ordinary life we know that these things do not appear to happen, and it is hard to bring our minds to accept that they do. Against this we have the testimony of serious and experienced researchers present at the time who were convinced by what they had witnessed. What we should avoid is any *a priori* assumption that things do not take place simply because we believe they cannot. Certainly, both in science and other disciplines where evidence is weighed and assessed such as history and law, there have been many complete and dramatic revisions and reversals of what were once considered secure conclusions and verdicts.

There are four possibilities which suggest themselves as regards the evidence set out in *The Scole Report*.

Firstly, that the principal report was a fraud by the authors themselves. This is rejected by anyone who knew directly or indirectly the authors and their work. Nor has it been advanced by anyone as a critique, since their deaths. Arthur Ellison died in 2000, Monty Keen in 2004 and David Fontana in 2010. All three maintained that they believed in the reality of the phenomena described and they issued no recantations or retractions. However, had any such evidence been produced I feel sure they would have been the first to do so.

The second hypothesis is that *The Scole Report* is the work of honest investigators who were duped by a complicated conspiracy. Effectively, this idea supposes that the organisers of the Scole circle engaged in fraudulent activity which, had they been charging the public to attend, would have exposed them to the risk of prosecution under the Fraudulent Mediums Act 1951. The authors challenge this suggestion, describing the protocols and tests which they applied to exclude fraud and deception and their reasons why they did not consider it to be an explanation. Many claims of spiritualist phenomena have collapsed with exposure of fraud, either unconscious or deliberate on the part of the medium but with the Scole phenomena this has not occurred. However, if the authors were victims of fraud in whole or in part and they were wrong, then it is a legitimate enquiry to identify why they went wrong and how they came to err. But the same principle should apply to science, being a self-correcting discipline, and if existing scientific models cannot explain a phenomenon, then the models will need to be revised.

This ties in with the third possibility that the events are true and that the authors were correct in advancing a spiritualistic hypothesis to explain them. If so, the phenomena at Scole may be considered as evidence of the survival of the human personality after bodily death and dissolution i.e. they establish that once living individuals are still able to achieve effects in the material world around us and interact with the living. As Raynor C. Johnson wrote in 1953 there can be no more important philosophical question to be answered than "Do the dead live?" (Johnson, 1953, 1957). If such a question could be answered affirmatively with irrefutable proof this would be the most significant discovery in human history carrying profound implications for every living individual and every society throughout the world.

A fourth possibility is that some or all of the phenomena did take place as described, including paranormal phenomena, but that the explanation adopted by the three authors, the sitters and some observers is the wrong one, and there is as yet no complete hypothesis that explains them. The late Maurice Grosse also sets down a short commentary where he stated that certain of the Scole phenomena reminded him of poltergeist manifestations. Similarly, could there be a relationship with the phenomena reported in Toronto during the 1970s with the so-called 'Philip' Group where a group of experimenters succeeded in creating psychokinetic effects which were attributed to an imaginary discarnate personality (Owen & Sparrow, 1976)?

The determination of which of these explanations to claims of such phenomena is the task of psychical research and the re-publication of the *The Scole Report* is a valuable contribution to work in this field.

Given that the events described at Scole occurred less than two decades ago, there is scope for further investigation and enquiry into them. Despite the deaths of the three authors opportunities still exist to investigate events behind *The Scole Report*, to collect further evidence, and to review the testimony of the surviving witnesses. Opportunities still exist to trace other witnesses and to seek out new data which may confirm or undermine the status of the *Report*.

Furthermore, *The Scole Report* is a valuable document for the wider study of alleged cases of spontaneous physical phenomena. If even 99% of the supposed data were proved fraudulent the 1% which was true would remain of profound importance for our understanding of the kind of world we live in.

The hope of psychical researchers is that analysis of cumulative data will yield deeper understanding of the factors at work or generate deeper theoretical insights, and *The Scole Report* provides potentially significant data both for the assessment of earlier cases, and for any cases that may arise in the future. Lengthy as *The Scole Report* is, there are many more questions and aspects of physical phenomena to be addressed and explored, including the dynamics of the phenomena under scrutiny in terms of the influence of the medium on the group and the influence of the group on the medium, and the extent to which phenomena may be shaped by the beliefs and demands of investigators. Perhaps, most crucially, *The Scole Report* may provide a stimulus and inspiration for experimental research in this field. A continual problem with groups producing physical phenomena is that their efforts eventually seem to reach a standstill on how the alleged phenomena may be further tested or examined. Accordingly, the hope is expressed that the republication of *The Scole Report* may act as a stimulus for creative and original thinking on as to how future cases may be treated and new experiments designed. There may well be wholly new directions in which research can be taken, as demonstrated in the analysis of acoustic signatures of anomalous raps recorded by investigators (Colvin, 2010).

Perhaps most significantly, it appears the Scole phenomena did not prove merely a one-off example for investigators of séance phenomena; rather it seems to have marked something of a revival in physical phenomena which continues this day. Since the *Report* was published a number of other experimental circles have been established which claim to have produced genuine paranormal phenomena and which have also been ascribed to the intervention of discarnate and spiritual agencies. Such circles have met and are meeting both in Britain and abroad at the time of writing and pose a challenge for investigators.

Certainly, the continuation of psychical research was the goal of each of the authors and it is hoped that the republication of *The Scole Report* provides just such a stimulus, providing valuable lessons for research in the future.

ALAN MURDIE LL.B, BARRISTER,
Chair, Spontaneous Cases Committee of the SPR.

REFERENCES

Broad, C.D.(1937) *The Mind and its place in Nature*. London: Kegan Paul.
Brookes-Smith, C. (1974) *JSPR 47*, 532-538.
Colvin, B. (2010) The Acoustic Properties of Unexplained Rapping Sounds. *JSPR 74,* 65-93.

Keen, M. and Fontana, D. (2006) The Scole Report Five Years Later. *Paranormal Review 37*, 20.

Johnson, R.C. (1953) *The Imprisoned Splendour*. London: Hodder & Stoughton.

Johnson, R.C. (1957) *Nurslings of Immortality*. London: Hodder & Stoughton.

Lustig, R. (1978, 28 January) Fraud charges rock world of the spirits. *The Observer*.

Owen, I. and Sparrow, M. (1976) *Conjuring up Philip: an adventure in psychokinesis*. Canada: Fitzhenry & Whiteside.

The following are all published by the Society for Psychical Research www.spr.ac.uk

JSPR Journal of the Society for Psychical Research

ProcSPR Proceedings of the Society for Psychical Research

Paranormal Review

EDITOR'S FOREWORD

When I first joined the Society in the 1960s, paraphysical phenomena of a dramatic kind already seemed to belong to a past era. The Schneider brothers, Franek Kluski, Eva Carrière, Helen Duncan and 'Margery' (Mina Crandon), and others of that ilk, all seemed to belong to a past era that would never recur. The emergence of the Scole Group in the late 1990s, however, has once again put such paraphysical phenomena back on the agenda. I only once attended a sitting at Scole but, as the Report testifies, less happened on that occasion than at any other sitting – thereby confirming my reputation as a psi-negative influence!

Be that as it may, this Report presents a formidable challenge, whatever one's presuppositions. For, either Robin Foy and his friends are consummate hoaxers – for which I may add I know no such evidence, or we are here confronted with an array of phenomena unprecedented in the recent history of psychical research. Some will ask whether the Scole Report strengthens the case for personal survival as the donors of the Tate Bequest, which generously helped to fund this investigation, might hope? Certainly, it looks here as if the spirit of our founder, Frederic Myers, was trying to tell us something (see Chapter V). However, it is, in the end, a matter of interpretation whether such messages emanate from a deceased individual or from some 'cosmic reservoir' where all past events may be stored. The authors decline to take a stand on this issue and leave it to the reader to make up his or her own mind.

The more fantastic the phenomena, the more will critics seek to demolish them. We may expect, therefore, a vigorous backlash from determined critics. Before authorizing this publication under SPR auspices, I put it to Robin Foy that we needed just one more sitting at a place of the Society's choosing and under conditions approved by it in advance, including the use of infra-red photography. Alas, the 'Team' (as he calls it – those on the 'other side') had decreed that the investigation had come to an end and so would not authorize another sitting under any circumstances. That being the case, we had either to veto the Report appearing under SPR auspices, despite the international interest it had already aroused, or accept the Report as it stands. In the event, we decided, for good or ill, that the latter was our better course. However, not all critics will agree, so although this report has the backing of our two referees, we decided that the critics be allowed to air their misgivings alongside the Report, together with the authors' reply.

6 Blacket Place   JOHN BELOFF
Edinburgh EH9 1RL

ABBREVIATIONS OF PERSONS MENTIONED

The following list of persons or entities appearing in quoted extracts is alphabetically arranged on the basis of first names. Members of the Scole Group are in bold face. The 'communicators', whether via the two mediums Alan and Diana or by 'direct voice', are italicised.

Communicators	Scole Group	Investigators	Other Sitters	Full Names
		AE		Prof. Arthur Ellison
			AG	Dr Alan Gauld
	Alan			**(medium)**
Albert				
			AR	Prof. Archie Roy
			BC	Prof. Bernard Carr
	BH			**Bernetta Head**
		DF		Prof. David Fontana
	Diana			**(medium)**
			DW	Prof. Donald West
EB				*"Emily Bradshaw"*
Edwin				
		HS		Dr Hans Schaer
			IGG	Prof. Ivor Grattan-Guinness
		IS		Ms Ingrid Slack
John				*"John Paxton"*
Joseph				
	KB			**Ken Britten**
		KS		Karin Schnittger
Lawrence				*"Reginald Lawrence"*
Manu				
		MK		Montague Keen
Patrick				*"Patrick McKenna"*
Raji				
	RF			**Robin Foy**
		RN		Ralph Noyes
			RS	Dr Rupert Sheldrake
	SF			**Mrs Sandra Foy**
SS				*"Spirit Scientist"*
		WS		Walter Schnittger
			YK	Yvonne Koch

ABSTRACT

This report is the outcome of a three-year investigation of a Group claiming to receive both messages and materialised or physical objects from a number of collaborative spirit communicators. It has been conducted principally by three senior members of the Society for Psychical Research[1]. In the course of over 20 sittings the investigators were unable to detect any direct indication of fraud or deception, and encountered evidence favouring the hypothesis of intelligent forces, whether originating in the human psyche or from discarnate sources, able to influence material objects, and to convey associated meaningful messages, both visual and aural.

INTRODUCTION

The investigation of physical phenomena associated with mediumship formed an important part of the Society's work and publications during its first sixty years; but not since the 1930s has there been any substantial evidence of séance-room phenomena which has merited the study and commanded the respect of those dedicated to the disinterested and thorough examination of these, perhaps the most controversial of all, aspects of the paranormal.

The present study, by three experienced investigators and long-standing SPR members, is an essentially descriptive and analytical approach in accordance with the Society's objective scientific traditions, and has no connection with any religious or spiritualistic organisation or belief. It is innovatory in several respects. It is, we believe, the first study to be made into the activities of a number of persons acting as a team; the first to link alleged oral communications via trance mediums with a variety of photographic, visual, auditory, tactile and tangible phenomena, and the first to investigate a range of tangible physical effects apparently not associated with ectoplasm, and which are susceptible to public inspection outside the séance room. The report is lengthy, not only because of the variety and abundance of matter to be described and evaluated, but because the potential implications of the evidence demand a careful assessment of the case for and against deception.

Hitherto, physical mediumship has been associated with a wide variety of questionable phenomena, ranging from ouija-board messages,

---

[1] Readers must be reminded at the outset that, although the SPR publishes and seeks to fund reputable research into psychic matters, in common with most scientific bodies it holds no corporate views. In consequence, all the material it publishes remains the responsibility of the authors concerned, and must not be regarded as being endorsed by the Society or even as necessarily representing the opinions or convictions of the Society's Council or membership. Thus, although the present investigation was conducted by three senior SPR figures, we were acting throughout in our individual capacities.

raps, table-movements, slate writing and trumpet-blowing, to the still more dramatic manifestations of purported levitation, transfiguration of mediums and the production of ectoplasmic materialised forms or figures. Mired in controversy, by no means all of it governed by the principles of dispassionate scientific inquiry, it has a history of research starting with the investigation by Sir William Crookes and Lord Dunraven in the 1860s and 1870s into the mediumship of D.D. Home, through the era of Eusapia Palladino, Mina Crandon, Franek Kluski and the Schneider brothers, to that of Helen Duncan in the 1940s. Controversy over the manner in which these mediums were investigated, and disputes about the reliability of the evidence, have continued to this day, despite the fact that many materialising phenomena were apparently produced in sufficient light to enable observers to see what was going on, and regardless of hand- and foot-holding precautions, or even the installation of electronic devices to guard against fraud. No matter how elaborate the equipment, thorough the precautions, intrusive the body-searches, vigilant the observers or impressive the witness testimony, it cannot be said that earlier examples of physical phenomena have commanded any significant degree of acceptance by the scientific community of the past, let alone those who now venture afresh into this corpse-strewn battlefield.

This would appear an unpromising augury for the present investigation were it not for the several novel features mentioned, notably the manner in which the evidential material, both physical and non-physical, is allegedly linked to the concerted plan by an intelligent agency (whether human or discarnate we leave aside at this time) to provide further evidence of the post-mortem survival of human personality. In the past, one of the ways of achieving a similar objective, ostensibly devised by deceased founder-members of our Society, was to provide evidential information by communicating messages immune to conscious fabrication by any individual medium, and in forms aimed at strengthening the case for survival by weakening the hypothesis that all linked messages and physical effects derive from the living human psyche. This collection of evidential messages, known as the Cross-Correspondences, was transmitted from 1901 until the 1930s. In due course we evaluate the suggestion that the present evidence may be connected to that prolonged and complicated effort to demonstrate that we survive bodily death.

This, then, is not a simple report on a single experiment or a series of related ones. In examining the supposed uniqueness and importance of a wide variety of phenomena produced under conditions aimed as far as proved possible at precluding deception, we have deliberately concentrated on evidence which is least dependent on subjective experience. It would be folly, however, to disregard phenomena not associated with tangible material, especially when such accounts have been confirmed and even amplified by many other apparently trustworthy witnesses, and when our own experiences have been accompanied by tape recordings whose transcripts reveal our comments as we were witnessing or experiencing the phenomena, thereby ensuring that our testimony was not solely dependent on recollection, and so minimising the dangers of exaggeration or misperception.

In addition to the admixture of evidence derived from oral mediumistic communications which we witnessed as investigators, and which are linked to various physical effects and material phenomena, there are a great many statements from others who have witnessed, and in many cases recorded, accounts of phenomena which appear to them to defy normal explanation. Here is another distinctive feature: most investigations into the claims of physical mediums have in the past been simply exercises in detecting or preventing deception by them through covert movement, collaboration with a confederate, the employment of secreted conjuring devices, etc. While such detection or prevention was clearly a principal objective of our investigation, it was not germane to the lengthy discourses we engaged in with purported communicators speaking through the mediums, or on occasions by apparent 'direct voice', which often claimed to provide evidence relating to the nature and interpretation of the physical phenomena.

In the following pages we describe the circumstances which prompted us to undertake this investigation; the origin, personnel and functions of the Group we investigated; our relationship with them, and the manner in which the investigation was conducted, together with the types of evidence we experienced, received or examined. We shall also note the testimony of many other witnesses; we actively collaborated with two of these (Dr Hans Schaer and Walter Schnittger) and describe them as co-investigators. In addition, and in particular, we propose to assess the case for and against fraud in relation to all the phenomena in the light both of the various measures taken to detect or preclude deception, and of the restrictions or limitations under which, often against our wishes, we frequently worked. We plan to examine the extent to which these constraints may be considered to vitiate the conclusions of our investigation. We aim to set the material in its historical perspective and, in addition to the possibilities of fraud, to evaluate it in the light of two major competing hypotheses. One comprises a range of theories broadly classified as 'super-psi', which would seek to account for the phenomena described by attributing to the individual or the collective subliminal minds of the mediums a wide range of co-ordinated paranormal powers. The other postulates the post-mortem survival of human consciousness.

However, we do not feel it appropriate to examine in the light of our discussions with the presumed communicators the nature and circumstances of a supposed afterlife. This would unduly extend the length of this Report and detract from its main function: that is the presentation and analysis of evidence. It was our hope and expectation that further sittings with the group who were the subject of our investigations would have allowed a more structured dialogue to take place so that later reports could examine these profound matters. But, as we shall show, this was not to be.

Throughout, we follow the customary practice of not littering the text with the cautionary qualifications of 'reputed', 'alleged', 'purported', 'supposed', 'apparent', etc. before such terms as spirit guides, lights, spirit Team, communicators, spirit advisers, and so on. However, these qualifications must be taken to apply in all cases. Likewise we have abstained from a liberal sprinkling of quotation marks when referring to spirit communicators by name, although for ease of reading we do italicise the names or pseudonyms of all spirit communicators when quoting them.

The reader must be left to decide whether, if deception is ruled out as an explanation for at least some of the communications and phenomena, there emerges an arguable case for suggesting the existence of a group of spirit entities acting through a number of collaborating communicators. Although a discussion of their apparent objectives may push us beyond the boundaries of this inquiry, this suggestion is consistent with the fact that earlier apparent attempts by discarnate personalities to provide firm evidence for survival have failed to sweep away all doubts. This failure falls into perspective when we note the introduction to the Countess of Balfour's classic analysis (Balfour, 1960) of A. J. Balfour's tragic lost love in the Palm Sunday Case, where she writes of the Cross-Correspondences:–

> It is not an ordinary case of evidence for survival; it was claimed that an experiment was being made by a whole group of 'communicators'. They were engaged in an attempt to produce evidence for their existence as a group through the automatic writings of several mediums at the same time but in different places. The object apparently was to refer to facts which would go beyond the normal knowledge of the automatists concerned, and which also when taken in their entirety were extremely unlikely to have been in any single mind.

The Palm Sunday Case was one of the last and perhaps the most celebrated of the Cross-Correspondences. Along with the huge volume of other evidence which began with the deaths of F. W. H. Myers and Henry Sidgwick around the turn of the century, its failure to produce final conviction was suggested to us as the ostensible motive which, on the hypothesis of survival, may have bestirred the personalities apparently communicating in the present investigation. Employing new technology in and for a vastly changed world, and using physical means rather than complex literary puzzles to act as their chief advocates, they appeared, if genuine, to be making an effort to overcome the formidable philosophical and psychological barriers to general acceptance of the concept of survival.

The evidence now provided falls uneasily into the following categories – uneasily because of its interlocking nature. First there are extensive, recorded oral communications from different entities normally through two trance mediums or, less frequently, by apparent direct transmission ('independent voice'). These are linked with comments on, explanations about, predictions concerning, or discussions on the meaning or significance of various physical phenomena. Then there are the extensive exhibitions of spirit lights, with which are linked apparent materialisations and touches by spirit hands or tangible substances. Next there is a range of apports and psychokinetic phenomena. These include visible movement and levitation of objects sometimes with and sometimes in the absence of spirit light and tactile accompaniments. Then there is what for the non-participant may be the most puzzling phenomenon: the creation of images and messages on unexposed, unopened rolls of photographic film, and the recording on a tape recorder from which the microphone had been removed of what were claimed to be directly transmitted spirit voices and music. Finally we record the circumstances in which an image appeared on a video film, albeit under conditions which fall short of ideal.

While each of these features is described and evaluated, we devote particular attention to those which are susceptible to independent examination, notably the film strips, especially those whose production, examination and interpretation are linked with oral messages and discussions between ourselves and the spirit communicators. However, we have described in some detail the demonstrations of light and associated phenomena, and exactly what else was experienced, together with a few illustrations from transcripts of passages of typical sittings.

As will be seen from the record of dates and attendances of sittings given in Appendix B, not all three of us were able to attend all sittings. Some of the reports cannot therefore be properly attributed to all of us. It would have been confusing, laborious and untidy had we attempted to issue separate accounts of what for the main part constituted the same body of evidence. What we have felt it sensible to do is to issue a joint report, but to make clear from the context those sections which can properly be ascribed to only one or two of us because only one or two of us were present on the occasion described.

Nor would it be reasonable to expect all of us to draw identical conclusions from the apparent purport of the oral and visual evidence, since that would go beyond the region of objective description and analysis into the realms of speculation. But we believe that, faced with our account of a bewildering array of strange phenomena, most readers would expect not merely a measured assessment of the case for a natural explanation, but would wish to know what we made of it all.

CHAPTER I: THE CONTEXT OF THE INVESTIGATION

The Scole Group and their Background

The group (hereinafter referred to as the Scole Group or the Group) around whom the phenomena comprising the subject of this Report took place consisted of four people, Robin Foy and his wife Sandra, and another middle-aged married couple, who prefer to be known simply as Diana and Alan (full names known to us), both of whom act as trance mediums. The Group resulted from the activities of Robin Foy, now in his late fifties, whose autobiography (Foy, 1996), cautiously reviewed in the *JSPR* (Barrington, 1996), explains how, and why, he was captivated by the direct voice productions of the well-known medium Leslie Flint (1911–1994), and how he devoted what spare time was left from the demands of a job as a paper-trade salesman to enlarging his experience and extending it to others. He sat as a member of a number of spiritualist circles in different parts of England. Foy describes (p.217) how on 21st April 1990 a group who were sitting at Ilkeston, Derbyshire, were surprised when "a new spirit entity spoke to us in the independent voice, one Noah Zerdin". Zerdin urged them to form an educational society "for the development, promotion and safe practice of modern physical mediumship, to ensure its survival so that current and future generations could witness its wonders for themselves". This led Foy in 1990 to found the Noah's Ark Society (NAS) in recognition of the name of the communicator and perhaps the biblical significance of the Ark. The NAS continues to flourish, publishing a journal and promoting the formation of private groups, of which there were said to be over 100 worldwide when we started our inquiry.

Neither at that time nor subsequently could we find anything in the background of members of the Group to support prior doubts about either their motives or their probity. Since what they were doing, and claiming, was being publicised through their own newsletter, *The Spiritual Scientist*, as well as more directly to numbers of sitters both in Britain and abroad, it seemed likely that any whispers of suspicion would have come our way. The fact that it was known that an investigation of the Group's activities by independent members of the SPR was in train, and that one of us had actually been named in *The Spiritual Scientist* as the SPR member who accompanied the Group to California for sittings there, would have made it all the more likely that any suspicions about them would have been conveyed to one of us.

In addition, as the leader of the Group, as a well-known figure in spiritualist circles for many years (although neither he nor other members of the Group are Spiritualists), and as founder of the NAS,

Robin Foy had achieved some national prominence. As his autobiography makes clear, his stated ambition was not to found a cult but simply to encourage the formation of small, independent non-commercial groups at which physical phenomena might occur, and discourses with spirits take place.

It might be thought that the background of the Group members and their personal histories and character have little to do with an objective examination of the evidence for the paranormal. But clearly our suspicions would have been aroused had Foy been previously apprenticed to a stage illusionist or had an impressive track record in professional deception, or had there been any suggestion that he had intended to pursue a career of deceit and had acquired the competence to execute it. In brief, we heard nothing to suggest that either he, his wife, or the two mediums are the stuff of which hoaxers or fraudsters are made. (It is perhaps worth noting that one of us, DF, is a highly qualified psychologist who has worked for over 30 years in the field of human personality and motivation.)

We had therefore to recognise that hoaxing so far as we were aware was at variance with the Group's known history, and that they appeared to have no motive for mass deception. Alan, the male medium, is a carpenter and a smallholder, a quiet, retiring, intelligent and practical man. He is responsible for the production of the Group's newsletter, *The Spiritual Scientist*, having had some experience of graphic design in his early years. His wife Diana, who has been psychic since childhood, and practises part-time as a healer, is more extrovert, but was as concerned as her husband was to keep out of the limelight so that the Group could concentrate on what they considered to have become their life's mission: the evidence of the phenomena and the reality of and messages from their spirit friends. The two mediums and their four grown-up children have been known as neighbours and friends to one of our scientifically qualified SPR members, Mrs Beverly Dear, for over twenty years, and she has sent us a letter warmly testifying to their integrity and simple life-style. When we first encountered the Group it included two other members: Ken Britten and Bernette Head. Ken, who left the Group after our first two sittings, having travelled 170 miles twice a week to Scole for two years, was at that time a maintenance technician at Stansted Hall, the headquarters of the Spiritualists' National Union, while Bernette, who regularly shared the long journey with him and who left the Group at the same time, helped run a local post office. It is pertinent to note that these ex-Group-members, when interviewed after leaving the Group, have steadfastly testified to the genuineness of the phenomena.

For the two mediums, and for Bernette Head and Ken Britten as for the Foys, a hoax for whatever motives would appear to have been pointless and self-defeating, both personally and professionally. To all outward appearances and personal testimony they appear to have dedicated themselves to the work they believe to be so important. It soon became apparent to the investigators that, far from enabling them to flaunt their skill at having deceived so many for so long, exposure or revelation would spell personal and professional disaster for all members of the Group. Their lives and reputations, closely bound up with the spiritist phenomenon, would be gravely compromised. Their prospects of attracting attention to their work would disappear. The people who had trusted their integrity, admired their achievements and marvelled at their claims would feel betrayed. Their only reward would be the censure of those they had deluded. These considerations are germane to our later examination of the fraud hypothesis throughout, and in particular in Chapter XV. Meantime we must return to the sequence which led up to our involvement.

The Origin and Circumstances of our Investigation

In his capacity as chairman of the SPR's Spontaneous Cases Committee, Maurice Grosse in 1992 had tentatively invited the NAS to consider co-operating with the SPR in a formal investigation of physical mediumship. He received a firm rebuff. The reasons became more evident in July 1995, when Malcolm Lewis (1995) proposed in an article in the *NAS Newsletter* (now the *NAS Review*) that the credibility of the NAS, and of physical mediumship as a whole, would continue to remain in doubt until serious scientific investigation of mediums was allowed. He argued that non-invasive and harmless image-intensification equipment capable of observing phenomena in total darkness was now available, and that full respect for mediums' wishes, and imposed conditions, could be assured. Repeated public demonstrations of physical phenomena to large, captive, but favourably predisposed audiences were neither "necessarily scientifically valid nor reliable".

Lewis received a rebuff with the publication of three articles. One was by George Cranley, the Editor of the Newsletter (and the NAS's Vice-President), a second by Stewart Alexander, the President and a physical medium himself, and the third by another physical medium known as Lincoln (Colin Fry). The Editor pointed out that the Society was primarily an educational body, and not a research organisation. "We leave that to well-established bodies such as the SPR and others." He disputed the statement that techniques existed to enable phenomena to be observed in total darkness, and referred to his spirit guide who maintained that even luminous strips on a trumpet were too bright for his medium. He quoted with approval the opinion of David Berglas, President of the Magic Circle, that scientists were the easiest people to fool, and argued that lawyers rather than psychical researchers, psychologists and magicians were better qualified to assess evidence. After dwelling on instances of danger and harm caused to mediums by some researchers during materialisations involving ectoplasm, and to the unconvincing nature of all photographs, he repeated a decision of the NAS taken in January 1994 that it was not their policy to encourage scientists and researchers to carry out tests with physical mediums; but that, should this view change, any tests would be undertaken only by "qualified people within the Society".

The response of Stewart Alexander, a good friend of the Foys, was equally reserved. Among his reasons was a view expressed by his spirit guide that photographs of partially materialised ectoplasmic formations were visually repulsive, and that to overcome this aesthetic objection would take time, and hence detract from desirable progress in other directions.

This response is understandable when one examines the questionable practices adopted by some investigators in the past, not least in relation to Mina Crandon, and the ease with which mere suspicion of malpractice has become so readily advanced as evidence of fraud. There is some evidence that it may have been further sharpened by reports of an SPR Study Day two years earlier when a highly inaccurate mock séance was held as part of a discussion on physical phenomena.

This general antipathy towards investigators also derives from a long-standing rift between the general body of spiritualists, and psychical researchers as represented by the SPR, a rift which some have traced back to the dismissive attitude taken by Eleanor Sidgwick to Crawford's work on the Goligher Circle (Inglis, 1984) more than 75 years ago, which helped to prompt the resignation from the Society of Arthur Conan Doyle. The uneasy relationship between mediums and Spiritualists (committed members of a religious body) and the posture of the SPR, which embraces all beliefs and none but is dedicated to objective scientific scrutiny of evidence, has persisted until recent times, when the attitude of mutual disdain had seemed to many on both sides to be outdated. It was this conviction that led Professor Archie Roy (AR), President of the SPR at the time, to discuss with mediums and with leaders of the Spiritualist movement the creation of a joint investigatory body. Comprising seven leading mediums, and an equal number drawn from the hierarchy of the SPR, although all acting in a strictly personal and non-representative capacity, the new organisation was set up in 1994 and found a suitable acronym in PRISM (Psychical Research Involving Selected Mediums). The objectives of the two groups comprising PRISM were dissimilar but compatible: smarting under constant attacks by sceptics on their probity, the mediums were eager to reinforce their position by the successful submission of mediumship to objective testing, while the psychical researchers for their part welcomed the opportunity

ıe a trail which all but a handful of researchers had abandoned
ᵌ advent of the Rhine revolution and the era of statistically-based
 ̲ ̲ ̲ratory-orientated research.

It is not the object of this Report to record the progress of PRISM. Its relevance here is chiefly because it was through PRISM that the existence of the Group came to our attention in the winter of 1994 in the shape of the first issue of *The Spiritual Scientist*, published by an institution known as the New Spiritual Science Foundation, operating from the Foys' home in Scole, near Diss, Norfolk, where experimental sittings of the NAS had been held from 1992. In his autobiography, Foy described how he established a small home circle in the cellar of his rented period home at Street House Farm in what had once been a dairy. By the end of August 1994, the development of physical phenomena at Scole had progressed so dramatically that Foy felt it necessary to resign as chairman of the NAS to enable him and Sandra to dedicate themselves to what, according to their spirit advisers, was to become the centre for the development of a new type of spirit energy, one which neither affected the health and safety of mediums nor involved the creation and manipulation of ectoplasmic forms.

Originally seven in number (one member dropped out for domestic reasons quite soon after the Group began meeting regularly), and sitting twice weekly since early 1993, the Group had started to experience physical phenomena on 4th October of that year. (These twice-weekly sittings, at which only the Group were present, and which we refer to in this Report as 'closed sittings', continued throughout our investigation, punctuated only by illness or absence abroad.) One of the first examples took the form of an apported gift, a Churchill crown which, they said, had dropped audibly onto the table in the centre of the séance room. By this time the Group had agreed to dedicate themselves to doing whatever the spirit guides asked of them. The results were recorded in considerable detail in the first issue of *The Spiritual Scientist*. Some 43 different types of physical phenomena were claimed to have been produced, ranging from levitations, apports and lights, raps and touches to materialisations of walking forms and voices appearing to come from different parts of the room.

There were two aspects of the claims made in *The Spiritual Scientist* which aroused special interest. One was contained in the statement that only now, when all the right factors and ingredients had come together to enable the work and plans to come to fruition, had it become possible to give effect to an objective originally planned by spirit communicators nearly 50 years earlier; and that this plan was to include "special sittings for intellectuals and scientists to quiz the spirit team and thus assimilate a wide range of knowledge about spirit communication and the exciting scientific experiments in the pipeline". The second was the description of 'photographic wonders'.

At a meeting on 28th January 1995 of the recently formed PRISM council, which included Professor Arthur Ellison (AE), Professor David Fontana (DF) and Montague Keen (MK), MK was asked to investigate, his home being little more than an hour's drive from Scole. Accordingly, on 18th February he visited the Foys' home, the official headquarters of the New Spiritual Science Foundation, and met the Foys and the two trance mediums, Alan and Diana. The aim was to establish mutual respect and confidence with a view to discovering the conditions under which the Group's activities could be the subject of an investigation. Following a lengthy discussion he circulated a report to PRISM, explaining that the members of the Group were not Spiritualists in the religious sense, but were all convinced of the reality of spirits and their messages. "In brief," he wrote, "what was shown to me was either the product of a conspiracy of outright lies, perpetrated with the aid of extremely ingenious and complex deception, or else it constituted the most impressive evidence of physical paranormality of which I have knowledge . . ."

The main reason for this hyperbolic verdict was the photographic material and its potential for objective examination. In the light of the investigations which have taken place over the succeeding three years, it is desirable to provide a more detailed description of these physical phenomena and the processes by which they appeared to have been produced, even though none had at that time been created under conditions involving any psychical researcher. Since our subsequent investigation not only failed to uncover any direct evidence of deception during the production of similar phenomena, but served to identify the difficulties of employing deception, particularly in the production of some of the later films, it would be inappropriate to ignore what was said to have taken place before the SPR members appeared on the scene.

The Scole Group's Claims

MK reported that the New Spiritual Science Foundation, under which title or aegis the Group operated, had no membership, and no intention of creating one. Nor did it then have any income. Its newsletter, *The Spiritual Scientist,* whose first free issue had been funded from the pockets of members of the Group, was by then in its second issue, with a circulation of some 300, and an annual subscription rate of £3.00 (later raised to £5.00 for four quarterly issues). All the Group's operations were undertaken from the Foys' residence, in whose cellar all sittings normally took place. At that time, and throughout the rest of 1995, the year which included the first two formal investigatory sittings, the two other members of the Group referred to earlier, Bernette Head and Ken Britten, were also present.

Although the Group expressed views on arrangements and direction, they were primarily guided both on procedure and policy by the advice and wishes of the spirit team (hereinafter referred to as the Team as distinct from the Group). Communications were claimed to be received from or through a number of spirit guides or controls speaking through the two entranced mediums. There appeared to be seven principal spirit guides, their pseudonyms and reputed background being described in the first issue of *The Spiritual Scientist*. At that stage no attempt had been made to validate their historical existence. What follows is excerpted from MK's report, updated where necessary to explain subsequent developments.

The 'spirits' were said to be under the aegis of one of the guides, 'John Paxton', described by the Group as an advanced or evolved spirit. The spirit guides were proceeding cautiously, first in establishing a rapport with the Scole Group and apparently others; then in familiarising themselves with the apparatus and the modus operandi of physical manifestations, of which the Group claimed to have witnessed 43 different types by December 1994, a figure which had risen to 51 at the time of the first meeting with MK. Of these physical demonstrations, the most spectacular, because the most readily evidential, was the development by stages of spirit photography, by now without the use of cameras, and in total darkness, save for the existence of pinned (subsequently Velcro-adhering) luminous wristbands worn by each member of the Group, together with luminous strips fixed at the cardinal points on the surface periphery of the circular table round which the Group and any visitors sat.

The stated motive prompting both the Scole Group and their Spirit Team was to bring about spiritual enlightenment by providing firm evidence of the reality of the spirit world, its concern for humanity, and its capacity to affect both our consciousness and our physical environment by means clearly outside the competence of the human participants: means inexplicable by commonly accepted physical laws. In view of the past history of spiritualistic evidence, however, the emphasis was to be on the production of physical effects rather than the traditional spirit messages, although there had been plenty of these too. The conditions in which the séances (which the Group preferred to call experimental sessions) were then being held, and the strict limitations enforced on the presence and the conduct of strangers, made it premature to contemplate installing various instruments to measure physiological or physical parameters (although the Group had in fact placed two instruments in the cellar to measure temperature change and air movement), or to introduce the sort of investigative apparatus which would ideally be required if every conceivable precaution against deception were to be taken. Thus, although sittings were in total darkness save for the luminous wristbands and table strips to enable movements of members of the Group to be observed, "the Spirit Team working with the Group have stated quite categorically that it is their eventual intention to introduce lighting of some description into the Group", to quote from an account of a typical sitting given on page 6 of *The Spiritual Scientist*. The premature introduction of artificial light would slow down developments.

That the phenomena were allegedly reflecting signs of development was apparent not so much from the (not uncommon) raps, taps and visual displays of spirit lights weaving round the room, or from reports of levitation of the central table, nor even from the appearance of apports, of which a motley collection were shown to MK, but from the films. The first 'photographs' had been taken in the dark by one of the Group with a camera using new 35mm film, and without a flashlight. The shutter button had been pressed at intervals commanded by the spirits via one of the two mediums, who remained in deep trance throughout, and were not concealed behind any cabinet or screen. This produced 11 separate images; some very clear, others less well-defined. The pictures, which had been developed commercially for the Group the following day, showed, for example, a familiar scene of St Paul's during the Blitz of World War II, surrounded by burning buildings, groups of soldiers apparently from World War I, architectural details, and a view of the Seine from the roof of Notre-Dame. For the next session the Group were asked by their Team to bring two cameras, both loaded with fresh spools of 35mm film, and to leave the cameras untouched on a chair. One was heard clicking, and winding on. The second appeared to have been levitated and to move round the room making similar clicking and whirring noises. When developed, each roll of 24 exposures was found to contain 11 pictures of various places and people, said (by the Team) to be copies of old and new photographs which existed somewhere in the world.

Most of the contents of the pictures shown to MK appeared to have no obvious significance but were clearly recognisable, although for the main part lacking the clarity or quality that might have been expected in originals or copies. Among them was a head and shoulders photograph of Sir Arthur Conan Doyle, which had appeared with a Sanskrit message, and the signature of Ivor Novello, a prominent pre-war song-writer. Both had been obtained on Polaroid Polapan black-and-white 35mm slide film (125 ISO), which, so the Group assured us, had not been removed from its factory-sealed and light-proof container until it was developed in a room upstairs at the Foys' home immediately after the relevant sittings, using a Polaroid Power Processor. Diana, one of the mediums, tracked down the origin of a (transliterated) Sanskrit text and showed MK a photocopy from a volume of the sacred text of Srimad-Bhagavatam (Canto 1, Ch. 5. Text 35) which contained both the original

Sanskrit verse and the translation into English. The message, which was intended to be spiritually uplifting, did appear to have a close relevance to the Scole Group's stated objective, and had been discovered when Diana chanced on a single volume of this 12-volume sacred text in a local Oxfam shop.

At around this time the Team asked the Group to abandon the use of cameras, and to leave the unexposed cassettes in unopened tubs of Polaroid 35mm film on the floor during sittings. The object was to provide greater safeguards against deception, since an almost instantaneous result could be obtained when the films were processed before witnesses, without the use of negatives or the introduction of any manual procedure. Immediately after they were taken from the séance room the spools were extracted before witnesses, and put through the automatic chemical mechanism of the Polaroid Power Processor donated by Polaroid to the Group. This extrudes the developed roll within less than two minutes. The pictures MK examined were said to be prints obtained from negatives made at a later stage from the original transparencies.

The interested official from the Polaroid company who had provided the Processor had also given the Group a quantity of 35mm Polaroid film of different exposure sensitivities, or film speeds. The initial success had come on black-and-white Polaprint film 125 ISO on which was seen a darkish image of a wooden Chinese idol. Later there appeared a monochrome picture clearly showing French airmen standing round a World War I aircraft, and the title page from a sheet of music called "When We're Together". The next significant film, this time on Polapan, produced the slides associated with Conan Doyle and the Sanskrit message. Subsequent experiments used faster film, ISO 400, and yielded a range of striking 'seascapes', comprising seaweed-like shapes. A later set, again said to derive from unopened tubs of slow colour film, Pola-chrome ISO 40, were akin to the patterns created in heated glass bowls containing coloured oils which constantly evolve into a succession of lurid shapes. All were different. The impression given from an examination of the films was that of a gradual progression towards ever more demanding and sophisticated technology.

The apports said to have arrived since the Group's first meeting in October 1993 usually comprised small gifts to sitters and guests, and were objects said to have been lost or discarded by previous owners, or once owned by the spirit world donors themselves. They ranged from sports medallions, tiepins, penknives, bracelets, a thimble and whale-bone spoons, to artefacts which appeared to have symbolic implications, notably a miniature silverine Noah's Ark vessel, and two old-style pennies dated 1936 and 1940 which related to the dates of photographs received during the previous week's experimental sitting. One apport, in the form of a sizeable piece of amethyst, was said to have landed with a thud on the central table, then fallen on the floor on a sitter's foot, and was warm to the touch when retrieved.

A more significant apport took the form of an apparently original copy of the *Daily Mail* for 1st April 1944, which reported on its front page the 'guilty' verdict after the lengthy and highly publicised Old Bailey trial of the famous physical medium Helen Duncan, whose prosecution under the subsequently repealed 18th-century Witchcraft Act was a *cause célèbre* in its day. The spirit of Mrs Duncan had allegedly announced her presence to the Group the previous September, when she said she wished to convey her good wishes and to bring something to verify her presence. The newspaper, on war-time newsprint, in excellent condition and showing no sign of ageing or oxygenation, appeared the following week.[1]

MK told the Group that, while he appreciated the desire of the spirit guides to proceed with caution as they became increasingly adept at their materialisation tasks, and to avoid premature publicity, this was difficult to reconcile with the fact that, although the great majority of the sittings were restricted to the six Scole Group members (closed sittings), some visitors had already been allowed to participate in others. At one session there were reported to have been 32 visitors when the Group had sat in a location in Felixstowe. In reply, the Group informed MK that an entity designated the 'spiritual co-ordinator', called Patrick McKenna, a former Irish priest who was later to become a familiar and amusing communicator, had felt satisfied by the previous September

---

[1] Following the discovery by Mr Tony Cornell, the SPR's Hon. Treasurer, that facsimile reproductions printed on post-war newsprint were commercially available, and therefore that the 'apport' might well have been obtained by this means, the Daily Mail confirmed that no original copies of the war-time issues were now available. Robin Foy, whose own expertise in newsprint matters led him to assure us that the paper was original, had been reluctant to part with it because he said, correctly, that it could not be regarded as evidential, having appeared at a private (closed) sitting of the Group of six in 1994, before our investigation started. He also feared significant damage to a unique artefact. When later assured that the Technical Services Department of the Print Industry Research Association (PIRA) International needed only a very small area of the margin, he immediately handed the whole paper to MK.

Visual examination under low-level magnification by PIRA in MK's presence showed clear evidence that the copy had been reproduced by letterpress, which has long since been superseded by more modern methods, while the fibres of the paper proved on chemical analysis to be identical to a contemporary wartime sample. PIRA concluded that there was no reason to doubt the war-time origin of the 'apport'.

The Scole Group say that the paper was in pristine condition when it arrived, although contact with light and air would normally have rendered it substantially yellow within a matter of weeks – far faster than newsprint made soon after the war when imported chemicals (which were not present in the samples analysed) were added to the pulp to improve quality and longevity. Further aspects of this 'apport' are discussed in Tony Cornell's critique and in the authors' response.

that sufficient progress had been made to permit the attendance of visitors. A Colchester medium, Bill Lyons, had been the first to be invited, apparently at the suggestion of the spirits, who presented him with an apport of a brass elephant on a plinth. There followed permission for the attendance of the spouses of the two members of the Group who subsequently left, Ken Britten and Bernette Head, and these visitors collected apports of a silver Peruvian bracelet and a semi-precious stone, obsidian, respectively.

On 21st October 1994, James Webster, a surgical chiropodist, described as a former member of the Magic Circle and a stage magician, attended a sitting. He provided the first issue of *The Spiritual Scientist* with a detailed account of an event which had included information about a deceased member of his family, the movement of lights akin to a fireworks display, a tap-dancing movement by a light on the surface of the central table, and the ringing of a string of small bells suspended from the ceiling. After discussing mechanisms by which modern stage magicians might achieve such effects – particularly the light displays – he concluded that . . .

> . . . one such *modus operandi* might be the employment of long, hollow strands of fibreglass with laser light projected through them. But this requires a previous set-up of props and gadgetry in the room and/or on the persons themselves which would immediately fail the test conditions which are required to be met by the genuine mediums and sitters.

The precautions taken at that stage were spelled out in a code of conduct for sitters, but they seemed more designed to ensure a harmonious atmosphere than specifically to guard against deception by any sitter. Sitters were asked to avoid wearing scent, to leave the contents of pockets and handbags outside the room, or locked in their cars, not to stand up or move around during a sitting or to try to grab any levitated object or move their arms around unless specifically asked to do so, to answer audibly and clearly any messages or questions addressed to them (since all sittings are tape-recorded), to avoid volunteering specific information, and to remain quiet while mediums recovered from their trances at the end of each session.

While expressing eagerness for some of his more experienced SPR colleagues to participate in sittings, MK ventured the view that any such participation would be more likely to produce evidential material if some of the restrictions imposed by the Team could be eased. It was very desirable, for example, to have video recordings of sessions so that independent examination of proceedings could be undertaken by others. Indeed, any investigation would be severely hampered by the absence of light unless infra-red cameras and other types of recording or monitoring instruments were allowed. He was told that it was the express intention of the spirit Team to introduce lighting of some description into sittings eventually, but that the existence of light would severely retard the progressive development of the phenomena. MK went on to express his concern that evidence suggestive of survival of human consciousness should not be dependent solely on the subjective experiences and personal testimony of participating investigators, no matter how eminent, qualified or numerous. Recognising this, the Group made it clear that their priority initially was to concentrate on those persons likely to bring scientific experience, and methodology, to the experimental sittings.

This initial meeting between the Group and MK was succeeded by an informal discussion at Stansted Hall, the SNU headquarters mentioned earlier, at which MK and the late Ralph Noyes (RN), at that time Hon. Secretary of the Society and subsequently a Vice-President, were present. They were shown a wider range of the still 'photographs' assembled over the preceding months. In July 1995 there followed a meeting at Stansted Hall with all six members of the Group, at which all the SPR members of PRISM were present save AE. They were treated to a formal presentation by Robin Foy, aided by Alan, the trance medium, and Ken, who operated the projector and gave a commentary. The upshot was an invitation for MK to bring AE to Scole, where he could examine the evidence and the séance room and enable the Group to satisfy themselves that his so-called 'vibes' would pass spiritual muster. Satisfied that those whom they proposed to invite had a positive attitude towards extra-sensory perception in general, the Group then invited three of the PRISM members, AE, RN and MK, to attend a sitting. This was our introduction to the investigation.

The Experimental (Séance) Room at Scole

The experimental science room (ESR), as the Foys' converted cellar was designated by the Group in order to distance it and them from traditional Spiritualist terminology and beliefs, is approached through a door and a flight of stone steps from RF's study. At the foot of the stairs are two identical chambers, that on the left having been converted into a refreshment room, and that on the right into the ESR. When sittings were held, the door at the top of the stairs from the Foys' study was bolted from the stairs side, while the door to the refreshment room was bolted from the outside. The door into the ESR was not bolted but could be accessed only by means of one or other of the two bolted doors just referred to. Additionally, opening and closing the door into the ESR made sufficient noise from squeaky hinges to be readily detectable. The only other opening to the ESR is a small former coal chute now securely blocked off from the inside by a stout wooden panel screwed firmly into the wall. A plastic sliding ventilation grid about 30 cm x 12 cm is fitted into this panel. Normally this remained closed. When open during daylight, a very limited amount of indirect light is visible. The room is almost entirely below ground level, and effectively sound-proof. The floor is of solid concrete, covered with hardboard to achieve a level surface, and the whole covered by a fitted carpet, and the walls and ceiling of uniform brick, coated throughout with dark gloss paint. There are several wall power points, and a central light operated by a dimmer switch from the left-hand side of the door. A string of small bells is suspended from the ceiling. The barrel roof springs from head-level walls, arching to a height of 2.25 m. The room is 5 m long by 3.96 m wide.

During the sittings we attended there were no curtains or 'cabinets'. The central table, around which the sitters were placed during all our investigations, was about 1.2 metres in diameter and a little over 60 cm in height, and had a compressed chipboard brown-painted circular top on a quadrant pedestal base consisting of ogee-sawn boards at right angles to each other, and extending almost to the edge of the table so as to divide the area under the table into four compartments, effectively obstructing under-table movement. A number of metal-framed armless sprung plastic stacking chairs surrounded it, with more of these chairs in the space between the sitters and the rear of the room. A small circular side table stood in the front right-hand corner of the chamber diagonally opposite the door. This carried a glass dome or bell jar of the sort once popular for housing stuffed animals, and was mounted on a glass shelf supported by six tubular Perspex legs, about 5 cm high. This was often moved to the centre of the main table prior to the sittings, and was so placed during the first few such sittings attended by the investigators. (See Figure 1.)

Depending on the instructions given to the Group by the Team at the closed sittings, various other items were present, although on overseas visits the Group relied on nothing more than a number of crystals, which were said to concentrate the 'energies' required. A large crystal, weighing nearly half a kilogram and said to have been apported for the purpose, sometimes rested on the central table. On occasion this table also carried a recently constructed 'fish tank', comprising a thick wooden plinth or base, and four sides of plate glass glued together, with a similar plate glued to the top, measuring roughly 13 cm wide, 10 cm high and 46 cm long. In addition, there was a section of a plastic Tupper-ware container used initially, according to Robin Foy, to amplify direct voice communication. On our first visit there was also a blank, unopened audio-cassette, left in the hope that the spirits would be able to record sounds on it (as to which see our description of the germanium experiment and the direct voice communication in Chapter VIII). Finally, there was a ping-pong ball carrying a small luminous strip which was usually left in the base of a translucent kitchen Pyrex bowl, about 20 cm in diameter, 7.5 cm deep, slightly patterned on the outside and plain within.

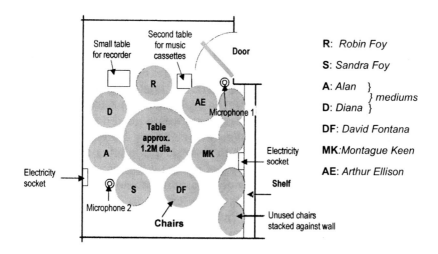

The SCOLE CELLAR Dimensions: Approx. 5m x 3.9m

Figure 1

Glasses of water were placed below the chairs occupied by the two mediums. Above RF's head and linked to a ducted electric cable serving the overhead lamp were four elastic loops to hold leads to microphones – normally two of these were located in different places. They were connected to the tape recorder placed next to RF on a trolley. On the wall behind RF were two small measuring instruments: a thermal probe to record temperature levels at top, middle and base of the room during a sitting, and a velometer to record any air movements.

Record-keeping

Fairly comprehensive contemporaneous notes were taken in short-hand by MK (with some difficulty because of the darkness) during the earlier sittings. Only when it was established, not without some persuasion on the part of the investigators, that we could have transcripts of the tape-recorded proceedings (since we considered them essential to our task), did the note-taking become less necessary. MK later compared his notes with the transcripts of the tape recordings to ensure that the latter reached a high level of accuracy and minimal dependence on memory. On the only occasion when no recording was made in sittings attended by one of us (by MK in California) he made more extensive notes, and these form the basis of his account given in Appendix C, which has been confirmed by the owner of the home in which the sitting was conducted, Richard Adams.

Transcripts of the tapes were prepared by Diana, one of the mediums. Considering the less-than-ideal level of acoustic precision, the varied quality, clarity and loudness of the speakers, the occasional changes made experimentally in the positions of the two microphones, and the not infrequent tendency for more than one person, or spirit voice, to be heard simultaneously on the tape, the transcripts are no mean achievement. Because we were usually encouraged to keep the conversation going during a lull in the sittings, as we were told that this helped to facilitate communication, there was a good deal of irrelevant chit-chat among ourselves, and Diana exercised her discretion in omitting much of this, although a reading of the transcripts creates on occasion the curious impression of an admixture of ephemeral gossip punctuated by serious discussions or reports on our observations and experiences round the table. Copies of transcripts were given to each of the three investigators, enabling us to confirm that they accorded with our recollection of events. In addition, AE and DF (who replaced RN; see below) forwarded to MK their own reports and comments on the sittings to supplement his own, while MK prepared extensive commentaries on the scripts and drew attention to material of apparent evidential significance or to the outcome of those further investigations which either the contents of films or the puzzles and hints from the Team (illustrated and discussed later) required.

One particularly valuable aspect of these records, as may be appreciated by excerpts from a few of the scripts in the next chapter, is the extent to which they eliminate those human failings – of misremembered sequences, imagined events, ill-recollected phenomena, etc. – which have so frequently justified great caution in accepting personal testimony. The fact that most of the events described were experienced or witnessed simultaneously by at least three seasoned investigators improves the probability of authenticity.

The Investigators

The principal investigators, and authors of this report, are all long-established members of the Society for Psychical Research. Ralph Noyes, who attended the first two sittings and subsequently acted in a consultative or advisory capacity, was at that time in rather poor physical health. He had a distinguished career in the Civil Service as an Under-Secretary at the Ministry of Defence, where he was in charge of a department responsible for monitoring UFO reports, a subject which gradually introduced him to psychical research (see Acknowledgements). A dispassionate but cautiously sceptical analyst, when at the end of the second sitting he announced his intention to retire and invite Professor David Fontana to replace him, he confirmed his satisfaction that what he had experienced was authentic.

At that time and throughout the period of investigation the President of the Society, and subsequently a Vice-President, Professor David Fontana, Ph.D. is an educational and counselling psychologist, a Distinguished Visiting Fellow at the University of Cardiff, a Professor at two universities in Portugal, and a Fellow of the British Psychological Society. Author of more than 20 books on psychology and related themes, translated into 23 languages, he is currently a Council member of the British Psychological Society and Chair of the Transpersonal Psychology Section of the British Psychological Society. He has published widely on psychical research, and chairs the SPR's Survival Committee. His interest in psychical phenomena and in methods of deception goes back to boyhood, and he has investigated and witnessed a wide range of physical phenomena in various settings.

Professor Arthur Ellison, D.Sc., an Emeritus Professor of Electrical Engineering at City University, a Past President (twice) of the Society and a Vice-President, is a member of its Council, Chairman of the Image and Publicity Committee and a member of several other committees. He has had direct experience covering many years of almost all types of physical and mental phenomena of psychical research. He is also a member of the Parapsychological Association, and a Vice-President and founder-member of the Scientific and Medical Network. He has had first-hand experience of the out-of-body and lucid dreaming states, and is particularly interested in altered states of consciousness, especially the possibility of human survival of bodily death.

Montague Keen began investigating paranormal phenomena in 1946, when he first joined the Society, of which he is Hon. Media Relations Officer and Secretary and Vice-Chairman of its Survival Committee. A former parliamentary lobby correspondent, agricultural administrator, technical editor and farmer, he has been responsible for much of the detailed work associated with the investigation and the preparation of this report.

In addition, towards the end of 1996, it was agreed that prominent researchers, mainly those on the Council of the Society, might be invited to attend as individuals after briefing by MK. As well as the several SPR Council members (Professors Robert Morris, Donald West, Archie E. Roy and Bernard Carr, Dr Alan Gauld and Dr John Beloff) who came singly or in pairs, three other members attended the one-day seminar sittings which the Group at that time organised independently (Mrs Rosemary Dinnage, Mr Leslie Banks and Mr Melvyn Willin). Two non-Council SPR members (Professor Ivor Grattan-Guinness and Dr Rupert Sheldrake) attended single sittings, while Ingrid Slack, a psychologist with the Open University, an SPR member and an experienced investigator of mediumship, attended three.

CHAPTER II: THE SITTINGS

Introductory note: Because the atmosphere, procedure and events of the first two sittings are relevant to an appreciation of the phenomena and of the circumstances in which they were produced, we describe them in some detail, even though they are not necessarily representative of all we subsequently experienced. As we became more familiar with the phenomena, and grew on easier terms with what presented themselves as personalities issuing from the mouths of the two mediums, so more attention was devoted by the Team to the production of the sort of physical evidence which appeared to command more of their resources, and demand more of their attention, leaving less time and/or energy for the mainly visual displays we also experienced.

Duration and Conduct of the Sittings

The investigation lasted from 2nd October 1995 to 16th August 1997. During this time the investigators held 18 sittings with the Group. In addition, one of us (MK) had two solo sittings, four sittings when accompanied by other SPR members and four sittings when accompanying the Group in California and Ibiza. In addition there were a number of sittings at which either Walter or Karin Schnittger, or both, were present with or in the absence of one or more of us. Full details of dates of sittings and the persons involved are given in Appendix B.

Most sittings lasted between two and two-and-a-half hours. The conduct varied little. The investigators would spend some time with the Group upstairs in the Foys' living room engaged in friendly conversation, during which there might be some discussion of the procedure envisaged by the Spirit Team and communicated to the Foys at a closed sitting for the conduct of a particular experiment. Frequently we were unaware of what was planned, but on several occasions we were invited to bring particular films, or security bags, or a padlock, in anticipation of an experiment of the types described in some detail later. In that event some time was usually spent in procedural formalities designed to guard against deception. The atmosphere was relaxed and friendly, and discussion of anything controversial avoided until after the conclusion of the sitting. We were invariably invited to take our time inspecting the cellar downstairs to satisfy ourselves that no hidden artefacts could be found, although we were asked not to interfere with the table, or the crystals on it, since these were said to be areas in which spirit energies had become concentrated. The investigators were always first to descend to the cellar; normally we subsequently ascertained that the doors at the top of the stairs and to the refreshment room had been secured against the possibility of an intruder or accomplice.

The usual seating arrangements were that Sandra Foy (SF) sat opposite her husband, with Alan and Diana between them on her immediate left. To the left of Robin Foy was the trolley carrying a cassette player and a selection of tapes laid out for easy selection in the dark, depending on what background music was requested by the Team or thought appropriate. On his other side a small table carried a tape recorder and spare tapes to enable a record of every sitting to be made. The visitors sat opposite the mediums and between the Foys and closest to the door. When, as was the case during the first two sittings (in October and December 1995), Ken and Bernette were also present, they sat, respectively, on the immediate left and right of the investigators. The three investigators always sat with MK in the centre, DF on his left and AE on his right, save for the first two sittings when Ralph Noyes was on MK's right and AE on his left.

Guest sitters were always asked to leave all electrical equipment behind in the living room, since it was feared that the introduction of such additional electrical equipment might imperil the communicating mechanism. Members of the Group wore Velcro wristbands carrying luminous strips which had been 'charged up' by exposure to electric light beforehand. They were made of strips cut from old trouser belting onto which were sewn luminous 'beads' with varying lengths of Velcro fixings at each end. We were told that they were originally worn above the elbow, but that when visitors to séances complained that this did not enable them to check hand movements, the Group made shorter versions, to be worn just above the wrist. In notes on our fourth sitting we recorded that "a very distinctive ripping noise was made when these armbands were removed". Later, when sittings were suspended or ended, we asked whether we could take them away in order to examine them more closely, and were immediately handed all eight.

Together with small luminous strips placed at the four cardinal points of the compass on the circular table, the luminous strips on the ping-pong ball when present, and a small luminous marker at the base of the string of bells, these were normally the only location guides that sitters had, save when sufficient 'spirit light' allowed some visibility. Any perceived changes in the position of a wristband would indicate to watchful sitters the movement of an arm or hand. Although the luminosity of the strips tended to decline during the sittings, the sound of the Velcro provided some safeguard against unobserved removal of the wristbands.

The Controls

It must be emphasised that we were present at the sittings of the Group as invited guests, albeit as investigators. It is not possible, therefore, to judge the procedure by standards and assumptions appropriate to experiments we ourselves had initiated in circumstances where we could exercise full control over events. There had been considerable discussion before our sittings began about the sort of controls which would be acceptable; and the Group made it clear that the conditions under which the sittings took place were those required by their spirit friends, and were not decided arbitrarily by members of the Group.

A central issue for the investigators was the absence of light. We had to be content with Robin Foy's assurance that it was the intention of the Team to "bring their own light" (as indeed to some extent they did), and that there was eventual but no immediate prospect of the use of video equipment, or infra-red equipment and/or image-intensifiers, enabling us to see what anyone was doing at any time. All of the precautions against deception, freely discussed not merely with the Group but with the Team, were therefore designed to compensate for this shortcoming. These we discuss in detail in Chapters XIV and XV, and associated Appendices (notably H to M), but it must be remembered that the chief objective in our investigation was the production of physical phenomena related to a series of experiments, and that procedures changed slightly as experience was gained or different security devices were employed. The reader who is impatient to learn more of these devices may find it helpful to turn to Walter Schnittger's account in Appendix D of three of the experiments which were very similar, although not identical, to those in which we were directly engaged.

The Procedure

Once all participants were seated in the séance room, the top (dimmer) light was turned off by whoever was nearest the door, usually MK. RF offered a brief invocation seeking the guidance and protection of the spirit Team. There followed a period of quiet meditation during which sitters were encouraged by RF to try to form a mental bridge with spirit communicators. After a few minutes RF asked whether everyone was OK. There were murmurs of assent. By this time (so we were told) both mediums, who were frequently heard to yawn, had entered a trance state, although we had no objective means of testing this. RF then switched to some jolly jingly melodies (Clockwork Classics), shortly succeeded by tranquil, music-of-the-spheres called "Sleepy Shores" to induce relaxation. The background music was played quietly throughout and was not infrequently changed in volume or content during the course of an experiment, or because a communicator asked for a different sort of music. One communicator specifically asked for some Elgar, whom he apparently knew, and a tape was duly bought by RF for the following session, when it was played.

The "Sleepy Shores" music was interrupted a few minutes into the sitting by the loud, distinctive and androgynous voice of 'Manu', who was invariably the first speaker, and who acted as the general prologue, mentor and impresario. He was shortly followed by Mrs Emily Bradshaw (EB). We were welcomed, with occasional comments on our states of health, absences or even preoccupations. Some forecast was given of what we were likely to experience that evening, and discussion followed. There was usually a pause while the 'energies' were built up, a process which could occasionally take several minutes, and which appeared to vary in length of time with the personalities of the sitters. A free exchange followed between sitters and these two communicators, who were then often joined by others. Both Manu and EB spoke through Diana. A clearer impression of events can be gained from a more detailed account of the first two sittings.

First Sitting: 2nd October 1995

The range of phenomena at this first sitting was particularly impressive, and our (AE, RN and MK) reactions to them were fresh and unbiased. All six of the original Group were present, having donned their luminously charged wristbands. Manu, whose voice sounded as though it came through a loudspeaker, warmly welcomed us through Diana in a very distinctive but mildly foreign accent, and proceeded to describe not only the spirit Team's objectives but what we were likely to see. Immediately after his withdrawal – to 'blend the energies' which we were invited to circulate sometimes clockwise, sometimes anti-clockwise in our minds – we heard Patrick, said to be a former priest, speak through Alan. He had a strong Southern Irish accent and a mischievous sense of humour. As with all those introduced to us that evening and during the subsequent months, there was complete consistency of both accent and mannerism in his speech. He initially sounded exhausted but promised it or he would 'unfold' as the evening progressed. He was comparing the process of communicating with the experience of jumping into a bath of custard, at which point Mrs Bradshaw, speaking through Diana, intervened by wondering "what the researchers will make of a bath of custard when it is written up," thereby clearly indicating their expectation of a formal report.

According to the account we were given by the Group after the sitting, EB had originally expressed a preference for being called Mrs Bradshaw rather than Emily (even though both were pseudonyms), since this was the custom in her day, which we suspected to have been Edwardian or inter-war. Mrs Bradshaw (EB) turned out to be the chief communicator. Her voice was clear and resonant, and somewhat formal, although in later months it appeared to soften as we got on Christian name terms with her. It was the voice of an upper-class English lady: melodious, *dégagé* and slightly stagey – and her attractive, intelligent and quick-witted personality left the impression of one accustomed to retiring from the dinner table so that the menfolk could circulate the port while she left to instruct the butler to see that the guests' horses were properly stabled. Emily remained with us throughout the sitting, not hesitating to interrupt or re-interpret the comments of others, even those of the elderly scientist who later appeared. But her interventions never seemed intrusive or bossy. The accent, intonation and mannerisms were idiosyncratic, consistent and readily recognisable, and quite unlike the medium's normal speech. (EB displayed an enthusiasm for the latest jargon, which she later told us she picked up in the course of her work a counsellor to young drug addicts who had recently died.)

A wide variety of entities and accents came through Alan in the early sittings. The communicators were hugely polite, and sounded excessively grateful for the fact that we had agreed to participate in an investigation. While there was plenty of teasing and merriment in this and subsequent sittings, there was never a hint of severity or rudeness: only on one or two occasions, during an animated discussion on a problem of evidentiality which worried us (or at least MK), was there ever a hint of acerbity.

As is customary, the Team appeared to be energised by music: hence the use of tapes. During a period of anything from a few minutes, as was the case during this first sitting, to fifteen or twenty minutes, while the 'energies' were said to be building up, we were encouraged to continue talking among ourselves, although occasional interventions and comments from Emily made it appear that she was part of the conversation. We were asked not to engage in disputes, or say anything which might disturb the harmonious atmosphere necessary for the production of phenomena.

An extract from the first tape will give the flavour of the event, as well as cast an interesting light on the relationships between spirit communicators and investigators, and the manner in which they sought to answer our questions (spirit communicators' names and utterances are italicised, for ease of understanding):–

MK [addressing the Foys, and referring to the music]: What does Emily Bradshaw like?

> *EB: I like a variety of music, so I'm quite easy to please, but I do like the classical music rather — jigs are not my choice, but it's the vibration of the music that matters for our purpose, rather than personal choice. I'm going out for a moment.*
>
> *Patrick: Lots of movement going on, lots of things happening.*
>
> RF: Yes, do chatter, it all helps.
>
> *Patrick: Thanks very much*
>
> Sandra Foy (SF): Not you, Patrick! . . . Better be quiet for a while.
>
> MK: Patrick sounded rather tired.
>
> RF: He always sounds tired; he'll be having a kip.
>
> *EB: Puts his feet up at any opportunity.*

Patrick: It's really . . . how it gets me. When I'm first called upon it makes me feel a sort of drowsiness. I haven't a clue what it is but if I stay in situ, *things do improve.*

RN: How do you know when it's time to come, you know about this meeting? Is time on your side like time here?

Patrick: Oh now you're getting into deep water already before we've started. We won't talk about time because that upsets a lot of people, but time doesn't really exist for us in the sense that it exists for yourself, but I know it's time to come, it's the moment I feel the pull.

EB: It's a sensing more than anything.

Patrick: Yes, a sensing like a pulling, and I recognise that pull and I know where it's coming from.

EB: Like a signal.

Patrick: Yes, like a signal [after further discussion] I feel the pull and I know I have to come and speak through the medium . . . it's a slowing down to the state where I can come and speak to you: having to put my thoughts into words. None of us have to do that, you see.

EB: It's totally instantaneous, you see.

Patrick: Yes, we don't have to. There's not many of us can do this, when you're talking numbers.

There followed an impressive display of lights (described more fully in Chapter III), a requested change of the tape to 'classical pops', apparently one of Mrs Bradshaw's favourites, and a sudden self-relegation of Patrick to make way for the first displays: "I've been told to get right back ... I'll be back." Then the string of bells started to ring. A hoarse, croaky, apparently independent voice was heard. RF announced him as 'one of our scientists' and we were told he was Joseph. A light then started to appear in various parts of the chamber. Emily predicted that it would be passing through the table for AE's benefit: "we thought he'd enjoy it". The spirit light, a small bright speck no larger than a pea, alighted on one of the tabs, then sequentially illuminated the Pyrex bowl from inside, settled momentarily on the ceiling, then audibly hit the fish tank and appeared beneath the table, then visited the tape recorder. Bernette observed that, were any of the Group controlling the light, "our arms would be all over the place". The conversation which followed a few minutes later gives some idea of the behaviour of the light:–

RN: Yes, it's touched my thumb, on my wrist.

MK: I'm holding out my hand like a Dickensian schoolboy . . . Oh, it's gone right through my hand!

SF: Yes, it can.

RF: Impressive isn't it? Look, little halos, figures of eight and zig-zags.

RN: Look at that!

SF: Giving all our sitters a halo.

Ken: Play with my bald head.

MK: It's got a variety of bald heads.

EB: It'll be over directly.

AE: Touched me on the top of my head!

EB: I did tell you it'd be over directly (laughter). You thought I was joking.

AE: Quite a tap! A very distinctive tap.

RF: Gone to the tank . . . Now the tub's lit up. We know all the shapes by now.

EB: It's two years this week.

RF: Exactly two years since the first phenomena. We didn't know how much it would build up from a single apport.

The light then went into the Pyrex bowl, tapped on the table and grew brighter. When RF said that we had to see the light going through the top of the table, the light immediately hit the table top three times. From time to time during these displays the voice of Lawrence, growing less croaky, promised to speak to us shortly. His was the independent voice, called an energy voice by the Group, and it appeared to come from a position on the table. RF said it was only about six weeks ago that they had received their first energy voice. While Lawrence was struggling to come through, another independent voice recognised as John introduced himself and exchanged greetings with Ken but, save to bid farewell, took no further part in the rest of the proceedings, which were henceforth dominated by the energy voice of Lawrence:–

Lawrence: It's coming better now. Not easy, you know. Can you hear me?

All: Yes.

Lawrence: I'm going to stay here. I found it very warm during the transition. There's a plumber here.

MK: I was talking about a plumber [MK had earlier described a scraping sound as resembling a noise produced by a plumbing operation].

Lawrence: I beg your pardon. I thought you were a plumber (laughter).

MK: I'm not clever enough for that.

Lawrence: You're being too modest I'm sure.

Sandra: He's trying to take notes in the dark, so he's quite clever!

MK: Or foolish.

Lawrence: He's not having much success! (laughter). He's got scribbles all over the paper . . . just a moment . . . who's that?

RF: That's me.

Lawrence: Who's that?

RF: That's Ralph.

Lawrence: I'm touching your right hand.

RN: My right hand indeed it was: a slightly electric touch.

Lawrence: You'd have an electric touch if you came from where I'm from (laughter). You get highly charged.

AE: You don't know your own strength.

Lawrence: Forgive my ignorance but I think I have a certain amount of static. Would you consider that a possibility?

AE: Yes, I would.

Lawrence: I'm going to discharge it in a moment.

RF: Going to discharge the static?

Lawrence: If you don't mind.

RF: That's interesting.

Lawrence: You might feel it, you might see it: I don't know if you realise, these three eminent gentlemen before us, that I'm speaking into a container. It has rather an echo.

AE: Yes.

Lawrence: Not literally, for that's not possible, but the vibrations you are hearing are emanating from within that container.

AE: Yes.

Lawrence: Now I shall place the container on the table and continue to speak.

RF: His voice is clearer when he uses it, but it fades away.

Lawrence was then prevailed upon to do his party piece, although he thought it must have got a bit boring by now: picking up the ping-pong ball. We then heard the sound of the Pyrex bowl as though it was being dragged along the top of the table. Then we heard the ball bouncing. Lawrence declared that he had dropped it. "It's slippery!" It then levitated, visibly so when its luminous tab faced any of us. As it hit the bells, they tinkled. A small light appeared and visited the ball, which dropped suddenly under MK's chair. He asked whether he should pick it up. As he tried to do so it moved away from his grasp into the corner of the quadrant below the table, a section quite inaccessible to any member of the Group, or indeed either of the other two investigators. Lawrence said it was electrically charged. The ball rolled out of the quadrant and towards RN's seat. MK contrived to grasp it, then exclaimed "No, it's gone again!" He finally managed to retain it (it had what he described as an immaterial feeling) and handed it to RN on his right. RN feared he might get another shock. "No, you've had it; you don't get two," said Lawrence.

RN then held the ball in the palm of his hand. A light approached. Bernette, on RN's right, asked whether it had sat on RN's hand. RN said it had run across his lower palm, like the end of a little rod. Lawrence asked what RN was going to do next. RN expressed puzzlement. Lawrence announced that RN would be showing us a trick. He should count to three and throw the ball back. RN did so, but the general atmosphere of hilarity was such as to make it uncertain what happened to the ball, except that its performance was described by

Sandra as Lawrence's party piece. This was followed by another and more brilliant display of the light describing large circles, and then appearing to perform acrobatics, including a series of ellipses. AE felt a peanut-like object hitting his finger twice, then appearing as a light above his head. AE declared himself dashed. Emily popped back to say he would be, shortly. There were "SPR this side, SPR your side: the place is alive with them". She declined to give names – at that stage.

The party atmosphere changed dramatically as Joseph, who had been speaking to us earlier via Alan, returned. He apologised for remaining anonymous, and offered to answer any questions, which turned mainly on the nature of the after-life, the extent to which it could be linked to lucid dreaming, the role of near-death and out-of-body experiences in relation to the next world, and several related ontological issues which fall outside the strict scope of this Report. The communicators seemed very touched by our offer to do what we could to help produce examinable phenomena under the right control conditions, and the sitting ended on a suitably elevated note as Joseph explained their mission: "We want to make people aware that there is something more to life than living, and death is nothing to fear, just an extension to life. It's a good thing happiness is involved in this work. It isn't all darkness and gloom. It is love and it is light."

EB suggested a series of sittings, some of them devoted to particular aspects of the varied work they planned.

Second Sitting: 15th December 1995

Since a wide range of the phenomena of the second sitting were similar to those experienced at the first, there is no point in repetition. We note the events of the second sitting (with the same participants) chiefly to indicate novel features or changes, and as a preface to our comments on some of the issues which they immediately raise.

RN first satisfied himself that entry into the room without detection was not practicable. Then, after complying as best we felt able with Manu's request to pass the energies mentally anti-clockwise (usually it is clockwise when there are no visitors, we were told), Sandra was asked to remove the 'fish tank' from the table centre and place it beneath her chair to be out of the way. Manu then invited us to enjoy the promised spectacle of light and other wonders, while reserving our more complex questions for later. After some fairly light-hearted discussion on the appropriateness of various pieces of music played on the background tape, RF said he discerned a change in the atmosphere. RN agreed, noting that there seemed to be a structure to it, like filaments of light, very faint.

The spirit voices soon emerged. Lawrence, a direct-voice communicator, came first. RF explained that his correct name was Reginald Lawrence, and he had been an engineer when on earth. One of the investigators whistled to the music. RF said this was out of order, since it might be coming from the other side. MK commented that it was also slightly out of tune. Mrs Bradshaw then intervened to observe amid laughter that those were two good reasons (for the ban). Sandra thought she saw a flash of light from the corner of her eye. EB noted with mock severity that Sandra was the only one being observant. Then the light display proper began, starting with the appearance of a thin filament inside one of the six Perspex supports to the plinth bearing the glass dome. RF said this was different from the lights we had seen during the previous session, as this was stationary and was introduced inside the dome at the base whence it would build up and spread. Its appearance on this occasion was like a quartz crystal, but (according to RF's explanation) it was simply the essence of a crystal that we could discern giving off light. RN noted that the light was sufficient to enable him to see the dome quite well.

Joseph, whose voice through Alan largely dominated the rest of the lengthy sitting, invited us to take part in an experiment: to place our hands on our knees and apply a little pressure. As we did so the light brightened significantly. (This simple test was later to be repeated successfully on two separate occasions in succeeding sittings.) MK bent low over the table to examine the light which had permeated the Perspex support legs, but was unable to see any filament, and he drew attention to the absence of any focal point in the light. AE likened it to a luminous cloud, then confirmed that the ping-pong ball was being moved around inside the Pyrex dish, or bowl. MK said he could see good reflections from the bowl. AE described it as shining on the plinth while the crystal or image of a crystal was brightening. We then observed the ball spinning round inside the bowl, and becoming much brighter. A hand was seen, dimly by RN, but initially not at all by MK, picking up the ball and dropping it. AE then saw the hand, casting a 'big shadow'. We clearly heard the sound of a ball bouncing. AE saw an arm going across the light. We discerned figures, but vaguely. From time to time these figures obscured some of the table tabs. However, we all believed we saw some form of shapes building up, with varying degrees of illumination.

The atmosphere changed when the display ended. It felt colder and darker. Joseph announced that he wanted to speak to us. He explained that he and his spirit friends existed in a land of pure thought and light, but light of an entirely different kind, not made up of material matter. He confessed it was very difficult to explain such concepts in terms we could understand. The rest of the session was devoted to the problems and techniques of communication. Discussion then centred on the extent to which 'negative vibrations' from sitters would inhibit the production of phenomena, and whether or not the use of infra-red photography, for which we were constantly pressing, would constitute a further obstacle, and also whether or not we could suggest or introduce some experiments of our own design.

In a statement which was intended to distinguish the entire investigation from any predecessors, and which both provided the explanation and established the limitations of the whole range of phenomena and associated experiments, Joseph continued:–

> *These experiments we have embarked on ourselves have been thought [out] and established as being interesting experiments by a team of spirit people from our side, the team working with the sole aim being to provide, as you say, evidence of an after-life. Now this indeed is what we are hoping will come to fruition, but up until this moment the Team have always thought it sufficient to provide their own evidence. It is not until yourselves have suggested that one might embark on other experiments that this ever came to the fore. It was never ever thought of. It was always thought that what we would produce would be sufficient, so you must understand that by your suggestions [of] other experiments which pose some minor difficulties on our side, that we do have to discuss in great depth sometimes just how these experiments might be carried [out]. But of course the main object of any experiments is to achieve successful results, and this is what we wish to do: to perfect our experiments to the point where we produce repeatable, successful results.*

The elaboration of this objective, in the light of the experimenters' proposals for the production of something akin to a permanent paranormal object, is best left to the stage when we discuss shortcomings and reservations. However, it was made clear (particularly by EB) that the Team did not wish to fragment their efforts. They were still in an experimental stage, and were intent at present on concentrating on the production of photographic evidence which would take us further along the road of evidentiality than the still frames which had been produced earlier.

It may be appropriate at this point to make it clear that in several of the earlier sittings one or other of us proposed specific experiments which we believed would, if successful under carefully controlled conditions, provide impressive evidence in support of a survival hypothesis. AE was especially fertile in his efforts to prevail upon the communicators to see whether they could read random numbers atop his study bookcase, or in his pocket during the sitting; and he was anxious to emphasise not merely the importance which the outside world would inevitably attach to the presence, and operation, of infra-red cameras to compensate for the darkness, but the apparent innocuousness of instruments such as image intensifiers, which were operated by the naturally-occurring infra-red spectrum of radiation from human bodies, without the need to use any fresh radiation or strong power. We were unable to make progress here, and had to reconcile ourselves to awaiting the promised day when sufficient light would somehow be provided by the spirit forces themselves to overcome the deficiencies of darkness. Nor were we ever able to understand how non-invasive instruments like image-intensifiers could have an inhibiting or adverse effect on the phenomena.

As for the specific experiments, including a recommendation of a book test (in which a psychic, or purported spirit, reveals the contents of a nominated line in an arbitrarily chosen page of a book in a specified location on a particular shelf in a library), Emily was dismissive. She pointed out that this had been done before – implying that it had not altered convictions – and that in any event they, the spirit Team, wanted to detach themselves from earlier experiments and to embark on something new, and more evidential. It was a disappointment to us that this reluctance, or inability, to undertake tests which we believed would have a substantial impact applied also to two simple devices which we had brought with us, which we left on a corner table of the room for the Team's inspection. Designed by Maurice Grosse (a member of the SPR Council, Chairman of its Spontaneous Cases Committee, and an inventor), they were intended to challenge a psychic claimant to change the position or alter the shape or location of an object sealed against any normal form of intrusion.

However, as the extract quoted above makes clear, there was reluctance to depart from the prepared programme, although a ready willingness to discuss and implement improvements in procedures to counter any accusation of deception. This was to have important consequences in the several experiments with sealed films.

Sittings Elsewhere

Since suspicion inevitably attaches to the fact that sittings were conducted in a specially prepared room in the house of the principal protagonist, it is worth recording at this stage that the Group have held sittings, with others present, in several different locations, mainly abroad during visits to Germany, the Netherlands, Switzerland, Ireland, Spain and the USA. Four of these sittings, two on the Spanish island of Ibiza (see Chapter XI) and two in California (see Appendix F) were attended by one of us (MK). In these cases the Group had no facility for preparing the room, beyond checking the black-out arrangements and placing luminous strips at the cardinal points of a central circular table.

CHAPTER III: THE PHENOMENA: LIGHTS AND TOUCHES

The Lights

The most immediately striking feature of the series of sittings we attended (see list of dates, Appendix B) was the occurrence of displays of light, several of which have just been described. Contemporary notes were supplemented by and cross-checked against transcripts of tapes on which the sounds and comments accompanying the phenomena were recorded. At every sitting, save those specifically dedicated either to a discussion (e.g. MK6, 4th March 1997) or to the production of films or messages on tape, light phenomena appeared. Invariably Manu came through first, and we had discussions with spirit voices. We give below a fairly comprehensive summary of the various phenomena involving light which all or some of us have witnessed, often on several occasions. We cannot, however, ignore the several written testimonies we have also had from others, including several members of the Council of the Society, Professor Ivor Grattan-Guinness, Dr Rupert Sheldrake and Ingrid Slack, individuals who have attended Scole seminars either at Scole or elsewhere, and in particular from Walter and Karin Schnittger and Dr Hans Schaer, of whose involvement more anon. All of these have testified to many of the phenomena we describe. The references given in brackets are to the relevant sittings and the pages of the transcripts where the phenomena are recorded or commented on. Sittings marked R relate to occasions where two or more of us were present. Those marked MK are sittings where only MK was present, with invited guest sitters or alone. That marked DF refers to a sitting on 11th November 1996, when only DF and Ingrid Slack (IS) were present with the Group.

The (normally single) light point would appear to:–

1 Dart around at great speed and perform elaborately patterned dances in front of us, including perfect, sustained circles executed at high velocity and with a precision which appeared inconsistent with manual manipulation;

2 Become visible to one of us but not the person next to him, and then reverse this arrangement as a demonstration of occlusion capacity and intelligent motivation (R8, pp.5–6);

3 Settle on outstretched hands and jump from one to the other (R5, p.3);

4 Respond to requests, such as alighting on and irradiating parts of our bodies;

5 Enter a crystal and remain as a small point of light moving around within the crystal, or permeating light throughout its structure;

54

6 While performing a perfect circle of light, switch on and off certain segments of the circle;

7 Diffuse light through a Pyrex bowl, upturned or otherwise;

8 Leave at the base of the Pyrex bowl a three-dimensional image of a glowing crystal which is found to be insubstantial when seized by the investigators, then converting the glowing essence of this crystal into a solid form which could be picked up and replaced – and repeat this procedure twice, to the satisfaction of three close observers, one of whom (AE) placed his head immediately above and close enough to the bowl to preclude the entry of a normal hand, his face being clearly visible to MK and DF in the light fromthe crystal (R12, p.13);

9 Strike the top of the table with a sharp rap, or the glass of the dome or dish with an appropriate ping, and do this repeatedly while remaining visible as a sharp pin-point of light;

10 Appear inside the ping-pong ball, which was ejected from its position inside the Pyrex bowl on the table to the far side of the room, to be discovered on the floor after the session;

11 Create a diffused glow on the ceiling, on the floor, on the wall furthest from the table about a metre and a half distant from the table, or around the hands and knees of sitters, sufficient to enable their hands and sometimes faces, as well as MK's notebook and pen, to be seen by the investigators; create the same glow in mid-air, unreflected from any surface;

12 Illuminate sitters' feet below the edge of the circular table despite the barrier formed under it by the solid quadrant compartments which effectively precluded contact with any of the members of the Group;

13 Settle on and apparently enter the chests of investigators, who reported internal sensations immediately thereafter, then leaving from a different part of the body;

14 Enter a glass of water held by an investigator (DF), and agitate the water visibly and audibly without being extinguished, his face being immediately above the glass, precluding unobstructed entry of any physical device (R14, p.12).

15 Illuminate simultaneously with a generalised glow six separate 5-cm high solid Perspex supports of the wooden plinth carrying the glass dome (R3);

16 Settle on the open palms of a guest investigator (Prof. Grattan-Guinness), who then enfolded the light inside his hands, momentarily, to satisfy himself of the absence of any physical link (MK7 p.5);

17 With the aid of a silhouette of the hand and fingers of an apparently discarnate entity, elevate a crystal illuminated from within by a spirit light, and transport it to the other side of the table;

18 Illumine from within a light bulb suspended well above the sitters' heads, with no light coming from the filament (R3);

19 Produce a glow in different parts of the glass tank, and move around there (R3);

20 Appear in a form similar to a large glass marble, which rolled across the table to one of the investigators, producing enough light to illuminate his hands;

21 Move in time to tape-recorded music (R14, p.11);

22 Produce 'lightning flashes' in an area of a large room some 3 to 3½ metres distant from the Group sitting round a table (MK Ibiza report);

23 Appear as two separate lights simultaneously (MK4, p.11);

24 Undertake several aerial 'bombing raids' on the table top, hitting it very audibly and visibly, and appearing to emerge from an area immediately below the table (USA Los Angeles report and at Scole, where the light typically re-emerged between one of the quadrants supporting the table);

25 Remain for a minute or more as a motionless, sharp, small, steady glow immediately above the table at head height;

26 Change shape from a pin-point of light to a generalised irradiation or glow;

27 Charge with visible light a ping-pong ball, which was levitated, dropped on the floor at the feet of a sitter, and moved away from his grasp into a dead-end corner of a quadrant beneath the table, having previously been stationary;

28 Markedly increase in brightness in apparent response to collective hand pressure on the knees of sitters;

29 Move at very high speed describing at times perfect geometric shapes within a foot or two of visitors' faces, but without making any sound or creating any perceptible air movement;

30 Illuminate the fingers of a full-size spirit hand which the percipient describes as soft and cool to the touch;

31 Build up from a faintly diffused glow into materialised objects on or floating above the table, the objects taking the shape of small, draped figurines, or a vague 'face' with apparent movement of lips, the various objects being subject to movement, some rising towards the ceiling before disappearing;

32 Instantly vanish on occasions;

33 Build up from nothing to a rock-like shape which rises in the air, passes in front of one investigator before halting in front of another, then returning to its place of origin and gradually disappearing (DF1).

The behaviour of the lights was sometimes akin to that of a shy young child ushered into a noisy room of grown-ups after dinner to perform: it seemed in turn nervous, coy, coquettish, mischievous and daring. It soon became apparent, and is evident from the preceding descriptions, that the phenomenon of light cannot be dissociated from many of the sounds and touches, and other visual phenomena. Nor, for that matter, can it be entirely divorced from the anticipatory comments of the Team and the contemporaneous remarks of the investigators. They offer further evidence of what is being observed or experienced. An apt illustration is the frequency with which luminous tabs on the table were momentarily shrouded or occluded, or when light phenomena were clearly apparent to and commented on by one sitter when his neighbour could see nothing. A passage from MK's note on the 11th sitting of 15th June 1996 (R8, p.3) is worth quoting:–

> Perhaps the most remarkable phenomenon of the sitting arose after RF exclaimed repeatedly how he could see a bright light in front of him which neither AE nor I could see. Just as I was attributing this in my mind to RF's imagination, a very sharp, bright light performed figures-of-eight and minor gyrations just in front of me. It did this on three occasions, for very short periods, while I described what was happening [R8 pp.4–5], surprised that others failed to see it. Shortly thereafter Sandra, on my left [DF could not attend this session], had the same experience: none of us could see what she was describing. Finally AE witnessed a similar light which, even though I bent towards him, I could not see. We concluded that the light in each case must have been occluded as though screens were placed in front of it and directed towards each of us in turn, with a fairly narrow arc of perhaps no more than 15° or 20°. The light was pin-point, very sharp and bright, not rays or glows, and moved swiftly.

Forms, Shapes and Touches

Before attempting any preliminary assessment of this evidence, or commenting on the explanation we were given about the nature of these lights, we should note some of these additional but apparently associated phenomena, apart from the sharp raps and pings which accompanied the kamikaze activities of the light spot and have already been commented on.

For the main part, forms were seen more or less dimly (R5, pp.3–4), but occasionally the silhouette of a graceful, full-sized hand was quite unmistakable as it grasped a crystal, or levitated a crystal, or gripped the upturned Pyrex bowl, illuminated from the inside by a spirit light, and moved it around. The fainter, self-illuminated forms, however, were generally much smaller than life-size – one investigator described one such manifestation as having the appearance of a figurine (MK 3) – while others saw and felt not only a hand but the fabric as of a gossamer dress or train as well (DF, AE). We experienced nothing which either resembled or rivalled the full-scale materialisations reported from traditional séances, but (as we were frequently reminded) this was supposedly not a séance but an experimental session in which a novel type of pure energy, wholly divorced from ectoplasm and its dubious physiological effects and dangers, was being developed. What we saw, indeed, had no apparent physical connection with either of the mediums: the figures appeared to float around, growing or contracting in size, sometimes above the table, sometimes elsewhere. Now and again the substance or image would be seen, albeit in its own dim, diffused light, to be changing shape, and was thus observed by one cautiously sceptical sitter (MK3, p.9). The angelic vision, as it was called by the Group, was particularly evident to DF at the previously mentioned (17th) sitting with IS when a bright area of self-illumination developed on the table in front of him, grew into the shape of a rock the size of a small grapefruit and, still brightly illuminated, was levitated, held out first towards DF, then towards IS, and finally placed in her hand. She commented that it felt like muslin (see Appendix G).

Occasionally we all experienced a gossamer-like brushing against our hands, sometimes accompanied by visible spirit forms, as during the 17th sitting when quite well illuminated essences built up to a height of about one metre in front of IS, who was sitting on DF's right. These made graceful movements in the air and trailed lace-like material across DF's hands. On more than one occasion two investigators, separated from each other by about a metre, and with another investigator seated between them, exclaimed when they were touched simultaneously. The aim, we were told by the communicators, was to provide evidence that there was more than one spirit entity responsible, and to show that the gap between the places touched was too wide for any one person to bridge (R13, p.9; R14). One guest sitter (Prof. Bernard Carr) reported having his fingers held and then his entire arm lifted up to its full extent above his head (R13, p.10). Simultaneously DF, sitting two places away, reported an identical experience. Once again, the gap between the investigators was too great for any one individual to bridge. On another occasion a spirit hand grasped the front of DF's sweater and pulled it gently but firmly away from him and over and above the rim of the table, an action only apparently possible if one of the Group had climbed onto the table. Several times objects such as film cassettes were placed in the hands of sitters on request, the sitters' hands being invariably found with unerring accuracy in the darkness. This ability to locate sitters with such precision, often in immediate response to specific requests, was in fact a feature throughout the investigations.

Not infrequently we experienced intense, very rapid and sustained table vibrations, accompanied on occasions by a distinct clockwise movement, as could be observed from the movement of the luminous table tabs. These were both felt and heard.

A fair example of the range of experiences encountered is given in the following verbatim extract of part of a sitting at which Dr Rupert Sheldrake (RS) was the guest investigator, with MK (MK4, pp.10–11). Question marks in brackets indicate inaudibility on the tape. Emily Bradshaw is the sole spirit communicator here:–

RF: [re the light] Just gone through your book, Monty?

MK: Yes. Seemed to, by the weight of it.

RF: Went through your book [MK's notebook resting on his lap] and appeared in the bowl. Here it goes again.

MK: Party trick. [Addressing RS] Did you hear that noise?

RS: Yes.

RF: Through the book and comes out from this side of the table.

EB: Is that 149, Robin? [RF keeps a record of every new example of physical phenomena]

RF: Yes, that's it.

MK: Sort of (?) act. And out again! I wonder if there will be burn marks on the book.

EB (with delicate sarcasm): What does he think the energy is?

MK: Eight or nine [counting light phenomena repetitions]: that seemed to come out on my leg. I've (got) it [the light] on my leg!

RF: Might have gone in.

RS: I was touched . . . Oh!

SF: Ask them to hold your hand.

RS: Will you hold my hand?

MK: These two things are happening at once. Simultaneously. Because this light has been sitting on me as well as my paper.

RS: Good heavens: whizzing round me now! Gosh!

SF: Display.

RS: Amazing! Now it's hovering.

MK: One thing you'll find interesting is there's no noise. You expect to see *[sic]* a noise, whizzing round at that rate.

EB: You're enjoying yourself now, aren't you?

RS: I'm fascinated. There's a hand, touched the light in front of me, (?) hand.

EB: Yes, quite often: various shapes and sizes and so on.

RF: Half an arc again.

MK: [pedantically]: Half a circle.

SF: Lit something up there (?)

EB: Yes it is, Sandra.

RS: You mean there's a whole body there?

EB: Yes, we don't have bits of people!

RS: Well it looks like bits.

EB: Well it isn't. Some parts are denser. The whole form is there.

RS: The hand – the whole form of the hand is there!

SF: A spirit hand.

RS: There's a hand.

SF: Yes.

RS: A hand near me.

MK: Do you think the hand is holding the light?

RS: The light seems to be lighting up the hand. It's like the palm, cupped hands floating in space.

MK: Oh yes, and the fingers just pointing down.

RS: Up I think.

SF: Yes.

RS: How many spirit people are here at a time?

RF: It depends.

EB: Two at the same time.

RS*: The same ones every time?*

EB: No, different people come to work and learn.

MK: They're experimenting on us (laughter)!

EB: Yes, absolutely.

RS: They are also gaining experience themselves, doing it again and again. Have they done it lots of times before on other circles?

EB: Oh no.

RS: So it's a new experience for them.

EB: A new experience for them, touching the earth energy and work with you. They come to serve.

MK: I only invite you to the most exclusive clubs!

A little later in the same sitting the following occurred:–

MK: I'm leaning towards you and I can't see it.

RS: There it is: it's coming down. Can you see it? [MK was on his immediate right.]

MK: No I can't . . . leaning towards you.

RS: No, it's gone now.

RF: The crystal's lighting up now.

MK: Oh yes! In front of me.

RF: Oh, I can see fingers on it. Someone picking it up.

MK: It's being moved, can you see?

RS: Yes.

MK: Going into the bowl. Hope they do that disappearing exercise!

EB: Sounds like a dare.

MK: An invitation (table vibrates)

RF: Oh, the bowl: lit up now.

SF: Oh, see the crystals in there?

MK: Did you see a hand coming over the top, picking it up?

RS: Yes.

MK: A hand, pointing very clearly! Did you see that! Extraordinary!

SF: Showing you.

EB: Can you see that, Rupert?

RS: Yes I can.

EB: Jolly good.

RS: The hand appeared to have a sleeve too.

SF: Did it? [Noise of crystals in the bowl].

MK: Oh, it's bashing me on the head: should I pick it up?

SF: No, you're probably leaning too far forward.

MK: That was very clear, wasn't it?

RS: Very clear (table vibrating again). I saw an actual sleeve.

SF: Yes, they have robes sometimes.

EB: You have felt the fabric before.

SF: Yes.

MK: Gossamer, lovely feeling.

No less interesting was a brief interchange which occurred (R12, pp.17/18) on 9th November 1996 during an experiment in which one tub containing an unopened, unexposed Polaroid 35mm film cassette was left in a sealed wooden box on the table, while a second film tub containing a Kodachrome 200 film was left there without any covering, as part of an experiment described in more detail later. There had been sounds of movement on the table. Then Emily spoke:–

EB: Looking at the other film. Got a new one for us to look at, haven't you?
     [This referred to the Kodachrome film, of which the Team had had no previous experience]

SF: They've taken the film out of the container! Just tapped my hand and put the film out of the plastic container. They've taken it back.

MK: Which one would it be?

SF: It wouldn't be the one in the box, I shouldn't think. Give it to Monty! [This was addressed to the spirit responsible for handling the film]

DF: [sitting next to her] Or to me. Yes! It's touched me. Can you put it on my hand — ah! That's it. It closed my hand over it gently. It's the film! [DF notes that it was his right hand].

RF: They're still rattling the container [i.e. the box with the tub in] over the table.

DF: That's absolutely mind-blowing. That felt warm, too.

MK: Putting it back (movement heard) [i.e. back into the tub]

During the previous sitting (R11, p.7), some time after the ping-pong ball (in DF's words noted immediately afterwards) had been "thrown violently out of the Pyrex bowl" in front of MK and AE, and the bowl had been heard to scrape and slide across the table until it came to rest a few centimetres in front of DF, both his hands were held. In a separate record of this event, DF describes how a ball of light, the size of a large glass marble, appeared on the table and apparently rolled towards him, remaining a few centimetres away on the table:–

> It illuminated my hands, palms uppermost, so brightly that I saw all ten fingers clearly . . . My right hand, palm uppermost, was touched. The fingers [of a dark shape he had earlier seen on top of the ball of light] then slid up towards my palm, so that with my thumb and finger I could hold them gently from above. The hand was small and delicate, like a woman's, and felt cool. On other occasions a spirit hand shook our hands on request, again finding us with unerring accuracy in the dark.

Although the foregoing examples raise many other questions relating to the luminous and tactile phenomena in particular (some of which we discuss later when we examine in detail the fraud hypothesis in the light of the evidence), it may be helpful to interpose some clarifying comments. The first relates to the exceptional nature of the tape recording itself. In this extract there are four people talking, plus a spirit voice, sometimes overlapping, and not in an acoustically ideal room. The voices were inevitably at different volumes and expressed with varying degrees of clarity. RF normally had the clearest and loudest voice, and made a practice of commenting aloud on the phenomena in order to get a permanent record. However, as a sensitive himself, with many years' experience of what are now called energy voices and of the appearance of shapes and visions in darkened rooms, he sometimes reported seeing or sensing things which others perceived not at all or only dimly. Not infrequently this difference in perception could be attributed to the position of the sitter, since on the hypothesis that there actually were spirit forms moving around the table, sometimes shifting or seeming to examine things (this was particularly true in the film and tape recording experiments described later), one person would see the tabs on the table, marking the cardinal points, temporarily obscured from the gaze of his neighbour.

The passage quoted above shows how EB did not simply act as part of the general conversation group, but made it appear as though she were sitting in their midst, able not only to 'observe' what was going on but equally to predict what was about to happen. That there was an apparent link between EB, together with any of her associates who came through, and the animated lights themselves, became obvious with longer experience, although the precise relationship between the collaborators and the lights was never clear. EB explained that the lights were themselves spirit forms which were there independently, but it had been found that they could be usefully employed in this way. We ourselves found it difficult to advance a convincing normal hypothesis for the range and variety of phenomena exhibited, and none was advanced, to our knowledge, by other sitters.

As is apparent from the foregoing descriptions, the light had a capacity to change shape, disperse radiance through crystals and Perspex cylinders, activate ping-pong balls, enter an upturned Pyrex bowl and an electric light bulb, collaborate in (or be wholly responsible for) the levitation of small objects, and enter and irradiate a glass of water. It was also heard and felt by AE to hit his spectacles, then his cheek (R14, p.9), but there was no pain or heat, even when it rested on a hand. Not merely the shape but the texture appeared to change. Those who reported having actually felt the light inside their cupped hands sometimes described a rough, rod-like texture; yet there was no evidence of any physical link with a transmitting agent, and on other occasions this rod-like texture was not present. DF reported that the light felt like a touch from a finger tip, and remarked on the similarity to phenomena witnessed by Geley (Geley, 1927).

Whether or not the spirit lights, if paranormal, were self-controlled or regulated from another level of consciousness, they behaved as though they could 'see' precisely where to go. During our first sitting, MK made the mistake of referring to 'direct voice' transmissions, and was promptly told by RF that this expression was no longer used. "If we use it we get our wrists slapped," he added. At precisely that moment MK felt a sharp but playful tap on the knuckles of his writing hand. Several months later (R12, p.15), following a similar misdemeanour, he expressed the fear that he might get his knuckles rapped again, but EB said there were other ways of showing disdain, at which point a sharp, clear sound of finger-snapping was heard in our midst. Finger-snapping was heard again at the DF sitting already mentioned, when raps described as "startlingly loud" were heard coming from the table.

Discussion

Any normal explanation – that is, one which complies with normal physical laws – presupposes at least two requirements. The first would appear to assume complicity by at least two and probably more members of the Group in deception of a highly skilled character. The second would require the existence of secreted apparatus to produce all these effects. Regular searches of the Scole chamber failed to produce any evidence of hidden artifacts. In addition, many of these phenomena were replicated in unfamiliar overseas locations in the presence of one of us (among a considerable number of other independent witnesses), and in circumstances which would have made prior installation of any such mechanisms impracticable. It is true that members of the Group were not body-searched before the sittings, but the possibility of their smuggling the necessary apparatus into and out of the cellar at each sitting, while under close observation and without detection, seems unlikely. In addition, if suspicion falls only on the two mediums, they would have had to smuggle this apparatus into and out of the Foys' house twice a week for a period of some four years. Nevertheless, although the presence of full body searches has never served in the past to allay the criticism of sceptics, the absence of such searches in the present investigation cannot be ignored.

However, the use of clandestine equipment would have required energetic and hence detectable movement by any of the arm-banded Group. The behaviour of the light or lights was generally inconsistent with the concept of a rod or manipulated wire or thread. Such hypothetical instruments or mechanisms would not only have had to create the lights but enable them to change form, move at great speed, and describe perfect geometrical shapes in the air at such velocities that the shapes appeared unbroken. Then, when still producing the shapes, the lights would have to remove a segment from view, replace it, then remove another segment. They would equally have to possess the competence to respond intelligently to requests, act in places or on things which were not in a direct line with any member of the Group, visit apparently inaccessible sites with great precision despite the darkness, irradiate objects such as Pyrex bowls, cylindrical Perspex supports and sitters' feet, and simulate the floating figures.

As already indicated, many of the light phenomena were associated with physical contact experienced by the investigators. Indeed, save for those later sittings where energy and attention alike were concentrated on the production of durable evidence, all of us frequently experienced touches, both by the entities of light themselves and by either unseen or perceived spirit forms. We have previously noted that the solid support quadrants of the table, and the juxtapositioning of the seats, made it impractical for many of the touches to be carried out by members of the Group, even had they been able to leave their seats without detection. Not only were touches experienced on feet and legs positioned within a quadrant of the table, and hence inaccessible to a groping hand or foot: they were quite often delivered with a precision which seemed inconsistent with the absence of light. A playful rebuke in the form of a light tap on the knuckles of the erring investigator, a gentle massage of an injured leg or a light brush over the cheek or on the head – these were the sorts of tactile phenomena regularly reported. Both MK and DF had the outside surfaces of their legs touched when situated in such proximity to each other that intrusion by a physical hand and arm between them would have been immediately detected. These touches were almost invariably gentle, including the soft sweep of gossamer-like substances from the illuminated figures clearly experienced by all of us.

Neither the frequency nor the impressiveness and variety of the phenomena appeared to be influenced by location. In the two sittings which MK attended in Los Angeles and San Francisco (a detailed account of which appears in Appendix F), lights, bangs, drummings, table vibrations and touches were reported by nearly all those attending, some 20 persons on each occasion. Among the more remarkable, and felt by more than half those present at a Los Angeles meeting, was the unmistakeable brush of a cat's tail against sitters' legs, when no living cat was present. (Since MK was unaccompanied by AE and DF on these occasions the controls were not those operative at the Scole sittings; but the opportunities for the Group or any member of it to attempt to tamper with the rooms in which these sessions were held were correspondingly less.)

One of the merits of publishing this factual report is that it constitutes an invitation to others to seek to replicate some of the effects described, and in conditions as close as possible to those under which the phenomena were produced. The authors wish to emphasise their readiness to co-operate in any serious attempts to this end.

CHAPTER IV: THE PHENOMENA: PUZZLES AND HINTS

One facet of the evidence from our sittings comprised the exchanges between the investigators and the Team, speaking either through the entranced mediums or, less frequently, by what were said by the Group to be energy voices, better known as direct voices in that they appeared to originate from above the central table area or from some object on the table itself. It cannot be said that the examples of these exchanges in this chapter bear the marks of any consistent plan, such as that which characterised some of the Cross-Correspondences. What plan or purpose is behind the present assortment of exchanges, if this disparate group of almost casual references and messages can be thus described, is far less clear, unless it be simply to provide us with a variety of apparently off-the-cuff observations, some of them appearing to stem from our own questions or comments, but their cumulative impact was intended to strengthen the evidence pointing to survival as the likeliest explanation. In a separate category, and assuming a greater importance in our eyes, are those discussions which relate to future or recent film material; and these we deal with in later chapters. We give some examples of these verbal exchanges and messages below:–

The Inversion

During the fifth sitting (16th March 1996) the "Classical pops" tape was being played as background music. A new (to us) Indian speaker, Raji, came through Alan, initially somewhat chokily. He commented briefly on the music, which consisted of snatches of familiar classical pieces melded after a couple of bars into another extract. He identified Gershwin from a snatch of the *Rhapsody in Blue,* then mentioned *William Tell,* as the Rossini overture was heard. Shortly afterwards, in the middle of a wholly different conversation, he tried with limited success to pronounce Paganini and Rachmaninoff, but then blurted out excitedly that it was the same at the end as at the beginning and went back to the middle. MK then remarked "That's interesting: it's reversed. Not many people know that."

MK later pointed out that a fragment of what he thought was the eighteenth variation in the Rachmaninoff/Paganini variations was being played at that moment. The melody is quite a popular one, but the fact that it is, technically, an inversion, i.e. written back to front (although the key and note durations may be changed), is not widely known. Indeed, according to views expressed to MK by musicologists, this was unlikely to have been recognised by those without musical education (none of the Group has any special leanings to classical music, although they may well have been familiar with the excerpt itself).

The Rayleigh Drop-In

The following sitting (13th April 1996), which was mainly concerned with a possible link with Frederic Myers (described in Chapter V on the Diotima film), provided another illustration of a message which had all the appearances of an unpremeditated and entirely casual remark, but which yielded results we found of interest. Towards the end of the sitting, Emily Bradshaw said "There's a gentleman here, used to be one of your sort" [ie SPR]. "Well, quite an important man – but you can't tell: they all say that, don't they? [laughter] . . . He's been before, used to live at 16 Terling Place, Chelmsford . . . Oh, a lord! We are honoured!" MK exclaimed "Really" in an affected accent which led Emily to conclude that he was on the track, and AE clinched it by saying "Rayleigh". MK, who has agricultural connections, said he'd be strutting up and down with pride. He later explained that he had recognised the name from his recollection of the Terling Herd of Pedigree Friesian cattle, which he knew to have been owned by Lord Rayleigh's farms, that the family name of the Rayleighs was Strutt, and that Lord Rayleigh's farms were associated with or managed by Strutt & Parker Farms, whose managing director, Sir Nigel Strutt, was an old friend.

When MK subsequently spoke to Sir Nigel Strutt, the current head of the Strutt family, which has long had close connections with the SPR, he was told, with some indignation, that the correct address was simply Terling Place (which is in fact a vast country mansion). At the next sitting, we raised the question of Lord Rayleigh's address, and EB immediately apologised for getting the number wrong: it was at the end of a sitting when the contact wasn't good, she explained. Then (R7, p.11):–

MK: Do you know which Lord Rayleigh it was?

EB: *The mathematician.*

MK: They both were.

EB: *I was told he was an awfully good mathematician.*

DF: A physicist would be.

EB: *Oh dear, I'll have to get more information.*

The following sitting she did so:–

MK: You may remember the noble lord: you corrected his address last time.

EB: *The third lord you mean.*

MK: Oh, the third lord, that was my question I was going to ask.

EB: *Well that's done that one, hasn't it (laughter)!*

MK: The two were very similar in accomplishments and reputation, but the third was more august.

EB: *We have only the best.*

John: [a spirit communicator] Argon.

MK: Yes, exactly. That doesn't mean anything to you, Robin?

RF: I've no idea what you're talking about (laughter).

The third baron Rayleigh, J. W. Strutt, who was President of the SPR in 1920 when he died, received the Nobel prize for the discovery of argon, and was one of the greatest scientists of his age. He was a colleague and friend of Frederic Myers at Cambridge University. His son, the fourth baron, was Professor of Physics at the Cavendish laboratory in Cambridge, and served on the SPR council for many years, being President in 1937–38.

There was a pleasant sequel to this exchange. During the course of a sitting on 23rd August 1996 with Walter and Karin Schnittger, together with MK, the following interchange occurred (EB's opening remark is of particular interest because it shows she had picked up on MK's pun at the sitting of April 13th):–

EB: We had an Admiral here earlier. Strutting about.

MK:Oh, was he AC or DC? [This was intended as a jocular if slightly obscure reference to earlier discussions on the effect which alternating as against direct electric current could have on the production of phenomena.]

EB: Honourable A. C. if you don't mind — well he'd mind.

SF: Do you know the face, Monty?

MK: I don't know the face but I know the name.

EB: He said he cared for the money.

MK:He did indeed. He was the Treasurer (laughter) — Treasurer for the SPR before the war. [In fact it was during the immediate post-Second World War years.]

WS: He's not going to collect money?

EB: He'd better not. He won't get any!

MK:Something to tell his cousin Nigel, who's interested in these proceedings.

Admiral the Hon. A. C. Strutt served on the Council of the Society, of which he was a Vice-President, for many years and was its Honorary Treasurer until shortly before his death in 1973 at the age of 93. He was the younger brother of the fourth Lord Rayleigh.

It is worth noting that the transcript of the first exchange, prepared by Diana the medium, indicated from the incorrect spelling of apparently unfamiliar names either a prodigious subtlety or else a forgivable ignorance of the extinct personalities involved. Thus:–

EB: . . . he was a lord. We're honoured!

MK: Really? *(sic)*

EB: Monty is on the track.

AE: Raleigh *(sic)*

Although it would take us too far into ontological territory, it is possibly worth speculating that, if Rayleigh (were it indeed he) had wished to identify himself, he could simply have given his name. Conveying an address, albeit 'heard' indistinctly by Emily as principal transmitter, suggests that Rayleigh was employing a tactic characteristic of so much of the Cross-Correspondence material: trying to convey to the recipient information in a form unlikely to be known to – and hence susceptible to distortion by the mind of – the medium. Rayleigh was not involved either as posthumous transmitter or as interpreter in the Cross-Correspondences, but he would certainly have been familiar with the many learned analyses of the scripts published by his close colleagues in the SPR Proceedings. However, as all the evidence involved in this exchange is in the public domain, it is interesting rather than evidential.

The GOM

If it is felt that the address at a stately home in Essex of a scientist who died 75 years ago is common enough knowledge, the next address clue is a little more puzzling. It occurred on 10th August 1996 during the 14th sitting, when we deliberately asked for some 'hints and tips', having had one (the Albemarle Club discussed next) already. Albert, another communicator, then responded:–

Albert: What about St James Square?

MK: Well, that's very near Albemarle Street.

Alb: You know who lives there?

RF: I used to work in St James's Square: Norfolk House.

Alb: I'm talking about long before you were born.

DF: Someone who lived in St James's Square.

Alb: Yes, don't worry.

SF: One of your colleagues.

Alb: Not mine. I should be so lucky!

DF: Someone very distinguished.

Alb: Yes.

RF subsequently not only volunteered that he had worked for a company located there but handed us a copy of a presentation book on the history of the Square which he had received at that time. Every employee had been given a copy. MK looked up the listed occupants of all the houses comprising the Square and found only one name which resonated in the context of psychical research. At the next session, not wishing to reveal the suspected identity directly, he said that he was *glad* to say he had left no *stone* unturned in his research into the St James's Square occupant, and requested that his respectful greetings be given to the GOM. He asked whether he was on the right lines. There was a slight pause, followed by a somewhat grudging "yes", Emily

69

declaring herself unwilling to risk her neck. RF said he had no idea what this was all about.

Gladstone, familiarly known to his contemporaries as the Grand Old Man, was made an honorary member of the Society in its early years, and was a great supporter of its work. Indeed he has been frequently quoted as commending research into survival as by far the most important question facing mankind. That fact would be quite widely known to students of the subject. However, most people would associate Gladstone with either 10 Downing Street or his principal London address at 11 Carlton House Terrace or, more likely, his Cheshire seat at Hawarden. The fact that he resided as a temporary measure for a few years at 10 St James's Square is not common knowledge and is not easy to discover: it is not mentioned in his official biography by Lord Morley, although Professor Roy later found a reference to this fact in Lord Jenkins' biography of Gladstone on page 566. The fact that RF provided MK with the book which produced the clue may be interpreted either as a disingenuous device to appear innocent or as an example of naïve honesty. It was, in fact, by no means the only instance where one or other member of the Group helped in this fashion.

The Albemarle Club

The relevance to the Society's founding fathers of the Albemarle Club, to which reference was made at the same sitting, was also initially unclear. During the introduction to this sitting, Manu said:–

> Somebody is nudging at my side, and says "Tell them to remember the Albemarle Club. Your colleagues used to meet there", he is saying. I know that the scribe over there [MK] will be putting these things down, and I thought that I would allow these things to come through while we are focusing. There are many, although on another side of life (who) follow with interest the progress you are making, unravelling the mysteries of the veil that is between. I hope that this will aid you, that you will be knowing who is helping. Many colleagues used to meet, that is what they are saying . . .

The Albemarle Club no longer exists. It was hardly prominent when it did, since a search through all the volumes on London Clubs at Westminster City Library's archive section revealed surprisingly little about it, and none of the principal reference books even mentions it. However, it was at this Club that Oscar Wilde received the famous letter from the Marquess of Queensberry which gave rise to one of the century's most celebrated and disastrous libel actions, so it must have been well patronised, even though it found no place among the 50 such establishments listed in *The Gentlemen's Clubs of London* (Lejeune, 1979) or other accounts of London clublife (e.g. Atkins, 1933; Darwin, 1903; Escott, 1914; Nevill, 1911, or Timbs, 1872). Still more puzzling, Dr Alan Gauld's check of the club affiliations of leading members of the Society listed in *Who Was Who* and *Walford's County Families* failed to mention the club. The Athenaeum and the Carlton were the most commonly listed. The Albemarle had a peripatetic existence, having been located in 1881 at No. 23 Albemarle Street, which runs north from Piccadilly. By 1885, however, No. 23 had become the National Union Club while the Albemarle had moved to No. 25. Here it remained for some years until moving to No. 13, later transferring to Dover Street nearby. No. 13 is now occupied by a restaurant whose owner informed MK that he knew nothing of such a club but suspected it might have flourished over the road at No. 46, an art gallery – but whose proprietor of 30 years' standing reported that he had never heard of it.

The significance for psychical research of these moves becomes apparent by examining the late Victorian neighbours of the club. No. 21 was occupied by The Royal Institution, and No. 22 by the London Society for the Extension of University Teaching, one of whose joint secretaries was the brother of F. W. H. Myers. The Royal Institution had as one of its leading members the third Baron Rayleigh, whom we have already met, and who was a founding member of the Society and a member of its Council for 35 years. EB told us much later in the same session that Rayleigh used to visit that Club too, which is hardly surprising since it was next door to the Royal Institution.

DF unearthed a link between the Club, Sir Oliver Lodge, and Lodge's close friend Myers (Lodge, 1909). A matter of weeks after Myers's death early in January 1901, Lodge had two sittings with Mrs Rosa Thompson, which he described as unexpected and unexceptional. The sittings were in Birmingham, where Lodge was Principal of the University. His wife was also present. On 19th February Myers apparently came through, and in the course of the communications the following transpired (taken from the Lodge transcript):–

> [Here there was an incipient attempt at a Myers control, and an incident at a club was referred to. Then another control said:]
>
> "Do you know he feels like a note-taker, not like the spirit that has to speak. I think he will speak presently."
>
> (A short interval of apparent discomfort, then 'Myers' purported to communicate)
>
> "Lodge, it is not as easy as I thought in my impatience.
>
> "Gurney says I am getting on first rate. But I am short of breath."
>
> (after some further reference to communication difficulties):–
>
> "Oh Lodge, what is it when I see you! Was it the Albemarle Club we went to when I talked about . . . oh, it leaves off.
>
> "Sidgwick knows I am with him. [It is likely that there should have been a full stop after "Sidgwick knows"] He said that he saw me in the morning of . . . Oh dear, it always leaves off in the interesting places."

From this it would appear that some incident took place at the Albemarle Club involving Myers and Lodge – and in which Sidgwick might also have been involved in some way – and that it was one of the first messages that Myers, if indeed it was his spirit, sought to bring through. DF observes that it is not clear from the transcript whether the words "oh, it leaves off" were from Myers, from Mrs Thompson, or from Nelly, Mrs Thompson's 'control'. Dr Gauld later discovered an entry in Myers's diary (deposited at Trinity College Library in Cambridge) for 1880 that says "Lunch Albemarle" (with his wife), but he does not say whether it was at the club or the hotel of that name, and Dr Gauld could find no further references to Albemarle in most of the diaries for that decade.

This apparently casual reference to the Albemarle Club is interesting but not particularly evidential. The link could have been guessed at by anyone aware of the references to the Club in Lodge's *The Survival of Man* (1909). We return at the end of this Chapter to the significance of this book.

The Myers Sealed Letter

Seemingly throw-away references were especially liberal at Sitting 14. They appeared to arise from conversations which we initiated. For example, we had been proposing to the spirit Team something . . .

> (MK) . . . that will link the physical manifestations with the after-life. At the moment there's no logical link – there might be if we had some successful book tests. If it were possible to read some buried archive letters in the SPR archives – letters which your own communicators many years (ago) deposited with the Society, which have not been looked at for a good many years.
>
> *EB: Myers left something in an envelope, didn't he?*
>
> MK: He did, not to be opened for 60 years, 1961.
>
> *EB: You've got it wrong.*

This interesting exchange had an important sequel. MK had indeed got it wrong, since he had been confusing the envelope with an auto-biographical volume which Myers did not wish to have published for 60 years – it was in fact published by the Society in 1961 (Myers, 1961). Emily was referring to a sealed letter Myers had left with Lodge to be opened after his death in the hope that his spirit would have by then transmitted a message confirming its contents, thus providing evidence of his survival. That this was certainly the case became apparent a few minutes later when DF asked EB whether there were any others on her side who wished to communicate (she had 'dropped' three names as though they were all present at a celestial party. We refer to these three shortly). EB responded:–

> *Just finding out . . . It was Mrs Verrall. She says they didn't get it right. They opened up the envelope and she was quite convinced she had the answer but*

she hadn't. Several months on from the passing.

DF: Myers's passing?

EB: Yes, but that's the way of these things.

MK: Back to Diotima are we? [A reference to the 'Diotima' film strip discussed in Chapter V and Appendix C.]

EB: Never guarantee results, and she was quite convinced she had the answer in a sealed envelope, so it was decided to open it up, and then it was disappointing, a bit like our test [a reference to an unsuccessful film experiment, discussed later].

As a former President of the Society (Salter, 1958) points out, the fact that Myers left a letter in a sealed envelope, which when opened nearly four years after his death was found to contain a message different from that claimed in the communication, was quite widely known. However, it may take some digging about in the SPR literature to discover Mrs Verrall's role. It is found in Mrs Verrall's 440-page analysis of her own automatic script writings (Verrall, 1906). In a discussion on varieties of the dramatic form of communications, she makes several references to this event. A script received by automatic writing on 18th July 1904 refers to "the supposed contents of a sealed envelope left by Mr Myers". It appears to confirm a message which had been received five days earlier. This said that the envelope belonged to Sir Oliver Lodge and would be found to contain a passage about Love from Plato's Symposium. The message was repeated on 24th November 1904. Accordingly Lodge, who had been given the letter by Myers fourteen years earlier, in 1891, and had banked it, called a special meeting on 13th December for the letter-opening ceremony. The hope and expectation was that it would prove substantially evidential. The event is recorded not in the *Proceedings* but in the SPR's *Journal* (circulated privately for the SPR's first 70 years) for January 1905. "It was found that there was no resemblance between its actual contents and what was alleged to be contained in it."

At a special sitting which MK had in company with Walter and Karin Schnittger on 23rd August 1996, EB said:

I have a correction to make. That envelope that was sealed. After his death, it was some years before Mrs Verrall was able to persuade them she knew the contents, and to open it. Not months – but it wasn't as long as you said. You were still wrong.

MK: Yes, I got that completely wrong.

EB: Yes, completely wrong, but he says it was some years not months. So I stand corrected.

The immediately preceding discussion had been about Myers. Emily's statement that "he says it was some years" could have referred only to Myers, of whose close involvement in our investigation we had already been made fully aware as a result of the Diotima film, discussed later.

Note that EB's information was entirely correct, since the letter-opening ceremony was indeed almost four years after Myers's death. According to Mrs Verrall's account in the *Proceedings* Chapter XII, page 301, the envelope was said to have been placed inside another envelope, which was initialled and dated before it was placed with other papers in a box and given to Lodge.

However, there is evidence that, although the envelope experiment was judged a failure by Lodge et al. at the time, several of the leading figures of the Society later concluded that there had nevertheless been a definite connection between the communication and the message, and a paranormal one at that. It was not until W. H. Salter's analysis of Myers's posthumous message appeared in 1958 that a fairly compelling case could be argued that various hints and disparate messages dropped by the Myers communicator through Mrs Verrall's scripts between 1901 and 1904 could reasonably be interpreted as a reference to the actual message, which read: "If I can revisit any earthly scene, I should choose the Valley in the grounds of Hallsteads, Cumberland."

That the message actually found in this sealed letter had indeed been indicated in various hints dropped into the Verrall scripts over a period is a suggestion skilfully and persuasively argued in Salter's memorandum, but it is not necessary for us to follow the reasoning which led him to this conclusion. What is relevant is the fact that the expected reference to the subject of love as expounded in Plato's Symposium forms part of the evidence produced in the first major film strip message obtained in the present investigation. The key word is Diotima, since something related to Diotima's message is what Mrs Verrall had confidently expected to be contained in Myers's 'posthumous' letter.

Brother Ernest

There are ample examples of less complicated and indirect references to the events which followed Myers's death. In the same sitting that gave us the clues about the Albemarle Club and the eminent tenant of a St James's Square residence, Emily was asked for some more crumbs or hints:–

EB: *You've had several already.*

MK: I know, extremely greedy I must admit, you've given us enough to work on but . . . .

EB: *Brother Ernest is here, he says, and they were all very attached to Homer.*

DF: That makes sense.

EB: *He did the translations, Ernest did, but his brother was awfully interested in the work. Then, of course, Andrew Lang. He's nearby. He was another colleague: they are coming together . . . . . Walter Leaf. He's here tonight. I am name-dropping tonight aren't I?*

Emily was, indeed, but the names were of people who had been closely

74

linked when alive. Dr Alan Gauld has pointed out that this very probably does refer to Myers's brother Ernest who translated the *Iliad* with both Walter Leaf (a long-serving member of the Council of the SPR, a classical scholar and a prominent banker) and Andrew Lang (an eminent classicist and author who was President of the Society in 1911). All were close colleagues and collaborators. Frederic Myers, himself a redoubtable classical scholar, would obviously have taken an interest in this enterprise.

These scatterings of specialist information gave the appearance of arising naturally from requests, and contexts, that could not reasonably have been anticipated by the mediums.

Mrs Holland's Recollection

During the 14th sitting, on 10th August 1996, we had been pressing Emily or her team to undertake book tests, but she had resisted this on the grounds that they would not avoid the super-ESP claim. Whereas our principal aim was to see whether the communications would provide irrefutable evidence of paranormal effects, Emily's, as she made quite clear, was to go much further, and to show that the messages were not merely paranormal but could not be written off as attributable to the subliminal minds of mediums reputedly able to obtain and reproduce the information through the operation of their presumed psychic powers. She added, however (R11, p.6):–

> *EB: Certain information does come from people who were in existence some time ago, that are assisting with the work now. We get the information from their memories of those times; we don't get it by rummaging through the books and having a look. Very misleading, if that's what you're thinking.*
> DF: I think it clarifies it, yes.

> *EB: Mind you, if you look in Proceedings Volume 21, page 213, you will see a reference there: "Oh, if only I could say" – no, "get, to you" – or something like that. There you are!* [N.B. The words "or something like that" do not appear in the transcript of the tape, but do in MK's contemporaneous notes, and have therefore been included here.]

> MK: That was said by whom?

> *EB: The medium known as Mrs Holland was telling me that, and she is saying "January 4th or 5th, 1904". It's all tied up somehow. India, I believe she was. Well, there you are. Off you go (laughter)!*

> MK: I can't wait to get out of the door.

'Mrs Holland' was the pseudonym employed by Mrs Fleming, sister to Rudyard Kipling, who with his family disapproved of her interest in such matters. It is therefore appropriate that Emily spoke of her as being 'known as' Mrs Holland. This lively and intelligent young woman, living in India, had developed the capacity to write scripts automatically while conscious. The scripts purported to be messages from Frederic Myers and his close colleague Edmund Gurney, who had predeceased Myers by some twelve years, and both of whom were apparently set on achieving what they felt they had been denied while alive: proof of the survival of human personality. Mrs Holland formed part of that small group of gifted mediums who contributed, albeit unawares originally, to the 30-year long Cross-Correspondences. Her early scripts, and their contribution to the build-up of evidence provided by these disparate but interconnected messages, were analysed by the secretary of the Society, Alice Johnson (Johnson, 1908), and published in the volume which was correctly identified by Emily.

Emily's quotation from the Holland script was almost exact. The script was obtained at a point where the presumed spirit of Gurney, with occasional interventions from Myers, was trying to correct the text of an earlier set of messages. Mrs Holland's insatiable curiosity, as her brother might well have described it, was posing difficulties for the communicators, who wanted her to suppress her own thoughts, questions and doubts, and to allow the messages to come through untrammelled. We reproduce the passage (written on Tuesday, 5th January, 1904) which ends with the words Emily quoted. We italicise the words as in the original, and show in bold type the phrase which she gave.

> You are very little good today – it is strange how soon you forget –
>
> Page 27, Para b – the third sentence needs reconstructing – it conveys a meaning that is misleading –
>
> The 2nd packet of proofs have still several errors that have escaped revision – Kindly go over them again with great care –
>
> **Oh, if only I could get to them** – could only leave you the *proof positive* that I remember – recall – know – *continue* . . . ..

This recollected quotation is interesting, not least for its highly specific character and accuracy (save that "get to them" was retailed by EB as " 'get to you' – or something like that", with the word 'you' appearing to be a synonym for 'them') and its further link with Myers and his contemporaries. The 1904 message, in expressing Gurney's frustration, would appear in the context of Emily's statement to be primarily an expression of desire to give us proof of after-life intelligence by communicating messages more effectively to us, or to the obtuse world beyond. However, once again all the information contained in this exchange is available in the public domain, and therefore cannot be regarded as evidential.

Founders' Day

At the next sitting (R11, p.24) we invited EB to comment on the intended significance of this last message. In response she gave us another crumb:–

MK: I was enormously impressed with the reference given about Mrs Holland – the precise page, and virtually the precise wording of the page in Proceedings. Absolutely spot on! I wasn't sure, though, what the significance was to us.

EB: *There wasn't really. It was just that you were talking about boring book tests, so we thought we would throw you a little snippet to whet the appetite for something better.*

MK: If you'd like to bore me again I'd be pleased.

EB: *Someone's going on about a meeting, 1886, January 6th . . .*

AE: January . . .

OTHERS: Ssh!!

EB: *Arthur's so quick to give me some feedback — is that the right word?*

MK: Yes, we're trying to gag him.

EB: *Trying to gag him! How naughty of you.*

DF: Couldn't hear what you were saying, Emily.

EB: *Well, somebody back here is on about a meeting. I think they said January 6th but give me a day or two either side. 1882. Great significance. They said they were present there.*

AE: I know.

MK: Foundation Day.

EB: *There you are!*

AE: Some of the people in your Team might have been there?

EB: *Hm! Gone quiet.*

Discussion: 5th January 1882 was the date on which Professor William Barrett convened a meeting at 38 Great Russell Street, headquarters of the British National Spiritualist Alliance, at which it was decided to form the SPR. The inaugural meeting was held in the City the following month. It is worth noting that this was not the only occasion when Emily appears to be receiving in sound terms a message she cannot always hear correctly. Her correction of the date from 1886 to 1882, and her earlier uncertainty about whether the word was "say" or "get", is characteristic of mediumistic statements, oral and written. The date of the formation meeting is relatively well known, and this renders the exchange, like preceding ones, of curiosity rather than strictly evidential value.

No. 5, Selwyn Gardens

Towards the conclusion of what was to be our final (36th) sitting, on 16th August 1997, when most of the time was devoted to a novel experiment in apparent trans-dimensional communication (described in Chapter XII), MK had been reporting with enthusiasm that all who had participated with him as observers at sittings of the Group in Ibiza the previous month had countersigned his account of the success of two experiments (described in Chapter XI). "I look forward to more of the same," he added. Emily said they were doing their best, and suddenly asked us who had lived at 5 Selwyn College Gardens. "Someone's just dropped in . . . .they are talking about an archway there: quite a feature apparently." MK said he thought this was referred to in Mrs Verrall's report in 1906. After some hesitation, during which Emily seemed to be listening to what was being conveyed to her from another entity, there followed a reference to Corinthians. There was a brief discussion among the investigators about whether Corinthians referred to the third Greek order of supporting piers, as MK initially assumed, or, as DF rightly concluded, to the New Testament. Then came a reference from Emily to "X – V – I – 13 (given thus in a mix of Roman and Arabic numerals). We (the investigators) then considered whether the inscription above the entrance to Selwyn College, Cambridge could be linked to Corinthians, but MK said the inscription was in Greek, and that Mrs Verrall had been conscious of some grammatical defect in it. Shortly after the sitting we discovered the quotation from 1 Corinthians XVI, verse 13, in the King James's translation but failed to recognise its relevance. MK thought it far too long to be the text over the entrance arch at Selwyn College.

The *New English Bible* translation is somewhat shorter:–

> Be on the alert; stand firm in the faith; be valiant, be strong. Let everything you do be done in love.

Also shorter is that in the Bible Society's standard biblical version:–

> Be alert, stand firm in the faith, be brave, be strong. Do all your work in love.

All of this became clear when, later that night, the references were found in Alice Johnson's classic work (op.cit.) on Mrs Holland's mediumship, and in which, at 11 a.m. on 7th November 1903, Mrs Holland reports having 'received' a script by automatic writing. This script was sent on to Miss Johnson, then Secretary of the SPR. In it Mrs Holland finds herself writing to "My dear Mrs Verrall", whom she did not know personally. She then tries to receive an address which, after some apparent difficulty, she writes down as "5, Selwyn Gardens – Cambridge." After some more sentences, she writes "Send to 5 Aylwyn Gardens." The "5 Aylwyn" is crossed out, and there follows: "5 Selwyn Gardens, Cambridge." Later this is repeated with a still more clear instruction: "Get a proof – try for a proof if you feel this is a waste of time without. Send this to:

Mrs Verrall,

5 Selwyn Gardens,

Cambridge."

There follows, on page 234, a further message dated Thursday, 17th January, 1904 (misprinted as 1901 in the *Proceedings*), in the course of which the following appears:–

> I am unable to make your hand form the Greek characters, and so I cannot
> give the text as I wish — only the reference — Cor. 16–13 . . .
>
> Oh I am feeble with eagerness . . .

This message purports to come from Myers. A footnote on page 234 gives the Biblical reference as "Watch ye, stand fast in the faith, quit you like men, be strong." As Alice Johnson explains on the next page, this text is inscribed, with the omission of the last two words, "Be strong," in Greek over the gateway of Selwyn College "which would be passed in going from Mr Myers's house to Mrs Verrall's, or to the rooms in Newnham College where Professor and Mrs Sidgwick lived. The road in which Mrs Verrall lived is named Selwyn Gardens after Selwyn College. The Greek inscription over the Selwyn gateway has an error in it — the omission of a mute letter — on which Mr Myers had more than once remarked to Mrs Verrall."

The quotation from the first epistle to the Corinthians appears again (see p.252) in a script dated Wednesday 1st March, 1905, on the first day of Mrs Holland's experiments with Mrs Verrall, whom Mrs Holland knew by name, but not as a practitioner of automatic script writing, let alone as a fellow experimenter in what had by then become apparent as one of the earliest of the Cross-Correspondences. It is odd, and perhaps worth noting, that we were given the reference to Chapter 16 in Roman numerals by Emily, whereas Arabic numerals were used in the first reference to this chapter in the Holland script. However, in the second reference to the chapter in that script, Roman numerals were used.

MK was mistaken in having attributed to Mrs Verrall rather than to Myers a sense of irritation over the incorrect Greek letter. This was thanks to his faulty recollection of the references in the 1908 *Proceedings*, to which he had recently had recourse in order to confirm the accuracy of the earlier Holland hint. DF has pointed to the significance of the fact that it was he, with no knowledge of the inscription, who had suggested that the words relating to Corinthians 16 might be linked to those above the arch, whereas MK, who knew about them, had initially rejected the idea, thereby making it less likely that there was telepathy between either of their minds and that of the medium.

Celestial Mechanics

Throughout the sittings we were constantly on the alert for communications which we believed unlikely to have originated from the minds, unconscious or otherwise, of the mediums. In this task we were aided by several factors, some easy to overlook. One was the frequency and content of such communications emerging by independent, or spirit, voice. These messages appeared to come from the centre of the table, or from above it, and were almost invariably preceded by low-level grunts and whispers as though the communicator had struggled physically amid unknown turmoil to get through, and needed time to generate his voice and recover his breath. In periods of animation, perhaps when we were experiencing some fairly dramatic visual or physical phenomena, there were occasions when several of us spoke or uttered exclamations apparently simultaneously with energy voices. Of more potential significance, however, were the varied contents of the communications, and their apparent spontaneity when the information given was in response to something we had said or asked.

On 13th July 1996, Archie Roy (AR), Emeritus Professor of Astronomy at Glasgow University, and a world specialist in celestial mechanics, was an invited guest. Under the pretext of asking him questions, Albert, speaking through Alan, raised the subject of stellar companions: whether our sun was one of a pair, and whether there was an association between this belief and the demise of the dinosaurs (the Nemesis theory). He went on to speculate on the triple star problem, with which AR seemed familiar. Albert then asked whether there was a rather large instrument – or a small instrument they were seeking to make larger – for research into gravity waves. AR told him that Professor Jim Hough and his group were working to build a kilometre-long gravitational wave detector. "This is for fluctuations of the gravity on earth," commented (or perhaps asked) Albert, and he went on to inquire whether star collisions, which this instrument was intended to monitor, would create a ripple effect.

AR has since told us that in his opinion it is unlikely that this exchange would have been initiated or understood by lay people, or indeed by many astronomers, beyond the score or so in this country whose specialisation was in this field. This view, however, has been strongly challenged on the grounds that any diligent reader of the popular press might have picked up the sort of information displayed.

Technical Responses

A possibly more impressive display of specialist knowledge arose in Ibiza during one of the two sessions at which MK, alone of the principal investigators, was present, and in which experiments culminating in electronic tape recordings were conducted (dealt with in Chapter XI and in the references to EVP, or transdimensional communications, in Chapter XII). The discussion in Ibiza on 29th June 1997, was initiated by Walter Schnittger (WS), an automotive engineer. It occurred towards the latter part of the first of the two tape-recorded sittings. The object was to obtain on a new tape messages which none of the sitters could hear, but which would subsequently be found to have been recorded, on a Panasonic tape recorder from which the microphone had been removed. Introducing the experiment, Manu had said they were creating two areas of "non-spin energy space". After the 30-minute tape had stopped,

Edwin (speaking through Alan), who was apparently in charge of the experiment, explained that 'they' had entered the recorder in order to influence the tape by causing an electromagnetic effect to take place on it.

WS: Is it right that you put on the tape as a normal recording, as we do in our world? Or using electro-magnetics: that's the way you describe it – getting a signal into it? Only, if you take out the microphone you take out the modulation part of it. I'm thinking of how you get the modulation part into the system – materialise something that replaces this modulation?

Edwin: That is how I understand it. I am not a technician with knowledge of wireless, and no electronics: I have no true understanding of such things, but what I am being impressed with here is that, deep within your recorder . . . by the way it is running on batteries? We forgot to tell you that . . . it runs on batteries because of the DC current. Even with some of these pieces of equipment, if they are used on AC, although the current is changed to low voltage DC, it still has an irregular modulation – is that right, Walter, do you agree?

WS: Yes.

Edwin: It is this that causes the problems of . . . gross fluctuations of the electro-magnetic field that is created using AC current – but we won't talk about that [?] because you were asking about influencing the tape. What they are saying is that, deep within the machine there are [??] small pieces of silicon – which is, I suppose, I am not sure, a sort of crystal. It is not made from silicon itself, but from sand: you think of all the sand you have in the desert: there is potential. This crystal substance is very hard, and where we enter – I am using words you can understand – when we can influence, make our impression (don't ask me how we do it because I don't know), that's whatever we want. An electro-magnetic field is created deep within the workings of the recorder which in some way activates the metallic tape that you used . . . yes?

WS: Ferrous oxide is used [on the tape].

Two days later, during the second session, WS asked for further information about the mechanism responsible for getting the spirit message on to the tape. Was it pressure or light? Edwin first confessed ignorance, and then continued with an explanation which struck us as technically advanced:–

Edwin: What I am understanding is that these devices have cut-off points. Do you understand that . . .?

WS: Yes [about to explain it] . . .

Edwin: Don't worry: don't explain it at the moment. They have a cut-off point and they become useless, ineffective for what they are designed for.

WS: Yes.

Edwin: Yes, what is happening: they – or those responsible – are in fact creating . . . yes, it is pressure I suppose. It is not physical pressure as you may imagine, but it is a pressure in as much as it is an expansion. This

81

expansion brings the silicon from [?very] near to its cut-off point. It is this point, near to its cut-off point, which is the sensitive moment. It becomes highly sensitive, and it is at that moment that they are able to create the desired entry and make a modulation, as you call it. You know our moves to use different materials in the future, and this cut-off point is a problem at the moment, a great problem to you. In the future there will be different materials which will enable these devices which you use, using silicon, to be used at much higher temperatures. This will open up a tremendously new area of technology in micro-electronics, and it is this area of micro-electronics at higher temperatures which will take man into far distant reaching areas that you don't think possible at the moment. And the first step, I think they are telling me, is "carbide"... Is it carbide? That is the first step; but there are others, other materials that will enable this process to be taken advantage of, this higher temperature. But in so doing, by raising this threshold this will also enable other – I use this loosely – will enable communication to take place.

WS: Very interesting. I am thinking about materialisation and   dematerialisation. Materialisation goes together with the effect on temperature, and dematerialisation is reducing energy and reducing temperature. Is that something you can agree to?

Edwin: Yes, because then you sense a coldness — because the heat has been withdrawn from your involvement or space during materialisation: the heat is extracted. That is why you feel cold.

This exchange has been quoted at some length because not only is it one of the rare apparent attempts to put into our terminology an explanation of the mechanism employed for an experiment: it goes much further by forecasting developments here in the realm of semi-conductors. While the somewhat diffuse technical discussion may be of questionable clarity and meaning, the prediction relating to semi-conductors was fairly specific. Whether the prediction will turn out to be warranted remains to be seen. What is certain, however, is that it is not nonsense. A detailed article by the executive editor of *Electronic Design Magazine*, published in *New Scientist* two weeks earlier and entitled "Crystal Powers", has as its headlined introduction the sentence: "It's ultrahard, loves the heat and could save billions in lost power all round the world. Has silicon carbide's time come at last? asks Roger Allan" (Allan, 1997). The article deals with the problems of overcoming the cut-off point at which semi-conductors become ineffective, and was not seen by MK until after his return from Ibiza.

We must leave the reader to conclude whether this has evidential value, or whether Edwin's information or prescience was a happy coincidence, or whether the medium, Alan, had absorbed the contents of this highly technical article in a somewhat specialist journal to which he reports that he does not subscribe, in order to anticipate questions he might be asked by the experimenters in Ibiza.

General Discussion

We have not included in these several extracts conversations which deal with the tangible evidence provided by the films, since these are to be described in the succeeding Chapters. Our concern at this juncture is to evaluate the evidence for paranormality of these disparate pieces of evidence against two competing hypotheses. The first is that the statements derive from the conscious mind of the medium through whom the voices are transmitted, that is to say, that pieces of evidence are fraudulent. The second hypothesis, assuming the first to fail, is that the material could reasonably be said to derive from the unconscious mind of the mediums, rather than from external sources.

Whether or not the mediums were consciously aware of it, the fact is that most of the mediumistic statements reviewed in this Chapter could have stemmed from a single volume, namely Lodge (1909). As we have indicated, it was in this book, *The Survival of Man,* that DF discovered the reference to the Albemarle Club. Dr Gauld subsequently carried out an analysis of its contents, which shows that the book has many of the details given in the eleven pieces of evidence quoted above: Rayleigh (but not his address or his discovery of argon); the reference to Gladstone's address; the Albemarle Club; the existence of and the disappointment resulting from the opening of Myers's posthumous letter; the linking of Ernest Myers, Andrew Lang and Walter Leaf with Homer; the *"If only I could get to you"* quotation, along with specific references to the *Proceedings of the SPR,* Volume 21, page 213, to the medium 'known as' Mrs Holland, to India, and to the dates 4th or 5th January (save that the correct Lodge reference is to 5th or 6th January) and to 1904. The same book gives 6th January, 1882, as SPR Founders' Day, quotes *"Ce n'est que le premier pas qui coûte"* and the stanza of the Myers's poem found on the Diotima film, and reprints Lodge's encomium along with Manu's reference to "Infinite progression, infinite harmony . . ." together with the short quotation in Greek (all of which are discussed later).

It would be stretching credulity to attribute all this to coincidence, although several of the pieces of evidence do not appear in Lodge's book, notably the Selwyn College archway episode and the additional information about Rayleigh. But as Dr Gauld points out, the archway reference is to be found in secondary sources, even in Spiritualist literature; and it would not be difficult to discover the information about Rayleigh from reference books.

None of this necessarily points to fraud, although it must undermine any claim to evidentiality that these communications might otherwise have had. The alternative normal explanation is that the information had been remembered from a reading of a limited number of not very obscure sources, and had been lying dormant in the mediums' subliminal consciousness – since both mediums were involved – ready to emerge when the entranced mind felt able to dramatise fictitious, perhaps secondary or tertiary, personalities. Indeed, we have been urged to omit these references entirely as of little value.

There are several reasons against this course. One is that we have a duty to report what we observed and to leave the reader to decide on the likelihood of fraud or of alternative normal explanations. Another is that, even if the communications did derive from the unconscious minds of the mediums themselves, they would comprise remarkable examples of the sort of information which the entranced mind is able not merely to retain but to dramatise with impressive consistency. If only on these grounds, it would be wrong to deprive the reader, let alone the professional psychologist, of his entitlement to make up his own mind.

There are also some complicating factors worthy of note. One is that both mediums must have read the same book or books, and in sufficient detail to have been able to commit to memory some very specific names, places and dates. Yet Alan, who describes himself as "not much of a reader", has told MK that he has not heard of or read the Lodge book, and has only a few books, mainly relating to healing, of his own. And whereas RF has an extensive collection of books on psychical matters, many of them quite rare, a snap inspection of his library showed that *The Survival of Man* is not among his three books by Lodge; nor were there any volumes of the *SPR Proceedings*. That is poor evidence taken in isolation, but it will be appreciated that it is inconsistent with the subliminal memory theory.

Then we have incidents like the identification of an inversion in the Paganini variations. This is not readily consistent with lack of interest in classical music. As for celestial mechanics, there is a clear difference of opinion on the degree of general knowledge likely to be required to engage Professor Archie Roy in a discussion of the subject. He has pointed out to us that, while his rôle as an astronomer would probably be well known to the Group, it would not be within generally available knowledge that his specialist field was celestial mechanics.

The final illustration in this Chapter, headed Technical Responses, is in a stronger evidential category in that the information arises from an unscheduled series of questions initiated by WS, and of which no one, not even the questioner himself, could have had prior knowledge. In the light of later illustrations dealt with in Chapter VIII describing, for example, the construction of the germanium gadget, and dealing promptly with technical questions by AE, the subliminal mind hypothesis would need to ascribe to the mediums a growing assortment of intellectual attributes and technical and cultural knowledge.

CHAPTER V: THE PHENOMENA: THE EARLY FILM WORK

We have already given a brief account of the films produced before our involvement with the Group. The process of learning and improvement which these films appeared to reveal was continued shortly after our investigation commenced in October 1995. We do not propose to give a separate account of the precise circumstances in which each of the fifteen or so film strips was produced. That would be both tiresome and repetitive, and involve us in descriptions of events in some of which we were not ourselves participants. Because of the progressive nature of the experimental aspect of the work, however, and the significance which may be attached to the several failures, we deal with the main films sequentially, and provide a synopsis in Appendix A. But we also propose to describe the general principles involved, and the nature and limitations of precautions.

From the outset it was made clear to us that the spirit Team were anxious to operate strict protocols to preclude charges of fraud. The reaction to our proposal to bring in infra-red video equipment, or even an infra-red viewer (frequently suggested by AE) which simply works on the natural infra-red radiation from bodies, has already been noted. Robin Foy had recorded in the summer 1995 issue of *The Spiritual Scientist* that the Team had said it was their immediate intention to illuminate the whole of the room so that everyone could see everyone else. This seemed encouraging, especially since we had been shown a number of still pictures taken during earlier sittings suggesting that there had been enough light to enable the central glass bell jar and plinth to be detectable. But this was no more than a beginning. We have to record our disappointment that in the succeeding two years no progress was made towards working either with infra-red equipment, or with sufficient artificial light to enable us to see all participants. Although on occasion the amount of seemingly spirit-generated light was sufficient to enable us to see one another, we were still far from enjoying an adequate degree of light up to the time of our final sitting in August 1997, although by that time we had been given reason to hope that ongoing experiments would enable video recordings to be made without the use of or need for infra-red facilities. However, in the absence of camera or video records, unsupported visual evidence risks being written off as mere subjective attestation. Particular attention, therefore, needs to be paid to the nature of the physical controls maintained by the investigators over the film cassettes/tubs during the sittings.

It should be noted that the presence of infra-red viewers or similar instruments would not in itself satisfy critics. It would be argued that, even in broad daylight, investigators risk being deceived by skilful conjurors. Our particular concern, therefore, was to control the point at which phenomena – in this case photographic phenomena – were actually produced. DF argued throughout for a four-step protocol in connection with these phenomena, namely the provision by the investigators of the film to be used; ensuring that the film throughout the sittings was in a secure container provided by the investigators; control of the container throughout the sitting by the investigators, and development of the film under their control. Such a protocol would remove any possibility of physical intervention. Neither the Spirit Team nor the Scole Group offered any objection to this protocol and, as we shall see in due course, it was almost – although not quite – fulfilled.

The films provided gratis to the Group by Polaroid (whose representative was reported to have shown an interest in the Group's work), and which we had inspected before formal sittings started in October 1995, were of four types, all Polaroid:–

Polaroid 600 Plus, the flat films suitable only for Polaroid cameras, and used in the Ibiza experiments;

PolaPan 35mm slide black-and-white films, ISO 125;

Polagraph 35mm, ditto, but faster, ISO 400;

Polachrome 35mm colour slide films, ISO 40.

The Star Film

Well before the first sitting on 2nd October 1995, MK had discussed with Dr Richard Wiseman (an SPR Council member, a former member of the Parapsychology unit at Edinburgh University, and currently a senior lecturer in psychology at the University of Hertfordshire, where he specialises in the psychology and practice of deception), the sort of protocol likely to pass muster with sceptics. As a result, Dr Wiseman provided us with a security bag, guaranteed to be fraud-proof, and made of opaque triple-layered polythene. In it we proposed to place an unopened tub of 35mm film in the hope of obtaining spirit messages. This bag was duly sent to the Group after the first sitting in October 1995, and there was some discussion about it with the Spirit Team during the next sitting on 16th December (R2, pp.18–19):–

> EB: *You have given us an excellent bag to look at. Took it all round the room and checked it out, didn't we, and it was really very good. I don't think we are going to have too much of a problem, but what we would like to do is to start to experiment with the Group and just yourselves, and not take it beyond that, just for a start, and see how we go with it.*
>
> MK: That was the intention: a dummy run as we might call it.
>
> [Later]
>
> Joseph: *Much of this that we present to you and present to many people will be very hard to be proved, and it will be hard to use some of these physical*

demonstrations as evidence . . . that is why these specific experiments, in this case the photographic experiments, are so perfect and so unique in the way they are done and the results achieved; and it has one ultimate aim in mind: it is not used as an experiment to attract people's attention as a trick, but to produce phenomena that will last . . . that is what we shall be doing in a photographic way in the next few weeks. If Monty – may I speak to you? – can purchase film rather than take it from stock, you know, Polaroid 12 pictures where we have done that before: that seems to work quite well.

RF: A colour one or black and white?

EB: Now then, Joseph, this is more your side of things.

Joseph: No it isn't!

EB: Well more than me. Perhaps we could let the Group know next time.

MK: I'll get both, so you can choose.

EB: Well yes, we're bound to use them both, aren't we? That will be all right. But what about the speed? What have we had good results with?

RF: We've had good results with . . . there's only one speed on the colour film: that's ISO 40, and the other one that I think we have achieved the best results is about 110, but that's black and white, but I'll check up.

AE: Then is the idea that Monty should bring one of each kind of film sealed in the same bag: is that the idea? And then you can choose which one to operate on?

MK: An internal experiment, not for the outside world.

Joseph: I am out of touch.

EB: We are not the photographic part of the team, you see.

KB: Perhaps we can confirm that within the group, and go back to Monty before he visits again.

At the succeeding sitting, on 13th January 1996 (Sitting 3), AE extracted from its packaging the tub containing a 35mm Polapan Polaroid film bought by MK, removed the chemical cassette to await development after the sitting, and placed the unopened tub containing the roll of Polaroid film in the Wiseman security bag. This he then sealed and took down for the sitting, placing it on the floor within one of the table quadrants. After the sitting we opened the bag, removed the film tub, extracted the roll of film and put it through the electrical developer machine upstairs. The results, projected onto a large screen in the Foys' library immediately afterwards, showed mainly star-like scatters with occasional lines inconsistent with any horizontal scratching which might have been ascribed to the development process. In one section there was a small cog-shaped light with a shadowy substance behind.

The outcome suggested paranormality, since images were certainly present when there ought, of course, to have been nothing at all visible. Although the results did not match our qualitative expectations, we could find no way in which this procedure could be faulted, because the security bag had been provided and sealed by us, and had been lodged inaccessibly between the feet of AE and MK throughout the sitting. The film had been provided by MK, and MK and AE had put the film through the developer. However, the poor quality of the film made copying difficult, and it later transpired that the original strip could not be found among the Group's burgeoning archives. It would certainly not have been suitable for reproduction, and its evidential value was clearly not appreciated at that early stage by the Group. There was to be a second star-scattered film in April of that year.

The Greek Film

The above procedure was varied at the fifth sitting (17th February). The film bought by MK was Polaroid 35mm colour, and purchased directly from Jessops of Leicester, the main suppliers. The package was again opened by AE, who removed the chemical cassette and gave the tubbed film to MK, who placed it on the edge of the table immediately in front of him in the séance room. RF explained that the spirit Team had told him they were having more difficulty than had originally been expected in getting through the black polythene security bag which had been used in the third sitting. Towards the end of the sitting:–

> Joseph: Let's hope you find something really interesting on the film, and bear in mind these are only the early stages. Progress will be made, believe me. Those responsible have explained to me their difficulties, and their confidence in achieving what they are setting out to do.
>
> EB: I do echo Joseph's words, that we have been able to give you something that will make you jump up and down when you get upstairs. We'll have a small wager: if you don't jump up and down I'll bring half a crown next time!
>
> AE: That's not legal tender
>
> EB: Oh dear. Still, you'd still like to have half a crown, wouldn't you – but I don't think I'll be paying up.

In the event Emily's half-crown was safe. The film was developed under our direction immediately after the sitting. While most of it was blank, three or four of what would have been frames had the film passed through a camera contained colour images, the most significant of which showed what in transliteration would be the word 'men' (μ ε υ) rather crudely written in lower-case Greek lettering. The letters were illuminated as though a searchlight had been centred on them, but with very faint indications of preceding and succeeding lettering. The initial line of the first visible letter μ was obscured. [see Plate 1].

Here there was no security bag. The tub containing the film was not marked and not visible during the sitting, even though it was only a few centimetres from MK, and very close to the other investigators on either side of him (AE and DF), both of whom were in positions likely to detect any attempt at switching tubs by the Foys, who would have had to reach across them and, assuming the absence of vision-enhancing equipment, grope in the dark. However, the control was not perfect, since theoretical possibilities for switching did exist.

The Myers Encomium and the Diotima Clue

For the sixth sitting, on 16th March 1996, MK brought along two more packs of unopened Polaroid films. A Polapan 35-mm Instant black-and-white roll (ISO 125/22) was intended for the principal test. He opened it, removed the chemical cassette and container, and handed the film in its tub to AE, who placed it in a new large plastic security bag provided by Dr Wiseman. All witnessed the enclosure and sealing. It was agreed that the second film, of Polablue 35-mm instant white-on-blue high contrast BN 135-12, a type not previously used, would be left on the table in its tub. DF signed a piece of white gummed paper which he affixed to the top of the tub. Along with its Polapan contents, the security bag, measuring 45 x 25 cm, was now placed by MK unfolded on the circular table of the experimental room, so that the front, lengthwise, edge just allowed the luminous table tab to be visible, while the opposite side of the security bag abutted the edge of the plinth bearing the glass dome. The film in the tub, sealed by DF with a signed piece of gummed paper, was placed under the glass dome in the centre of the table (in conformity with instructions said to have been given by the Team at one of the Group's closed sittings).

During the sitting we heard several scuffling sounds as though something was entering and exploring the contents of the bag ("sussing it out," Emily explained); then there was a noise of dragging, as though the whole bag had been transferred to the other side of the table. Emily said it had been lifted over the top of the dome (R5, p.5), and when the session ended it was indeed found to be on the other side, still flat. It was agreed to leave the bag on the table, placed below the plinth, for the supposed spirit energies to work on, since most of the sitting had been taken up in discussion and light displays.

Accordingly, in the next (seventh) sitting, on 13th April, we had two existing film experiments to complete, namely the Polablue film, which DF had marked with a signed, gummed seal, and the Polapan film in the black polythene bag. The bag was found to have been scratched in places, but was not otherwise marked in any way. When the Polapan film it contained was developed immediately after the sitting, it proved a disappointment. True, there again were night-sky stars on what would normally have been the first two or three exposures, and to that extent it was evidential; but qualitatively speaking we felt this to be unimpressive, and we concluded that if the Team were involved they were indeed having difficulty in penetrating the plastic. We were later informed (R10, p.16) that the three layers of plastic were an obstacle. However, we noted that the film leader, which normally projects a few centimetres, appeared to have been wound back into the cassette, and it proved necessary to extract it with a pair of stamp tweezers. By contrast, the other film, which was found at the end of the sitting to be still in its paper-sealed tub, signed by DF, was seen on development to contain handwriting along almost its entire length.

We named this the Diotima film. The handwriting consisted of two closely related messages which provided further possible evidence of the role, relevance and pervasive influence of a purported Frederic Myers. It constituted, in fact, the first substantial example in which the physical impression of messages on a sealed, unexposed film was closely linked with orally delivered information. It will be recalled that the tub containing this film (brought by the investigators and sealed with a piece of signed white gummed paper by DF) had been left immediately under the glass dome on the central table. When we returned for the 13th April sitting we found that the tub had been placed (prior to the sitting and by unknown means) several centimetres away from the dome and on the black plastic security bag which contained the other film. Since the type of film in the signed tub was novel to the spirit Team, it was regarded as a pilot experiment, hence warranting a less rigorous protocol, and it had apparently been left in the séance room between sittings. However, in the light of (a) subsequent film experiments where the controls were better, (b) the communication it contained, (c) the oral hints given to us about its contents, and (d) the relative success of the Star film experiment just discussed, it would be inappropriate to ignore the film solely on the grounds of these acknowledged weaknesses in experimental procedure.

Immediately after this sitting, the three investigators had supervised the development of the tub's contents by opening it after examining and removing the paper seal (which appeared on careful inspection not to have been tampered with, although complete reliance cannot be placed on this precaution). After a four-minute processing time in the electrically-operated developing machine under our observation, the images on the film were clearly seen through a viewer, and its contents copied into a notebook. Not all the words were immediately legible or understood, although the writing was for the main part quite clear. The first message consisted chiefly of a poem written in four lines across the length of the 12-frame film strip, with no signs of any vertical divisions. On the extreme left was the word Diotima. This was followed by the sentence, *Ce n'est que le premier pas qui coûte.* Then came the following stanza, written in script across the four long lines:–

> That hour may come when Earth no more can keep
> Tireless her year-long voyage thro' the deep;

Nay, when all planets, sucked and swept in one,
Feed their rekindled solitary sun; –
Nay, when all suns that shine, together hurled,
Crash in one infinite and lifeless world: –
Yet hold thou still, what worlds soe'er may roll
Naught bear they with them master of the soul;
In all the eternal whirl, the cosmic stir;
All the eternal is akin to her;
She shall endure, and quicken, and live at last,
When all save souls has perished in the past.

[Note: a few of the words were difficult to decipher, but the correct ones have been printed here. In only one case was a word missing: 'world' in line 6.]

A second message which followed this consisted of cursive Greek letters the reproduction and translation of which are given below. At the end of the film were two names. The former looked originally like *Cora las Seguain*, but was difficult to decipher, especially since it was in mirror-image. The latter, written more clearly, appeared to be *Will Rallings*.

The interpretation of these messages occupied some weeks. The Group made arrangements for the film to be copied, but it transpired that the images were fading rapidly after only three weeks. Although the transparency of the roll produced a clearly visible image on the screen, a contact print proved legible only with great difficulty. This was the first, and fortunately only, occasion when this fading was known to have occurred. Inquiries of the technical department at Polaroid elicited the information that fading of the images on Polablue 35mm BN 135-12 film would occur only over a longer period than three weeks and then only if the film had been exposed several times to bright light in a projector. We had no projector capable of exhibiting a complete film strip, and the film had had minimal exposure even to daylight, so the fading presented a considerable puzzle in itself. Thankfully, a computer-enhanced impression later enabled most of the original to be rendered legible (see Plate 4).

The name Diotima was not recognised by any of us, but we shortly established that she was a character in Plato's *Symposium*. At that stage the significance of the reference to her in the film message was not apparent. However, before the next sitting, on 18th May (R7), RF said the name of Cora Las Seguian had at last rung a distant bell, and he found he had a book in his collection entitled *Discourses Through the Mediumship of Cora L. V. Tappan* (Tappan, 1875) which included her signature. Although a subsequent examination of the signature on the film message showed similarities with that in the book, notably in the formation of the 'T' in Tappan (which we had mistaken for an 'S'), Foy informed us that, when he had sought further information from the

Team at a subsequent closed session, he had been given confirmation that, although the name was Cora L. V. Tappan, the signature on the film had not been made by her.[1]

Before we had had opportunity to probe further into the possible meaning and origin of the messages on the film, we were given some significant hints in the eighth sitting (18th May), which followed. We had not at that stage discovered any particular significance in 'Diotima', and had not been able to translate the Greek, some letters of which were far from clear. The hints came at the opening of the sitting, introduced as always by Manu:–

> *Manu: With our photographic work we caused you to scratch your heads and ponder on what we had done. So again we are preparing another milestone to pass, and you are thinking about 'What now? What more puzzles shall they give us to think about?' This is part of the plan: no doubt you have decided that for yourselves, for it is reminiscent of other times when spirit came and gave you something to puzzle over. That in time [turn?] caused it to be a great part of the evidence for all. I think you know what I am meaning. So the time has come once again to beat the drum and say "Aha! it is more fine evidence that is coming", for it is our intention to bring evidence that you can take with pride to your colleagues, that they may also have to scratch their heads and ponder much and change their minds somewhat, and that will bring you great joy, just as we are in great joy when we watch you solve your puzzles.*
>
> *I would add to the puzzle a bit more! There are more clues to come, and this will aid you. I will just say this, for it has been used in connection with the man from our side of life, who looks upon you as our ambassadors, and because he is experienced in doing this communicating work, then he will be of great help to you, and I do not think it will be very long before all is revealed. At the time when he had passed away to our realms and left your earthly life and someone was giving a um how you say . . .?*

---

[1] Cora Tappan (1840–1923), to whose feats as an inspirational mediumistic platform speaker from the age of 16 onwards Nandor Fodor (1933) devotes much space, is recorded under different names as she acquired successive husbands, four in all. Her full title is Cora Lavinia Victoria Scott Hatch Daniels Tappan Richmond. According to Janet Oppenheim (1985) she had no opportunity to prepare her lectures, of which she reportedly gave 3,000, and her orations "appear to have been genuinely improvised on the spot", although another commentator, Owen (1989), described her inspirational addresses as "rarely innovative and often obscure, rambling and repetitive". However, even the arch-sceptic Podmore (1902) acknowledged that her trance utterances were characterised by an unusual degree of coherence. She visited England in 1874, and is described by Braude (1989) as a brave, pioneering spirit. She founded the National Spiritualist Association but was fairly hostile to dogmatic religion. It was never explained what this lady had to do with the messages, apart from a word from Emily, our principal communicator, that Cora was with them. The signature may be safely placed for the time being in the category of loose ends: interesting but apparently pointless, and for which no explanation is offered, and perhaps none deemed necessary, although her detachment from the trammels of orthodox monotheism would convey an appropriate, since spiritual, kinship with the Group.

MK: Encomium?

Manu: Probably. And he said these words: "Infinite progression, infinite harmony and infinite love". I could not put it better, and so I repeat these words that they may be another part of the puzzle. It will fall into place shortly, you will be pleased to know. Think of those words: they have much meaning, and I would like you to ponder on them in your meditations.

Although the clues given later that sitting, and discussed below, related directly to Diotima, it was clear by the end of the session that Manu could have referred only to the encomium to Myers published by the SPR shortly after his death in January, 1901 (Lodge et al., 1901). This was dedicated solely to Myers's memory, and comprised five encomia, the first by Oliver Lodge. On page 8 of Lodge's encomium appear the same words in Greek –

ονπω εφανερωθη τι εσομεθα

– seen on the Diotima film, and which translate roughly as "It is not yet apparent what we will become". With minor punctuation differences, the precise reproduction of the stanza on the film, later traced to a verse in one of Myers's poems *The Renewal of Youth* (first published in 1882), immediately precedes a paragraph by Lodge which he introduces with the very words Manu had given to us in the sitting:–

Infinite progress, infinite harmony, infinite love, these were the things which filled and dominated his existence.

In addition, the expression,

Ce n'est que le premier pas qui coûte [It is but the first step that counts] is a direct quotation from a passage in Myers's posthumous *Human Personality and its Survival of Bodily Death* (Myers, 1903). This link with Myers was later strengthened by a 'crumb' from Emily when, at the end of a lengthy sitting on 9th November 1996, apropos a reference by MK to Myers's work, she said:–

EB: While you're there have a peep at Human Personality *Volume 1, page 250.*

DF: Page 250?

EB: That's it, where you'll find another little clue for you, Monty. I know you're fond of these clues. Another little tease for you. I hope your French is good. That was another clue.

MK: *Ce n'est que le premier pas qui coûte!*

DF: Your French isn't very good (laughter).

MK: I was quoting from one of the clues that was given to us,

EB: I'll leave you with that so I can tantalize you a little longer.

This quotation does in fact appear on the page Emily mentioned. The incident was subsequently referred to by RF (who knows some German, but no French) in the Spring 1997 edition of *The Spiritual Scientist*, but oddly enough the sentence was rendered meaningless by being quoted as *"Ce n'est que le premier pas des coute"*.

The intended meaning behind the Diotima reference might well have continued to elude us but for hints later that session from Emily Bradshaw. These are in bold type in this extract of the transcript:–

EB: While there is a (?) of energy in the centre of the room, I'm going to have a tease with you. What have you made of our test word?

AE: Diotima?

EB: Arthur knows, a test word.

AE: A character in Socrates.

MK: Plato.

*EB: Do you not remember **the reference before**?*

AE: Wasn't it at the beginning of the message?

*EB: Yes it was, **but at the beginning of another message.***

AE: Ah! Another message, not necessarily to us.

EB: Indeed! You've got to go back quite a long way.

MK: About four (?) years.[1]

EB: Not quite as far as that!

AE: Eighty or ninety years.

*EB: Don't go too deep. It was a **test word**, received before. Look through your dusty records.*

SF: A test sitting in the past that the word was used?

EB: That's right, Sandra. It takes a woman, doesn't it!

SF: They'll have to go back through their records and check up the references.

EB: Do you want another clue?

SF: Go on, tell them (laughter).

EB: This is wonderful! I do enjoy this job so much; makes it worth coming here, to tease these boys.

MK: Gives us a sense of sitting at the back of the form, while the girls . . . .(?)

SF: I don't know who it is! No idea.

EB: Sandra hasn't got a clue, but she's just being logical about what I am saying.

DF: Can you give us another clue?

*EB: I can tell you **Mrs Verall** [sic] and **Mrs Forbes had the test word** from a certain gentleman. There, now the cat's out of the bag!*

DF: From Myers?

EB: Quite right!

DF: Dionisis [sic] [2]

---

[1] The reference could not have been to four years.

[2] DF was thinking of the Ear of Dionysus cross-correspondence, although, as will be seen below, Mrs Forbes wrongly assumed that a word beginning with Dio would be a reference to the Greek god.

EB: No, the Diotima word.

DF: Diotima, in the Cross-Correspondences was it?

EB: Well, you hold them up in such admiration, don't you?

AE: Yes we do..

EB: Well, as Robin puts it, 'you ain't seen nothing yet!' (laughter).

DF: So, Emily, when we solve this, what are we actually looking for?

EB: I'm not going to tell you all that! Gracious me!

DF: Is it a classical allusion of some kind?

EB: When these Cross-Correspondences took place, they were of great importance at the time: a great step forward, and still held in high esteem by a great many people. They are difficult to explain away.

DF: (?) . . . **after forty years.**

EB: Yes, I daresay, but now we have a further opportunity with people who are excellent communicators, to (?)[1] modern technology. You've never had correspondence on a film before, have you?

AE: I am wondering, Emily, whether 'Diotima' could be interpreted in a different way, meaning 'through time'.[2]

EB: I haven't got that information, Arthur, so I can't help you.

DF: Myers is involved, then?

*EB: **Very much so.***

DF: That's nice to know. We have such admiration for that man.

EB: So you should have; so have we. There's a great need at this time . . . men with his sort of mind are thin on the ground, aren't they?

DF: Yes, giants (?)

EB: He will be of great assistance to you. I believe Arthur has thought it was him [ie Myers] for some time.

DF: Is that right, Arthur?

AE: Yes, I have.

DF: The first time we got the Greek letters we immediately thought of him, as Myers was a Greek scholar.

EB: Well just you go and check some of your dusty old books, and all will be revealed.

MK: May we engage the services of others in the SPR that may be knowledgeable about the documents, the archivists?

EB: I think it would help you to discover the truth for yourselves: you had best attend to it. Obviously, don't jump and shout about it, but I'm sure those that work within the organisation can be discreet.

Towards the end of the sitting:–

[1] The missing word was probably 'use' or 'employ'.

[2] This was not the only effort of the sitters to find alternative meanings in the word. We had toyed with DF's ingenious notion that it might be interpreted back to front as *ami to id*, or *friend of the spirit*.

*EB: Now, because I'd like to help you as much as I can I'll give you one more piece of information. Get your pen out, Monty![1] The first time the test word appeared, in my information, was **December 18th, 1902.** Not so many dusty books to go through!*

MK: Thank you.

EB: That should be a help to you, go and check. We do want you to do it for yourselves, but as you do set a lot of store by information from us, leading you to the right place I hope will add some value to what you are doing.

These clues shortly allowed us to solve the mystery without recourse to outside aid. We referred briefly in our introduction to the Cross-Correspondences. The Diotima case, the details of which are quite lengthy and involved, was one of the first fruits of what purported to be a message derived from hints separately received by, and bewildering to, Mrs Verrall and Mrs Forbes. An account can be found in Mrs Verrall's lengthy *Proceedings of the SPR* (Verrall, 1906) and in Alice Johnson's analysis (Johnson, 1908). Our own summary, which we have withdrawn in order to shorten the Report, is available to interested readers from the SPR Library.

The controls associated with the production of the Scole Diotima film were, of course, imperfect; and we have made it clear that this was due to the essentially pilot nature of the operation in which this 35mm Polaroid film cassette had been left for a month at Scole with only a signed sticky label over the tub as security. Nevertheless, it is right to examine its contents in some detail on the basis that, as much of the rest of the film evidence was produced under tighter conditions of control, this particular film may also be of possible significance. On the assumption that it is, the following points are of interest:–

a) The contents of the film are closely linked with the early years of the SPR.

b) There is a link between what was orally transmitted in the session following the development of the Diotima film and the additional information conveyed by that part of Manu's introductory message when referring to Myers.

c) As with the incorrectly spelled names in the Rayleigh case, so RF's misreporting in *The Spiritual Scientist* of the French phrase would appear to be an indication that he was unaware of the existence, as well as the meaning, of the original.

d) In the long history of the Cross-Correspondences, the Diotima case does not rank among the more celebrated or significant clues or puzzles, although it was certainly among the first. The selection of something relatively obscure, and long forgotten, presupposes a familiarity with the literature which may be possessed by none of the Group. RF, the

---

[1]   MK consistently took shorthand notes, albeit in darkness.

most likely candidate in view of his treasured collection of old books on spiritualism and allied subjects, allowed us unfettered inspection of his library, and he clearly believed he possessed old volumes of the *SPR Proceedings*. In fact the latter turned out to be relatively modern volumes of the *SPR Journal,* which would have been of very limited value for nearly all the clues which had a bearing on the contents of the early Proceedings cited.

e) However, Lodge's *Survival of Man* mentions virtually all the clues in the film material — the French and Greek quotations, the Myers poem, the Diotima reference, the quotation given by Manu of *Infinite Progression, Harmony* . . . and the reference to *Human Personality*, along with the fact that Mrs Verrall and Mrs Forbes had the Diotima word from "a certain gentleman", the discarnate Myers. All these considerations strengthen the case for presuming a connection between Lodge's book as a principal source material, and the agency, whether human or discarnate, which created the film.

The Latin Mirror Image Film

While none of us was present when the next film was produced, it is worth recording that everyone who attended the seminar for ten people, held on 25th May 1996, approved and signed a detailed account of the proceedings given to us by Mr Denzil Fairbairn of Raunds, Northants. His statement is reproduced in Appendix C (and is intended to be lodged with other records available for inspection at the SPR office by serious students). Mr Fairbairn records how he was invited to select one of a dozen or so Polapan black-and-white slide films from a boxed package stored in the Foys' study. He describes his approach as being "100% sceptical of the claims made in the first five issues of *The Spiritual Scientist*. After closely examining the outer box of the film pack to ensure that the ends had not been tampered with, and finding it still sealed with the several spots of machine-applied adhesive, he removed the chemical developing cassette, took out and examined the film itself and then replaced it in the tub. He then made an identifiable mark on a sticky address label sealing the cylinder, and was asked to retain the sealed film, which had been touched by no one else, and to place it anywhere on the table before the sitting commenced. He put it behind the glass dome and towards the edge furthest away from the Group, and in such a position as to make retrieval by any of them in his view impossible, having regard to the visibility of their wrist bands. When light was restored the tub was still in the same position. He placed it in his pocket. After refreshments he removed the seal, which appeared to be intact, and opened the tub to recover the film roll and subsequently supervise the development process. Two 'frames' of film had clear messages and designs, the first having the appearance of a Christmas tree on its side, but which, on being projected, was found to comprise a Latin message:–

Reflexionis, Lucis in Terra, et in Planetis [Of reflection of light on the earth and the planets].

Not only was this in (vertical) mirror-image, but the adjoining frame appeared to be a mirror image of its (horizontal) opposite (see Plate 2). During the sitting, an apparently relevant message was received (verbally, through Alan's mediumship):–

Joseph: Someone mentioned a light centre a while ago. A centre of light. It has been indicated there may be something on the film that is relevant to this. What it can be . . . some way it is tied in. Some symbolic way, I'm not sure. I hope it is successful.

EB: Denzil will be jumping up and down!

Although this experiment was not one conducted under our supervision, the obvious normal explanation of the results would appear to involve the switching by a member of the Group by one of two methods: either the film would have to have been removed from its container and replaced by a previously prepared film, or the entire tub, with its contents, would have to be substituted. But neither explanation can be reconciled with the existence of the paper seal since, although removal and replacement of such a relatively crude precautionary device can be easily accomplished in normal circumstances, it would have to be effected *in situ,* in complete darkness, undetected, and after first removing or obscuring luminous armbands during a sitting – unless the paper had been very poorly stuck down so that the tub could be abstracted, the seal removed noiselessly and without damage, the lid snapped open unheard, a replacement film substituted, the lid closed silently, the paper resealed and the tub restored to its original position. Alternatively Mr Fairbairn, despite the testimony of other independent witnesses, most of whom he had never previously met, was in secret collaboration with the Group, a hypothesis which would have to be advanced for similar phenomena when other experimenters are involved.

The Golden Chain Message

The progress of these film strip experiments then took a temporary downward trend. After the eighth sitting (18th May 1996) MK had placed two metal safety strips (provided by Richard Wiseman) over the lid of a black tub of Polaroid film he had bought, and which he had then sealed inside the plastic security bag, to be left to work on. It had been expected that this film would be ready for processing by the time of our next (eleventh) sitting on 15th June 1996 (the ninth sitting was the Fairbairn seminar, and the tenth was for Walter and Karin Schnittger). For this meeting, attended only by AE and MK of the investigation team, we were invited by RF to select one of the three remaining Polaroid films left from his old stock, although they were already getting past their viability date, and seal it with a sticky white label. This we did. Both MK and AE signed and Sellotaped the label around the middle of the tub. They took it down to place on the table, but at the Team's request it was left there. We were told that there had been no opportunity to work on it, since many other things had been happening that evening. Thus there were two films awaiting processing after the eighth meeting. A message from Robin Foy the following week informed us that the spirits had finished work on the films. AE, Professor Archie Roy (AR) and Mrs Trish Robertson, of the Scottish SPR, who all chanced to be staying with MK that weekend, hastened with him to Scole on 22nd June to videotape the development of the two films, only to find them both blank. It is worth noting that, despite the fact the the precautions taken for the second film were particularly poor (Foys' stock film, and tub left for several days, unprotected but for a poor paper seal), the result was negative.

We made the next attempt to obtain photographic evidence on 13th July, the twelfth sitting. This was attended by AR in addition to AE and MK, who had brought a new, unopened package of Polachrome 35mm 12-exposure colour transparency film. AR cut open the sealed package, removed one carton, broke the seal and extracted the black tub, leaving the chemical cassette behind as usual. MK affixed a luminous adhesive tab to the side of the tub. AR then pocketed the tub and later placed it on the séance room table immediately adjacent to one of the four luminous tabs on the edge of the table, and with a crystal pointing towards it. The tub was in the same position at the end of the sitting, although we reported frequent temporary occlusions of the luminous tabs as reputed spirit forms moved around the table. The subsequent development of the film, which AR supervised, revealed a large, scrawled message which appeared to read:–

Perfectio consummata feu quinta Ellantia Universalis

(see Plate 8), followed by a roughly drawn circle with a dot in the centre: a symbol (AR pointed out) for the sun, theories about which had just figured in the astronomical discussion he had been having earlier with the spirits (see "Celestial Mechanics" in preceding chapter). It was a friend and neighbour of Diana's, Beverley Dear, who found the reference in *Magic Symbols* (Goodman, 1989), which reproduces illustrations contained in a German publication of 1747: *Aurea Catena, Oder eine Beschriebung von dem Ursprung der Natur und Naturlichen Dingen*. This contains an illustration of the Golden Chain of Homer (Aurea Catena Homeri). On this chain are attached or suspended a number of symbols, one of which has a circle with a dot in the centre and a small cross below. At the base is:–

Perfectio consummata, feu Quintaessentia Universalis

99

This was translated by one adviser as 'From chaos to the highest summit of mankind', but Dr Gauld considers it should more accurately be rendered as 'Completed perfection or the fifth universal essence',[1] part of the highly symbolic device which begins the chain with chaos and confusion and ends with perfection, representing man's progress towards the light. The antique style of the film script was identical to that of the eighteenth century reproduction of the alchemical symbol. Ms Dear, a member of the SPR, informs us that she had bought Goodman's book from a local second-hand bookshop some months earlier, thinking she might be able to use some of the illustrations as source material for a textile design project (DF also has a copy). It was Diana, however, who actually found the illustration in Magic Symbols from which the film impression appeared to have been taken. What we had initially supposed to represent the sun, a circle with a dot in the centre, was now seen more clearly to have a cross underneath it, matching the bottom symbol of the *Aurea Catena Homeri*.

The experimental procedure under which the film was obtained was less than perfect, since the periodic occlusions of the luminous tabs on the table, although very brief, might be considered as suggesting the removal of the tub so that it or its contents could be switched, even though all such manoeuvres presuppose an ability and willingness by one of the Group to risk detection by concealing both armbands in order to stretch over –perhaps even climb upon – the table to abstract and replace the tub. However, the same considerations apply here as in other cases where the protocol was less than perfect: if even one procedurally unassailable experiment of this nature takes place, it can be suggested that it is inappropriate to dismiss on grounds of protocol imperfection the results of similar film material. Apropos the failure of both the earlier films, it is indeed worth noting that failures are inconsistent with the belief that slacker controls necessarily correlate with better results.

The German Poem

Success attended one of the several experiments which Walter Schnittger (WS), who was later to work in close co-operation with us, undertook at a sitting on 26th July (No.13), and about which he has given us a detailed signed report (see also Appendix D, describing the protocol related to three other sittings where films were produced). The film was clearly a second and more accomplished attempt to reproduce the text of a German poem. At the earlier attempt during a sitting at

---

[1] These versions assume that feu, meaningless in Latin, is a mistranscription of seu(or),with the 's' of seu written as the long obsolete *f* extended version of 's'. However, if this is a mistranscription it appears as such in the 1747 German *Aurea Catena*, and does not appear to be a mistake originating with the Team or the Group.

which he was present on 31st May, only the first few words were legible, and then followed a gradual blurring into a void. WS's wife, Karin, had held the film in her hands during the session, but apparently shook it either from excitement or when laughing. A wry reference to this event was later made to us by Emily when she counselled a somewhat indignant DF not to shake a film he was holding.

For the 26th July sitting, WS states that he selected a fresh pack of Polaroid Polachrome film from the remaining manufacturers' stock in the Foy store, affixed a self-gluing label to the tub and signed it. He then held the tub in his own hands throughout the session, neither putting it on the table nor allowing anyone else to touch it, and then supervised the development procedure. Short of an accusation that he participated in a fraud, the only defect perceptible in this procedure was that the original film, in its packaging, had come from the Foys' dwindling stock. The charge could thus be made that it had been tampered with by them, despite all appearances to the contrary. However, the film which had been used at the Schnittgers' May sitting, and which had carried the less complete effort, had been selected by the Schnittgers from a larger number of films, rendering tampering less likely – unless one argues that all the films in the Foys' stock had been subjected to fraud, then expertly re-sealed to disguise the fact: a difficult and potentially hazardous procedure.

The poem produced at the July sitting, with a translation opposite, is as follows:–

Ein alter Stamm mit tausand Aesten	An old trunk with a thousand branches
Die Wurzeln in der Ewigkeit	The roots within eternity
Neigt sich von Osten hin nach Westen	Bends over from East towards the West
In mancher Bildung weit und breit	In many forms far and wide
Kein Baum kann bluthenreicher werden	No tree can become more richly blossomed
Und keines Frucht kann edler seyn	And no tree's fruit can be more noble
Doch auch das 'Dunkelste' auf Erden	But even the 'darkest' on earth
Es reift auf seinem Zweig allein	Ripens on its branch alone

There were three interesting features about this film. First, the poem (see Plate 5) was written in what the Schnittgers and other German speakers considered good German of the type, and in a style, characteristic of the period around 1840. Secondly, it is a poem considered to be of high quality, and despite extensive inquiries made in Germany by

101

the Schnittgers, Dr Kurt Hoffman and others, its authorship remains unknown.[1] Thirdly, according to Robin Foy, the Team have suggested that it was written or found by an ancestor of WS, thus providing further possible evidence of a link between a sitter and film content.

Eventually there were to be three films with German messages; in all cases the Schnittgers were the sitters, either alone or with others. We refer to the significance of these in our examination in Chapter XV of the fraud hypothesis. The German poem film described in this section also contained coloured symbols representing the planets and one or two Chinese ideograms, all very precisely drawn, clearly visible and in brilliant colours.

---

[1] Dr Kurt Hoffman has written to inform us that German experts he consulted identified the poem as characteristic of the style of Friedrich Rückert (1788-1866) but, so far as they were aware, had never been published. Rückert was a popular poet and was the inspiration for many of Gustav Mahler's songs. He was also famous for translating the Koran into German, and was greatly interested in Eastern mysticism. Extensive inquiries more recently made of leading German scholars in 16 UK universities have failed to confirm the authorship (although Rückert is considered a likely candidate), and no one has yet found whether or where it has ever been published. It is not among the anthology of Rückert's verses available to scholars, and is considered 'very obscure'. More recently, we have heard from the curator of the Friedrich Rückert Museum that a search of some 20,000 poems in German libraries and museums has failed to identify its origin or authorship. However, a number of authorities have drawn attention to the hand-writing on the film, since authors at the time wrote in Gothic script, whereas the film script appears to have been written in the 1920–1950 period style, perhaps by 'someone brought up on German hand and using Roman for the occasion,' to quote one authority.

All this may be thought to have a bearing on the general fraud hypothesis, to the extent to which this hypothesis relies on relatively easy access to material already in the public domain.

CHAPTER VI: THE FILM PHENOMENA: NEGATIVE AND POSITIVE RESULTS

To appreciate both the significance and the protocol attending the next major piece of evidence it is desirable to revert to the narrative style, so that the reader may better understand the context in which the two related film strips discussed in the next chapter appeared and were investigated.

The fourteenth sitting, on 10th August 1996, was another setback.

On this occasion, however, it was possible that there was a defect in the mechanism of the spool containing the developing chemical, which spoiled the first 12 or 15 cm of the extruded film, so that a fresh development cassette had to be inserted to enable the rest of the film to be developed. It proved to be blank, but it is possible that, had there been any images, they might have appeared on the first strip of the film, and thus become lost. The Team had asked DF to be responsible for this film, which was brought by MK, and it remained under his physical control throughout. DF had indeed been specifically asked to keep his finger on the tub (on which he had previously made several secret marks with a penknife), while it was placed on the table.

Some indication of the problems experienced with film work was given to us during a discussion at this 10th August sitting on the nature of the supposed energy transfer which resulted in the creation of these films. Within what we were given to understand were the severe conceptual and linguistic limits imposed by our physical terminology, Albert, speaking through Alan, attempted to explain what happens (R10, p.16):–

Albert: These forces are being used much like a carrier wave is used: transmitting; and these forces can penetrate material in our world and your world . . .The thought process or imagery is carried by this [carrier] wave, that's how I think of it. These carrier waves are used to carry signals like modulation, frequencies modulating.

AE: Correct. Radio waves, making a high frequency, go up and down. The high frequency will carry the energy, and the lower frequency is the intelligence being carried.

Alb: I'm glad you said that. This is what I feel is a good example. When I use the analogy of radio I get into trouble. You will agree that there is some material that radio waves have difficulty with.

AE: Yes, metal.

Alb: . . . they do have difficulty penetrating other substances, not necessarily metal. As [these forces penetrate different materials] a change takes place. These transformations during this [process] are lost sometimes; part of the information is lost, and is unpredictable. We have nothing to gauge our findings on because of the unpredictable nature of this phenomenon. Now added to this complication, the different substances affect these waves themselves, and we have different losses, and different changes taking place with different materials. In relation to the films: the films are in a metal container. Can you confirm this?

DF: Yes.

AE: I thought it was plastic.

MK: It's in foil.

Alb: It's not in foil; it's metal, about ten thou' of an inch thickness.

AE: That's fairly thick.

Alb: That's no matter. We have adjusted for it long ago, but what caused us problems is when the films are placed inside other objects. At the moment there are two layers. Black too is a problem — there is no problem now, but it does give us a problem from time to time; but when other layers are used, this caused problems, to be overcome with further experiments. This is why we had a negative result when faced with another layer. In time it could have been rectified, but it was thought we'd return back to where we started: move forward in a slightly different way.

We were told that, to improve security, the Team, at a closed session on 1st November, had asked the Group to make a wooden container just large enough to hold a tub. The Team wanted the box made with a hinged top lid and a sturdy hasp. The aim apparently was to improve evidentiality, in anticipation of those occasions when it might be necessary to leave the box for some days or longer for the spirits to work on, particularly since non-photographic activities might have absorbed available energy at any single sitting.

Alan duly asked one of his sons, who has a workshop where he makes boxes and equipment for fishing tackle, to make such a box. This he did in time for use by us on 9th November (16th sitting), when MK brought along an experimental Kodachrome 200 film, which was left in its tub on the table for the Team to inspect (see Chapter VII). For that sitting MK, having been asked to buy his own padlock, also randomly selected one of the two remaining Polaroid Polachrome 35mm films from the Foys' stock. One of these we had obtained and left at Scole the previous month; the other was a replacement of the defective film from the abortive DF experiment in August described in the previous chapter. It had been sent direct to Robin Foy by the suppliers, Jessops of Leicester. Before this sitting, MK placed the selected film in its tub and unopened in the box, padlocked it, retained the keys and put the box on the table in front of DF. During the sitting there were lights and noises around the box. Both DF and Sandra reported that they had film cassettes placed unerringly in their hands. Before the sitting ended, DF was instructed by the Team to take the locked box containing its film away with him. There was some discussion with Emily whether the padlock keys should be left at Scole or entrusted to DF, who undertook not to open the box while it was in his possession. Since DF was due to have a special sitting two days later (11th November), it was finally agreed that he should retain both the box and the keys during this time. The fate of this film is described in Chapter VII dealing with the Wordsworth poem, since it was found on being processed immediately after the 11th November sitting to contain the first of a two-part 'Wordsworth' script. It was at that sitting, too, that Ingrid Slack (IS), who accompanied DF, reported receiving into her hands a film out of its tub. The circumstances surrounding the second Wordsworth script contained on the first experimental Kodachrome film, and both relating to the poem *Ruth*, are also described there.

In the event, the initiative of the Team and the carpentry skills of Alan's son, who made a neatly crafted box proudly illustrated in constructional detail in *The Spiritual Scientist* (March 1997, No.10, p.10), complicated life for investigators and Group alike. The investigators considered that a box with exposed screwheads would be unsuitable if at any time it was to remain unsupervised at Scole. The Group at our suggestion therefore arranged to seal over all the screwheads with a lacquered paint which they and we believed would fracture were any attempt made to interfere with the hasp in order to open the lid or with other aspects of the box. This was done, and the painted seals deemed satisfactory by the investigators. MK meantime undertook to have a similar box built, but with no exposed screws. Thus there were later two boxes, referred to hereafter as the 'Alan' and the 'Keen' boxes respectively.

The fact that in subsequent months successful films were produced only from the 'Alan box' rather than the 'Keen box' gave rise to fears that critics might argue for the existence of a secret panel in the former, or claim that it would have been possible to open the hasp, lift the lid and substitute another film tub, or even that it was possible to produce a duplicate Alan box and substitute it for the original during sittings, although an examination of the sequence of film production events would appear inconsistent with most of these supicions. However, they are examined more closely in that part of Chapters XIV and XV which is devoted to criticisms of perceived defects in procedure, and in more specific detail in Appendix K. Others are implicit in the accounts of the next three occasions when the box was used.

On 22nd November Walter and Karin Schnittger, accompanied by SPR member Dr Hans Schaer (HS) from Zürich, held a sitting (No.19) at Scole. As with other Scole sittings he attended, WS has provided us with a detailed, signed record (see Appendix D), summarised as follows. He used one of a package of three Polachrome films picked up by KS direct from Jessops the previous day. At the same time WS, who is an engineer specialising in analysing automotive problems, bought a new padlock in Norwich. On arriving at Scole he was given the Alan box to examine, which he did thoroughly, checking the metal joint on one side, the painted seals, the locking mechanism on the other and the wooden parts inter-locking and glued, and additionally secured with nails. He removed his lock from the manufacturer's packaging, selected a 12-exposure film from the package bought for the experiment by KS, opened it and placed the plastic tub immediately into the box which he then locked, taking it with him while he locked the keys in his car and handed his car key for additional security to HS. His report continues:–

> During the whole evening the film was not touched by anybody except myself, and it was all the time in my hands: from the moment of locking it in the container [ie the Alan box] until the film was processed, including the processing action itself, the wooden container and the film were always exclusively in my hands, and nobody ever touched them and I never let them go or stand alone.

WS thus had full control of the film and the box before, during and after the sitting, right through to the conclusion of development. While he was holding the box with both hands on his knees during the sitting, Edwin asked him to take it in one hand only, having ascertained that he was right-handed, and to place the box in such a way that his forefinger was on the lid feeling the locking mechanism with the lower middle of the finger, while the padlock itself was in the palm of his hand, the thumb holding the left side of the box and the remaining three fingers gripping the right side. He thus not only possessed the box but grasped it in such a way as to control all possible points of entry to it. Holding it thus, he was asked to place it on the table, so that its base was squarely on the table top, and his right arm to the elbow was resting on the table. While in this position for the next few minutes he experienced phenomena virtually identical, as far as hand position and box-shaking are concerned, to those later described during a similar experiment in which MK was invited to hold the Keen box, but which failed to produce a successful film.

WS experienced vibration of the table, sometimes so pronounced that the crystals on it were heard to rattle, a light sensation in the arm and leg similar to a low-voltage reaction, and frequent touches on the right hand holding the container both around his finger-tips and over the back of his hand. On one occasion the pullover and shirt on his right arm were pulled up, he records, and he felt a finger encircling his wrist, then the pullover and shirt sleeve were pulled down again. He had the impression of several hands touching his right arm, sometimes quite strongly, as though efforts were being made to wrench his fingers away from the box, or apply such force to it that he had to exert some effort to keep it still and resist the pressures.

WS supplied a contemporaneous commentary on these experiences for the benefit of Edwin, who was eager to know how he felt. On responding that he felt well, he received a 'good boy' pat on his left shoulder from the Team. After several minutes he was told to relax and return the box to his lap. Then the experiment of placing the box on the table while holding it securely was repeated, but this time with less touching, and with no battling for it as before. After the sitting and retrieval of the padlock keys, still locked in his car, WS inspected the film developing machine to ensure that it was empty, inserted the developer cartridge himself before unlocking the box, taking out the tubbed film, extracting it and placing it in the developer. The film, reproduced on Plate 6, had German words resembling Wie and Staub in handwriting, and strange semi mirror-image letters and ambling lines throughout, puzzles which were to give us ample scope for investigation and speculation over the next few months, and which we briefly list in the short Chapter X on unsolved mysteries.

On 6th December the Schnittgers had another sitting (No.20), this time without Dr Schaer, but at which the procedure was virtually identical to that just described, save that there was less force applied to WS's hand holding the box. The result on the film was a series of what appeared to be X-rays of WS's fingers and thumb (see Plate 7). We could not and cannot fault the protocol for either of these WS films.

On 17th January 1997, the Schnittgers had a further session (No.24), again with their own Polaroid 35 mm film in the same (Alan) box and with WS's own lock, but on this occasion WS was asked by Robin to place the locked box in the centre of the table so that the corners were directed towards the north and south table tabs. A sheet of plain A4 paper had already been placed in the centre of the table to allow him to draw the outline showing the exact position of the box and the location of the padlock, which hung down onto the paper. Both the Schnittgers checked the room before the Group descended. During the sitting they satisfied themselves from their observation of the Group's wristbands that no one left his seat. When the sitting finished WS confirmed that the box was in precisely its original position. Subsequently it was touched only by the two Schnittgers, who supervised the developing. WS marked the film before it was developed and checked afterwards to ensure there was no substitution. What emerged is seen on Plate 9, the Dragon film.

The role of the Schnittgers in the production of filmic evidence produced during the sittings discussed here is particularly valuable, since the precautions against deception were of a high standard, and the Schnittgers, who had been fully briefed by MK, were very much aware of the need for meticulous attention to all details in the control of the films and box. It would seem easier to suspect the Schnittgers of deception rather than inattention to detail; but we would not support such an accusation. The Schnittgers, together with Hans Schaer, worked so closely with the three authors of this Report that they became part of the investigative team. We never doubted their integrity.

The Dragon strip proved to be the only film to be devoted solely to apparently hermetic symbols. The strip, however, gave rise to some puzzlement and even concern. In part this stemmed from the broader doubts expressed by critics over the fact that all the successful films produced in connection with a locked box occurred when the Alan and not the Keen box was used. However, these doubts are not relevant to the results achieved when a sealed security bag was employed or when the film tubs were hand-held (see Chapter V). More substantially, the concerns derived from the discovery by Alan Gauld that the picture of the dragon and other markings were consistent with those likely to have been made had the film been produced naturally. We examine this view in detail in our discussion of the fraud hypothesis, and in Appendix D, but mention it here to remind the reader that our presentation of the evidence is accompanied at each point by a critical look at the perceived flaws in protocol, and at all the doubts which have been advanced in connection with the evidence.

As mentioned earlier, one of us (MK) expressed to the Team during a solo sitting with the Group on 4th March 1997 (No 29), that he was concerned lest the ambiguous and hermetic nature of the drawings would lead critics to conclude that we were being coaxed back into occult realms, making acceptance of the evidence by the sceptical world outside more difficult, even though such a lack of acceptance would be without logic. (It must be said that MK's concern was not shared by DF or AE.) While all the symbols may be familiar to students of hermetics, and indeed were shortly found reproduced on various pages in a relatively modern *Pictorial History of Magic and the Supernatural* (Bessy, 1963), the message they were intended to convey remains unclear. Unless they comprise little more than a random collection of post-medieval drawings, it does appear, however, that their objective is to be spiritually uplifting.

Plate I (Greek letters).

These Greek letters appeared on a film that was bought and handled throughout by the investigators, and developed at Scole on 17th February 1996. It had been placed unopened in its tub on the séance

table immediately in front of one of the investigators. The colouring and images stretched over three or four frame lengths, of which the part reproduced here was the central feature

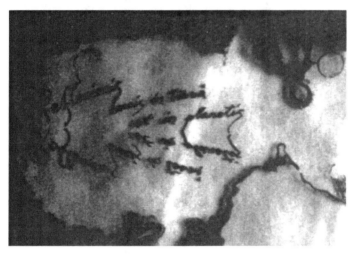

(Above) Plate 2 (Reflexionis). Details of the manner in which this mirror-image film (above) bearing a Latin inscription was produced are given in Appendix C, which contains the testimony of Denzil Fairbairn, the principal observer, supported by nine others who attended the seminar sitting of 25th May 1996.

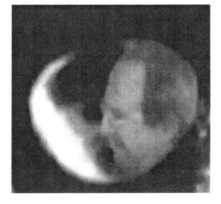

(Right) Plate 3. The slowly moving image of a man's profile in a bubble appeared for several seconds on part of a video in the experiment described by Hans Schaer in Chapter XIII.

109

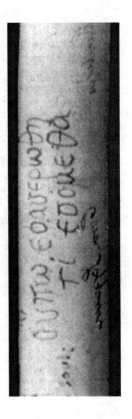

Plate 4 (Diotima). This Polablue film, developed by the investigators on 13th April 1996, faded rapidly before it was copied. This reproduction has been computer enhanced and shows both Greek and French messages (see Chapter V) in addition to a stanza from a lengthy poem by Frederic Myers, a mirror-image signature of Cora Tappan (a Victorian inspirational medium), and the enigmatic reference to one of the earliest of the Cross-Correspondence puzzles, the Diotima clue. The level of control in this case was not high, however.

Plate 5 (German poem). After a false start on 31st May 1996, in which the first line only of this poem was shakily reproduced on an earlier film (held in the tub by Karin Schnittger), this very clearly inscribed poem, complete with Chinese ideograms and astrological symbols in various hues, was developed by the Schnittgers after their 27th July 1996 sitting. The Polachrome film came from the Foys' dwindling stock. Despite extensive inquiries (Chapter V and Appendix D) no trace of the original, either in script or print, has been found, and the authorship is unknown.

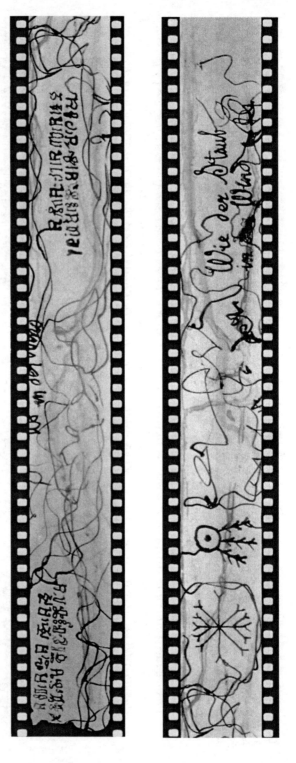

Plate 6 (Wie der Staub). These strange images, with clearly discernible though rambling German phrases, originated from a Polachrome film bought and controlled throughout by the Schnittgers after it was placed by them in a locked box held in Walter Schnittger's hand and developed the same evening after a sitting attended also by Dr Schaer on 22nd November 1996 (Chapter VI and Appendix D).

Plate 7 (X-ray film). This Polachrome film was bought by the Schnittgers, placed in the 'Alan' box and held throughout by Walter Schnittger. Developed by him that evening, it appears to show X-ray-type impressions of his fingers and thumb (6th December 1996).

Plate 8 (Perfectio). Bought and handled throughout by the experimenters, the tub containing this unopened roll of Polachrome film had a luminous strip attached to it when placed immediately in front of the experimenters near the edge of the séance room table. It was developed immediately after the 13th July 1996 sitting.

Plate 9 (Dragon film). The controversial Dragon film, comprising a number of disparate hermetic or alchemical symbols, appeared on 17th January 1997. The film was Polachrome, bought by the Schnittgers and padlocked inside its tub in the 'Alan' box, placed on marked paper at the centre of the table. It was developed the same evening (Chapter VI and Appendix H).

114

Plate 9 (continued). Third section of Dragon film (see page above).

Plate 10 (Ruth 1 film). This Polachrome strip was developed from a Scole film pack on 11th November 1996, having been retained by Professor Fontana in the newly-made and padlocked 'Alan' box. The origin and possible significance is described in Chapter VII and amplified in Appendix M. It should be read in conjunction with Plate 11.

Plate 11 (Ruth 2 film). Produced two weeks later, and the subject of several hints and much debate between investigators and communicators, this was the first Kodachrome film to be created. With various aberrations it completed the stanzas of Ruth which Wordsworth introduced into the ephemeral second edition of his Lyrical Ballads in 1802. Below: complete strip (reduced-size); overleaf individual stanzas, enlarged by 10%.

115

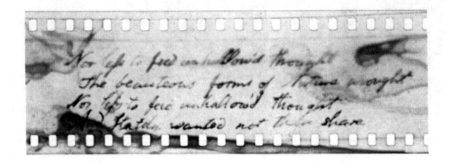

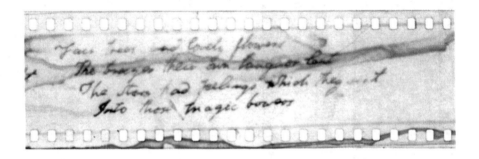

(Above) Plate 12 (Ruth 2 film). Divided into three sections to show the individual stanzas. The whole film (reduced-size) is shown on the preceding page.

(Right) Plate 13 (Ruth script). Reproduced by kind permission of the curator of the Beinecke Rare Book and Manuscript Library of Yale University Library, this page is taken from the family copy of amendments to the 1800 edition of Wordsworth's second volume of Lyrical Ballads, and was reproduced in Christies' catalogue for their miscellaneous book and manuscript auction on 12th December 1965, when it was sold by Matthew Wordsworth and bought on behalf of Yale. The film script bears a close similarity to the original, in Dorothy Wordsworth's hand.

Whatever in those climes I found
Irregular in sight or sound
Did to my mind impart
A kindred impulse, seem'd allied
To my own powers & justified
The workings of my heart.

Nor less, to feed unhallow'd thought
The beauteous forms of Nature wrought,
Fair trees and lovely flowers
The breezes their own languor lent
The stars had feelings which they sent
Into those magic bowers

Yet in my worst pursuits, I ween
That often there did intervene
Pure hopes of high intent
My passions and forms so fair
And stately, wanted not their share
Of noble sentiment.

So was it then and so is now:
For, Ruth! with thee, I know not how
I feel my spirit burn
Even as the East when day comes forth

Plate 14 (Electrical diagram). This Kodachrome reel was developed from one of the two films bought by the investigators and locked respectively in the 'Alan' and newly-made 'Keen' boxes on 11th January 1997. The latter proved blank; the former yielded a diagram which the communicators said was to enable Professor Ellison (who was absent from this sitting) to modify the 'germanium gadget' which he had helped to construct as part of an electronic communication experiment (see Chapter VIII).

A represents the Germanium B and C Coils to high Resistance. This would help improve Conductivity. JCC

The whole being enclosed in box.

118

Harrison, N. J.
February 4, 1925

adoweroft
on Laboratory
w Jersey

roft:

losing herewith our suggestions for improv-
quipment in the Laboratory Library. You
tried to be extremely practical and
to produce a first class
thers connected with

Plate 15 (Edison signature). Compare the photocopy on the right (courtesy Edison National Historic Site office, New Jersey) of Thomas Edison's initialled signature on a 1925 letter to that appearing at the end of the electrical diagram (Plate 14), reproduced above (actual size).

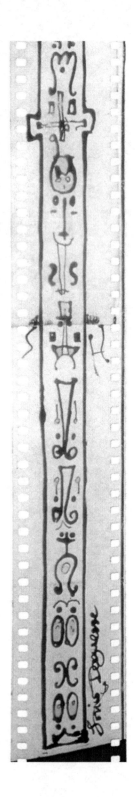

Plate 16 (Daguerre film). The two parts of the film, and same-size sections of these. Full caption on facing page below.

Plate 16 (Daguerre film). The last, and longest, film produced during the investigation gives an apparently symbolic message, the name of a pioneer of photography, Louis Daguerre, some mysterious and as yet unidentified initials said to be related to Daguerre and his work, and a totem-pole drawing of glyphs which invite expert comment and analysis. This is from a 36-frame roll of Kodachrome 200 film taken from the padlocked 'Alan' box (see Chapter IX and Appendix K)

121

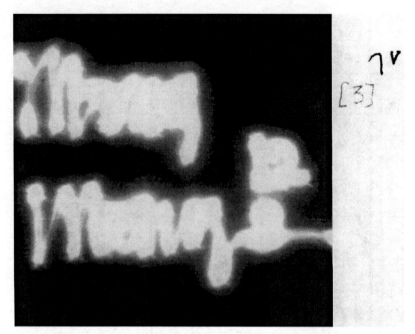

Plate 17 (Ibiza films). These two images were found on numbers 3 and 4 (code marked on the right, with square-bracketed explanatory numbers subsequently printed below) after the experiment described in Chapter XI. Tony Cornell has shown how similar impressions could be produced by the surreptitious use of a small LED pencil. This is discussed in Appendix J and in his comments and the authors' reply.

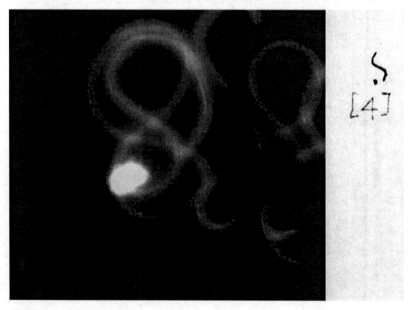

 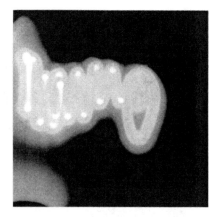

Plate 18 (Ibiza and Cambridge polaroids). The two images above were produced at Cambridge with the aid of an LED and should be compared to those in Plate 17.

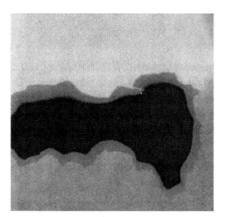 

Above and Below: Compare, in each case, the image on the left, which was received at the Ibiza sitting, to the one on the right, produced with an LED at Cambridge.

 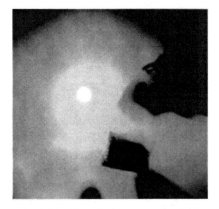

Publisher's Note: In Plates 17 & 18 the lightest grey is vivid yellow, darker greys are shades of green (from lime to emerald); black is black, white/white. See front cover for example.

Plate 19 (Ibiza sitting). Apart from the investigator (MK) who conducted the two repeated experiments described in Chapter XI (see also Appendix J), and who would have occupied the vacant chair on the right, this is the seating arrangement at Dr Hans Schaer's house in Ibiza. It shows the 'apported' candle found on the table at the end of the first of the two sittings.

Below: The room without occupants shows the disposition of chairs, central gate-legged table and side tables more clearly.

CHAPTER VII: THE PHENOMENA:
WORDSWORTH'S AMENDMENT OF *RUTH*

The two films we term Ruth 1 and Ruth 2 were produced at separate sittings, and it is important to get the sequence of events clear, because the oral spirit communications via the mediums, and indeed the discussion between visiting sitters and the Team, comprise part of the evidence. It is also arguable that the evidence on the second Ruth film, developed later (after the 18th sitting, on 18th November 1996) and examined below, may have been in part a product of a discussion which took place before and during that sitting.

Before the start of the 16th sitting on 9th November 1996, MK randomly selected one of two Polaroid Polachrome 35mm 12-exposure films. One of these films he had bought and left earlier at Scole; the other was a replacement for the defective roll which the investigators had tried to develop on 10th August after the 14th sitting. It had been sent to Scole by the Polaroid film suppliers, Jessops of Leicester. Both packages were examined by the investigators and both appeared pristine. In our presence, and in front of the Group, MK opened the selected package, removed the chemical (developing) cassette, and without opening the lid placed the tub containing the film in the newly made 'Alan' box, as described in the previous chapter. He padlocked the box, retaining the keys in his pocket. Before the sitting began, he placed the box on the central circular table 12 to 15 cm in front of DF.

At the same sitting MK produced a carton containing one 35mm roll of Kodachrome 200 film, which he had purchased from Boots and brought with him. At the request of the Team, as conveyed to us by the Group, he had removed the tub from its package but without opening it, and he was asked to leave it on the table for 'spirit investigation', Kodachrome being a novel technology for the Team.[1]

Following some procedural discussion with the Team, the Alan box was handed to and retained by DF, who was given the keys on the understanding that he would not open the box or touch the contents, pending his return. He took the box away with him and kept it in his possession until his return two days later for a special sitting from which AE and MK were absent, but which was attended by IS in addition to DF. At that session (Monday, 11th November) DF had the Polachrome film inside the padlocked box (with the keys safely on the

---

[1] The reasons why Kodachrome had been suggested, originally by Maurice Grosse, as an alternative or addition to Polaroid, and readily agreed to by the Team, are not strictly relevant here, but were thought to convey an improved level of perceived authenticity as a result of having a more independent and locationally detached protocol for developing films.

key-ring in his pocket) immediately in front of him on the table throughout the sitting. After the sitting he supervised its processing in the special developing machine supplied by Polaroid for 35mm film, and with the routine for which he was already familiar. The chemical cassette was placed on one side, the Polachrome film on the other, the lid closed and the film developed automatically within two minutes.

As DF pulled the strip from the machine and examined it beneath a magnifying viewer, the text of extracts of a poem, which included a reference to Ruth in one line (see indented extract below of the spirit message), was found in script characteristic of early 19th-century handwriting. The text is given below and reproduced in Plate 10, together with annotations which may be safely ignored for the moment. Along-side it is the text printed in the current Oxford University Press edition of Wordsworth's collected poems, and which, with minor textual changes, appears in all those Wordsworth anthologies we examined which contained the poem Ruth – and not many did. This latter 'official' version was soon identified after the sitting. It will be immediately apparent that the chief difference between it and the version obtained from the Team is the switch from third to first person.

During this (11th Nov.) sitting, and before the film (henceforth termed Ruth 1) had been processed, the following conversation between DF and the Team took place:–

> *Joseph: It's a little like what you will see on the film. There's some teasing there. I don't know what it is, if anything at all, but I do have some information. It comes from a gentleman who was very fond of words. That's all I should say . . . The scientist you refer to isn't a scientist . . .but the film, the gentleman who is rather fond of words, says he's unable – I don't know why: perhaps because of where he is at the moment – is unable to convey what he was hoping to. He's unable to show you exactly what he wanted to show you. It's as if he's lost touch with his thoughts, I suppose. Whilst living – that may seem strange – but he was rather evolved when he came to the earth while he lived, so therefore on his return I feel he's gone on rather quickly.*
> *EB: That detaching that I was telling you about before, David, do you remember?*
> *DF: Yes, I do.*
> *Joseph: This has perhaps caused him some . . . not unhappiness, because I'm sure that's not an emotion or feeling that he has: he was disappointed that he couldn't produce (that's a good word) what he wanted for you. Do you understand? I haven't made it quite clear, but it's difficult to express something on behalf of someone else.*

[Several minutes later, apropos a discussion of the contents of the box]:–

> *Patrick [another spirit communicator]: I think it's going to be a picture, or in writing.*

RF: Oh, right.

Patrick: I think it's going to be black and white, or colour (laughter).

SF: In other words he doesn't have a clue!

Patrick: Is it a colour film? Then it will be black and white.

EB: Your clues aren't as good as my clues.

RF: No.

Patrick: Well, I've got something here . . . strewth . . . no Ruth.

DF: That's a clue to the writing?

Patrick: Not a clue, but someone called out "Ruth" when I wanted some clues about the film. I said "strewth" and he said "no . . . Ruth", so perhaps Ruth is on the film. Perhaps they've got it wrong.

DF: It's called hedging your bets.

Patrick: Might be 'truth'.

Note that this was an unusual interchange, since up to that date no hint of content of films had been given during any session in which the spirit influences on the unexposed film appeared to be operating. The Team had twice emphasised their desire to ensure that any images or messages stemmed, and could be seen to have stemmed, from them, rather than from the subconscious hopes, expectations, images or wishes of the sitters. The playfulness of the interchange and the teasing repartee are typical, however. So too is the punning, as seen in the references to someone fond of words. Note too that the word Ruth appears in the text of Ruth 1, thus making Patrick's hint superfluous, but much in the spirit of his earlier teasing 'clues'.

Once it had been established that the Team's version of the poem on the Ruth 1 film showed departures from the Oxford University Press version, the immediate problem was to see whether there existed a manuscript of the spirit Team version, which we supposed must have been Wordsworth's earlier, discarded, draft. Proceeding in the belief that this manuscript had been written in the first person, but that after-thought had prompted Wordsworth to amend it, and that this first-person version had never appeared in print, MK initially failed to do what hindsight clearly commended: to examine all available versions of the text in all successive editions of Wordsworth's poems. Instead, he looked at the text in the light of what were taken to be Wordsworth's own feelings and attitudes, a process which was to lead to a significant dispute with the Team.

The story of the poem itself has an important bearing on the film message. Covering 43 stanzas, it is an account of Ruth, an abandoned orphan girl, a child of Nature, who is captivated by a dashing young American "of green Savannahs". He finds himself unable to escape from the lure of his free-roving and perhaps somewhat dissolute past, and abandons her just as they are about to set forth on a new life together.

She goes mad and is thrown into prison, from which she eventually escapes to live out the wandering life of a beggar, playing on her flute, sleeping rough, ageing fast.

It was initially assumed by MK that a first-person draft of this passage in a poem written by Wordsworth in Goslar, Germany, in 1799, reflected (in Ralph Noyes's words) a "kind of rueful, belated, repentance-cum-defensive explanation for an episode in Wordsworth's life about which he must always have been ambivalent – his affair with Annette Vallon in France in 1791, which begot him an illegitimate daughter, Caroline, and his failure to make reparation despite meeting Annette again in 1802". A good deal of further research was required to show how perceptive, or unfair, this assumption proved to be.[1]

Here, on the left, is the script version of Ruth as seen on the 1st Ruth film on the night of November 11. On the right is the version appearing in Palgrave's Treasury. The latter is in all essentials identical to the wording found in other volumes and in all other editions of Wordsworth's work, save one:–

The Ruth 1 version (as originally read)	*The Palgrave Treasury version*
Stanza 22	
Whatever in these climes I found	Whatever in those climes he found
Complete (?) in sight or sound	Irregular in sight and sound
Did to my mind impart	Did to his mind impart
A kindred (?) spirit seem'd allied	A kindred impulse, seem'd allied
To my own powers justified	To his own powers, and justified
The workings of my heart.	The workings of his heart.
For Ruth with thee I know	

---

[1] An examination of works in the British Library dealing particularly with the Vallon episode established fairly conclusively that Wordsworth need have had little reason to feel guilty about his affair with Annette. The affair was known to his family, notably to Dorothy his sister and later to Mary his wife, albeit little publicised. However, there is also evidence that this early love affair – he was 21, and Annette a few years older – did have a profound effect on him; and in the light of subsequent spirit information it is certainly reasonable to suppose that the first person version did reflect this episode, even though, as Professor George Harper has noted (Harper, 1921), 'every fresh fact, makes it more and more apparent that . . . it [the Annette affair] was openly acknowledged and its consequences honourably endured.' DF has, however, pointed out that, since Wordsworth deals exhaustively with his affair with Annette in Vaudracour and Julia, written in 1805, a communicating Wordsworth might better have been expected to have referred to this poem rather than to Ruth, a poem which may reasonably be accounted fairly obscure since it is not even mentioned in Mary Jacobus' (1976) analysis or by H. W. Garrod (1922, 1927), Jared Curtis (1971) or even W. J. B. Owen (1969).

Stanza 23

(Stanza omitted
from first film)

Nor less, to feed voluptuous thought
The beauteous forms of Nature wrought,-
Fair trees and gorgeous flowers;
The breezes their own languor lent;
The stars had feelings, which they sent
Into those favour'd bowers.

Stanza 24

Yet in my worst pursuits I ween	Yet, in his worst pursuits, I ween
That often there did intervene	That sometimes there did intervene
Pure hopes of high intent	Pure hopes of high intent
My passion amid (?) forms as fair	For passions link'd to forms so fair
	And stately, needs must have their share
WW	Of noble sentiment.

(Note: some words were difficult to read on the film. Only in the light of the subsequent discovery of the printed text did these become more apparent.)

MK was the sole investigator at a sitting with the Group on 18th November 1996. When the poem issue was being discussed in the Foys' sitting room before the session, RF informed him that the spirit Team had been emphatic that the poem on the Ruth 1 film had been written in 1800. MK said that this could not be squared with the fact that, in the definitive version of his poems which Wordsworth had worked on in 1843, he had authorised the date as 1799. (Indeed, his dictated notes in Vol II, page 123, recorded below the title Ruth, tell us that the poem was "Written in Germany: suggested by an account I had of a wanderer in Somersetshire", and dated "1799".) MK told the Group that he could not understand how the version of the poem on the Ruth 1 film, and which appeared to be an early draft, could have been written after what was assumed to be the final version (that on the right above) had been published. This proved a useful blunder on MK's part, for a short way into the subsequent (18th) sitting (MK2, 18th November 1996) the following discussion took place. Edwin's remarks were not preceded by any reference to MK's doubts.

> Edwin: Now recently, did I say 1800? — this is a question that needs to be answered. Mr Keen, you have some trouble in your mind with regard to the date of 1800. Why does this trouble you so?

> MK: Because the authorised version of Ruth by Wordsworth himself dates it 1799, the year when he was at Goslar in Germany writing a number of lyrical poems. It seems difficult to imagine that he produced an earlier

version of it after the original version seems to have been written. Clearly there is a confusion here.

Edwin: There does seem to be. All I know — perhaps I misunderstood — let's not worry or concern ourselves too much. I shall . . . yes . . . thank you, I'll give you what I've been told. There was a first edition to his lyric I understand, and a second edition. I think — don't take this as a hundred per cent but I think what has been misunderstood . . . these writings that you have are merely vibrations: thought, as you know, feelings and memories of alterations that were made to the first edition and subsequently additional verses were added, and this I believe was done.

What you have witnessed was written in 1799 as well. Some that wasn't published, only a little, but he felt it was lacking somewhat. There is a certain, well quite a lot, of change which we can't express to you. A lot of emotion, and a lot was changed. It isn't my place to explain. You have something which is extremely interesting and it is unlikely you will be able to find it. You may. It would be wonderful if you did. I believe it is somewhere unusual. I don't know where or I could help. We help if we can, even if it's only clues, but I'm not privileged to know where, but it does exist. It was in the family until some years ago. It isn't now; perhaps it was . . . I don't know what happens to these things. Does that help?

MK: That helps enormously.

Edwin: 1802, the final edition, and it didn't contain all that you have. Do you feel, Mr Keen, quite . . . quite drawn towards this lyrical poetry? Is it taking up a lot of your thought?

MK: It is — because it is taking up a lot of my time — intrinsically fascinating.

Edwin: Well we can use your fascination. It will be clear to you, not this evening but on another evening if you are that enthusiastic: if you have that mind for it, we can take advantage of your thoughts and vibrations.

MK: Thank you very much. I have a question, but I won't attempt to pose it until you invite them.

Edwin: We can interact with you with regard to this poem, and perhaps in some way that can be made evident to you also. Perhaps we can answer your question.

MK: I'm not certain of the degree of autobiographical evidentiality that there is, of the alterations that were given on the film, and whether the significance relates to Wordsworth or more indirectly to Myers.

Edwin: I can't answer that; I can't help you. I can tell you it is indeed . . . and it was the gentleman himself, his own feelings when he added those particular verses changed prior to publication.

MK: I think I understand: they appear to be inspired by his recollection of Miss Vallon. I wondered if it had been indirectly inspired by Annie Marshall.

Edwin: I can't help you with that but you may have your answer in some obscure way (laughter).

EB: That was my feeling too.

MK: I'm sure it would be obscure.

The conclusions that could justifiably be drawn from this exchange, assuming paranormality, were:–

a) that Edwin had either overheard the pre-séance conversation or had read MK's thoughts; or that the subconscious mind of Alan, the medium, was being dredged;

b) that Edwin interrupted his speech momentarily while some message was conveyed to him by another spirit, information which took but a second or two for him to receive but far longer to impart;

c) that MK had mistakenly assumed, and had researched on the basis, that the film version was an earlier but discarded draft written while the poet was, so to speak, identifying himself and his conflicting emotions of spiritual purity and carnal desire with the attitude and conduct of the deserting lover portrayed in Ruth;

d) that the employment of the first person had an autobiographical significance for Wordsworth, and

e) that the answer lay in an examination of the earliest editions of the lyric poems, or ballads.

Before that examination could take place, however, the second film was developed. This was the Kodachrome 200 35mm transparency film which had been left on 9th November on the central table, inside its black plastic tub, for the spirits to examine experimentally. The communicators asked MK to take it away and get it developed, along with another similar film which he had brought with him, and had inserted, still in its unopened tub, into the Alan box, which he padlocked (locking away the keys in his car). In the event, the development of both films by expedited arrangement at Kodak's developing centre in Wimbledon (the only place in the UK where these films can be processed) the following Monday morning revealed nothing on the boxed film, but a further Ruth script (now referred to as Ruth 2) on the Kodachrome 200 film.

Neither of the two Ruth films could thus be claimed to have been produced in wholly fraudproof conditions. In the case of the Ruth 1 film, fraud could be postulated only if either both DF and IS, as well as the Group, were parties to an elaborate deception, or if a prepared film had been placed in their store by the Scole Group after carefully re-sealing it to make it appear wholly new and thus deceive the three investigators and IS. The Ruth 2 film, dependent on a wholly different technology, had been left with the Foys for examination and possible treatment by the Team. In that case, too, the conditions were not fraudproof. What appeared on the Ruth 2 film (reproduced in Plates 11 and 12) was the following script:–

To
Ruth[1]
1880

So was it then xx [2] and so is now
For Ruth! with thee I know not how
I feel my spirit burn[3]
Nor less[4] to feed unhallow'd thought
The beauteous forms of Nature wrought
Nor less to feed unhallow'd thought
And Stately[5] wanted not their share
Fair trees and lovely[6] flowers
The breezes their own languor lent
The stars had feelings which they sent
Into those magic[7] bowers

As in the Ruth 1 film, these stanzas were written along the length of the roll with no sign of vertical divisions. The Ruth 2 film is a transparency, and copies appear as opaque positives, as do the photocopies of it. The smears and blotches which appear opaque in the photocopy of the positive are therefore translucent in the original, and do not obscure the message significantly.

MK wondered whether there was a published version which contained the first-person stanzas of *Ruth* and, if so, what significance if any attached to that change of person? Subsequent research convinced him that the sequence of editions of the poem was crucial. The first edition of the *Lyrical Ballads*, known as the Bristol edition and containing anonymously some of Coleridge's verse, including *The Ancient Mariner*, was published late in 1798 in one volume. It did not contain *Ruth*. Its success encouraged Wordsworth to publish a second edition of this volume in 1800, but he added a large amount of new material, including

---

[1] Some explanatory comments are required:–

[2] This looks like the beginning of a word, but is crossed out, although it could equally well be a dash. In the light of later discoveries, this apparently trivial feature was to prove among the most significant of all the pieces of Ruth evidence.

[3] The word 'burn' is struck through and was rendered illegible, but has been restored here because subsequent investigation shows it to be correct.

[4] The first 's' in 'less' in both the first and third lines of this stanza is the old extended *f* which the Wordsworths used, although it was dying out in the early 1800s.

[5] This line does not belong to the 23rd stanza, which had been omitted from the first film, but belongs to the end of the 22nd. Its inclusion makes sense of the 22nd stanza, although there ought to be a comma after 'stately' to make the meaning clearer.

[6] Lovely' is transformed to 'gorgeous' in later versions, and

[7] 'magic' is changed to 'favoured'.

Perhaps more emotionally telling is the use of 'unhallow'd' rather than 'voluptuous'. The signifcance of these and other differences between the Yale MS and the film versions, and between the Yale MS text and subsequent, standard, versions of the poem, are commented on later.

Ruth. This new material was collected in a separate volume with a separate index but bound together with the first volume. That first volume was now marked as the second edition, but the second volume had, quite correctly, no such ascription and is properly described as the first edition of the additional poems. In 1802 there appeared a revised edition which embraced both the first and second batch of the earlier material. Again, the two volumes were bound together, the first being described as the third edition, and the second (containing *Ruth*) as the second edition. When yet another, combined, edition was published in 1805 these confusing distinctions disappeared, and the whole was now called the fourth edition. It is with the alterations made to *Ruth* for the second, 1802, edition, that we are concerned. The 1802 printed text, with emboldened words to indicate changes, reads:–

Stanza 22

Whatever in those climes **I** found

Irregular in sight or sound

Did to **my** mind impart

A kindred impulse, seem'd allied

To **my** own powers, and justified

The workings of **my** heart.

Stanza 24

Yet in **my** worst pursuits I ween

That often there did intervene

Pure hopes of high intent

My passions, **amid** forms so fair

And stately, **wanted not** their share

Of noble sentiment

This is essentially the same as the script in the film. The original manuscript of these amendments, which MK later discovered to have been in Yale University since 1965, has the misplaced and truncated line

---

[1] A footnote appearing on p.176 of Brett and Jones' (Brett, 1963) study of the *Lyrical Ballads* refers to the insertion in 1802 of seven new stanzas into the original 1800 text of *Ruth*. This footnote is repeated in the paperback edition of Brett and Jones, and cannot therefore be considered obscure. However, few other than specialists would have recognised from this note that it was in this 1802 text (i.e. the second edition), and only in that ephemeral edition, that Wordsworth used the first person variation in these stanzas. By far the most authoritative analysis of the revisions to the *Lyrical Ballads* appears in the most recent volume in the Cornell series (Butler & Green, 1992), a work not on the University of London Library shelves in December 1996, and not available in the British Library. (Save for minor verbal alterations the original third person wording was restored to, and remained in, all subsequent editions.) Nowhere has research thus far revealed any authority who noted any particular '*significance*' in these amendments. Even the Brett and Jones footnote relating to all seven new stanzas fails to draw attention to the nature, let alone the significance, of that change.

"For Ruth with thee I know" inserted at the end of Stanza 22, and it omits the last two lines. Further clarification is found in Brett and Jones' above-mentioned footnote. They point out that some of the seven stanzas inserted by Wordsworth into the 1802 edition, including the first, were removed from later editions; others remained, but with alterations; and the order of stanzas was changed. The last of the seven is also swept away, but in the fourth edition of 1805 two of the new stanzas were included. The second of these reads:–

> But wherefor speak of this? for now
> **Sweet Ruth! with thee I know not how,**
> **I feel my spirit burn –**
> Even as the east when day comes forth;
> And to the west and south, and north
> The morning doth return.

The two lines in bold are those which appear in our second film and partly in the odd line at the end of Stanza 22 in the Ruth 1 film. 'Sweet' has been supplanted by 'For' in our second film. Brett and Jones simply reproduce the new verses and note those which survived and those which were dropped. The verse we have just quoted disappeared after the 1805 edition.

It is quite clear from the historical evidence that the answer given to MK, after his query about the date, corresponds to what he subsequently discovered. What may seem puzzling is the absence of comment, by any of the leading Wordsworth authorities consulted, on the significance of these amendments. In a technical note later (see Appendix M), we attempt to explain this omission.

The existence or whereabouts of the original Wordsworth manuscript of the poem was not known to the investigators until a letter from Prof. Jonathan Wordsworth confirmed Edwin's hint that it may have gone "out of the family". Dr Wordsworth reported that the Wordsworth family MS of this version of *Ruth* was an amended copy of the first, 1800, edition of the additional *Lyrical Ballads* which had been sold to Yale University by his Uncle Matthew. (Printers customarily sent authors two proofs, one to amend and return; the other to retain. We are here concerned with the latter, the former having long since been lost sight of.) It transpired that this amended copy of the *Ballads* had been auctioned at Christies in London on 9th December 1965 and bought by a bidder acting on behalf of Yale University, where it has since been lodged in the Beinecke Rare Book and Manuscript Library. The Beinecke Librarian has sent us photocopies from the Yale MS of the amendments made to the original 1800 text of *Ruth*. Broadly, although as we have already noted not precisely, these correspond to the script on our two films (see Plate 13). The Yale Library Catalogue index describes this proof copy as "annotated throughout with manuscript corrections and revisions by William and Dorothy Wordsworth and an unidentified person in preparation for the edition of 1802". (See Plate 13)

This leads us straight to four questions:–

1 In whose hand were Wordsworth's original amendments written?

2 Is it the same as that seen on the films?

3 Could the films have been made in ignorance of both the text and the handwriting of the Yale MS?

4 If not, has the Yale MS page on which the manuscript changes appear been available for someone in or connected to the Scole Group to see and copy?

As a tantalising supplementary question, one might also ask whether there are differences in the text, punctuation, corrections, etc. between the Yale MS and the two Ruth film versions, to which significance may be attached. Five questions have to be considered separately. A positive answer to the second, and more particularly a negative response to the third, may counter doubts arising from the defective safeguards against deception either when the Ruth 1 film was received or when the Kodachrome roll which subsequently yielded the Ruth 2 film was accessible at Scole.

Q1. Whose hand wrote the film scripts?

Wordsworth often dictated his poems, or employed others to amend his rather illegible handwriting. According to Hale White (White, 1897), quoted in a lengthy article by Frederick A. Pottle (Pottle, 1966) in the *Yale University Library Gazette*, these corrections were mainly in Dorothy's hand. There exists, indeed, a pencilled note in the Yale MS in the hand of Wordsworth's literary executor, Christopher Wordsworth (1807–1885), that the MS corrections are "by the hand of the Author's sister Dorothy Wordsworth and by the Author himself in some cases". Dorothy herself records in her *Journal* that she wrote out *the original version of Ruth* (our italics) on 27th July 1800, and her brother read it after supper on 22nd August. Most of the alterations which went into the second, 1802, edition – these are the ones which concern us – were made in the spring and summer of 1801. According to her Journal record, Dorothy spent the morning of Sunday, 7th March, 1802 writing out *Ruth* and reading it "with [these] alterations". Next day she records rewriting the alterations and posting them to the printers, from whom the first copies of the new edition were received on 22nd June that year.

Q2. Is the MS handwriting the same as in the Ruth films?

According to Pottle, Dorothy transcribed these changes for the second edition clearly and neatly on her brother's proof, copying the transposed stanzas, with the alterations and additions, on both sides of a pasted-in leaf of the same size as the pages of the printer's proof copy. The loose sheets in the proof copy sent to the printers, on which these extensive amendments were written, have long been lost. The only extant copy of the additional verses in handwriting, therefore, is that sold more than thirty years ago at Christie's, i.e. the Yale MS. The relevant page showing alterations opposite page 106 of the 1800 edition, photocopied by the Beinecke Library at our request, is reproduced by kind permission of the Library in Plate 13. It will be seen that the film script corresponds very closely although not exactly with Dorothy's handwriting.

Q3. Could the Ruth films have been made without seeing the original?

A comparison between the handwriting on the films and that reproduced from Dorothy's revisions shows that, whoever or whatever produced the films must have had a copy of Dorothy's script before him. If that is not apparent from the general similarities, it should be from observing that both the Yale MS and our Ruth 2 film include the deletion mark (which, of course, does not appear in any text) in the line: "So it was then xx and so is now".

Q4. Was the Yale MS copy accessible to the Scole Group?

The Christies' catalogue of the 1965 sale when the Wordsworth family MS was sold to a bidder acting for Yale University, and in which the *Lyrical Ballads* was Lot 149, was embellished by three photographs. One contains all the material found on the two Ruth films. The only other copy of the Yale MS traced by MK was made in microfilm by Kodak on the orders of the Board of Trade for depositing in the British Library, where it is available for study by approved students. An inspection on the microfilm projector in the British Library of the script, however, shows the handwriting to be faint and extremely difficult to read, let alone copy, especially the top verse. Some of the words at the end of longer lines, which have been all but eroded by two centuries of handling of the MS, are barely legible.

There is no easy way to discover whether scholars admitted for research to either the British Library or the Beinecke Collection at Yale are able to work from either a microfilm or (in Yale) the original version, but we note that the curator of the Beinecke Collection, Mr Vincent Giroud, has pointed out that, while the identity of researchers must remain confidential, the normal outcome of research is publication. We are not aware of any recent relevant learned publication on the subject of Ruth. Nevertheless, the answer to our fourth question must be that access by the Group to the relevant extract of the Yale MS was possible and cannot be ruled out. We leave to Appendix M the questions arising from this conclusion.

Q5. Are there significant differences between the two texts?

A comparison between the Yale MS and the contents of the two Ruth films does indeed show a number of differences, although what significance should attach to them must remain a matter of opinion. The first, and perhaps the most important, is the appearance on the extreme left of the Ruth 2 film of the words *"To Ruth 1880"*. We examine the meaning and significance of this later. Suffice it to say for the moment that these words are not in the Yale MS. Several of the words which appear in both the MS and the films are in the wrong place or incomplete in the latter. In one extreme case we have "For Ruth with thee I know" in the Ruth 1 film, and the words *"For Ruth! With thee I know not how"* (which is more accurate) in the Ruth 2 film. Similarly the Ruth 2 film repeats the line *"Nor less to feed unhallow'd thought"*, and then renders the meaning obscure by following it with the remainder of the uncompleted final line in the Ruth 1 film . . . *"And stately wanted not their share"*.

We deal in Appendix M with the question whether these differences are evidentially important. At this stage we can obtain a more balanced assessment of the significance of the films and their contents by looking at what the investigators were told by one or other of the Team, and the extent to which it was accurate. On the left is what one or other of the Team said. On the right is our comment.

11th Nov. sitting:

Joseph: It comes from a gentleman who is very fond of words.	This is correct, taking it to be a pun on Wordsworth.
He is unable to show you exactly what he wanted to show you.	There are obvious signs of this in both films.
It's as if he's lost touch with his thoughts.	The juxtapositioning of stray lines from different stanzas supports this.
(From Patrick) . . . he said no, "Ruth"; so perhaps Ruth is on the film.	This is correct.

18th Nov. sitting

Edwin: There was a first edition to his lyrics, then a second edition.	This is also correct.
Alterations were made to the first edition.	True.
. . . subsequently additional verses were added.	True.
It was in the family until some years ago. It isn't now.	Correct.
What you have witnessed was written in 1799 as well.	The revisions were certainly worked on in 1801 and 1802. We do not

137

know whether the 1802 version was conceived around the time of the original 1800 publication. The first version was certainly composed in 1799, as Wordsworth has confirmed. This is ambiguous. Some projected changes may not have been published. Although all seven verses were in the 1802 edition, not all survived. This is the case

Some that wasn't published: only a little.

1802, the final edition, and it didn't contain all that you have.

Not all of the Team's statements were of equal significance, of course, but in relation to the complications attending the various editions of *Ruth* and the changes made, Joseph, Edwin and Patrick appeared well-informed, *not least when responding to questions of which they had no prior notice.* Some of these responses, notably those touching on Wordsworth's emotional state, require the more detailed explanation we provide in Appendix M.

It is perhaps interesting to mention a few further Wordsworthian references conveyed to the sitters (DF, Bernard Carr and MK) on 14th December 1996. The principal control, Manu, who always introduced the sittings, commented in passing that *"our birth is but a sleep and a forgetting"*, recognised at the time by DF as a quotation from the poet's *Ode on Intimations of Immortality*, which evoked particular and highly personal memories for Professor Carr. Later, Joseph conveyed the author's (presumably he meant Wordsworth's) apologies for his lack of ability to communicate as he would like. According to the transcript Joseph then hinted that we should be able to identify the handwriting. He urged the sitters not to give up: it was important that they try their best (to identify the handwriting): he was merely passing on what he had been told; but it was "indeed a wonderful piece of evidence, even if I say so myself. There is to be more, of course . . . "

On 1st July 1997 there was an unexpected footnote. Two days earlier, at a sitting of the Group on the Spanish island of Ibiza, MK, asked by a spirit communicator how things were going with his Wordsworthian researches, had replied that he had pretty well completed the research, and thanked the spirit communicators for what he described as an impressive piece of evidence. He was duly thanked in turn. At the opening of the next sitting two days later Manu, addressing him, said:–

Someone wants me to say something to you, but they are not able to, as I am, to come . . . one moment (pause): "Prelude, or growth of a poet's mind".

During that day MK had been reading that passage in Gill's recent biography of Wordsworth which refers to the early development of his great autobiographical poem *The Prelude* as a "selective account of the poet's development". DF has noted that Manu's words are the subtitle of the poem, a fact of which MK had been unaware.

There remains one more puzzle: the significance of the date 1880 which appears on the second, Kodachrome, film. At the 21st sitting, on 14th December 1996, which immediately followed that of November 18, MK asked whether the date of 1880 was (as we had naturally assumed) an error for 1800:–

> *Edwin: I don't think so.*
>
> *EB: You'll find out.*
>
> *Edwin: I don't know.*
>
> *EB: It will all be made plain to you quite soon. Oh yes, you'll get a bit of help, Monty. You'll be inspired.*
>
> *Edwin: It may refer to something else you've been considering that relates in some way to the poem itself and the contents of what the poem is suggesting. It is a possibility that Ruth, and that date, are not intending to relate directly to that poem but indirectly.*

This was taken by MK to be a broad hint of Frederic Myers's involvement. Previous sittings had very specifically linked at least one of the films produced in the summer of 1996 with Myers, and there had been several references by the Team to his influence and presence. The earlier (Diotima) film had clearly been intended to be associated with one of the original Cross-Correspondences, in which the recently deceased Myers appeared to play a major role. Myers had written a biography of Wordsworth, but it had been published in 1881. A chance comparison of two copies of this work found in the London University library, however, proved this date to be ambiguous. The first edition of Myers's biography was indeed published by Macmillan's in that year, but the identical volume, described as one of the *English Men of Letters* series (also by Macmillan's) has 1880 as the publication date. Macmillan's produced a library edition in 1902 and reprinted the volume in 1905, 1908 and 1912. Unlike the original, these reprints had indexes, and they record three references to the poem *Ruth*. Two of these are incidental, passing notices. However, on pages 139/140 Myers quotes a stanza from *Ruth* describing the hot-blooded, tempestuous temperament of Ruth's lover, and contrasts this with the "healing powers of those gentle and familiar presences which came to Ruth in her stormy madness with visitations of momentary calm".

A strong case has been put to us that the 1880 date was a mistake for 1800, and that the assumptions which led to the suspicion that the discarnate Myers might somehow have been involved are too flimsy. While these issues will be examined in more detail later, in the context of a wholly different account of the authenticity of the films (see

Appendix M), we here proceed on the assumption that the inclusion of 1880 in the Ruth 2 film is unlikely to be accidental, even though Wordsworth had by then been dead for 30 years, and Myers was only six or seven when the poet died. There were close connections between the two, not just in poetic style and ardour, but in their mutual love of the Lake District where both were born, and in their connections with the Marshall family at Hallsteads. This was the place that had been etched on Myers's heart, the subject of his posthumously opened message, and the location of his tragic love for Annie, his wife's cousin, whose suicide in 1876 left a mark of guilt and remorse which is apparent in many of Myers's subsequent poems. Could Myers, a handsome, sensual man, have identified himself with the conflicting emotions of Ruth's lover, just as Wordsworth may have done when reflecting on changes to the original version of *Ruth*? And since we were given many other hints from the Scole sittings that the spirit of Myers may have been an important influence, not least in orchestrating if not actually producing some of the communications, oral and physical, MK concluded that the 1880 date could be a characteristically subtle, almost devious, way to link Myers with Wordsworth. Echoing Flaubert, one may imagine Myers saying of his great compatriot, "Wordsworth, c'est moi!"

The preceding analysis enables us to answer with some confidence the five questions we have posed. The first asked in whose hand was the original amendment to Ruth made. There is general agreement that it was in Dorothy Wordsworth's writing. Secondly, was it the same as the handwriting in the Ruth films? The answer is most probably 'no'. For this there are two reasons. One is that at least one expert has discerned some minor stylistic differences, in the formation of certain capital letters, between the film and the original version, and this alone must cast doubt on whether the deceased Dorothy could have actually reproduced her own handwriting on the film. The second reason is that it presupposes something which the Team have more than once asserted: that a name on a film is not necessarily to be taken as an authentic signature. What appears, we are told, is a thought-impression. There can be no doubt that the film writing is very similar to Dorothy's, but there is some evidence to support the notion that this could well represent an effort to impress a somewhat confused visual recollection onto the film. Hence the misplaced lines, the uncompleted fragments, the odd repetition. We cannot therefore say that the same intelligence that was responsible for Dorothy's handwriting was equally responsible for the film, since the impression the Team appeared to seek to convey was that it was the spirit of the poet himself which had transmitted

---

[1] The 'confused visual recollection' has a possible earthly parallel in Ted Serios's 'thoughtography' image on film of a Canadian airport, where, in the image, Canadian is spelled Canaidian.

the images. One possibility entertained by MK is that Wordsworth, having agonised in life over the draft amendments and finally noted with satisfaction Dorothy's all but perfect (note the significance of the deletion after "*So it was then . . .* ") transcription of his scribbled draft, found that this version was the one that lodged in his memory.

The third question, could the film scripts have been made in ignorance of both the text and the handwriting of the original, must surely be answered in the negative. The most vital clue here is the minor deletion just referred to. Finally, it is not possible to answer the question whether the page on which the manuscript amendment appears, which was reproduced in Christies' catalogue, has ever been seen by the Scole Group or any possible confederate; but we examine in Appendix M, and in the light of a wholly different interpretation of events, some of the assumptions required to make this the basis of a fraud hypothesis.

CHAPTER VIII: THE PHENOMENA:
THE TAPE RECORDINGS AND DIAGRAM

The sequence of events which led to the production of alleged spirit voices on audiotape extended over several months. It embraced the production of a Kodachrome film of outstanding clarity, this time containing a strictly prosaic message and an instruction diagram, closely linked with the discussions between members of the Team and ourselves, and between the Team communicators and an unknown entity apparently charged with the task of getting a message onto a blank tape running inside an amplifier with no microphone. Since the film and these electronic voice production experiments were inseparable, we have given an account of both. We were to experience further significant developments in apparent EVP, or 'transdimensional communication' as the Group preferred to call it, in subsequent months, however.

The experiments started with a request from Joseph to AE on 14th September 1996 (15th sitting):–

> *Jos: Can you get germanium?*
>
> MK: Do you mean bring it here?
>
> *Jos: Yes.*
>
> AE: I should think so. Semi-conductor, used for making chips: germanium — before silicon was used.
>
> RF: Never heard of it.
>
> *Jos: Strange, but a small amount placed in a shallow receptacle upon the table has been requested.*
>
> AE: I'll see if I can get that. I'll take that on.

Then, shortly after a period of light displays:–

> *Jos: Did someone mention a coherer?* [N.B. no one had]
>
> AE: The coherer was invented by Sir Oliver Lodge.
>
> *EB: (sardonically) Well, that's a surprise!*
>
> AE: Radio, before the crystal.
>
> *Jos: Before germanium.*
>
> AE: Long before germanium.
>
> *Jos: For the same purpose, I believe.*
>
> AE: Yes.
>
> *Jos: Yes.*
>
> AE: Semi-conductor, yes, scientists on the other side too.
>
> *Jos: Perhaps there are.*

And a good deal later in the same session, after Joseph had explained that only enough germanium to cover a fingernail was required:–

AE: If you can do things with a germanium crystal, electronic voice production might be possible.

Jos: That's right; it might well be.

AE: That's the end product, perhaps?

EB: Don't spoil the surprise, Arthur. Put your logic away. Wait and see.

Jos: It's very interesting how things have parallels in other dimensions. What you term electrical fields, electrical energies, magnetic energies, all have parallels in other dimensions.

And shortly thereafter:–

AE: If you can move a piece of germanium around and press it in a certain way, you might produce electric charges which might be used to speak, when amplified and put through a speaker.

Jos: Yes, we know (laughter). We've done it!

This was an interesting start. The reference to a coherer was puzzling, not simply because no one had mentioned it, but because only AE appeared to know what it was. EB's response to AE's statement that it had been invented by Lodge had an undoubted tinge of sarcasm. A coherer is an early form of detector of magnetic waves in which the resistance of an imperfect contact is abruptly reduced and to some extent made unidirectional by the passage of high frequency currents. Germanium was discovered by Winkler in 1886, and Lodge is reported to have developed his system of wireless communication in 1894. It struck us as relatively unlikely but not impossible that members of the Scole Group would be familiar with this specialised area of scientific history or terminology.

For the next (No.16) sitting, on 9th November 1996, AE duly brought a very small quantity of germanium, placed it in a saucer and left it on the séance room table. A hitherto unknown communicator, speaking as an energy (or direct) voice, and recorded as SS (Spirit Scientist) in the transcript, took over, although once again he said he was relaying messages rather than speaking from his own knowledge. Nonetheless, in response to AE's query whether or not silicon would have served instead, he immediately said that it would not, and explained that the germanium was intended to enhance communication:–

> . . . but communication of a totally different nature: communication that has never, we believe, been attempted or achieved before. Voices from other areas or dimensions of life . . . but not necessarily of the afterlife as you think of it.

At this juncture there was an intriguing interruption in his comments as he continued: "These communications . . . do I understand the gentleman is writing?" RF told him that MK was, and that they were also recording it. "Is that allowed?" he asked. RF assured him it was.

SS said it was hoped to transmit messages through the germanium using it as a focus, but not simply a focus. We were not dealing with electromagnetic waves, only pure spirit vibrations and waves – if we wanted to think of them in that way. SS continued:–

(SS) There will be a need . . . someone has already volunteered their help in the manufacture of small devices . . . something will be needed to hold the germanium.

RF: Oh right.

SS: And I see, he's referring to a piezo effect.

AE: Yes.

SS: He wants you to mount the germanium and apply a degree of pressure, a constant pressure between the two threaded screws. These can be used as terminations.

AE: Yes. Should they have points or flat ends touching the germanium?

SS: One flat and the other pointed.

AE: Like a crystal radio set.

SS: There's some polarity involved.

AE: Yes, when the radio waves hit it they are rectified, when they can be made audible.

SS: Well, I don't know if we can rectify anything because I don't anticipate the need here.

AE: Rectify means take out half the waves; it doesn't mean put something right.

SS: Very well. Robin, I'm asking you if you could get this done: to mount the crystal as has been suggested.

RF: Yes, we'll get it done.

SS: Professor Ellison, you mentioned something that was gratefully received in our side before. They wish to take advantage of this. Amplification: if in some small way – not a great deal will be necessary – some device could be brought here to amplify what will be heard.

AE: With a microphone or speaker?

SS: No, I don't think so. No, not a microphone but purely an audio input but a relatively high impedance input.

AE: Yes, I understand.

SS: The gain does not have to be a considerable amount.

AE: The gain is the number of times the output is of the input.

SS . . . The two terminations upon the germanium will be used as an input.

AE: Yes I see.

SS: Hopefully the output will be heard.

AE: There will be a small loudspeaker.

SS: Yes, we are now talking of voltages. There is some concern as to the amount of electricity. Could this be of low voltage?

AE: I should think this would be.

SS: . . . Unfortunately you will not be able to use any other electrical equipment.

RF: Right.

AE established that they wanted an amplification operating on a "very low, extremely low voltage". "Microvolts or millivolts?" he asked. "Millivolts" came the immediate response. AE expressed satisfaction and said "We can do something with that." Then shortly afterwards:–

SS: I just wanted to relay some word, not mine but others. There was some laughter, but someone was referring to a grid, cathodes and anodes and grids.

AE: Terms used in triode valves, long obsolete now.

SS: He was laughing in reference to table-tennis (laughter) with regard to this grid . . . He says the grid was on top of the envelope.

AE: The grid in an old valve used to be between the cathode and the anode, controlling the number of electrons between cathode and anode. These days we do it with a bit of silicon.

This has been quoted *in extenso* partly to give readers an idea of the manner in which instructions for the operation of the germanium gadget, as it became known, were transmitted and received, and partly to enable them to form an estimate of the likelihood not only that this degree of technical know-how would be within the normal knowledge of the Group, but also that prompt responses would be given through the mediums to unscheduled technical questions put by a professor of electrical engineering. The responses also help to account for AE's puzzlement. He was worried about what he perceived to be the employment of wholly outmoded techniques, and invited DF, who was to have a special sitting two days later (on 11th November 1996), to raise the matter. DF reported back to MK and AE as follows:–

> . . . I raised Arthur's query re the possibility of substituting the proposed germanium rectifier for a diode version containing silicon. Joseph was adamant that it was not a rectifier and should not be thought of in that way. He and Emily stressed that germanium was required because it had spiritual and healing qualities, and that the proposed device (like the glass dome on the table) is not essential to the desired effects, but helpful. I raised the problem of the fragility of the germanium, and inquired if pressure from a pointed screw was necessary. Joseph replied that it needn't be too pointed. He stressed we should not think in terms of 'cat's whiskers' (or rectifiers).

In designing the germanium apparatus, AE specified a pointed conductor resting lightly against the metal around which was placed a small insulating frame, with strips of copper to make connections to the underside of the germanium and on the top of which rested the pointed steel screw. AE reports that he was concerned lest the pointed screw when screwed down on to the brittle plate of germanium might crack it, and he had considered making the point of the screw rest on the end of a piece of coiled wire to add a measure of resilience. Then he realised he was reinventing the crystal detector from the early days of radio, and designing a rectifier (which allows for the current to pass in only one direction). "I asked the communicators whether a modern, more reliable silicon diode would not be better," AE continues (9th November sitting): "They informed me that the device was not to be used as a diode and should be made exactly as described. A piece of rubber was therefore placed under the germanium to give it a measure of resilience."

Unexpectedly, AE was unable to attend the sitting on 14th December 1996 (Sitting 21). EB regretted his absence and said they had something up their sleeves for him. Joseph, the latest communicator with Emily, said someone had "this coherer . . . great importance to what will be produced, but how?" MK explained that AE was very anxious to take part in whatever experiment was planned, but the amplifier which the Team had also asked for was not yet ready.

However, by 3rd January 1997 (22nd sitting) all was in place. AE brought along a box containing an amplifier, which included a tape recorder, attached it to the germanium box, constructed as had been requested, and we awaited results.

Since both the tape player for background music and that used for recording the event were receiving alternating current from the mains, AE was baffled to understand why the spirit Team had also told us that a relatively small additional alternating current from an amplifier should cause problems. Nevertheless, he had obtained batteries to replace the mains as a power source for this amplifier. He was also told that white noise (a noise containing all possible audible frequencies) would probably come through the speakers.

We had been joined on 3rd January 1997 by Professor Bernard Carr (who had also attended the December 14 sitting), before he began his sabbatical year in America. When the device was switched on with the volume control at maximum, there was, as expected, no sound from it. However, when the communicators started their work, "crackles and bangs rather like electrical sparking came from the speakers. A sound like a steam train accelerating from a station was also produced, and finally the rushing sound approximating to white noise" in AE's words. To MK's less professional ear it sounded as though someone was knob-twiddling a defective radio to locate a distant station. AE and Prof. Carr (BC), an astrophysicist, were particularly intrigued by the source of the noise, since they said that no normal explanation would appear to account for it. Although inaudible to MK and AE, whispers were reported by DF and other sitters, apparently stemming from the amplifier.

Edwin emphasised that the spirits were still at the exploratory stage, and were confident that, with time, the combination of amplifier and germanium box would result in clearer and better speech, and that eventually it should be possible to get through without employing mediums at all. He stressed, however, that some of the spirit communicators might not be able to hear us directly, and we would likewise not be able to communicate with them directly: it would have to be done through personalities like himself. He then appeared to listen to a colleague, and then said we could expect a request to make some minor adjustments in the apparatus.

It was apparent that the Team's attempts to communicate a clearly distinguishable message were encountering considerable difficulties, despite a good deal of inarticulate utterances, whistling sounds and even some musical notes. The communicators concluded that there was something wrong with the amplifier, but told us there might be a sketch on one of the films, which would be used at our next sitting on 11th January.

The films concerned (Kodachrome 200 35mm 36-exposure) were part of a batch bought at the request of the Team by MK (from Jessops of Leicester) on 5th December 1996, and lodged at the Psychology Department of Hertfordshire University in the care of Dr Wiseman. MK had retained one package of five, and on 11th January took two of the cartons to Scole where the investigators were DF, IS and MK (AE was unable to attend). DF and IS each removed one of the films from its packaging and placed the unopened black tubs (each of which they secretly marked) containing the film cartridges in the two small wooden security boxes which had been made for the purpose, that is, the Alan and the Keen boxes. DF and IS closed the lids and MK padlocked both boxes. The Alan box (held by DF) had a combination lock; the Keen box (held by IS) was key-operated by padlock. MK alone knew the combination lock number of the Alan box, and retained the keys of the Keen box. The boxes were then taken downstairs by DF and IS and placed on the circular table close to where they would be sitting.

After the sitting, MK immediately unlocked the two boxes, and IS, having checked the secret markings together with DF, placed each in a separate Jiffybag, which she marked externally to distinguish the box which she had held from that held by DF. She sealed each bag on the gummed flap with sealing-wax on which she imprinted the chasing of her ring. This she also impressed into sealing-wax on a separate sheet of paper so that the person opening the Jiffybags could first satisfy himself not merely that the seals had not been broken or the surrounding paper marked in any way, but that they corresponded in impression with that on the paper.

Next morning (Sunday, 12th January) MK faxed a message to Ralph Noyes, the then Hon. Secretary of the SPR, in order to have dated confirmation of the above facts, and in particular of the predictions made by the spirit communicators. The essential passage read:–

147

It was made clear by the spirit communicators that their intention was to link the message on the films with the events of that evening, and more particularly with the problems of the electronic equipment, possibly including a diagram, or some message or request to or affecting Professor Ellison. This was a response to a request I had made at a previous sitting for such an evidential link.

MK arranged for the two films to be developed by expedited procedure at Kodak's works in Wimbledon, where David Cobb, production manager, inspected the seals and, having satisfied himself that they had not been broken or interfered with and that they matched those stamped on the paper, signed the authentication note. Before MK returned to collect the results, IS telephoned Mr Cobb and ascertained that there was something on one of the films. (This was an additional agreed safeguard to ensure that MK could not be accused of substituting a faked for a blank film.) The film from IS's box proved blank; the other had on the middle section of the 1.3 metre-long roll a precisely drawn electrical diagram together with a clearly written message subscribed by a monogrammatic signature which we were unable to decipher. The message was essentially a guide to or comment on the diagram and was in generally easily legible handwriting, with one short word crossed out (here printed as *mmm*), as follows:–

A represents the Germanium, B and C Coils of high Resistance. The whole being *mmm* enclosed in Box.

This could help recepsion [?] Considerably

The message is reproduced in Plate 14. It should be noted that the main preoccupation that evening was in trying to get intelligent noises onto the amplifier which AE had provided, which was linked to the germanium gadget. MK's contemporaneous account of the event, endorsing DF's record, was that:–

. . . the investigators (DF and IS) had control of the films from start to finish. At no stage did any of the four members of the Scole group touch either the films or the boxes after the latter were handed to the investigators for inspection and film-insertion. The boxes, one of which I designed and had made to ensure that there were no externally accessible screws or attachments, remained very close to the experimenters throughout the sitting and could not have been removed by human hand without their knowledge. In addition, the door at the top of the stairs leading to the basement experimental chamber was bolted on the inside *[see Chapter I]*, as was the adjoining cellar room, while the door of the séance room itself cannot be opened silently. Even had it been possible to replicate the different constructions of each box, to have concealed these fake boxes and to have substituted them for those in front of the experimenters, those responsible would have had to have possessed precognitive powers [ie in correctly anticipating the absence of AE, for whose benefit the drawing appeared to have been made there and then]. Regardless of the origin of the handwriting and the signature, this does appear to be an example of veridical communication.

More to the point, perhaps, in view of the theory that a member of the Group might have simply leaned over and extracted a film tub from a hitherto unsuspected and undetected secret panel in the Alan box, or levered open the hasp without breaking the paint seals and substituted a prepared film, was the existence on this occasion of a highly visible red LED on the amplifier, for whose manipulation RF was receiving instructions from the Team. This light was sufficient to facilitate detection by the investigators of any groping hand. The authenticity of the possibly precognitive phenomena referred to above, however, was seen in retrospect to have been weakened by recalling that a future message for AE had been forecast at the previous week's session.

At this sitting the Team also apparently intended to communicate using the germanium device plus the amplifier. A couple of typical extracts from the unedited transcript of this session will enable the reader not only to obtain a clearer idea of how these communications in fact arrived, but also to note the close interrelationship between what we were saying, what the communicator Edwin was telling the sitters, and what Edwin was trying to convey to the unfortunate entity called Thomas, of whom more later:–

RF: Here we go! Hear the white noise? [from the germanium device plus amplifier]

(Sea-like noise.)

RF: Fading in and out.

(Louder noise like white noise but stronger.)

RF: That seems to be the transmission tone. Very faint on top of it.

IS: (?) . . . trying to do this . . .

MK: Like a force twelve gale.

RF: Fascinating.

(Can't hear, but mention of 'tabs' by sitters.)

(Change of tone through amplifier.)

RF: Sounds like knocks on a microphone.

MK: Yes, it did.

Edw: I don't think they are using a microphone (laughter).

RF: Just how it sounds.

IS: I'm sending out good (?) thoughts to help.

EB: Thanks. Much appreciated.

RF: Oh! Talking . . .!

(Repetitive signal-like noise.)

EB: Try the recording out.

RF: The only thing we get is flashing lights.

EB: That's not such a problem. We can adjust for that.

Edw: Wait a little while.

(Sound like a gale-force wind blows from amplifier.)

EB: Listen carefully Robin, won't you?

RF: Yes.

(Change in tone.)

RF: Background noises there. Sounded like . . . (?)

(Gale sound and tapping sound.)

RF: Oh, voice then.

OTHERS: Yes!

(Loud, repetitive signal.)

(and shortly afterwards:–)

RF: "How are you?" Can you hear the voice?

Edw: Thank you for adjusting, that was the machine. You will have to adjust for optimum results.

RF: OK

(Continuous noise.)

Edw: You could try to record on the tape.

EB: Try the tape now, before it's too critical.

RF: It's not coming on properly. Gone off again. It was doing that earlier.

Edw: Keep on trying; it's important.

RF: I know, yes.

Edw: Yes, there's going to be an attempt in 10-15 minutes.

MK: Can you hold it?

RF: Yes, trying to keep it on.

EB: You may have to. We'll adjust to the light.

Edw: The voices you can hear are not the communicators, the closer . . .

EB: Technicians.

RF: Oh, right.

Edw: You might hear them.

EB: Won't understand them, of course.

RF: I may have to hold the button [ie of the amplifier] in.

EB: If you wouldn't mind.

RF: No, of course.

(Voices)

Edw: Come along my friend.

EB: Yes, do come along.

SF: That's wonderful!

(Attempt at repetitive sound.)

Edw: We can hear you!

RF: That's good.

(Repeating something.)

EB: Call . . . get clearer in a moment.

(Repeating sound.)

Edw: Oh I see! What you are hearing is a link in the chain: communicating with the next link.

EB: Not the close link yet. This is like a relay in the chain.

It was apparent that the Team or their helpers were attempting to improve reception and eliminate faults, for immediately after this exchange Edwin asked RF, whose hand was on the amplifier making volume adjustments as requested, to press the recording button because (according to Edwin) a contact had been made. RF did so, but despite much encouragement and the sound of a voice, Edwin had to inform the putative entity within that we could not hear him. The volume was turned up. EB announced that Thomas was making a further attempt, but every time RF pressed the recording switch to obtain a permanent record, the switch flipped back. Edwin, who appeared capable of hearing Thomas and Thomas's problems, assured him that his message was understood by those in the spirit realm, and that there would be something in writing on the film for AE. And so it proved.

Since the tape recorder inside the amplifier had worked correctly when tested on the mains, AE concluded that the problem when subsequently reported to him might lie with inadequate battery voltage. However, he received the diagram (Plate 14) and was duly baffled by it. So was DF, who considered that the proposed modification would be likely to attenuate rather than strengthen any signals, if normal physics applied. AE's note on the subject records that no mention had been made of the inductance of the two high-resistance coils, and that the direction indicated for positioning the coils showed that, if one of the input leads was positive and the other negative, then opposite poles of the small coils would be in juxtaposition, giving maximum inductance and little spreading out of the electromagnetic field. As indicated in the diagram, the coils would act like an aerial, picking up electromagnetic waves; if the other way round, the pick-up of one side would cancel out that from the other, as DF had supposed. AE's failure to see what purpose the germanium gadget was therefore serving must be viewed in the light of the Team's emphatic preference for germanium over silicon, and Joseph's observation that the germanium device was not essential for the production of voices on tape, but had other non-physical qualities. Evidence that recordings could indeed be produced on tape running in an amplifier from which the microphone had been removed, and which was not attached to any such device, was to come six months later. It also became apparent that the germanium gadget, whatever its function, was not essential to the production of voices on such a tape recorder (see Chapters XI and XII).

The changes required by the diagram on film (Plate 14) were duly made, however, and the machine was collected by MK from AE's home and transferred to Scole on the weekend of 18th/19th January via the Schnittgers, who were visiting MK that weekend and had previously attended a sitting at Scole (17th January: see Appendix D). Walter Schnittger undertook to instruct Alan, the medium, on the correct soldering of the wires, shown in Plate 14. It must have resulted in an improvement, since the Group at one of their closed sittings on 21st January produced a tape carrying an audible message purportedly obtained, albeit with great difficulty and against the background of gusts of white noise, from the mysterious Thomas. Thomas spoke of his pride in having been able to establish at last a historic communication link from a distant dimension, and promised future attempts at similar communications. The Group attributed this message to none other than Thomas Edison. However, we were not ourselves party to this experiment.

Nevertheless, attention was now given to a closer examination of the signatures shown in Plate 14. There was to be a long pause before voice experiments were resumed. Most of the sittings which followed were designed for the benefit of such visitors as Dr Alan Gauld, Professor Donald West, Dr Rupert Sheldrake, Professor Ivor Grattan-Guinness, Dr John Beloff and Professor Robert Morris, when no further experimental work could usefully be undertaken with the recording apparatus. It appeared from closed sittings of the Group, according to RF's reports, that there was dissatisfaction on the part of the Team with the amplifier, which had been adapted by one of AE's Ph.D. students. It was never wholly clear what was wrong with it, except that it was blamed for the excessive white noise. The Group later handed it back, and replaced it with a simple, cheap, tape recorder of the type used in the Ibiza experiment the following June/July and, more strikingly, at Scole in August.

Efforts to identify the monogram below the words 'high resistance' on the film (Plate 14) ran into immediate problems. There had been a reference to Fox in the sitting of 11th January, and then another to Talbot, which led MK to suspect that, granted paranormality, the 'spirit' of Fox Talbot, the pioneer of photography, might have been connected with the diagram. The suspicion was enhanced by the resemblance to the letters FOX of the monogram below the writing. At that stage we ignored the tailpiece figure of 888 (which has been repeated elsewhere, and continues to represent an unsolved riddle) on the extreme right, and what appeared to be a fairly meaningless squiggle after it. But even had inquiries of the curator of the Fox Talbot museum in Lacock, Wiltshire not given us grounds for rejecting the theory that Fox Talbot might be involved, a comment from Emily that MK would be better employed looking elsewhere clinched it. RF conveyed to MK a nudge from the Team that he should look more carefully at the whole message.

This led to a closer examination of the hitherto ignored terminal squiggle shown on the extreme right of Plate 14, as by that time, prompted by the references of the Team to Thomas, we had become aware of the suggestion that Edison might have been the spirit technician.

A tracing of the final squiggle signature was sent by MK to the Edison National Historic Site office in West Orange, New Jersey, where Douglas Tarr, the archives technician, responded with samples of Edison's handwriting, including an initialled comment by him on a letter dated 1925. It proved virtually identical with the film squiggle (see Plate 15). With hindsight, the carefully drawn monogram could more readily represent the initials TAE than FOX, or indeed any other combination of letters, although it has not been recognised as similar in any way to Edison's own fist. Edison's reported interest in extending communication beyond the boundaries of the earth has long been the subject of speculation, since his own statements on the subject were, at best, ambiguous (Edison, 1921). We have not asked that the tape recording purporting to convey a message, apparently from Edison, be submitted to any form of acoustic examination, particularly since it was not recorded when any investigator was present. Our hope was that this might be done later.

The most obvious normal explanation of the EVP (electronic voice phenomena) would be the prior production of a recording transmitted into and appearing to come from the amplifier via a radio signal beamed in from some unknown external source. That theory is difficult to square with the apparently spontaneous nature of the events occurring, the unpredictable timing of interventions by one or other of us, and more especially the odd snatches of conversation with explanations and comments to us to explain what was going on. Nor would we have been likely to hear a radio transmission beamed from outside the séance room and specifically intended for us to pick up.

It is possible to entertain widely differing estimates of the likely level of technical knowledge which may have been needed by the mediums were they conscious and play-acting (note that both male and female mediums contributed communications during the technical discussions at some stages). The ready responses to unforeseeable specialist questions posed by the investigators about constructional details of the germanium gadget impose some strain on the theory of deception. At the least they add significantly to the lengthening list of cultural and academic attributes which must be ascribed to Alan and Diana.

In addition, the presence of the LED illuminated on the amplifier throughout the 11th January sitting and mentioned earlier must be kept in mind. LEDs vary in luminous intensity; but in pitch darkness the LED attached to the amplifier, as already made clear, seemed bright enough to have enabled the investigators to detect any hand or instrument removing or seeking to tamper with the locked Alan box located a few centimetres from them, or with the tape recorder receiving the EVP material.

To maintain a semblance of continuity, the sequels to the experiment of 11th January are recorded in Chapters XI and XII dealing with the further tape-recording experiments in Ibiza and Scole in June and August respectively. Before these experiments are described, we turn in the next chapter to the last of the film strips.

CHAPTER IX: FILM PHENOMENA:
DAGUERRE, THE LAST FILM

What turned out to be the last of the film strips, and in at least one respect the most puzzling, derived from another 36-frame roll of Kodachrome 200 film. We have called this the Daguerre film because the written name of Louis Daguerre, pioneer of photography, appeared after the script which read: *Can you see behind the Moon?* (Plate 16). The film was developed following a sitting on 24th January 1997 (Sitting 25), attended by Prof. Donald West (DW), Dr Alan Gauld (AG) and MK, as part of what had been intended to be a series at which distinguished SPR researchers and others were to be invited to participate in experiments, or witness phenomena, or perhaps both. The sitting was prefaced by what by now had become a familiar procedure, in which the two visitors were invited to place two new Kodachrome film tubs (part of the batch bought by MK, stored at Hertfordshire University, and dispatched thence by Dr Wiseman direct to Prof. West) into the Alan and Keen boxes. MK produced his own padlock for the Alan box, locked it after DW had placed his film inside, and put the key in his car. The second tub was placed in the Keen box by AG who secured it with the combination lock MK had bought. AG memorised the four-figure setting number, and kept it to himself.

When DW, AG and MK entered the séance room, they placed the two boxes on a piece of plain paper in a central position on the table, as determined by alignment with the luminous direction-indicator tabs. The boxes abutted one another, and DW traced their outlines onto the paper, including the irregular shape made by the padlocks resting on it. After the sitting, DW, AG and MK each checked to ensure there had been no sign of movement of either box. Because the Group wished to retain the Alan box for further experiments, the investigators opened it after the sitting, removed the tub containing the film and placed this in a Jiffybag, which AG sealed and signed and handed to MK, together with the padlocked Keen box, so that they could both be taken to Wimbledon the following Monday for development. Having been requested accordingly, the manager at Wimbledon certified that the Jiffybag seals were intact, obtained the combination from Dr Gauld by telephone, and opened the Keen box.

In the event the film in this box proved blank, whereas the Alan box film carried 1.3 metres of drawings, hieroglyphs, abstract imagery (for want of a more apposite description), the initials RS in two places, and some monograms. This film, which as indicated we have called after Daguerre, has generated considerable research, several further hints from later discussions with the Team, and thus far a failure to establish the full relevance or significance of the message or of the hieroglyphs, or the identity of RS and his supposed relationship to Daguerre. We examine the fraud hypothesis in some detail in Chapters XIV and XV. Here we are primarily concerned with the circumstances relating to the film's production and our attempts to discover the meaning of its message.

We proceeded on the assumption that the message was not intended as a meaningless game devised by the Team, but had been as carefully thought out as the Wordsworth films appeared to be, and that it was designed to demonstrate the Team's declared intention to bring further and better evidence of survival, and of the capacity of deceased souls to communicate by a method reflecting their thought-forms rather than our own. This assumption could, of course, have been mistaken, and in that case it would have been pointless even to attempt to discover a meaning. However, earlier films certainly had meanings, or reflected intentions, even though several were by no means entirely clear to us. But that meanings were in fact intended in the Daguerre film was evident from conversations with EB and Edwin spread over three sessions, that on the evening when the films were introduced and apparently worked on, 24th January 1997, and two subsequent sittings, on 8th and 28th February. The first, which of course took place two days before the film had been processed, contained the following exchange:–

> Edwin: I believe that someone, a Frenchman, has . . . perhaps that's all I should say: Monty does like a puzzle.
>
> EB: He's going off them!
>
> Edw: Well, I don't think it's going to be too difficult . . . when you know who it is. When you look at his work a few more puzzles will fall into place. Just one other word, well two words — "the moon" . . . Oh, I must tell you, it's probably the longest attempt they have made, in length.
>
> [Later]
>
> EB: Someone is saying the initial 'R' is there.

While all these hints accurately forecast what was to appear on the 1.3 metre-long film strip, they contributed little to explaining its meaning. Time spent subsequently by MK in the print room at the Victoria and Albert Museum in London showed that the writing bore no relation to Daguerre's normal signature. A subsequent sitting on February 8th, at which DF, IS, WS and MK were all present as investigators, contained the following:–

> Edw: Can you see behind the Moon? [a repetition of the first message in the Daguerre film]
>
> MK: No, I can't see where it comes from.
>
> Edw: Well Louis can.
>
> IS: Louis Stevenson?
>
> MK: No!

DF: Louis Pasteur?

MK: No, Louis Daguerre — but it isn't his signature. That's one of my complaints. I don't mind being teased, but I think that's misleading.

EB: We said there was a Frenchman there.

MK: If he was, and he signed it . . .

EB: Who said so? Not the same at all . . .

DF: His name was just written there.

Edw: There is another signature who was responsible.

MK: The RS? That was there, certainly.

Edw: Not in the hand of RS, even.

RF: Did RS have a French connection?

MK: There is one other letter.

Edw (slightly impatiently): "Can you see behind the Moon": that's where you must look.

MK: Right.

Edw: It was all because someone was in prison.

DF: Oh, that was a clue to that.

[Later]

EB: Think about the work, the work of the signature.

Edw: Have you found any of his work?

MK [on the assumption that 'his' referred to Daguerre]: Oh yes, I looked up Daguerre's work, quite a bit of it. I saw nothing that was the back of the moon, but maybe I didn't look carefully enough. I haven't done as much research into it as I really ought.

EB: Look into his other interests.

MK: Daguerre?

EB: Yes, you see I'm being awfully sweet to you.

MK: If you could manage to put a little more saccharine into the tea . . .

DF: Other interests?

MK: Fox Talbot had other interests, and Louis Daguerre, but I haven't tracked down the Fox Talbot reference yet.

DF: That may not be a reference.

EB: I wouldn't put too much money on that. Not yet. Wait for something further.

RF: Do you know if RS had a French connection at all?

EB: I'm not giving that away!

[after indications that RS was not connected to poetry or children's books . .]:

MK: Very much like the Paris Metro, the writing, 1890's style.

EB: Oh well, not surprised.

MK: Ah!

Edw: Yes Monty, you have to look beyond what the text books tell you, beyond the obvious career of the person involved . . . something a bit deeper, more obscure. Then you will find your answers. Find out about the work of the man, the Frenchman. Then you will find out a lot more about that particular experiment.

MK found some of these hints so ambiguous as to be almost meaningless. Daguerre (1787–1851) was a brilliant painter for the stage, and invented the hugely successful Diorama before collaborating with Nicéphore Niepce (and with Isadore, his son, after Niepce's death in 1833) to improve and perfect Niepce's photographic invention, the rights for which were bought by the French Government in 1839. Daguerre retired shortly afterwards. He had been responsible for some dramatic scenic effects during the 1820s and 1830s at several Paris theatres, most notably at the Opéra. But no connection with anyone with the initials RS could be found, or indeed any connection with a spell in prison, or with a close collaborator, other than Niepce and perhaps a little with Fox Talbot in England, with whom he was in fairly close touch. Talbot's own photographic process was virtually contemporaneous with the development of the Daguerreotype, but based on a different technology. The Daguerreotype became all the rage, and dominated the reproductive process at least up to the time of the 1851 Exhibition, having become a major craze in the USA. Some of Daguerre's impressive photographs include moonlight scenes.

On February 28th (a sitting attended by MK with Dr Beloff and Professor Morris), the following conversation was recorded:–

Edwin: Can you see behind the moon, Monty?

MK: I'm afraid not.

Edw: Some can, Louis can.

EB: We told him that last time.

MK: I've been puzzling over that for two days in the British Library.

Edw: I don't know any more than you.

MK: My learned colleagues may help. I could find nothing of Daguerre or his photographic sessions. This is my moaning session!

Edw: No, I won't tell him. I was going to say this — this applies to many people: everyone has their skeleton in the cupboard. Some have more than one. Some are quite horrendous to others; therefore they may keep them well hidden. Do I need to go on?

MK [foolishly]: No, I've got the drift of this. I must go back to this.

Edw: We don't make the puzzles easy or you would never believe where they came from.

MK: True, I can't complain about that.

Edw: It's not of our doing. We merely pass on 'crumbs'.

MK: Whose doing is it then?

Edw: Some of what is presented is by those who are named. In this case the

the gentleman named was very close in that experiment, but I think Monty knows.

MK: Well, I think I know most of the people involved in his career, but RS and the prison sentence don't seem to add up.

Edw: Unfortunately you were given too much information at the same time, and naturally you got your wires crossed.

MK: I will make further inquiries.

Edw: There was a reference to I Ching. This was the prison sentence, not 'behind the moon'.

EB: Perhaps we could clarify this some other time. We'll share our crumbs on another occasion and concentrate our energies on the build-up.

Edw: There is something here which is unfamiliar. Someone on our side is experiencing something unfamiliar to them.

MK: [During a conversational lull] The design reminds me of the Paris Metro about 1890, Art Deco [This was a blunder: MK was thinking of Art Nouveau]

Edw: The Metro?

MK: Yes, the Metro, but Daguerre died in 1851, well before the Metro was conceived.

Edw: Well! [said in a tone which implied: well, there you are]

MK: Oh, I must look at the Paris Metro, but the first was run in Budapest or London in the 1860s. He may have designed something: he was a great designer.

EB: We did say look beyond the obvious.

MK: Yes, I'll look at the stage sets of the operas he designed, but not the prison sentence in that context.

Edw: No, no.

[Later]

EB: One of our communicators mentioned "Laurels". More crumbs later.

MK: Laurel wreath, the King of France giving it to Daguerre for services? Or perhaps it's a horticultural metaphor?

EB: No, nothing as boring as that.

DF wondered subsequently whether the reference to the 'laurel wreath' was unconnected to Daguerre, but linked instead to the Cross-Correspondences. MK's suspicion that the Metro was involved had all the appearance of a red herring, since Daguerre was safely in his grave several years before the first plans for a Metro were drawn up, and construction did not start until some 30 years later. The two earliest European metros, in London and Budapest, did indeed open in the 1860s, but there is nothing in the official history of the Paris Metro (Robert, 1983) to suggest any involvement with Daguerre or with anyone with the initials RS. Indeed none of the 17 entries under Daguerre's name in the main catalogue of the British Library could be found to yield anything connecting him to anyone with these initials. Nor did the Maison Européenne de la Photographie in Paris provide any further clues than those apparent from the Gernsheims' biography (Gernsheim, 1956), which mentions in the context of Daguerre's work on the Diorama two booksellers bearing the suspicious names of Reeves and Spooner (i.e. R & S). However, Emily's 'crumbs' had made it clear that we were to look for a single individual.

Our searches thus far have drawn a blank. We could find nothing on or about the film which relates to the I Ching or the Yin and Yang with which I Ching is associated. It may be noted that at the end of the Daguerre film there appears, decorating the box shape, a large ornate letter T or F, together with what seems to be a small capital 'A' suspended on the top horizontal stroke, but its significance has thus far escaped us. To make matters worse, the only other signature on the film, to pursue Emily's clear hint, appears on the extreme top right end, pock-marked with sprocket holes. To MK's imaginative eye this signature represents Marconi, but having extensively checked the Marconi archives, he has had to admit that it bears but slender resemblance to Marconi's signatures. In any event Marconi, even though he may have shared Edison's interest in communicating with the Hereafter, could have had no connection with Daguerre. This remains a mystery.

Although our research into 'RS' and Daguerre has thus far proved unprofitable, the time and trouble spent may turn out to contribute to the level of evidentiality we require, since if the correct identity of RS were to be discovered, and it proved consistent with the clues provided by the Team, it could be shown not to have been information readily accessible. As for the meaning of the *Behind the Moon* message, we feel it more prudent to leave this on one side until more work has been done on the clues, and a wider range of expertise can be harnessed as a result of the present publication. However, the 'hieroglyphs' accompanying his signature provide a different challenge. Although a number of leading experts on alchemy gathered at an international conference in Prague in September 1997 were unable to cast light on the strange glyphs when consulted by MK, our attention has since been drawn to the fact that many of the symbols can be found in Nigel Pennick's *The Secret Lore of Runes and other Ancient Alphabets* (Rider 1991). However, far from being set out readily available for anyone to copy, they are not only scattered around the fifty different alphabets and glyphs in this specialist and scholarly volume, but buried within illustrations which themselves contain large numbers of crowded designs, some of which do not bear too close a resemblance to the glyphs seen on the film. A number of presumptions, some imagination and considerable scholarship appear to be required to obtain from this series of designs a coherent message, which our learned informant has interpreted as representing the names of the apostles. If his interpretation is correct, then prior familiarity with the symbolism associated with gematria would be required by the artist responsible. We mention this not to comment on the validity of this interpretation, but the fact that, like the Schnittger's German poem, the material in the film cannot be said to be easily available.

Although the Daguerre film was the last strip to be produced for us by the Team, it was not the last photographic experiment. That, together with an account of the later developments in recording spirit messages, will be described in Chapters XI and XII. For the present we gather up a miscellany of further physical occurrences or manifestations experienced during our sittings.

CHAPTER X: APPORTS, MISCELLANEOUS MESSAGES . . .

Objects mysteriously coming from apparently nowhere, generally called apports, were not common in our dealings with the Scole Group, although the Group themselves reported receiving many at their closed sittings. In only one or two cases of the few apports received by us could it be fairly said that the circumstances in which they were received were such as to make normal fabrication extremely difficult. We have earlier referred to the wide range of apports claimed by the Group to have been found before our arrival on the scene, many of them as gifts for the (then) six members of the Group, or for visitors. They consisted mainly of small objets *d'art* or *bijouterie*, some of which, e.g. an ark, appeared to have some symbolic significance. Probably the most extraordinary, since the least susceptible to a non-paranormal explanation, is the pristine copy of the Daily Mail (see Chapter 1) which featured an account of Helen Duncan's prison sentence under the 18th-Century Witchcraft Act.

The first apport we experienced as investigators was during an eventful sitting (12th) attended by AE, MK and Archie Roy on 13th July 1996. This was the occasion at the end of which the 'Golden Chain' quotation in Latin appeared on a film strip. We had been invited to bring three empty plastic film spool tubs, to which we fixed three luminous tabs, and to place one on each of three of the cardinal points between the table tabs and the crystals adjacent to them, which pointed towards the table centre. The Group said they had been asked to ensure that we left the tubs on the table for an hour at the conclusion of the sitting, and then return to examine them. This we did, to find the west tub about one-third full of greenish crystals we could not readily identify; the south tub with a similar quantity of liquid we presumed to be water, but did not taste, while that placed by the east tab had a substantial deposit of grey ash. Unwisely, not knowing what to expect, we had failed to take the elementary precaution of leaving the room after rather than before members of the Group, and securing it. This naturally undermined the evidentiality of the experiment. RF said the Team had asked that the contents should not be removed until further instructions. We were later told that, at the next sitting of the Group (at which we were not present, but the Schnittgers were), the tubs were found to be empty.

Rather more impressive from a veridical viewpoint, however, was an apport which appeared, during the same (13th July 1996) sitting, in the translucent Pyrex kitchen bowl placed on the séance room table, into which on several occasions a light entered and swirled round fast and bright enough to reveal any contents and to make the bowl glow. When the room light was turned on we found a screwed-up piece of paper in the

Figure 2

centre of the bowl. AR opened it carefully and found it to carry some
writing and to contain three ammonite shells and some dust, two of the
shells being entire, one broken. The material was carefully removed and
stored, and the paper opened up. As may be seen from Figure 2, the
paper, measuring roughly 13 x 2 cm, was torn all round. One side bore
scorch marks around a burnt section. The writing was indecipherable.
There was a date, or a number, 1881, immediately below what might
have been a signature containing the letters either P or D, and a, g and
h. Below that was what we took to be a single word, part of which, with
a considerable stretch of the imagination, might have been "johnny", but
the remainder of the lettering looked more Greek than English. Above
the signature was a capital Omega, at the right foot or serif of which
was sketched an arrow pointing to the circumference of a circle with a
dot in the centre. It was concluded that the circle might represent the
sun, and that Omega, the last letter of the Greek alphabet, is associated
apocalyptically with the end. We could only speculate that this might
have had a bearing on the nature of the discussion which AR had just
had with Albert (see Chapter IV).

During the sixth sitting, on 16th March 1996, we were given advance notice by Reginald Lawrence, one of the communicators, that the spirits intended to present us with two pieces of metal for an experiment. At the seventh session (13th April 1996) they duly arrived. Some quite sharp noises accompanied what we presumed to be the delivery of these objects. We were not told where they would be but were invited, mischievously as it transpired, to search the room. At the end of the sitting one of us noticed that they were facing the investigators and inside the glass dome which rested on its plinth in the centre of the séance table. The two flat oblong pieces of metal, weighing an ounce or two only, could have been placed under the bowl normally during the sitting only if someone had leaned over and lifted or tilted the bowl before slipping the pieces inside unobserved, which would have involved covering both luminous arm tabs. Not impossible, but decidedly risky, and ideally requiring two hands to lift the delicate glass dome while an accomplice inserted the metal pieces below it. Raji, a communicator, explained that they were pieces of ordinary metal — nothing complicated. One of them had been created by an electrical process, and both of them were found on earth. One was clearly a strip of aluminium, which could be said to derive from an electrical process; the other of some ferrous material. We were given detailed instructions regarding what to do with them. They were to be weighed and carefully measured, then returned to Scole. This was done by AE at City University. They were wrapped up and returned to Scole in a sealed envelope and in due course returned to the same laboratory to see what, if anything, had changed (we had asked for but been given no clue as to what to expect). In the event, nothing had changed, and whatever the experiment was designed to demonstrate, it proved a failure.

Another failure was responsible for the next apport. Emily Bradshaw was given to betting half a crown on the successful outcome of an experiment, and had reminded us more than once that she had yet to lose a bet. She was equally confident about the outcome of one of the film tests, which chanced to be in MK's hands, but which turned out to be negative. We gently chided her for this. Towards the end of Manu's introduction at the 15th March 1997 sitting there was an oblique reference to something for MK. A moment later there was a loud bang, a good deal noisier than would be expected from the delivery of a coin, however violently it was thrown. This was accompanied by a triumphant exclamation from Emily "Debt paid!" After the sitting we discovered an 1890 half-crown on the floor next to the table not far from Diana's seat. If effected by one of the Group, this would have required a vigorous arm movement, difficult to perform without being observed, especially since this took place very early in the sitting, when the luminous armbands were at their brightest.

The final incident may not qualify as an apport so much as a paranormal transference. The background to this incident is described in Chapter XI, detailing the two sets of experiments which were conducted in Ibiza by MK in the spacious blacked-out living room of Dr Hans Schaer's converted farmhouse on the island of Ibiza. Towards the conclusion of the first sitting, when MK was feeling round the top of the table to make certain he had not left behind any of the Polaroid film frames with which the experiment was concerned, he knocked over a long candle which had somehow been moved undetected from its rightful position in a candlestick holder several feet away from the table.

...AND UNSOLVED RIDDLES

It would be wrong to conclude that our principal occupation was solving puzzles set by the Team. If paranormality is assumed, it was clear that the Team's apparent main object was to add to the volume and variety of evidence pointing towards survival rather than towards ESP from other sitters. Whatever its source, some of this evidence had clearly been worked out well in advance; other parts of it appeared to be throw-away observations, or occasionally tendered to us rather casually and seeming to arise naturally from a conversation the direction of which could not have been foreseen. A few were too vague to enable us to follow up; and in one or two cases our informants sought to back-track, as though they had blundered into prohibited territory. While it was made clear that they wished us to concentrate on the phenomena and not on the personalities of the communicators, or on those transmitting information through them, there were many names dropped, not all of them prominently associated with the early years of the Society. During the sitting (R8, p.14) at which Emily confirmed that she had been referring to the third Lord Rayleigh (see Chapter IV), thus completing that little puzzle, she added:–

> EB: *While we are talking about puzzles, Monty . . . Yes, you are a bit of a Bragger, aren't you?*
> MK [somewhat taken aback]: Absolutely, whenever the opportunity is given!
> EB: *Now you know what I'm talking about, don't you?*
> MK: [cottoning on]: Yes I do: Lawrence.
> EB: *My lips are sealed.*
> AE: Oh yes! Lawrence Bragg.
> RF: This is over my head.
> AE: Yes, I understand that.
> MK: Thank God for Emily's occasional indiscretions (laughter).

While this may have been no more than Emily's off-the-cuff revenge for MK's crude pun on the name of Strutt, it could have been a hint for us that Sir Lawrence Bragg, who died in 1971 and won the Nobel prize with his father for work on X-rays and crystals in 1915, might still be interesting himself in the rôle of crystals as energy centres. He was a close associate of Sir Oliver Lodge, although not notably associated with the SPR. Emily's reaction suggested that she could not altogether resist dropping slightly more hints than discretion ought to have permitted. Indeed, she suggested that she had gone further than she ought when giving us information about Mrs Verrall and Mrs Forbes in connection with the Diotima case, and in particular when giving the date of 18th December 1902, which made it easy for us to trace the Cross-Correspondence reference ("I nearly got ticked off for having given away too many clues", she told us).

Misleading clues were not the only obstacles faced. On 20th September 1996 there was a reference to 'St James Place' (R11, p.25). Much time was spent in a vain search through Kelly's Directories to find some person, perhaps less exalted than Gladstone but more intimately connected with the Society in its early years, who might have dwelt there during the last two decades of the 19th century, or a little beyond. But no inhabitant of that street seemed relevant. However, on 18th November 1996 (Sitting 18), Edwin referred to St James Row. We subsequently found that Eveleen Myers, widow of Frederic, and with Mrs Sidgwick about the last survivor in the 1930s of the SPR's original membership, lived during her later years in widowhood in Cleveland Row. St James' Row does not exist in the district known as St James, but Cleveland Row, a small but exclusive near cul-de-sac running along the north side of St James's Palace, is very close to St James's Place. From the manner in which Emily accepted MK's link-up with Mr Myers's lady, it would appear that the Team may have got the street names slightly confused. Perhaps an interesting illustration of memory-lapse, or maybe the inhabitants of Cleveland Row in the 1930s referred to the street simply as The Row. Its location in St James's may therefore have led to the error.

From time to time one of us would make remarks or ask questions intended to establish whether the responses could be attributable exclusively to the mind of the spirit communicator rather than to the medium. Prof. Grattan-Guinness tried this out chiefly to see whether communication was by telepathic rather than cognitive linguistic mechanisms, but with limited success. He asked questions in French, Italian, German and Russian, but received only a belated acknowledgement, *do svidanya* in correctly stressed Russian from Emily. On another occasion (R10, p.4) MK, having established to his satisfaction that the spirit of Myers was around, was still less successful. He had spent some time trying to get to the bottom of the Diotima film messages, and said that, when he was looking at the Latin and Greek references, there were times when he felt more like Thrasymachus than Glaucon in his search for clues. "If you can convey that to Mr Myers, I'm sure he'll understand", said MK, to which Albert intriguingly responded: "I can't say. I'd love to say more". He was invited to comment. There was a pause. MK then asked whether this was understood, and the male communicator hesitated and asked for the recording tape to be switched off. The impression conveyed was that he, or someone, had recognised the significance of the names, but the rules did not allow him to comment. (Glaucon and Thrasymachus were two fictional students of Socrates in Plato's *Republic*; the former was always bright, right and top of the class, while Thrasymachus was inclined to throw tantrums when frustrated).

The chief areas of perplexity, however, were in the interpretation of symbols, or initials, appearing on three films: the (Schnittger) Wie der Staub drawing with its apparently random scribbles and juxtaposed lettering which we suspected was somehow associated with Easter Island; the coherent message, if there is one, conveyed by the apparently random collection of hermetic symbols traced or impressed onto the (Schnittger) Dragon film, and the mysteries linked with Daguerre, his shadowy associate RS, and the Moon, in addition to the extensive symbolism, in the Daguerre film. All of these, along with earlier mysteries, we are happy to offer to a wider circle of students in the hope that others, more expert or industrious than ourselves, will suggest their interpretations.

CHAPTER XI: THE IBIZA EXPERIMENTAL EVIDENCE

The Sunday, 29th June, 1997 Experiments

Although there were a number of sittings, mostly with invited distinguished guests, which followed the production of the Daguerre film on 24th January 1997, these were chiefly dedicated to the production of visual and tactile phenomena designed to give the visitors sufficient personal evidence to help them pronounce on the genuineness or otherwise of the phenomena. Towards the end of March 1997, the Group spent three weeks in California, where they responded to a long-standing invitation from Brian Hurst, an American medium, to hold sittings in his converted garage. MK accompanied the Group in order to arrange a sitting in San Francisco with a number of interested scientifically qualified guests. These various sittings were not designed for the production of films or tapes, but the results merit recording, and an account of them appears in Appendix F. Not only did the visit to the USA prove fairly exhausting for the Group, who had also committed themselves to visits to the Netherlands and Germany for sittings arranged by the Schnittgers; it also appeared to persuade the Team that the succession of sittings primarily for the purpose of repeating displays of lights, touches, etc. was delaying the production of more durable evidence, undermining the Group's concentration and dissipating their energies. The upshot was a decision to hold no more meetings with us or with any other outsiders for the time being in order to enable the Group to concentrate on the provision of fresh evidence. Only many months later did we learn that preparations for work with a video camera were being initiated around this time, and would take more than a year of closed sittings to bring to something approaching fruition.

Fortunately, another of the long-planned overseas visits was a relaxing week at the holiday home of Dr Schaer in Ibiza, which the Group had visited twice previously. MK was invited to join them for the purpose of conducting two experiments, which took place in the evenings of 29th June and 1st July 1997. What follows is taken from his notes. The sittings were held in the principal sitting/dining room of Villa Estancia de Bourgainvillas near St Eulalia on a wooded hillside set well back from the main road and hence quiet and relatively isolated. Those witnessing and/or participating in the two experiments are listed in the key to the sketch plan of this room in Appendix J and in Plate 19. They comprised our host, Hans Schaer (HS), the businessman/lawyer referred to earlier, who became an SPR member and is a leading figure in the Swiss Parapsychological Association; Walter Schnittger (WS), with his wife Karin (KS), a translator; Yvonne Koch, a Swiss teacher

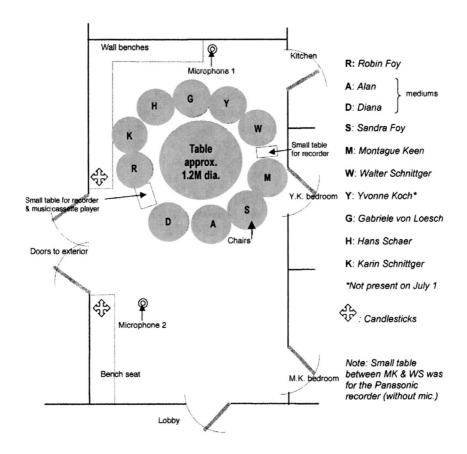

**Seating plan for Scole Group experimental sessions in Ibiza:
June 29 and July 1. 1997**

Figure 3

(who attended only the first sitting); and Gabriele von Loesch, a psychotherapist from Hamburg. In addition there were the four members comprising the Scole Group. Of the six sitters, HS had attended several sessions since October 1995 either in Ibiza or most recently at his home in Zürich, to which he had invited the Group. WS and KS were also relatively frequent sitters (and we have already made it clear that we consider HS, WS and KS as our co-investigators), but Yvonne had attended only one previous sitting (in Zürich), and Gabriele none. This was MK's 27th sitting. What follows is drawn from his report.

The evenings were very warm. The men were in shirt-sleeves or T-shirts, the women in summer dresses. The room was some 11m by 5m, with three doors leading to two bedrooms, a lobby giving on to a bedroom suite and exit to the patio, a door leading to the kitchen and, in the centre of the wall behind RF's seat, large double doors as the principal entrance. A rooflight and two small clerestory windows, the only sources of natural light, were thoroughly blacked out. Rugs were placed at the base of the doors to block any light filtering in from the shuttered windows in adjoining rooms. The ceiling, some 4m high, was supported along its length by a substantial beam, with two large cross-beams beneath, one of them immediately above the circular gate-legged table around which we sat, so that the height from floor to lower beam was around 3m.

MK took photographs of the room as it looked when prepared for the sitting, chiefly to show the eccentric disposition of the chairs (those occupied by HS, Yvonne and Gabriele being at the furthest arc of an oval); and also, after the sitting, to indicate the position of a candlestick from which a 20cm-long candle had been transported at some point during the sitting to the centre of the table (as noted in Chapter X). Fluorescent tabs had been placed by the Group on the edges of the table at the four cardinal points, the table having been carefully aligned with the aid of a compass earlier in the day by WS and RF. Similar tabs were placed on the 'play' button of a tape recorder used in the second experiment. Each of the four members of the Group wore armbands with fluorescent strips enabling the sitters to note if or when their arms moved. RF, as usual, taped all the proceedings on a machine placed on a side-table on his right. A second recorder played background music. The chairs were placed some 60 or 70cm from the table, save for MK's, which abutted it. The seating arrangements are clear from Plate 19.

The Two Polaroid Experiments

Having been forewarned by RF before his departure from England on the previous Wednesday, 25th June, that the Team had informed the Group on Monday 23rd June that they wished him to undertake two experiments requiring equipment, MK bought three packs of Polaroid-600 film, of the type used in ordinary Polaroid cameras, from Boots of Sudbury, Suffolk, and a packet of three 30-minutes-a-side audio tapes. The more elaborate, and troublesome, of the two experiments related to the films and involved the following procedure which, RF told MK, had been requested by the Team at the last closed sitting they had held at Scole. As the principal investigator, MK was to open a new pack of ten Polaroid films and extract the cassette in which they were held. Then, once it was dark, and seated immediately in front of the luminous tab on the edge of the table indicating the north magnetic pole, he was to extract six of the ten films, marking a secret numerical code on each one with a pen suitable for plastic, then place them face downwards on the table.

170

This was to be done at the commencement of the sitting. Towards the end, he would retrieve the films and re-insert them into their cassette, finally replacing the protective board covering it, so that the entire reloaded cassette was ready to be dropped into its slot in a Polaroid camera for development after the sitting and in the light, the camera first having had its lens cover effectively blacked out by layers of opaque black tape. Finally MK was to press the exposure lever six times to expel the first six films, the protective board being automatically ejected as soon as the camera was closed up after the insertion of the cassette.

Before the lights were switched off MK explained precisely what had been asked of him, and added that as a further safeguard he would scribble something in black indelible ink on the back of the cassette using the marking pen he planned to employ in order to identify each film. He would make a separate, identifiable mark on the white plastic edge of each film (see technical note at end of this Chapter), using a code a copy of which he had hidden in his bedroom so that it could be later retrieved for checking against the six marks. He explained that the intention, as conveyed to him by RF, was to see whether the Team could produce images on any of the six films, after taking precautions aimed at countering error, deception or cheating of any kind. While the lights were still on, he then displayed to the other sitters the unopened pack, the outside of which he had also marked beforehand, then opened the top flap to expose underneath it the freshly torn strips of paper adhering to the opened flap and revealing a metallic protective foil which concealed the cassette. This he tore open, a process involving some force which inevitably creased and severed the metallic foil to an extent and in a fashion which (as he pointed out) would have made restoring it to its original, smooth appearance impossible. Without this rupture, he pointed out, there was no way in which the film cassette could be extracted. He then removed from inside the foil covering the instruction leaflet which was folded over the top, discarded it, and then removed the cassette itself, which he then marked at the base, pointing out that the mark could be seen and identified only by holding the cassette at a particular angle to the light to make the black ink visible. Then he placed the cassette on the side table on his right, well away from the nearest member of the Group, and between his and WS's seat, pending the commencement of the sitting proper.

As soon as the lights were switched off, and soothing music began to be played on RF's tape player, MK picked up the cassette and extracted the protective board cover, which he placed on the small table on his right, then pushed out six of the ten films, each of which he marked as they partly emerged. He placed each face down on the séance table, aligning them with the edge where a flap extension joined the central part of the table. This was done so that he could feel this edge when

171

retrieving the films, and as an additional safeguard against anyone else moving the films. Towards the end of the sitting he reversed the process, first ascertaining by touch that the cassette had not been moved, and then replacing each film into the cassette slit, ensuring that the plastic pouch containing the chemical developing fluid was on the right-hand side. He had earlier privately rehearsed this tricky procedure in the dark with a sacrifice pack of outdated film. He then replaced the protective card.

Since MK experienced some difficulty in re-inserting the films and protective cover, he became uncertain whether he had collected all six. He therefore explored the table immediately in front of him gently, with one hand, and found that he had, but was startled to touch something which produced a sharp, loud clap. He explored it a little further, and reported that he was grasping a cylinder, about eight inches long. When he felt the ends he concluded that it was a candle. The apparent apportation of this candle from its candlestick, situated some two metres behind Alan, had not been part of the planned or expected experiment, but added to the amusement of the sitters and the evidentiality, since the following advice had been heard towards the end of the sitting from Edwin (his statements, recorded on tape, were independently noted by MK in shorthand during the sitting, and subsequently checked on the tape recording before the transcript was made):–

> Edwin: Be careful how you handle the table. There may be some changes that have been made. We don't want to disturb anything that someone has done. Just take the films and nothing else. If there is anything else there just leave it alone.

Earlier during the sitting Edwin expressed:–

> . . . every faith in Monty getting all the equipment back together and duly passed though the various mechanisms and processes necessary for the development of these films — but only Monty must be involved in this because of the evidentiality that is required. We feel you will be amply rewarded on this occasion, and on the next. That is why we emphasise the necessity for strict protocol to be observed — the secret marks, etcetera, and examining the necessary equipment . . . I believe it will be hard to debunk.

As for the films themselves, he predicted that these were not the sort of images they had been expecting. They were "rather abstract in nature because some of them are related to the energies present." One would be rather different from the rest. He thought it would be number six. The only other direct reference to this experiment came as a footnote to the sitting, almost at the end. There had been a number of flashes, akin to lightning, of widely varying levels of intensity and in different parts of the room. Edwin assured the sitters that none had been sufficient to have had any effect on the plates lying exposed on the table. No one had raised this question, but the appearance of flashes was, of course, commented on at the time by all who witnessed them.

When the lights were switched on, MK placed the refilled cassette in the standard Polaroid camera (belonging to the Group), drawing attention to its blacked-out lens cover and having ensured that his marking at the back of the cassette was still there. The procedure of putting the cassette into the camera was necessary solely for the purpose of developing the films. When the cover of the camera was snapped closed, the ejection mechanism failed to operate. It was well over an hour before MK succeeded, with much advice from Alan, who was now restored to consciousness but did not touch the camera, and WS (who assisted in the process of eliminating all possible sources of error), in operating the exposure lever as planned, and ejecting the first six films. WS retrieved the marking code from MK's room and checked it to ensure that it tallied with MK's marks on the films. It was unfortunate that the last film, No.6, was ejected simultaneously with the seventh film. As a result, the developing chemical failed to extend over the whole emulsified area. But it was also apparent that, as forecast by Edwin, this film was somewhat different from the rest, which were vaguely psychedelic and wholly abstract. To provide a control print, MK ejected another film, which remained black, showing that it had not been exposed. WS then removed the thick layers of plastic covering the lens and took normal flashlight pictures with the remaining three films.[1]

All present were satisfied that the approved protocol — with the additional marking safeguard in the form of a pre-written code — had been observed, that the experiment was successful and almost certainly unique, and that no other safeguards against deception or error were needed or could have been suggested.

The second sitting was in all essentials similar to the first, save that, since Yvonne was unable to attend, the seating arrangements were adjusted on the west side, leaving the sitters somewhat further apart (see sketch plan). Prior to the séance, HS, WS and MK carefully reviewed the protocol but could find no way in which the results of the previous sitting could have been faked. In particular they noted that, even had

[1] Technical note: Since not everyone is familiar with Polaroid photography a brief description of the mechanism involved may help to make this report clearer. Each of the ten films in a cassette is composed of an emulsified sheet sandwiched between two sealed layers of smooth plastic. Immediately a new cassette is inserted into the Polaroid camera, and the flap which exposes the cavity containing the cassette is snapped shut, an electrical contact in the body of the camera activates a battery at the base of the cassette, providing the power to operate a motor. This in turn propels a cogwheel forward so as to eject the protective covering board, thereby making the first film ready for an exposure. Every time thereafter that a slide button is pressed on the side of the camera, a film is exposed with the aid of a flashlight powered by the cassette battery, and then immediately ejected. As it passes out of the camera twin rollers exert sufficient pressure to break a membrane holding the developing fluid in the flattish sac (on which MK had written his code markings), pushing the chemical over the surface of the film and initiating the development process.

the Polaroid pack been accessible to the Group or any agent, and even had it been possible to have opened the pack, detached the metal foil covering, accessed the films, substituted treated, i.e. exposed, plates and reversed the process so as to render the interference undetectable (or alternatively to have substituted a totally different pack containing pre-exposed films), this would have been of no avail, since MK had placed indelible marks on each of the six films extracted, replaced and finally ejected. These were the marks he and WS subsequently checked against his prepared code known only to him before and during the sitting.

The only significant procedural change in the second experiment was, therefore, to accord with the wishes expressed by Edwin at the conclusion of the first sitting, namely to reverse the positions of the tape and the film equipment, so that the films would be left, with the film cassette, on the small side table on MK's right, alongside WS, rather than placed on the séance table. Edwin made clear that MK could do what he liked with them – i.e., it did not matter whether they were face down or up, in a tidy pile or scattered. The tape recorder (from which the microphone had been removed, as described below) would be placed in the centre of the séance table, where it would receive more concentrated energies. The film marks, which were again in accord with a (different) code subsequently retrieved this time by HS from MK's bedroom, and checked by him and MK against the first six expelled films, can be seen on the right-hand side of the prints reproduced in Plate 17. These films, which MK stacked on the corner of the small table wedged between WS and himself, were ascertained by him to be in the same position when he retrieved them for reloading into the cassette.

This time four of the six films were blank. The images reproduced are on the remaining two, the third and fourth films of the six. During the sitting there was at least one event which not only bore on the image of film No.4 but appeared to be clearly related to conversations recorded on the normal tape recorder (under RF's control). As the transcript confirms, Emily advised Gabriele at one point not to grieve over her late husband. Then Edwin said:–

> . . . it's many . . . "many, many" — he's saying "many, many" . . . It does not seem long.

Emily then asked Gabriele, whom she addressed with permission as Gabby, whether Lutz, her late husband, had been very interested in his family history, and Gabriele confirmed that this was so. The following conversation then ensued:–

> EB: He is trying to convey something of himself to me . . . let you know he is here. There is a certain pride at his connections [Gabriele agreed]
> Edwin: They (?he) had a lot of relatives.
> Gabriele: Yes.
> Ed: "Many, many", as a reference to many in his family.

When the films were developed after the sitting, and efforts were made to read the words on the fourth picture, it was not apparent to the participants until they played the tape recording of the sitting that there was a clear link between the message to Gabriele and the image on the picture shown in Plate 17, which appears to represent the word 'many'. They were unable to discover what the number 12 represented, however.

The Tape-Recording Experiments

Before the first sitting began MK inserted a pre-recorded music tape into a tape recorder from which, he had been told, Alan's son had removed the microphone. To check this removal in front of the sitters, MK pressed the 'play' button and they listened to Mozart for a few moments, showing thereby that the playback system was working. Having removed the music tape, he then inserted one of the pack of fresh tapes he had brought with him, showed the company that it was fully rewound, pressed the record/play button in full view, and spoke into the recorder for a couple of minutes, with others commenting. He then pressed the 'stop' and 'fast rewind' buttons followed by the 'play', to demonstrate that nothing had been recorded or was recordable. Finally, he rewound the tape to base and left the machine on the small side table on his right, next to WS, and with his index finger resting lightly on the fluorescent record button tab so that WS could watch him when he pressed it. This he did, simultaneously with RF (who was operating the recording machine opposite him), as soon as the voice of the principal spirit guide, Manu, came through. The tape remained on until, thirty minutes into the sitting, a click was heard. There was no attachment to the tape recorder.

When replayed after the sitting, nothing beyond the hissing noise of the mechanism was heard on the tape until nearly half way through, when, for a period of about 15 to 20 seconds, there was a very distinctive heavy breathing sound and an attempt made to communicate a brief message in what was quite discernibly a voice. In order to discover whether the RF tape which recorded all the proceedings might show some evidence of interference at this point, three of the sitters (WS, HS and MK) noted the counter number indicating the time of message transmission, and then played the recording tape on the same machine, to ensure synchronicity. Although there did seem to be some audible though minor interference with the quality and clarity of the recording, there was nothing substantial enough to suggest a clear relationship between the two sets of sounds on the two tapes. During the session there were several references by the spirit communicators to this experiment, and the means by which it was effected, notably in statements by Edwin in answer to invited questions by WS. These questions and answers were mentioned in Chapter IV.

Second Sitting, 1st July 1997

For the second sitting, when the tape recorder on the instructions of the Team was placed on the séance table in front of MK rather than on the side table, MK went through the same procedure, but inserted the audio-cassette so that the reverse side of the tape used in the first sitting would play. (He had hidden this tape in his room since the previous sitting.) MK then gave WS and HS the opportunity to fast-forward and play the tape at any point to show there was nothing on it. This they did, returning the tape to its starting point.

In this second sitting there was far more audible activity. While the participants heard nothing during the sitting that on playback was subsequently heard on this tape, precisely half way through the tape they heard two sharp clicks, followed by several more close together, a slight whistle, more atmospheric crackling, then a high-pitched signal-like noise followed (at 291 on the counter) with a loud puffing and (at 295) an attempt at communication, with the high-pitched sound still in the background. At 302 the voice whispered noisily, but unintelligibly. There followed four more efforts to communicate, and then a longer sequence in which what sounded like "Barry" was heard. At 375 there was something like "tip, tip tip-in-the-sea", but it was not clear enough to be fully distinguishable. At 380 they heard what sounded like "bye-bye".

During the sitting Edwin had been addressing an unknown entity and telling him (sometimes raising his voice, apologising for having done so) that "these good people" would not be able to hear his message (on the tape player), and he (i.e. the entity trying to convey a taped message) should try to make himself clearer. At the moment when Edwin said "I can hear someone; you can't but I can", MK noted aloud that the background music played by RF on a separate tape recorder throughout the sitting was playing a few bars of the first movement of a Mozart symphony, and said that would help to locate and link with the point on the spirit message tape. (When the sitting record tape was played back on the same machine as that used for the spirit message, this point turned out to be at 314). A few moments after saying he could hear someone, Edwin shouted "Barry!" and then added: "It is not at all clear, Monty. You may just have to accept the fact that it is just an attempt rather than a clear attempt, but you never know . . . we never know . . . "

Although the quality was poor, and the messages not clear enough to be comprehensible, the fact that non-random messages were recorded from a machine lacking any microphone struck all present as strongly suggestive of a paranormal origin.

With some minor textual modifications, this account has been seen and approved by all participants in the two sittings as an accurate record. The present authors later examine some hypotheses which have been advanced to account for these phenomena by normal means.

CHAPTER XII: THE RACHMANINOFF RECORDING

The last major experiment to be conducted before the Group held (with one exception) only closed sittings was conducted by MK, AE and DF on 16th August 1997 (Sitting 36), and proved to be one of the most productive sittings thus far from the criterion of objective evidence. It directly reflected the wishes MK had tried to express at Ibiza when asking for recordings of 'spirit messages' on tape in circumstances which would enable us to hear, independently of our own or of the mediums' voices, exclusively 'spirit' voices. Hence, the following is a detailed description of the procedure followed to produce two simultaneous tape recordings, only one of which carried 'spirit messages' exclusively; the other carrying these messages together with the human and Team voices normally heard at sittings.

Prior to the sitting of 16th August, MK provided DF with a packet of audio tapes bought by himself and retained in his possession. DF opened it, selected one tape at random, and in a vacant room made secret identification marks in four places on the cassette surface. (These he verified on the cassette after the sitting in the presence of the other two investigators.) AE then opened and examined the Panasonic tape recorder which had been used in the Ibiza experiments the previous month, and confirmed that its microphone had been removed, and that there was nothing in it which could record sound. He then handed it to DF, who closed it. AE then replaced the batteries which he had removed during his investigation, and handed it to MK, who then demonstrated the recorder's capacity to play a pre-recorded music tape. To confirm AE's findings, he then inserted DF's blank tape, talked into the receiver grid and played back the result, to show that nothing had been recorded: a double-check safeguard. AE returned the machine containing the re-wound DF tape to DF, who descended the flight of stairs leading to the séance cellar, where he "carried out a particularly exhaustive check of everything, including the undersides of the table and chairs", to quote his own account, for hidden electronic equipment or other artifacts. He was followed by MK and AE, and the four members of the Scole Group. DF then plugged in a lead connecting the microphone-less recorder to the primitive semi-conductor (germanium) apparatus which AE had designed some months earlier to the specification of the Team (see Chapter VIII), and which AE now re-examined. DF kept the microphone-less recording machine under his manual control or on the séance room table immediately in front of him and under continuous visual observation throughout the sitting. As with the two Ibiza experiments, the microphone-less recorder had two bright luminous tabs on the start and play keys, enabling DF and MK, seated immediately on his right, to ensure that it was not moved or otherwise tampered with at any time. At an early stage in the session, when requested by Edwin, DF co-ordinated pressing the 'start' button on this microphoneless machine with a similar action by RF on the recorder recording the sitting. Thus the two machines ran together for the next half-hour. There shortly emerged from both mediums messages of encouragement to the unknown communicators:–

EB: *I don't think that they can hear you but I think that they are aware of us being aware of them.*

RF (and SF): Right, we'll have to tell you what we hear.

DF: Faint, distant voice [emerging from the microphone-less recorder], Emily. Can't quite seem to work yet.

EB: *Hearing you.*

Edwin: Oh, someone's here.

RF [Quoting what he believed he could hear from or in the microphoneless recorder]: "Can you hear me?" "Can you hear me?" "Can you hear me?" "Yes".

EB: *Yes, they are aware of you. [Apparently addressed to the recording entities.] Come closer.*

Edwin: They are trying to bring some music.

RF: Oh lovely . . .

EB: *Can you hear, Arthur? Are you all right over there? You are farther away, aren't you?*

AE: Yes . . . white noise.

DF: You can't hear a voice within the noise?

AE: No.

MK: I can't either.

EB: *Give them a chance.*

DF: I can hear it, repeating a saying.

RF: Yes, "Can you hear me?"

EB: *Repeating a pattern.*

RF: Yes [they are saying], "Can you hear me now? Can you hear me?"

DF: Yes, we can hear you.

EB: *Monty's going to have a treat tonight.*

SF: Oh!

DF: [jocularly] Monty's always having treats. You gave him half a crown. What about the rest of us?

EB: *He'll know why. It will all be made clear.*

[After a few more exchanges:]

Edwin: Yes, someone's going to . . . yes . . . we understand (CLUNK) yes . . . thank you. He's going to bring some music, but it's very special . . . Very

178

special. Oh, I see! The composer's going to play it himself!

RF and SF: Oh!

EB: It's a projected memory for him.

RF: Yes.

Edwin: I hope it isn't a banjo!

DF: Is it what we hear now playing on the tape?

EB: What you are hearing should be going onto your tape recording, because it's going straight through.

Not only was the harsh 'white noise' clearly coming from the microphoneless recorder, but so too now was music and a voice message over it. The music was almost immediately recognised by MK as part of Rachmaninoff's Second Piano Concerto. He was clearly deeply moved: "Fantastic! This means a tremendous amount to me!" He later explained that this was one of the earliest pieces of classical music he knew, and that he had been raised on Rachmaninoff's own recording on 78s before the war. Long before it became popular as background music to the film *Brief Encounter*, it had assumed a particularly poignant relevance to boyhood days spent as a lonely evacuee. He was certain he had never mentioned this fact to anyone (DF and AE confirmed that he had certainly not mentioned it to them), least of all to the members of the Scole Group, none of whom appeared particularly interested in classical music. The music faded somewhat while a declamation which we were unable to interpret, but which was obviously in English, overlay without obliterating the music. The second movement of the concerto then returned to fuller power.

At the conclusion of the sitting, both the DF tape and that from RF's recorder were labelled and handed to MK. DF checked that his marks were still on the DF cassette. At no stage did it appear that any member of the Group had access to DF's microphoneless machine or to the DF tape. When the three investigators played back the tapes, the DF tape, instead of being silent, was found to have recorded the Rachmaninoff as well as the declamatory message, to say nothing of a large amount of white noise, but none of the voices or background music from the room itself. All present, except for the two entranced mediums, had clearly heard the Rachmaninoff and the declamation emerging from the machine controlled by DF during the sitting. The tape operated by Robin Foy (the RF tape) recorded all that was on the DF tape, and in addition all the observations made by the participants during reception of the spirit music and messages, none of which appeared on the DF tape. This RF tape, recorded by means of RF's open recorder, therefore included the Team's messages to the sitters, the Team's instructions or advice to or encouragement of the entities responsible for overcoming the technical problems of sound transference onto tape, our own and RF's comments and his background music, in addition to Rachmaninoff's Piano Concerto and the uncomprehended oration which was recorded on the DF tape. The tapes and DF's microphoneless recorder were taken away by the investigators for independent expert examination.

This, too, would appear to be an experiment without obvious precedent. However, any outcome whose veridicality turns to some extent on subjective factors, such as the special meaning of a phenomenon for one of the investigators, is bound to be considered less persuasive to others, and there will be doubts, which we examine in greater detail in Chapters XIV and XV, about the degree of safety with which alternative explanations, which do not invoke paranormal influences, can be eliminated.

CHAPTER XIII: THE VIDEO FILM

The sitting in August 1997 which produced the Rachmaninoff tape was to be the last in which the authors participated; and indeed with one important exception it was the last sitting of the Group attended by outsiders before the Group reported, more than a year later, that they had received a request not from the familiar Team but from a reportedly more elevated set of 'communicators' to cease sittings as a Group. Shortly after the August 1997 sitting we had been informed that the Team wished to concentrate on other experiments and were unwilling, or perhaps unable, to repeat earlier experiments. They considered we already had ample material from which to prepare our Report.

At our final sitting in August 1997 we had noticed that a curtain rail had been fixed to the roof about one and a half metres from the external wall. The Group, having been pledged to secrecy, were at that stage reluctant to give further details, merely observing that novel experiments of a far-reaching character were in train. It later emerged that work had for some months been in progress in an attempt to obtain images on video, using a camera which Dr Hans Schaer had provided. Subsequently we learned that the Group or the Team were having considerable difficulties in fixing images by pointing the camera at an angled upright mirror. The fact that difficulties were being encountered was apparent from the lengthy period during which the Group reportedly tried first two, then one mirror at various angles as proposed by the Team. Accounts illustrated with diagrams later appeared in *The Spiritual Scientist* of an experiment known as Alice, perhaps in tribute to looking-glass land (or because Lewis Carroll was an early supporter of the Society for Psychical Research).

We had appealed to the Group to be allowed to repeat two or three experiments introducing modifications which would take into account some shortcomings in the earlier experiments. For example, it had been argued by critics (see Chapters XI and XII and Appendix I) that sounds present on the tapes in Ibiza or Scole, where the recorders had been divested of their microphones, might be attributable to external radio signals. As we point out, the nature of the transmissions, together with the circumstances, timing and personnel of the sittings concerned, do not appear to support this suggestion, but we nevertheless felt it important that some form of screening be installed. Better still, we considered it desirable for us to receive responses to questions posed at the sitting itself – a development which we were assured had indeed taken place during the Group's tour to the Netherlands and Germany. Similarly we wished to repeat the Polaroid film experiments held in Ibiza, taking even more stringent measures to preclude any possible access by any members of the Group to the films during their development (as to which, see Appendix J). Other examples were DF's repeated request for further photographic images involving the four-step protocol which he had urged throughout, and AE's continuing and insistent pleas for the use of infra-red or image-intensifying equipment.

However, the door was metaphorically closed, and a lengthy meeting with the Group subsequently failed to open it. We had no option but to accept their decision, although with considerable reluctance. The Group themselves emphasised that they would have been happy to comply with our requests, were it within their competence to do so. We pointed out (to the Group, since we had no further opportunity of direct discussion with the Team) that absence of replication, or something akin to it, would be seen as weakening the evidence they said they were eager for us to experience. We made it clear that replication under further controls would give extra weight to their claims and thus further their mission. We emphasised that they and the Team would appear to have every-thing to lose and nothing to gain by declining our requests. However, the decisions apparently did not rest with the Group, and we therefore had to content ourselves with the assurance that it was the firm intention of the Team to invite us to return, once they had perfected the new experiments in what was a technically difficult area. They had promised adequate light: they would give us adequate light. We had wanted video evidence: this was what they were striving to produce.

We had hoped that upon the resumption of our sittings we would be able to supervise the experiments and witness successful results, but weeks passed, then months. Our expectations were sustained by reports from the Group of images appearing on video film through a type of psychomanteum, the origins of which date back to the ancient oracles of Greece. But our concerns were sharpened by fear that prolonged delay might result in premature and uncontrolled publicity, which could undermine publication of our own findings. We were aware that the Group had been asked by the Team to abandon their periodic public seminars, from which they received a modest financial reward, and to make no further plans for overseas tours or lectures. Moreover, we were conscious of the fact that members of the Group were subsidising the production of *The Spiritual Scientist* from their own limited resources, and we knew that they were eager to further their work by seeking to publicise their experiences in the media, to which end they had received approaches from television producers. Accordingly, at the end of 1997, the Council of the SPR made tentative proposals for financial assistance, but these were politely but firmly rejected by the Group. They made it clear that they could make no guarantees of results within any specified period, and did not wish to be beholden in any way to us, or to the SPR. Whatever view one may take of this reaction, it does not suggest cupidity. In the event it became evident that the Group were continuing to experience difficulties in getting the physical arrangements right, and in ensuring that the 'energies' were balanced and blended in a manner destined to produce the desired results. Word of these experiments appeared in *The Spiritual Scientist*, but it was not until Dr Schaer was invited to participate in a sitting that any evidence became available through one of our co-investigators. What follows is his account:–

Hans Schaer writes:–

The first part of the sitting in the Scole cellar took place on Saturday, 28th March, 1998 in excellent visibility. A curtain rail had been fixed to the roof of the cellar at the far end, but the curtains attached to it were both drawn back. Alan, the medium, had bought from a local shop a duo-pack comprising two sealed video-recording tapes. They were packed together in a sealed plastic wrap and were 45-minute JVC-type EHC (extra high grade) cassettes. The package was sealed by foil or sealed plastic. He handed it unopened to me. I inspected the package, opened it and selected one of the cassettes. This I signed and dated. Alan showed me how to insert it in the video-camera, which I did entirely by myself. No other person present had touched the cassette.

The camera (a JVC compact VHS camcorder, model GR-AX600 registered at 3 lux (1 lux in slow shutter mode), with an f.1.6 lens [which HS had earlier supplied to the Group] was already mounted on the tripod when I inserted the cassette. It pointed towards the upright mirror across the room, which was slightly bent backwards, located approx. 3½ metres from the camera lens. There was bright electric light (from an estimated 60-watt bulb) at this stage. The curtains suspended on the cellar ceiling were open. I switched on the video camera.

All five of us sat round the central circular table on the outside part of the curtain. Robin inserted into his tape recorder an audio tape consisting of meditation music which Sandra had put together. After exactly five minutes' meditation, Alan got up and sat in the chair which had been placed between the video camera and the mirror. He gazed into the mirror for five minutes. He returned to his seat and Diana then took her turn to gaze into the mirror. After five minutes it was my turn, then Sandra's and finally Robin's. Robin then closed the curtains, returned to his seat and switched off the light. We remained seated in the dark for approximately an additional three-quarters of an hour (during which time Alan and Diana went into trance). At the beginning we had the usual type of trance conversation through the mediums, with the familiar entities Manu, Emily Bradshaw and, briefly, Patrick McKenna coming through and addressing us.

Then a new entity from a far-away dimension introduced himself whose name nobody could clearly understand. Although we listened to the tape various times after the sitting, the closest we understood of the name was something like . . . Darti.

During this sitting it was indicated by the spirit Team that the phenomena which had been produced in the past would not be continued and repeated, because the energy must be used for the development of new phenomena. Towards the end of the sitting Emily Bradshaw told us that she believed this sitting had produced a remarkable, successful result, i.e. that the spirit Team had succeeded in producing something substantial on the video tape. She also said that if there was anything on the tape it would be pretty much at the beginning of the tape. If there was nothing at the beginning it would be unlikely that there was anything towards the end. This meant that if there was any result on the tape, it was produced on it during the time (the first 30 minutes) when the video camera had been run in full electric illumination.

Once the sitting was closed with a prayer by Sandra and the light was switched on again, we were all surprised to find that the curtains, which had been closed prior to switching off the light before starting the dark séance, were drawn back and opened by about 50 cm.

I removed the video tape from the camera, checked my signature, and brought it upstairs (carrying it myself) and inserted it into the television set at the Foys' sitting room. Hardly had the tape started to run than we saw in the lower right part of the screen a picture, very clearly recognisable as the profile of a man aged between 50 and 60, slightly bald in front, with dark black hair and possibly a black moustache, wearing metal-rimmed spectacles. This portrait appeared to be almost as inside a water bubble. This portrait was on the tape for about six seconds. There were many coloured blurs on the tape, some of them in movement. One of the blurs started to move towards the bubble, entered it and formed a second man's head behind the portrait of the first one, but still very well recognisable. The second man wore something like a Russian fur hat. The picture with the second face lasted for about three seconds, and then both portraits vanished.

We were not (and still are not) able to identify these two men that evening. No specific explanation as to their identity was given by the spirit Team either.

The Scole Group were kind enough to produce a postcard-size enlargement of one sequence of this video-tape which shows these two men in profile very clearly (see Plate 3).

CHAPTER XIV: AUTHENTICITY: PRELIMINARY DOUBTS EXAMINED

We cannot give an account of the varying procedures which attended the production of evidential material during our investigation of the Scole Group and their phenomena without referring to some of the more obvious shortcomings, and the criticisms to which they give rise. Many of these we have briefly discussed, but it is of the utmost importance that all reasonable criticisms of the phenomena, the Group and of our approach as investigators, be rigorously examined. During the extended period when we were awaiting our return to Scole to participate in what we had hoped would prove to be the culminating experiment (see previous chapter) we had several opportunities to receive and respond to criticisms from those who were aware of our work and had in some cases themselves participated in it, either as invited experts for sittings with one or more of us, or as members of ten-strong seminar sessions unconnected with us, or simply as readers of the Group's own publication, *The Spiritual Scientist*. A number of talks, three of them involving extended presentations of the film material, were given by MK to audiences in Britain, Germany and the USA during this period, and they included a special informal meeting of members of the SPR Council, augmented by the presence of our four co-investigators, Dr Schaer, Walter and Karin Schnittger, and Ingrid Slack. Briefer accounts were given by MK on behalf of the investigators at the 22nd Annual International Conference of the SPR in September 1998, and at a meeting of the Scottish SPR, as well as at two local branches of the Scientific and Medical Network. In addition there has been a lively exchange among a closed-circuit group on the Internet, in which the authors have participated. While at none of these was it possible to give more than a summary of the principal evidence, they have provided us with an opportunity to anticipate several of the commonest questions, and criticisms. Many have been briefly touched on above. Others raise more general questions of evidentiality, and to these we devote the next chapter and a number of associated Appendices. Here we think it timely to pose, and attempt to answer, several of the doubts which have been most frequently expressed.

The 'Communicators'

If they are genuine, should they not identify themselves, enabling us to check their authenticity?

a) We could discover no phenomena or statements whose evidential value depended solely on our knowing the identity of the purported spirit communicators. In most cases the evidence would have been neither supported nor undermined by our being told the names they claimed, although naturally our curiosity was aroused.

b) Past efforts to test the credentials of named communicators have produced varied and confusing results. In some cases communicators appear to show a remarkably unclouded recollection of names, events, persons and places; others do not. But there is no apparent relationship between the strength of their memory of earthly lives and the accuracy of the information imparted. The personality may not have a regular consistency, but may wax and wane, so to speak, in coherence, recollection and intensity. An ostensible communicator, the distinguished classical scholar Frederic Myers, failed to recognise the Lord's Prayer when read to him in Greek, or correctly recall several classical references which would in real life have caused him no difficulty; yet on other occasions (Verrall, 1910), he could in response to questions display arcane knowledge well beyond the subliminal reach of the medium (Mrs Piper).

It is a well-established but strange fact that communicators often have difficulty remembering or pronouncing their own names, but can recall people, events and places in accurate detail. It may not be surprising that 'Lord Rayleigh's' apparent casual hat-doffing to us on 13th April 1996 (sixth sitting) was accompanied by a note of his address, and an indication of title, but no name, although this is the reverse of what we might expect. Nor can we say how far the ability to communicate, and the facility with which it is accomplished, may depend on the quality and state of health of the medium, the temperament and tactics of the interlocutor or the presence or absence of friendly or querulous participants.

c) However abundant the evidence of identification they might have provided, it would simply be attributed to the very hypothesis the spirit Team seemed eager to undermine, since anything which turns out to be accurate will be known, immediately or eventually, to the inquirer. It may therefore be ascribed to mere precognitive telepathy on his part. If the information cannot be confirmed, then it is not relevant evidence.

d) The Team more than once insisted that they wanted us, as well as outside critics, to concentrate on the evidence, not on unresolvable arguments about the nature of those responsible for its origin.

Why did the investigators not insist on book identification tests, or the correct identification of hidden numbers?

When these were proposed, they were described by the Team as 'old hat', and as having failed to influence mainstream scientific opinion. These well-established experiments were made famous by (among others) the Rev C. Drayton Thomas in the inter-war years when sitting with Mrs Gladys Osborne Leonard (Thomas, 1922, 1928, 1935, etc.). A communicator would specify a message which would be found to appear on a page in a book located in a described position and shelf in a sitter's library. Some two thousand trials, in which the place, book and page were selected at random for the spirit communicator (Drayton Thomas's father) to identify rather than leaving the communicator himself to provide the details, resulted in a success rate of no less than 62%, and some successes were so specific and remarkable that they sufficiently overwhelmed the doubts of the sceptically cautious Mrs Eleanor Sidgwick as to convince her that, at the very least, clairvoyance was in operation. But there's the rub. Even had the Scole entities conceded our request, diverted their efforts to a series of book tests, and achieved no less a level of success, it is unlikely that any conclusion would be drawn beyond that admitted by Mrs Sidgwick. The avowed aim of the Scole communicators, after all, was to produce evidence of survival, not of an essentially psychic quality like clairvoyance.

Nonetheless, we would be the first to acknowledge that, for all their limitations, successful book tests (which for this purpose would include correct extracts from or close references to documents not generally publicly accessible) would have been a considerable improvement on the information conveyed, and on those images printed on film which appear to have been lifted, so to speak, from one or more books accessible to the public. True, we were never misled as to their sources, although some question mark hangs over the purported attribution of the authorship of the German poem (see concluding passages and footnote in Chapter V), the original of which, if it indeed exists, has yet to be traced; and it was well recognised, even before our arrival on the scene, that most of the films already produced were 'reproductions', using that term in its broadest sense. However, as we have made clear, we were not permitted to insist on anything: merely to propose.

If the Team's aim was indeed to produce definitive evidence of survival, why could they not create a permanent paranormal object (PPO)?

A PPO is inherently paranormal, i.e. something which by accepted standards is impossible, such as a pair of unbroken but interlocking rings made of two different types of wood, or an X-rayable substance inside a new tennis ball. We do not know why the Team were unable to achieve this feat, but at an early sitting we did present them with two devices which had originally been designed to test the powers of a well-known psychic. Both involved creating changes in physically inaccessible objects. Both were admired by the Team. We were commended for our initiative, but the team preferred to pursue their own agenda. We neither pretend that this satisfies us nor expect it to appease critics. However, we devote Appendix H to a detailed examination of the case for categorising the series of film strips as presumptively permanent paranormal objects.

Why could not the team be asked to provide solutions to recondite mathematical problems, or give information which could not have been known to anyone?

The response to this applies equally to the preceding question. We had no means of knowing what limitations the Team were under. Assuming paranormality, such tasks may have been beyond their competence, or within their competence but against their wishes, or compliant with their wishes but contrary to constraints imposed upon them. This raises the problems of ontology and presumption touched upon in the next chapter. Whatever the reasons, the absence of such information does not detract from or alter the value of other pieces of evidence, which should be judged on their merits. As for providing information not currently known to anyone, this (as we were told by the Team) invites the objection recited earlier: when the information is eventually confirmed as accurate, it can be attributed to precognitive clairvoyance or telepathy, a faculty which need not import any suggestion of survival.

If the Team really were seeking to elevate mankind's spiritual consciousness, why would they engage in such trivial pursuits as playing around with illuminated ping-pong balls, vibrating tables, pretending to wrest boxes from the grip of experimenters, playing trumpets badly [see Appendix E], and suchlike childish tricks?

Whatever moral disapproval one may express at the failure of many manifestations to accord with our expectations of gravitas, it is only the genuineness of the phenomena themselves which matters, if we are concerned primarily, at this stage, with the evidence as distinct from its implications. The wide range of phenomena we have described was apparently designed as an attempt to demonstrate not only the survival of human personality but also the capacity of some of these survivors to influence tangible objects in our world, no matter how trivial, amusing or serious. Taken to its extreme, moral disapproval implies the sort of reasoning which led one critic, on hearing the tape recording at which a trumpet was played and drumming was heard during a sitting at which Hans Schaer was responsible for the controls, to dismiss the episode on the grounds that the trumpet was badly played. Such observations may be accurate, but they simply reflect disapproval of method, not a criticism of genuineness.

Control Over The Mediums

Surely the absence of infra-red equipment, and the fact that the experimenters could not see what was going on, make the whole operation suspect?

This is one of the commonest criticisms. We have recognised the absence of this equipment as a weakness, and have described the attempts we made to introduce either IR video-cameras or image intensifiers, pending the expected development of sittings in reasonable light. We were puzzled by the Team's unwillingness to contemplate even the latter, since their introduction would import no new energy but merely utilise the existing IR radiation from sitters' bodies. We were never clear whether this reluctance arose from the Team's belief that IR viewers would be incompatible with the development of physical phenomena, or because they might, perhaps, reduce the intensity or variety of these phenomena. None the less we must point out that:—

1   The existence of wristbands, and luminous strips at the four cardinal points on the central table, in addition on occasion to luminous strips on such pieces of equipment as film tubs and ping-pong balls or bells, did provide an important though less than perfect check on unauthorised movements by any member of the Group for most of the duration of the sittings.

2   The degree of light created by what gave the appearance of spirit forms was on occasion sufficiently bright and sustained to enable us to see one another, and hence to observe any intrusive form had it been reaching across the table or manipulating any piece of equipment.

3   There is no guarantee that the use of such equipment would have satisfied resolute critics, since there would have been no certainty that those viewing would be looking at the right tricksters at the right times. There have been claims that even in broad daylight clever illusionists can outwit any form of surveillance. A century of exposure to photography of one sort or another in séances in which materialised forms appeared (e.g. Edwards, 1962; Barbanell, 1959) has not removed doubts, let alone provided proof acceptable to determined critics. The various measures taken to ensure that the film rolls could not have been tampered with or be substituted by the Group can be judged on their merits; and it is questionable whether those merits would have been considered improved if one or more of the sitters had had infra-red equipment at his disposal. Our view is that the most important control was that which we were able to assert over the production of the film evidence itself.

Why was there no form of electrical circuit-breaking equipment to detect any untoward movement by those under surveillance, or instruments to record such factors as air pressure changes, rates of vibration, alterations in temperature, acoustic profiles, brain wave patterns, changes in electromagnetic fields, electrocardiagram fluctuations, etc.?

The exhaustive examination of the Schneider brothers (Gregory, 1985) does not support the assumption that the use of elaborate equipment of this nature would remove doubts. Even were the business of wiring up and plugging in the mediums not considered to be intrusive and inhibiting, its introduction would hardly be compatible with maintaining the atmosphere of harmony which is widely believed to be a prerequisite for a successful sitting. However, it is worth noting that the Group themselves had installed a device to measure air flows, or 'psychic breezes', and a thermometer to record variations between internal and external temperatures. But we were not at that stage concerned overmuch with the measurement of parameters within which the apparently paranormal appeared to operate, conceiving this as a task which could be more thoroughly tackled once the preliminary responsibility of establishing authenticity had been fulfilled. Nor were we in a position to impose, although we could certainly suggest and discuss, additional measuring devices, but we considered many of these would prematurely complicate our work. Once again it must be emphasised that our concern *was to control the point of production of the photographic evidence.*

Many of the mediums claiming to produce physical phenomena have submitted to thorough body searches. Why was this not done here?

It is indeed the case that quite elaborate body searches were carried out on such prominent mediums as the Schneiders, Helen Duncan, Eusapia Palladino and Eva Carrière. But despite the thoroughness with which such searches were undertaken, attempts have still been made to question the authenticity of the phenomena (e.g. recently Wiseman, 1992, Polidoro & Rinaldi, 1998).

There were several reasons why we did not propose, let alone insist on, searching the mediums. Body searching is not merely invasive of human privacy but currently pointless. It derives from the days when the raw material of materialised spirits was ectoplasm, which appears to emanate from various parts of a medium's body and assumes a life and shape of its own, infinitely malleable, of varying density and solidity, and often rather suspect. Widely dismissed as nothing more than butter muslin, or some crushable material capable of being squeezed into a very small space and regurgitated by the medium when it has not been retrieved from various bodily apertures, it has been controversial for over a century. Its production is also attended by symptoms of physical exhaustion, in consequence of which mediums would often have to be helped from the séance chamber, drained of energy by the ordeal.

The conditions at Scole were entirely different. There was no ectoplasm, or anything like it. A thorough body search would have required the presence of a medical practitioner, possibly two; the members of the Group would have had to be stripped naked and examined, to quote the delicate phraseology of former times when referring to women mediums (they were never ladies), *in rectum et vaginum.* Ideally, X-rays would have to be applied or emetics administered in case a regurgitation theory might be advanced by sceptics. A dentist would be needed in view of the manner in which false teeth could be used to hold micro-transmitters. Pocketless garments would then have to be donned in the place of the clothes worn not just by the two mediums but by the other members of the Group. All this while maintaining that attitude of relaxed friendliness without which the phenomena would be unlikely to emerge.

Of course it could be argued that the purpose of body searches would be to detect the smuggling of any illicit equipment into the séance room. However, the ethical objections to body searches still remain. In addition, as we pointed out earlier, the notion that the extensive equipment necessary for faking could have been smuggled undetected into the séance room at each sitting over the entire length of our investigation can be contested. And we must again emphasise our view that if the point of production of the photographic evidence could be fully controlled, the matter of body searches, like circuit-breaking equipment, becomes irrelevant.

If body searches were considered inappropriate, or unnecessary, why not physical constraints in the séance room?

There were several reasons:–

a)   Some of the considerations which relate to body searches equally affect the application of physical constraints.

b)   All known cases of physical constraints have been applied to a single medium or claimant, and most involved the physical detention by one or usually two investigators of the arms and legs of the medium. With four people under surveillance this would have been physically impossible in the available space, even had we been able to provide the necessary number of investigators. There were in fact six members of the Group under examination in the early stages of the investigation: that would have made the imposition of any sort of effective physical controls even less feasible.

c)   We were never prevented from searching the séance room both before and after sittings. Indeed we were positively encouraged to do so.

d)   To the extent to which we might have suspected that equipment required to create some of the phenomena, notably that concerning light, may have been secretly introduced, we were aware that in at least three places where such phenomena were witnessed, in Los Angeles, San Francisco and Ibiza, all the Group wore only the lightest garments, which would have precluded the safe concealment of any but the smallest item.

How could you tell that the mediums went into trance?

Only by deduction. We had no means of assessing this objectively. Nevertheless if they were not in trance they would of necessity have been fully conscious. That would mean that everything they said must have been fraudulently contrived. They would be imitating voices from wholly fictitious personalities whose language and accents they were able to produce with a consistency and spontaneity which never varied or gave rise to suspicion by any investigator over dozens of sittings. They would be inviting and responding intelligently to questions which they could not have foreseen, and contriving to persuade cautious investigators that the sounds appearing to emanate from a point in front of them on the table, or even from a tape recorder within inches of the investigators, were not in fact issuing from their own larynxes.

In addition, the mediums would have had to display a conscious familiarity with literary and technical subjects in a degree of detail which presupposed careful prior study. Also relevant is the fact that even though any enhancement of the investigators' controls clearly militated against the practice of deception of any kind, the Group nevertheless engaged in several discussions with us as investigators on ways by which safeguards against fraud could be strengthened.

Since discovery of deception was a prime aim, why did the investigators not bring in experts, like professional illusionists?

The decision whom to invite to accompany us rested with the Group as apparently advised by the Team (although there were some unrehearsed discussions between the investigators and the Team about the names of potential invitees). We put forward names of people, mainly our professional colleagues, whose participation we believed would both augment and check our own conclusions. Nearly all were accepted, although later there were difficulties in finding dates when they could attend, because the Team meantime decided against further demonstration sittings in the apparent interest of developing and perfecting other experiments on their agenda.

While we would have been happy to have invited all manner of experts, therefore, the decision was not ours. But if it were, we would have been deterred by the knowledge that, from time to time, critics have argued that lawyers were more suitable than scientists, that investigative journalists would be shrewder in detecting duplicity than psychologists, or that it was no use inviting professional magicians unless we could be certain that their specialist expertise was appropriate to the means of deception suspected to have been employed. Magicians, like other professionals, tend to be specialists in their own fields and relatively inexperienced in others. We know of no magician who has specialised in the kind of séance room phenomena in evidence at Scole. In any event, while not practitioners, the three investigators have for many years made studies not only of séance room deception but also of the illusions devised and operated by magicians. We should also point out first, that one of the first sitters (Webster, 1994) to record his impressions following a seminar sitting (with ten members of the public) before we arrived on the scene was or had been a practising magician; and secondly that one of the most celebrated expert investigations ever undertaken of a physical medium, the Naples sittings with Palladino (Feilding et al., 1909) was carried out by three investigators (Feilding, Carrington and Baggally) with formidable qualifications in the field of illusion and deception, and produced very positive findings; but this has not stopped the investigators from being assailed on the grounds that they were ill-qualified and incompetent.

The investigators appear to have had every opportunity to discuss and agree a procedure for the production of film strips, yet the record shows that no two procedures appeared to be identical. Surely this was an unsatisfactory feature of the controls?

This is an understandable criticism, but based on the assumption that we were conducting an experiment where all the parameters were predetermined by us and under our control. A careful study of the sequence of events recorded in earlier chapters, and summarised in Appendix A, shows precisely where and why these changes in procedure were made. For example, we introduced a fraud-proof bag with which the Team (and of course the Group) had not previously experimented. It was found to have features which the Team found difficulty in overcoming, even though the results were a technical success. We introduced a new type of film (Kodachrome 200), and there was no merit in operating a strict protocol until we had discovered whether the Team could cope with its different technology. In some cases secret markings were applied to film tubs as a safeguard against substitution. It should also be remembered that initially we were invited as guests in our individual capacities because of our considerable knowledge of the subject and our experience in the field. We could not insist on conditions which ran counter to the programme or plans of the Team, or press for changes which they considered incompatible with their powers or likely to add to their difficulties, since we could have no understanding of either.

Several detailed questions have been raised by our colleagues about the film strips (Appendix H), the tape recordings at Scole and in Ibiza (see Chapters VIII and IX and Appendix I), the efficacy of the controls during the Polaroid film experiment in Ibiza (Chapter XI and Appendix J), the manner in which the security box made by the Group themselves might have been employed to deceive us (Chapter VI and Appendix K) and about the lights and touches described in Chapter III and Appendix L. These are important but detailed matters and we feel they are best placed in separate appendices. We turn now to more general considerations affecting the evaluation of the Scole evidence.

CHAPTER XV: THE POSSIBILITIES OF FRAUD

Unique Features

Before examining, in greater detail than has so far been appropriate, the general arguments for and against fraud, we first note several claims of uniqueness in the present investigation which have an indirect bearing on the hypothesis of conspiratorial deception. To the extent to which such claims withstand scrutiny, they may be considered to cut both ways: on the one hand the unprecedented requires a particularly exacting standard of evidence and an even greater draught of credence; on the other, it appears to make deception more difficult to achieve successfully, safely and consistently.

With rare exceptions previous investigations into physical phenomena have concerned themselves with the work of individuals. As we pointed out in our introduction, never to our knowledge has a group of four (originally six) people been under collective scrutiny, such that suspicious behaviour on the part of any one of them, whether during sittings or at any other time off-duty, would strengthen doubts about the honesty of them all. In an investigation extending over two years in three countries, and involving varying levels of thoroughness and depth and a dozen senior members of the Society for Psychical Research in their private capacities, no inadvertent, off-guard remark which might be thought to reveal a deception has been noted by any of the principal investigators or reported to them. In addition MK has been able to watch the Group in informal surroundings, sharing the same hotels with them while in the USA, and the same holiday home in Ibiza as a guest of Dr Schaer, and entertaining them to dinner or visiting the homes of both couples while enjoying their hospitality. The fact that he has observed nothing suspicious in any of these contexts is not to be readily dismissed as a mere subjective impression by an investigator who may have got a little too close to his subjects, since these experiences have been shared by such other observers as Dr Schaer and the Schnittgers, who know members of the Group well, Brian Hurst, in whose Los Angeles home the Group were guests for two weeks, as well as the other two principal investigators.

Another claim to uniqueness for the investigation resides in its collaborative nature. After the first contact had been made on the initiative of the investigators, and mutual confidence had been established, the invitation to participate in the sittings came from the Group acting, as they were constantly to assure us, by and with the consent of the Team. Our own discussions with the Team, extending over many sessions and covering a wide range of subjects, were fully consistent with the impression that the Group's programme, schedules, activities, contacts and policy were all substantially influenced, if not positively determined, by the advice they received from their apparent spirit communicators.

The Group themselves played an essential part in what were to prove lengthy, sometimes intricate and often fruitful discussions between the investigators and various members of the Team, primarily through the entranced mediumship of Diana and Alan, although sometimes by independent voice. However, the relationship between the investigators and the Team was characterised and increasingly animated by a desire to explore the most effective means by which the Team felt their objectives might be achieved: i.e. to provide better, newer and more tangible evidence of survival. While investigators' suggestions for reaching this goal were frequently either not accepted or considered incompatible with the Team's claimed technical limitations, our active involvement in the carrying out of experiments designed essentially by the Team themselves was a novel, and striking – if at times frustrating – feature of the investigation. We are reminded by Professor Archie Roy that Feda, Mrs Leonard's 'control', herself suggested book tests, but nevertheless it is rare for mediums or their spirit guides to spell out and discuss with investigators improvements in controls. If we must therefore suppose these discussions to be a subtle means of gaining our confidence and diverting our suspicions, they represent a remarkably risky strategy.

The fraud case must necessarily presuppose the elimination of any difference between the Group and the spirit Team. The latter would have to be considered a deliberate figment created by the fully conscious mediums with the active complicity of other members of the Group. That would make remarkable the several discussions we had (including the significant passage quoted from MK's sitting in Ibiza recorded in Chapter XI) showing the apparent eagerness of the supposed deceivers to improve the protocol in order to eliminate the very deceptions they were intent on practising.

A further claim to uniqueness is the nature of the energy said to be responsible for the physical phenomena. Assuming paranormality, whatever this energy is, howsoever constituted or transformed into communications, shapes, sounds, lights, and substances, it appears to differ entirely from that supposedly responsible for ectoplasm. This was not merely what we were told: it seemed consistent with our observations. Indeed the Team themselves inclined to place the novelty of this form of energy at the head of their list of claims to uniqueness, and they underscored it by constructing a new vocabulary to describe the different ways in which it manifested itself. It is a moot point whether the production of so-called ectoplasm is more or less easy to fake than the so-called pure spirit energy (albeit admixed with the energies said to be derived from members of the Group, and sitters), which has purportedly been used for the creation of the range of phenomena experienced at Scole. It is undeniable that ectoplasm has a murky history, that many photographs of ectoplasmic forms bear remarkable similarities to crude paper masks, and that impersonation by confederates has been alleged as often as has the medium's regurgitation of butter muslin. However justified or unfair such charges may be, they have been the staple of physical mediumship controversy for over a century. By contrast, the great diversity of functions performed by the energy at Scole makes it more difficult to identify mechanisms by which this energy could be simulated by normal means.

The final claim to uniqueness, and a further possible argument against fraud, is that whereas many of the films were created in circumstances designed to preclude interference by those under investigation, they nonetheless yielded externally examinable evidence. Apart from apports, about whose genuineness there is invariably controversy, there are precedents for physical phenomena of an apparently paranormal nature available for external study (e.g. the wax impressions of hands created during sittings with the Polish medium Franek Kluski, and photographs portraying alleged spirit extras), but there has been little which has proved durable, and certainly nothing in the public domain in modern times which gets any closer to the Holy Grail of psychical researchers, the permanent paranormal object.

No less important to buttress the above claims to uniqueness are the contents of the films themselves. Not only do they display diversity of information, albeit most apparently taken from existing sources, but they contain material whose existence appears unlikely to have been known to the Group.

There are several other features of this investigation which, while not unique individually, may be argued to be so collectively. One is the subordinate role of the investigators, a condition dictated by the fact that the Team's capacity to produce phenomena was beyond the expectations of the investigators. Restrictions had to be accepted by them, albeit with reluctance and sometimes puzzlement, as the price of obtaining results. This meant that procedures devised by the investigators to prevent deception had to be discussed and made consistent with the abilities, limitations, prior plans and wishes of the Team, the Scole Group themselves playing a largely passive role in this respect. This may, of course, be regarded as a weakness of the investigation. However, it is worth remembering that a wide range of human behaviour, from making love to writing poetry, can only reliably be produced at the behest of the creators rather than that of their investigators.

Then, at the request of one or other member of the Team, there is the direct employment of individual investigators to undertake specific tasks, e.g. the purchase of films of a particular type (MK and WS), the obtaining of a small piece of uncommon metal such as germanium (AE), the construction of an electrical device and the provision of electric coils in order to improve the efficacy of this device (AE). In addition there were instructions, down to the precise position of fingers and thumbs on each hand, given to WS on one occasion, and to MK on another, as to the manner in which a locked box containing a tub of unexposed film was to be held so that neither lock nor surfaces were accessible to possible fraudsters. Likewise we were told when and whether a sitter could 'invite' a spirit light to approach him or settle on his hand (although frequently these things happened in response to our direct requests), and were given the exact procedure which one of us was to follow when conducting an experiment. While all such experiences do not of themselves weaken the fraud theory, they clearly presuppose total consciousness on the part of both mediums if fraud were indeed practised. Alternatively it can be argued that, by acting as masters of ceremony, the Team (or the Group) could manipulate things to their own convenience.

Value and Weaknesses of Testimony

Past investigations into claims of paranormal physical events have usually been more or less dependent on subjective testimony, or less frequently on the production of photographs which have generated more controversy than agreement. No matter how eminent the investigator, how numerous his or her collaborators, how thorough the precautions or elaborate the instruments of detection: so long as testimony is ultimately dependent on what was thought to have been seen, felt, remembered or heard, regardless of its intensity, critics will pay little heed, and the wonder (even were it to penetrate beyond the purdah of academic publications) will last but nine days. Not infrequently the familiar morning-after affliction has led some witnesses to retract in the light of reflection and perhaps peer disapproval the evidence to which they had earlier given their unqualified approval. While we are not aware of any such cases relevant to the Scole Group, it is certainly true of some of the most carefully conducted experiments on outstanding mediums, such as Rudi Schneider (Gregory, 1985) and Mina Crandon (Inglis, 1984). Hence the avowed objective in the present instance of both the investigators and the Team was to minimise, where we could not entirely dispense with, dependence on the frailties attendant on human observation.

Since the investigators' primary rôle was to take all practical steps to guard against deception, the chief aim of this Report has been to present evidence allowing the reader to decide whether the phenomena described are explicable by normal means or not. In the absence of that other Holy Grail of psychical research, conclusive proof, we can simply present the evidence and allow readers to reach their own conclusions on the balance of probability. For some critics, the possibility of fraud, however remote, is enough to condemn all the phenomena, no matter how substantial the contrary evidence. We may consider this reasoning spurious, but it is sufficiently pervasive among critics of paranormal claims to justify our detailed study. The point has been astutely summarised by Paul Beard (1966):–

> A favourite method of the negative sceptic is to examine evidence which is many years old, and was observed by somebody else. He then invents some possible alternative explanations, and looks around for supporting facts which might have been present. He does not produce any direct evidence to show that this alternative really took place. It remains speculation and is unprovable. However, it cannot be shown that it could not have happened, so the sceptic claims that the factual evidence, the product of direct observation on the part of his predecessor, is unreliable. However, we submit that logically it requires no more than the successful accomplishment of a single cast-iron test to disprove the argument that the mere possibility implies the probable practice of fraud.

We clearly had no option but to work within the limitations the Team felt it necessary to impose on us. To have insisted otherwise would have led to an end to our sittings. Hence our concentration on security measures relating to the purchase, handling, safeguarding and development of the films. There were hints, too, that the Team or their advisers were all too familiar with the fate which had eventually attended the introduction of the impressive system of controls, manual, physical and electrical, used when phenomena of wide variety and striking appearance had been witnessed at sittings with such as Eusapia Palladino or the Schneider brothers, much of them in conditions of ample visibility.

Usually the problem for investigators has been to apply constraints so secure, and monitoring equipment so reliable, as to leave the medium under test with no way to fake phenomena by physical manipulation. But no matter how elaborate the precautions, history shows that to rubbish these precautions requires no more than the mere suggestion that fraud might have been possible. It needed only Harry Price's apparently false accusation (see Gregory, 1985) that Rudi Schneider had cheated to consign to oblivion the testimony – including his own – derived from a decade and more of one of the most comprehensive investigations ever undertaken into physical mediumship.

The tasks facing the Scole Group, were they responsible for fraud, would be more challenging than those confronting an individual deceiver. The Group have produced a large variety of physical phenomena accompanied by mediumistic and direct voice messages without apparent props, preparation or accomplices, and in locations in six or seven different countries. They (or their spirit Team) have displayed a wide range of specialist knowledge and accomplishments.

Our investigations were primarily concerned to discover whether evidence for paranormality could be reliably obtained. As already made clear, we had confidently expected to continue our sittings with the Group in order to pursue a more structured course of questions and answers, to examine in more detail the evidence for and against a survivalist hypothesis, and to consider the ontological implications, but this was not to be. Nevertheless, some reflections are relevant.

It may seem reasonable to argue that if the camel of a film strip produced in the circumstances we have described can be swallowed by the discarnate scientists, they should not find themselves unduly strained by the gnat of the fabled interlocked pair of rings made from different woods. However, this simply reflects our estimate of the relative difficulties; and for all we know there may be limits imposed on celestial conjuring tricks as there are on earthly ones. Whatever the reasons, they have no logical bearing on the measures taken to preclude deception, and hence no relevance to the case for genuineness. What is indisputable, unless all is fake, is that whatever or whoever was responsible in the present instance for the rolls of film, the tape messages and the video impressions, encountered difficulties and setbacks en route which resulted in a number of totally or partially failed experiments, and may well have been responsible for the subsequent months of experimentation to find conditions reliable enough to secure images on video film. Whatever conclusions may be drawn from this painful progress, it may undermine the argument that if X can be produced, why not Y; and that if there is no Y, then it must be assumed that X is of distinctly suspicious origin.

"The experiments which are being made are not the work of earthly skill," wrote Frederic Myers in *Human Personality* (Myers, 1903):–

> All that we can contribute to the new result is an attitude of patience, attention, care; an honest readiness to receive and weigh whatever may be given in our keeping by intelligences beyond our own. Experiments, I say, there are, probably experiments of a complexity and difficulty which surpass our imagination; but they are made from the other side of the gulf, by the efforts of spirits who discern pathways and possibilities which for us are impenetrably dark.

The argument still holds good after the investigatory experiences of a century. Our own investigation has shown that, once we had witnessed a wide range of the show-piece phenomena which have so impressed visitors to Scole, the available time and energy became concentrated on either experiments or discussion, or normally both. The cosmic conjuring tricks had served their purpose; they were clearly not an end in themselves. One of the reasons given for calling a temporary halt to further sittings with those on our list of selected participants was that the Group informed us that such sessions were obstructing progress in improving and extending the range of experimental evidence.

As for the varied, eccentric and sometimes baffling contents of many of the photographic images, it is certainly true that some do appear meaningless to us, even with the familiarity DF has with hermetic symbolism; and it is not easy to understand what purpose is served in creating patterns which are purely abstract, or contain symbols which we are told have never been interpreted. For what it is worth, we can record the explanation we have been given, that they are the work of various communicators, and that the degree of freedom of expression permitted in the discarnate world enables them to experiment as they wish. It is not necessary and it may well be thoroughly mistaken to conclude that each one is the product of a long-pondered plan of some of the apparent communicators whose pseudonyms and style we have come to recognise. No more is it reasonable to assert that an experiment in visual or oral communication must appear wholly free from procedural defects from the outset in order to be evidential. All the signs are that in both categories the Team have stumbled forward, encountering failures and obstacles along the route, in much the same way that they might have done on earth. In the process they appear to have illustrated an observation of Frederic Myers, that it is as unreasonable to expect those 'born' into the next world to be immediately seized of all its mysteries as it is to expect those born into this world to understand all the mysteries of life on Earth.

Motivation of the Scole Group

We have already pointed to the absence of precedents for a comprehensive investigation of a Group rather than an individual. It helped us to know that, while the Group held small paid-for seminars once a month, there was nothing to indicate that they were exploiting their mediumistic abilities for financial gain, although some sitters have expressed distaste for the Group's efforts to cover expenses by the sale of crystals or glass domes to those wishing to establish similar Groups (one of the Scole Foundation's declared objectives). But it is difficult to think of any other realm of life where those who display their particular talents and achievements are frowned on for using them to defray some part of their outgoings. Indeed, it soon became apparent to us, and somewhat critically so by the time we began preparing this Report in the autumn of 1997, that they were making considerable financial sacrifices, having been asked by the Team to discontinue even their monthly seminars for a period, and to invite no visitors or investigators, in order that more and better physical phenomena of a novel type could be developed between the Team and the Group. Such a development, by voluntarily limiting this opportunity to defray their costs, does not suggest pecuniary motives.

MK observes that a striking illustration of the Group's lack of commercial incentive to perpetrate deception was apparent during their visit to California in the Spring of 1997 in response to an invitation from Brian Hurst to conduct a series of sittings in his garage, which he had specially converted for the event. (An account of this visit is given in Appendix F.) The Group had originally agreed to travel to Las Vegas, nearly 300 miles distant, accompanied by MK, in order to give two (free) sittings over a period of three days to a gathering of scientists at the University of Nevada at Las Vegas. At the last minute arrangements for their accommodation in Las Vegas fell through, and the plan was scrapped. Anxious nevertheless to afford USA scientists the opportunity to experience the phenomena at first hand, MK prevailed on the Group to travel to San Francisco for a single sitting. This they willingly did, at their own expense with neither fee nor reimbursement for an 800-mile car journey and most of their hotel accommodation. In the process they sacrificed the opportunity to conduct at least two fee-paying seminars for sittings for 20 people in the Los Angeles venue. In this context it is also well to remind readers (as mentioned in Chapter XIII) that when, at the close of 1997, there was a tentative SPR proposal to offer financial support, they firmly declined.

If deception for monetary gain appears to be ruled out, what other motive to promote an elaborate fraud might there have been, one powerful enough to have encouraged all of them to take repeated risks of detection and exposure? Since we could find nothing in our experience which would be consistent with the motives which normally underlie hoaxing, could we not attribute it to the more subtle lure of fame? Yet there is much in their conduct to suggest that they contemplated the prospect of fame with apprehension, borne of the conviction that some critics of the paranormal would be bound to denounce them and their works as spurious. It says little for the fame motive that the two mediums have constantly avoided the limelight, even to the extent of withholding their surnames. In sum, we have been unable to find a motive, certainly none consistent with the Group's behaviour and background, beyond a professed belief in the genuineness of the phenomena and of the spirit Team, and their own rôle and responsibilities in promoting a wider knowledge of the consequent implications. There has never been any suggestion from either of the two former members of the Group that deception occurred. On the contrary, they have firmly upheld the genuineness of their experiences at Scole. Fortunately, the very existence of a group of first six then four people, all of whom must have been party to any deception that may have taken place, made in some ways the task of detecting and precluding fraud easier, since the involvement of several individuals increased at times the likelihood of detection.

Implications of Fraud

We have tested the evidence identified during our investigation against two criteria. Unless these remain clearly understood and differentiated, the outcome of the investigation will be vitiated. As investigators, our primary task was to establish *whether or not* the phenomena, and the people responsible for their production, appeared genuine. Only when we had done so was it relevant or sensible to examine whether the communications and the phenomena would collectively weaken the super-psi hypothesis and strengthen the alternative hypothesis of the continuation of human personality beyond death.

The limitations imposed on us by the Team meant that we did not have to plunge ourselves into the sort of considerations that have both characterised and marred so many of the earlier investigations into the activities of physical mediums. For example, did the medium slip his hand out of the knot; could he (or more frequently she) not have wriggled a foot in such a fashion as to cause the chair to be ejected from the cabinet, the table levitated or the curtain to billow out? Can we be certain that the prestidigitating medium did not manage the hand-substitution trick and delude the investigators on both sides, thus leaving one arm free to perform the requisite miracle? Did the investigators suffer a momentary lapse of concentration after more than an hour's intensive scrutiny? Can we be certain with hindsight that there wasn't some hallucination, some momentary delusion . . .? Our concern was to satisfy ourselves (and others not present as witnesses or participants) that the evidence was strong enough to overcome the limitations, to which we devote considerable attention in what follows.

Our working hypothesis was that fraud, if it existed in the case of the Scole Group, would have to be a carefully prepared collaborative operation, one moreover which could be attempted only if the mediums were fully conscious throughout and with their eyes open (whether or not they had any part in the physical effects), since their voices were constantly commenting on or giving advance notice of the impending appearance of lights and objects, and of the precise destination of lights in response to invisible sitters' requests during the sittings. Even if conscious deception were practised, it would still be difficult, without crediting the mediums with infra-red or image-intensifying equipment, to account for the precision with which spirit lights or hands were able to find us unerringly in the dark. On the fraud hypothesis the two mediums would also have to be wholly responsible for engaging in discussions on matters often initiated by ourselves or by other accompanying sitters, and involving areas of knowledge they were unlikely to possess – and doing so with an unvarying consistency of accent and physical immobility. We have given a good many examples of these wide-ranging samples of knowledge.

In assessing the physically examinable evidence, we think it proper not to ignore the unqualified testimony of many experienced witnesses, apart from ourselves, who have been persuaded that what they saw,felt, heard, and occasionally received information about, was not produced fraudulently. Nor to disregard the antecedent improbability of dishonesty, or the difficulty of creating the illusion of or conjuring the phenomena which we have recorded.

General Considerations About Deception vs. Authenticity

The experimenter effect has long been recognised as a factor in parapsychological research, and it has a bearing on our work at Scole. It was clear that our desire to be invited to Scole sittings would not have been well received had we been overtly hostile to the very idea of paranormality. Both the Group and their Team were convinced that a negative attitude, rather than one of open-minded scepticism, which they appeared to welcome, could inhibit the results. To the extent to which in some fashion our own 'energies', for want of a better term, were utilised to blend with those of the spirit forces, or 'earth energies', in order to produce phenomena which must derive from energy of some sort, such conviction makes sense. At any rate it has been a commonplace in the history of psychical research for over a century that a hostile approach is liable to attenuate any paranormal displays, even if not positively to prevent them.

The selection process, in which names of prospective sitters had first to be approved by the Team, did not – and clearly could not – apply to those who attended the paid-for seminars (which included at different times three members of the SPR Council acting in their individual rôles), since they were not regarded as formal investigators, even though their attitudes appeared to have had some bearing on the phenomena. Thus when a sitter who suffered from mild claustrophobia found herself immured in a darkened cellar, her distress, which was perceived by Emily in spite of the darkness, was said to have reduced the variety and impressiveness of the displays. On the occasion when two senior SPR members attended as guests (Professor Morris and Dr John Beloff) one of the mediums was feeling under par, and one of the visitors subsequently felt unwell, although he experienced no ill effects during the sitting. The phenomena that evening were the weakest of all the 26 sittings MK, who was present, experienced. There has very recently been interesting evidence that the personality of an experimenter may affect an experiment to test ESP (Wiseman, 1998), and hence can in some way be a contributory factor to its success or failure.

It was noteworthy, too, that in the two Californian sittings MK attended (see Appendix F), one mainly for interested scientists in the San Francisco area, and the other in Los Angeles, where many of the sitters were associated with local spiritualist churches or their friends, the phenomena were more spectacular in the latter, although in both cases the sitters were unknown to the Group, and the controls were identical. Some of this difference might have been attributable to the fact that the former sitting was in a wholly unknown location and room, and was anticipated with no small apprehension on the part of the Group who felt themselves to be on trial before a number of sitters likely to be more critical and suspicious than those in Los Angeles. Although both sittings were deemed successful by all the sitters with whom MK discussed the event immediately afterwards, in that both produced remarkable phenomena apparently defying normal explanation, it would not be unreasonable to attribute at least some of the superiority of the second to the more positive, or perhaps less critical, attitudes of the participants.

Throughout this Report we have felt obliged to discuss a criticism the underlying assumption of which we must challenge, even though it is perhaps the commonest of all the implicit doubts: that the detection of one or more defects in the protocol for an experiment is good enough evidence that not only that experiment but scores of others in the series of which it forms part are therefore flawed, and consequently valueless. Even those who acknowledge that it is essential to consider evidence in its entirety find it difficult to do so in practice. To examine each item for perceived defects is not only permissible but essential, since the detection of fraud at any stage and in any experiment could quite properly cast doubt on the authenticity of the lot. But to examine each one with the aim of showing that some additional safeguard was desirable – even though no evidence has been found to show that it would have affected the outcome – and on this ground to reject the entirety is unacceptable. Such a basis would make it virtually impossible ever to provide convincing evidence of anything in the spontaneous case category.

The questionable logic of such an approach can best be illustrated by a close look at the film strip experiments. For reasons which it would be necessary to reiterate only for those who have failed to study the foregoing Chapters, there was no consistent protocol. It is acknowledged that in all the instances in which the principal investigators were involved, there were departures from the ideal. In some cases the films had been bought by or given to the Group rather than bought by the experimenters. Despite care taken to examine the packaging for signs of tampering, that fact is an acknowledged procedural defect. Likewise the fact that in some cases the film cartridge remained inside a box, one made by the Group themselves, and placed on the table rather than held in the hands of an experimenter, might be considered similarly defective, despite the obstacles to interference presented by the padlock and, in some cases, the circumferential drawing round the base of box and padlock to preclude physical displacement (see especially Appendix K). Had a single, identical flaw been common to all experiments there would be merit in the argument that all must be rejected. But this was not the case. Whatever ruse was adopted to overcome the precautions attending one such experiment would have been useless for others. The fraud argument, in other words, must presuppose a range of different methods of effecting the tricks, for none of which we found any direct evidence.

This point has been expressed most forcefully in G. N. M. Tyrrell's celebrated study of apparitions (Tyrrell, 1973, p.30):–

> All the evidence we come across in real life is faulty to a greater or lesser extent; and the only question of importance is how good the evidence is; not whether it is perfect or imperfect. Evidence is a matter of degree.
>
> Since we are bound in this imperfect world to deal with evidence which falls short of theoretical perfection, the question of whether or not cases may rightly be regarded as forming a faggot would seem to depend on the standard of evidence which they reach individually. If the sticks have any strength in them at all, they will be to some extent stronger collectively than singly. But if every stick is entirely rotten, then the faggot will be just as rotten as the individual sticks.

This lengthy examination of what may be considered by readers a remarkable range of phenomena was originally prepared in the confident expectation that, once the initial task of establishing authenticity had been completed, an indefinite series of further sittings would enable us to examine more deeply some of the ontological and perceptual aspects associated with such phenomena. Our expectations, and to all appearances those of the Group, were dashed by the inexplicable events of the autumn of 1998. These form no part of this Report, and do not affect its conclusions, but we must record our deep sense of disappointment that so promising and fruitful an investigation had to be prematurely terminated.

CONCLUSION

It is now two years since we had what proved to be our final sitting with the Scole Group, and a good time to attempt to sum up our feelings at this distance about the investigation. We mention initially a number of unanswered questions. Many of these have been touched upon in earlier chapters, and are summarised now to emphasise that they still concern us.

The first question relates to the identity of the supposed communicators whose messages the Team claimed to relay to us. Were they, as we were led to believe, past members of the SPR, in particular F. W. H. Myers and others involved in the Cross-Correspondences? If so, why were they reluctant fully to reveal their identities? Why were we never able to speak to them directly through the mediums, but only through the intermediary of members of the Team? We were given to understand that if they revealed their identitities we would waste time speculating on whether or not they were who they said they were, rather than devoting our attention to the actual material produced. However, such speculation was inevitable anyway, and the more information we were given, the more fruitful it would have been. In addition, as we have shown in Chapters IV and V, we were frequently given clues (or 'crumbs' as they were called) designed to lead us to the work of these very communicators. If this was an attempt to help us discover their identities for ourselves, and thus to provide evidence of their survival, the attempt attracts a number of criticisms.

Chief among these is the fact that the clues we were given related to material which was reasonably accessible in the public domain. Many of these clues related to information in Sir Oliver Lodge's *The Survival of Man* (see our Chapter IV). Lodge's book, although first published in 1909, went through numerous reprints, and copies are therefore not difficult to obtain. Further, if one of the intentions (as with the Cross-Correspondences) was to eliminate the possibility of telepathy from the living, why choose this book, which was and is in DF's library? By the same token, why were we given clues which could be solved from the *SPR Proceedings*, complete copies of which are available in the SPR library visited regularly by all three of us, and many copies of which we have in our own libraries? Why did the SPR communicators, if such they were, not give us clues to obscure material hidden in the SPR archives in the Cambridge University Library, and which was accessible only to SPR investigators such as ourselves? It could be argued that discarnate individuals have little memory of earth life, and thus can draw only upon things with which they were very familiar, such as perhaps the Lodge book and old copies of the *Proceedings*. But although the evidence from other investigations (see e.g. William James in Murphy & Ballou, 1960) is that earth memories, if they exist after death, are quirky and incomplete (see also our Chapter XV), we cannot fall back upon this as a clinching argument. All we can say is that our evidence, although some may feel it points towards survival, will not carry conviction in this area for everyone.

Similarly, the two Ruth films raise unanswered questions. If Wordsworth himself (or one of his admirers such as Myers) was attempting to communicate, why did he give us a version of the poem *Ruth* which, although obscure and not anthologised, happened to appear in the very material photocopied in a 1960s Christies' catalogue? It is right to argue that this catalogue is difficult to come by, but equally right to argue that this is so only if one sets out deliberately to find a copy. It is not difficult to come by if one already chances to have a copy, or happens to have seen it on a friend's bookshelves (it is not fanciful to suggest that people tend to keep Christies' catalogues). Why not give us material which escapes this criticism of availability? It could be argued that the poem was given to us because – in particular as reflected in the changes between the different editions – it has particular autobiographical significance for Wordsworth or perhaps for Myers (see our Appendix M), but this remains speculation. It may appeal to some as a possible explanation, but hardly to others. And it is worth saying that although it took MK time and diligence to solve all the clues given in connection with the Ruth films, clues which are hard to solve are not necessarily hard to set.

Turning to the films, let us first consider the Alan box, in which some of the images were produced. Why did we obtain positive results when films were placed in the Alan box but not when they were placed in the Keen box? The former, in spite of the precautions with the paint seals, was arguably not fraudproof; the latter certainly was. The manual controls over the Alan box during certain of the sittings seem sufficient to discount the possibility of fraud, but many would contend that they do not eliminate it as conclusively as the Keen box would have done. It may be argued that a box made by the Group was (leaving aside any possibility of manual access to the contents during sittings) more in tune with the 'energies' that the Team appeared to be using, and thus easier for them to work with. There is some evidence from research into psychometry, however debatable, that objects in ways unknown to science may carry some vestige of their owners or makers (e.g. Beloff, 1993). In that case, the Alan box might have been less of an experimental obstacle to the Team than the Keen box, made as the latter was by a professional carpenter unknown to the Group. Again we can speculate, but we cannot reach unequivocal conclusions.

As for the films themselves, there is the disappointment that we did not quite achieve DF's four-step protocol (e.g. Chapter V). It could be said that we got near enough to it to remove all but the most obstinate of doubts. It could even be said that with the Star film, produced when the film was placed in the Wiseman fraud-proof bag, we actually achieved it. But the Star film was of very poor quality and the images on it of inadequate definition for satisfactory reproduction, and hence considered by the Group not worth bothering to retain. So why, when we were so tantalisingly close to the four-step protocol, was it not achieved? The Team expressed themselves ready to provide us with the irreproachable evidence that they claimed to know we needed. They appeared to recognise and accept our requirements, and to be more than ready to meet them – and more than confident that they could. Yet a small loophole in the evidence always remained (DF is reminded of William James's pronouncement that it seems as if the Almighty has decreed that this area should forever retain its mystery).

Why did the Team not return to the experiments with the Keen box when we suggested it following our final sitting in August 1997? Were they unable to do so? Were they governed by their own wishes to move on in order to obtain even more impressive evidence? Were they concerned about the amount of time that was passing, and the demands that the work was making upon the Group? (Two sittings a week for four years are not undertaken without great commitment and sacrifice.) Were the Team working with a succession of groups of 'scientists' in the afterlife, each of whom were anxious to hurry things forward to their own sphere of interest? Or, if fraud is suspected, did the Group proceed to new tricks (as conjurors would do) each time they suspected we might be close to identifying their methods of deception? Readers will wish to make up their own minds.

On a similar issue, why did the Team not take more account of our concerns regarding controls as the investigation progressed? Each time new phenomena were produced we suggested ways of tightening these controls. Such progressive tightening is part of the scientific method. One obtains results, then submits them to ever-increasing rigour to see if they continue to hold up. We naturally expected that if there were scientists on the other side they would be very well aware of this method, and thus sympathetic to our requests. Yet we sometimes received the impression that by advancing these requests we were seen by the Team as in effect moving the goal posts. And why were experiments not always explained to us beforehand, so that we could make some of our suggestions for adequate controls at the outset rather than subsequently? Yet again, why were our own proposals for experiments not taken up? Perhaps the demands they contained could not be met, yet we were never told the parameters within which the Team were working. Perhaps the Team were themselves unaware what these parameters might be, and were exploring and advancing the boundaries of what was possible. If so, it would have been helpful if this had been explained to us. Instead, we were frequently denied explanations on the grounds that we wouldn't understand them.

While on the subject of controls, the Team's refusal to allow infra-red viewers or image intensifiers into the séance room remains a mystery. Such pieces of equipment, as AE frequently pointed out, only register existing energies; they do not add to them. Thus we could not understand how viewers or intensifiers could interfere with any of the psychic processes used by the Team. Why therefore were we refused leave to employ these elementary safeguards? Was the embargo against them perhaps psychological rather than physical? Were the Team concerned that while using them our attention would be distracted from the phenomena, with the result that we would disrupt the subtle emotional and mental harmony upon which the production of psychic phenomena seems in part to depend? Again, we were never told. It is true that we did not ourselves feel them to be of great value. Even had we used them we would have been reminded by determined critics that conjurors can fool people (particularly – according to oft-repeated but unsubstantiated claims – scientists) under their very noses in broad daylight, let alone in the restricted vision provided by viewers and intensifiers. But all the same, we would like to have been allowed them.

Nevertheless, we did not have particular problems in accepting the need for darkness during sittings. Many known and perfectly normal physical operations, such as the germination of some seeds, can take place only in darkness. For unknown reasons darkness may be necessary for certain psychic phenomena, and darkness should not therefore automatically cast doubt on their reality. Indeed darkness, to the experienced investigator, is not without its advantages in that when vision is restricted the other senses can become more acute. Furthermore, in darkness opportunities by tricksters to distract the attention of investigators (one of the skills of the conjuror) are greatly lessened. In addition, although we were in darkness we had the partial safeguards of the wristbands worn by the Group, and the sporadic illuminations from the so-called spirit lights themselves.

Turning to the content of the films, despite the fact that, as we say in Appendix H, botching is no more evidence of fraud than perfection is evidence against it, could not the Team have anticipated that some of the marks on the photographic images which they produced, and some of the sounds on the tape, would attract the suspicion of critics? Our task and that of the Group to present convincing evidence would obviously have been eased had more care been taken to avoid these artifacts. Perhaps such care was not possible. The very fact of obtaining marks on films under controlled conditions should be remarkable enough in itself. Unfortunately, if even the smallest loophole exists in these controls, critics are bound to subject what appears on the films to particularly detailed scrutiny.

It is as frustrating to us as it must be to readers that we are forced to be left with so many puzzles at the end of this investigation. We would have wished that this were not so. To be so close to final success and yet to have it elude us is an enduring disappointment. Yet in spite of falling short of our ultimate aim, we have we hope presented enough evidence to persuade readers that at the very least the investigation bears comparison with certain other intriguing cases published by the Society, and thus is well worth bringing to wider attention.

It is fair to conclude by taking a further look at the motives for fraud on the part of the Group, and the possibility of effecting it, since fraud is unequivocally the only alternative explanation to genuineness in the present instance.

Often it is said that the motives for fraud in the production of psychic phenomena are so difficult to identify that the apparent lack of them is no argument against its involvement. Yet motives are one of the most important considerations in a court of law, which at the very least suggests they are always worth consideration. We have said (Chapter XV) that in the present instance money does not seem to come into it. In spite of their difficult financial situation (occasioned in no small part by the time devoted to their psychic interests) the Group never asked us for money, and indeed turned down a quite generous offer from the SPR. They have refused to set up a membership list with attendant membership fees for their Spiritual Science Foundation, and have chosen instead simply to sell their magazine, almost certainly at a financial loss, to subscribers. They have made no secret of their methods for producing apparent psychic phenomena, and indeed have compiled a 69-page book, *A Basic Guide to Physical Psychic Phenomena Using Energy*, detailing these methods, which they sell (again probably at a financial loss) to anyone interested. The crystals and glass domes which they offer for sale are priced so modestly that it is clear that the concern is to make these items readily available to other experimenters rather than to profit from them. The Group gives free advice to anyone interested in trying to produce phenomena by the methods they have pioneered. And as we made clear in Chapter XV, they forfeited without hesitation the small income accruing from their seminars at the apparent insistence of the Team.

If money isn't a motive, could fame have been? If the Group could establish the existence of physical phenomena beyond reasonable doubt, their work would compare with that of researchers such as Lodge and Crookes and the other giants of the past. However, the two mediums in the Group showed no taste for personal publicity. As for the Foys, Sandra remained modest and self-effacing throughout the period of our investigation, and although Robin was clearly anxious that the Spiritual Science Foundation should make its mark, it seemed clear to us that this anxiety was due to his belief in the importance of physical mediumship rather than to any desire for self-aggrandisement.

Were there other, less obvious, motives? We made some reference to the qualifications of the investigators in Chapter I, but it is relevant to add at this point that one of us (DF) is a psychologist who has not only specialised in the field of personality studies throughout his professional career but is also qualified in psychological counselling. The career of another of us (MK) was spent working with journalists, the media and politicians, while AE for many years worked and liaised with industrialists and businessmen. All three of us therefore have some professional experience of assessing the motives of others and in identifying their propensity for deception (including self-deception). The two co-investigators who worked most closely with the Group are respectively a lawyer and businessman (HS), and a well-qualified mechanical engineer (WS). Thus like the authors both are hardly strangers to human behaviour. At no point in the experience of any one of us did we detect hidden motives or a hint of duplicity on the part of any member of the Group. On the contrary, it would be difficult to imagine a more open, forthcoming and straightforward group of people. Never once did they even show an inclination to question us about our private lives – with a possible view to feeding the information back to us during the sittings in the guise of mediumistic revelations. As further evidence of the apparent probity of their motives, it is worth quoting their objectives as printed on the opening page of *A Basic Guide to the Development of Physical Psychic Phenomena Using Energy*:–

> [This book] is offered to the public with our combined love for
> mankind and the spirit world, in an effort to help others to
> understand about their own spirituality within the greater scheme
> of the spiritual realms, and to experience for themselves the very
> special spirit-world phenomena in an atmosphere of love and
> harmony as we ourselves do at Scole on a regular basis.

Sceptics may scoff at such sentiments. Others may prefer to treat them with respect.

On the question of fraud itself, it must be understood that for it to take place two things remained essential throughout the sittings, namely *equipment* and *movement*. The Group would have had to operate the former and engage in the latter. Could they have done so? Again the reader must be left to reach his or her own decision, but there are certain considerations upon which such a decision should be based. The first is that the Group would have needed to smuggle the equipment into the séance room (which was invariably available for our detailed inspection at all times) for each of the sittings we attended during the two years of our investigation. They would also have been forced to carry this equipment to the various sittings they held abroad, including those that took place at Ibiza under the watchful eyes of MK and of our fellow-investigators HS and WS, and those that took place in the USA when MK was again present. In addition, as we have stressed already, the equipment required would have had to be elaborate, ingenious, and in some cases expensive and bulky. It would have had to include contraptions (which even AE, as a leading and highly experienced professor of electrical engineering, cannot explain) for fabricating balls of light that audibly struck the table and then reappeared in the quadrants under the table, that rolled across the table top, that varied in size from that of a pea to a large marble, that entered crystals and a light bulb and a glass dome, that could submerge in a glass of water held by DF close to his mouth and directly underneath his inclined head and that could be held by Professor Grattan-Guinness between closed cupped hands, that responded to requests, and that rested on and travelled across the palms of sitters and apparently entered their bodies and produced sensations as of internal movement. It would have to account for diffused patches of light that travelled slowly across the room, that formed small seemingly robed figures which floated above the table, touched the investigators, and then ascended rapidly to the ceiling before disappearing, and that simulated transparent face-like images complete with what appeared to be moving lips.

In addition, the equipment would have had to include the infra-red viewers or image intensifiers essential in order to find the hands etc. of the investigators unerringly and time after time in the dark. It would also have included of necessity extending rods, pseudopods, cassettes of duplicate films, batteries, LEDs, the pieces of lace-like material that were felt when the illuminated figures brushed across our hands, the electric motor (or similar) needed to vibrate the table at very high and sustained frequency, possibly duplicate illuminated armbands, and on occasions the equipment needed to transmit messages onto an audio tape in a microphone-deprived recorder. Not impossible, perhaps, but something of a tall order, and presupposing a lack of elementary observation on the part of the investigators which, if present, should prompt their shamefaced resignation from the Society.

The second consideration to keep in mind is that the movement needed in order to operate this equipment would also present major difficulties. As mentioned in the text and as he would be the first to concede, Robin Foy is not exactly built for agile and stealthy movement around a dark room. In addition, he occupied a seat at each sitting only inches away from AE, who was free to reach out and touch him unexpectedly at any time. Hemmed in as he was on the other side by the unit bearing not only the tape recorder that recorded the sittings but the tape recorder used for the background music and the array of music tapes (which he changed frequently and at precisely the appropriate moments), silent movement of any kind would have presented him with many challenges. Sandra Foy, the other non-medium member of the Group, was invariably placed on DF's left, again only inches away and vulnerable to touch by him at any moment. To remove her armbands and frequently absent herself undetected by him would have presented her with challenges only marginally less than those facing her husband. In addition, as neither Robin nor Sandra Foy was in trance, they could be – and frequently were – without warning engaged by the investigators in conversation. Unfailingly they replied immediately, and from their correct positions. Sceptics may argue that in the darkness the investigators could not identify the positions from which the Foys were speaking. In reply we repeat that senses such as hearing become more acute when one is accustomed to sitting for long periods in darkness. More importantly, as already made clear, Robin Foy was almost rubbing shoulders with AE, while Sandra was in similar proximity to DF. Thus it would have been difficult even for those with less experience than ourselves consistently to be deceived as to their positions in the room.

What of the mediums? If they were responsible for the movement, they would without detection have to manipulate lights at ceiling level one moment then at table level the next, then dive down and circumnavigate the table (the ogival supports prevented access from underneath) in order to touch the thighs of investigators sitting inches from each other. They would have to levitate crystals under the noses of the investigators, fabricate illuminated materialisations on the opposite side of the table from their chairs and allow these materialisations to speed up to the ceiling, kneel soundlessly on the table in order to fake direct voices and masquerade as spirits by shaking – on request – the hands of the investigators, and to put cassettes in these same hands (again on request and without fumbling). They would also need to lean across the table to do nefarious things with films in a locked box (opening and then closing the latter by means of its defective hasp), then replace the box in exactly the marked position from which it had been taken.

They would have variously to produce lights which appear to enter the sitters' bodies and simulate internal movement, manufacture the diffused patches of light that travelled the length of the room in mid-air, materialise – inches from the sitters – perfectly formed hands which appeared to end at the wrists and which picked up crystals and were clearly visible in accompanying 'spirit' lights, and lift up, simultaneously and to full stretch, the arms of two investigators separated from each other by the third investigator (a feat which, due to the distance between the two investigators, would need both mediums acting in concert). They would have to perform perfect and sustained circles in the air with pinpoints of light at some distance from their seats and so fast that the circles appeared unbroken, illuminate large crystals from within, then apparently dematerialise them while leaving perfect illuminated simulacrums behind to be seen and their emptiness 'felt' by the investigators, swivel the table around soundlessly and then vibrate it at high speed under the fingers of the investigators, and much more besides. On each movement from their positions they would have soundlessly to remove their luminous wristbands and leave them on the table (or obscure them and provide duplicates to place on the table), and then replace them around their wrists on their return. And they would have to accomplish all of the above movements while commenting upon the phenomena (and responding at a moment's notice to unexpected questions about them) in simulated trance from their normal seated positions across the table. And all this by mediums who lack the slight figures best suited for clandestine movement.

We are not saying that any of this undetected movement is impossible: we are simply asking the reader to assess the balance of possibilities. In leaving readers to assess this balance for themselves and to draw their own conclusions we are well aware that determined sceptics will always insist on normal explanations. They 'know' that psychic phenomena cannot happen, and are therefore unprepared to countenance even the possibility that they might. And it must be confessed that, life being what it is, there are always loopholes for such sceptics to identify in any investigation. Even had we achieved in full our coveted four-step protocol, it would fail to satisfy all of them. We would be asked if we could be sure the employees of the commercial outfit responsible for developing the films were above suspicion. Might not one or more of them be in league with the Scole Group? And what about the shop where we purchased the film? Could we be sure that another confederate hadn't sold us a prepared film, or that one of the Scole Group hadn't tailed us undetected to the shop and covertly switched the film at or just after the point of sale? And how could we be sure that the fraud-proof box or other container into which we put our film wasn't switched once we arrived at the Foys? After all, we spent some little time in conversation with them before each sitting, and a good conjuror can pick a pocket with impunity. How did we know this hadn't happened to us, and the box or container abstracted and replaced with a duplicate, or opened by some expert locksmith and a substitute, suitably marked film inserted? Did we take the precaution when in the Foys' home of always standing and walking in a circle, so that MK could guard AE's pockets while AE guarded DF's and DF guarded MK's? (The potential for humour in such a set-up would almost have made it worth contemplating.) And how do we know that we didn't fall asleep during the sitting, so that our precious box could be taken from our nerveless fingers? Could we perhaps have been slipped a sleeping potion to ensure we dozed off? (Incidentally, sleepiness was never a problem for any of us during the sittings.)

Horror of horrors, could one of the investigators be suspect? Could he have formed a romantic relationship with one or other of the female members of the Scole Group? If the charge could be directed against Sir William Crookes, why not against one of us? Could either or both these ladies have used sexual charms to distract the investigators at critical points during the sittings? If the accusation could be made in all seriousness against the portly 50-year-old Palladino, surely it could be levelled against the unquestionably more comely Scole ladies? And so on and on.

Whatever our defence, the determined critic would ultimately offer a sad shake of the head and utter the words that have formed the epitaph of so many past investigations – "If only you had thought (or been able) to control for . . . " Field work in psychical research is so vulnerable to this kind of dismissive verdict that one may well question if in fact it is worth the major investment of time, energy and money which it involves. Our answer is that in any area of human behaviour, effects that are only observable under the tightly controlled conditions of a laboratory are not really of enduring use or interest. If psychic abilities exist, then they may reasonably be supposed to happen not just in the laboratory but in real life, whether in the séance room or in more familiar surroundings. If they do, it is equally reasonable to propose that they are worth looking into, that efforts be made to find the ways in which they are compatible with the rest of our known science: indeed ways in which they may not only add to our scientific knowledge, but augment our understanding of what it is to be human, and whether or not life carries meaning outside that attributed to it by reductionist philosophies.

It was with these considerations in mind that we conducted the Scole investigation, with these considerations that we have compiled this report, and it is with these considerations that we would undertake further such investigations should the opportunity arise. In the meantime, we will be more than happy to co-operate with any conjurors who wish to try and replicate in our presence, accurately and under comparable conditions, the effects we witnessed at Scole.

Our final word is that whatever is made of our investigation by others, now and in years to come, we feel privileged to have been allowed to undertake it.

APPENDIX A:
SUMMARY OF FILM SITTINGS AT SCOLE

Explanatory Note: The numbering in the first column relates only to those sittings at or from which films were produced, whether successful or failures. The figures in square brackets in the date column refer to the investigators' original transcript numbers. Not all sittings have transcripts. Those marked MK refer to sittings where he was not accompanied by DF and AE; that marked DF1 relates to a sitting where AE and MK were not present.

No.	Date	Film type	Present	Developed	Details
1	13/1/96 [3]	Polaroid	AE, MK, DF	same evening	MK-bought Polaroid film. Placed in sealed safety bag (ex-Wiseman). Star-light images and cog-wheel shape. Evidential but poor quality. Safety bag said to create problems.
2	17/2/96 [4]	Pola-chrome	AE, MK, DF	same evening	MK's own film (ASA 40, very slow). Tub on table 5–8 cm from MK. Result mainly blank, but with Greek lettering on green background.
3	16/3/96 [5]	Polapan (B&W)	AE, MK, DF	next sitting	Film brought by MK, sealed in Wiseman's large security bag by AE. Second, Polablue, film left in tub on table.
4	13/4/96 [6]	a. Polapan	AE, MK, DF	same evening	(a) 16/3 security bag film developed: only 'night star' patterns.
		b. Polablue		next sitting	(b) left on 16/3 with signed sticky label cover for one month, produced Diotima film.
5	18/5/96 [7]	Polapan	AE, MK, DF	next sitting	MK bought film. Safety strip sealers placed by MK on tub, put in Wiseman security bag, signed, and left (see 22nd June 1996, ChV reference to blank results.

6	25/5/96	Polaroid	D. Fair-bairn & 9 others	same evening	Fairbairn selected one of about 12 Foy Polaroid packs. Marked the tub. Retained possession. Placed tub in-accessibly on table. Produced Latin message in mirror image.
7	31/5/96	Polaroid	W.& K. Schnitt-ger	same evening	Polaroid ex Foy stock. Opened by WS. Tub held in his or KS's hands. Blurred first German poem film result.
8	15/6/96	Polapan	AE, MK	next sitting	One of three remaining Foy Polapan stock. Selected by MK, left on table with sticky label, Sellotaped and signed; together with Polapan from 18/5 sitting. Both blank.
9	13/7/96	Pola-chrome	A.Roy, MK, AE	same evening	AR opened MK-bought pack of three and selected one, placing luminous tab on tub side. Tub on table adjoining north tab (MK's seat). Unmoved through-out. Produced Latin Golden Chain *(Perfectio)* message.
10	26/7/96	Pola-chrome	WS, KS	same evening	Film drawn from Foy's remaining Polachrome stock. Tub held in WS's hand throughout. Second (clear) German poem film produced.
11	10/8/96	Polaroid	AE, MK, DF	same evening	Film drawn from Foys' remaining Polaroid stock. Held throughout sitting by DF in tub marked with penknife, but unsuccessful development. Machine or film malfunction suspected as cause.
12	9/11/96	Pola-chrome	AE, MK, DF	2 days later	(a) one of 2 remaining Foy Polaroid packs at Scole opened; tub put in new Scole (Alan) box, padlocked, left with DF until his return on 11/11 (see below). (b) Experimental Kodachrome 200 film, MK bought; left in tub on table.

13	11/11/96	Pola-chrome	DF, I.Slack	same evening	The (a) film from 9/11 was retained in locked box by DF throughout, opened and developed: it produced first Ruth film.
14	18/11/96	Koda-chrome	MK	next Monday	This was the (b) film left on 9/11 experimentally. It produced second Ruth film when developed by Kodak at Wimbledon.
15	22/11/96	Pola-chrome	WS, KS, & Dr Schaer	same evening	WS's own new film, own padlock. Locked box in WS's hands throughout. *Wie und Staub* film produced.
16	6/12/96	Pola-chrome	WS, KS	same evening	WS's own film. Placed in Scole box, padlocked. Held by WS throughout. Developed showing X-ray-like reproductions of fingers and thumbs.
17	11/1/97	Koda-chrome	DF, IS, MK	next Monday	MK bought 2 films, padlocked by DF & MK in Alan and MK boxes, left on table. Drawing to help AE improve germanium gadget promised on film. Un-padlocked films put in sealed Jiffybags and developed by Kodak. Film in Alan box successful: electrical diagram, instructions and signatures
18	17/1/97	Pola-chrome	WS, KS	same evening	WS's film. Alan box locked with WS padlock. Keys in WS's car. Box on table on marked paper. Film marked before processing. Dragon & *Quadrans Muralis* etc. film produced.
19	24/1/97	Koda-chrome	MK, A.Gauld D.West	next Monday	Two new MK films ex-Wiseman to West, padlocked in Alan and MK boxes by DW and AG. Left on marked paper in centre of table. Tub in Alan box removed after sitting for Jiffybag sealing and taken with MK box with combination padlock to Kodak. Latter blank; former produced Daguerre, etc. message.

APPENDIX B: DETAILS OF ALL SITTINGS

No.	Date	Persons attending	Special notes
1	2nd Oct. 1995	Ralph Noyes (RN) Arthur Ellison (AE) Montague Keen (MK)	Plus all six members of the Group
2	16th Dec. 1995	RN, AE, MK	Plus all six members of the Group
3	3rd Jan. 1996	David Fontana (DF) AE, MK	Four Group members henceforth
4	13th Jan. 1996	AE, DF, MK	
5	17th Feb. 1996	DF, AE, MK	
6	16th March 1996	Ditto	
7	13th April 1996	Ditto	
8	18th May 1996	Ditto	
9	25th May 1996	Denzil Fairbairn et al. (see App.C)	A 'seminar' sitting
10	31st May 1996	Walter & Karin Schnittger (WS, KS)	
11	15th June 1996	AE, MK	
12	13th July 1996	AE, MK, Archie Roy	
13	26th July 1996	WS & KS	
14	10th Aug. 1996	DF, AE, MK	
15	14th Sept. 1996	DF, AE, MK	
16	9th Nov. 1996	DF, AE, MK	
17	11th Nov. 1996	DF, I Slack (IS)	First 'Ruth' film
18	18th Nov. 1996	MK	The second Ruth, first Kodachrome film
19	22nd Nov. 1996	WS & KS, Hans Schaer (HS)	'Wie der Staub' film produced

20	6th Dec. 1996	WS & KS	X-ray-type imprints on film
21	14th Dec. 1996	DF, MK, Bernard Carr (BC)	
22	3rd Jan. 1997	DF, BC, AE, MK	
23	11th Jan. 1997	DF, IS, MK	
24	17th Jan. 1997	WS, KS	Dragon film produced
25	24th Jan. 1997	MK, Donald West, Alan Gauld	Daguerre (Moon) Kodachrome film
26	8th Feb. 1997	DF, IS, MK, WS	
27	21st Feb. 1997	MK, Rupert Sheldrake	
28	28th Feb. 1997	MK, Robert Morris, John Beloff	
29	4th March 1997	MK	
30	7th March 1997	MK, Ivor Grattan-Guiness	
31	15th March 1997	DF, AE, MK	
32	27th March 1997	MK	San Francisco sitting
33	5th April 1997	MK	Los angeles sitting (Appendix F)
34	29th June 1997	MK, WS, KS Hans Schaer et al.	First Ibiza sitting
35	1st July 1997	MK, WS, KS Hans Schaer et al.	Second Ibiza sitting
36	16th Aug. 1997	DF, AE, MK	Rachmaninoff tape

Note: There was a special sitting on March 28th 1998, at which Dr Hans Schaer was the sole investigator.

APPENDIX C: THE FAIRBAIRN TESTIMONY

This account of the precise circumstances in which the Latin mirror image film (Reflexionis; see Chapter V) was made was written by Denzil Fairbairn and circulated to and signed by all other participants. The wording is therefore his own.

1   The following account relates to an experimental sitting with the Scole Group (i.e. the New Spiritual Science Foundation) on Saturday, 25th May 1996, following a seminar conducted for ten people by the Scole Group, which comprised Sandra and Robin Foy and two trance mediums known as Diana and Alan. Although we witnessed and experienced several phenomena, including energy lights, direct voice communication and various touches from apparently materialised forms during the sitting, which took place in a cellar beneath one of the ground floor reception rooms in the Foys' home, I am confining myself to facts of which there is tangible evidence not dependent on subjective experience or testimony. I am confining this statement to the facts surrounding the production of two exposed frame-lengths on a sealed roll of 35mm film which is tangible, can still be viewed (and has been copied) and which in my view could have been brought into existence only through Spirit intercession. My fellow sitters, who had not previously met as a group, and some of whom were therefore unknown to one another, were Kay and Joan Fairbairn, Derek Cooper, Graham Marshall, Sue Goodson, Alan and Barbara Mayze, and Norbert and Marguerette Wehling.

2   During the seminar which preceded the sitting, Robin Foy announced that the Spirit communicators had agreed that a roll of unexposed film should be taken into the cellar, and that I had been selected to be instrumental in facilitating this experiment. Just before the sitting Robin Foy invited me into an annexe room adjoining the living room where I was followed by Derek Cooper and Norbert Wehling. Both witnessed what transpired. I was asked to select one unopened 12-exposure 35mm Polaroid 'Polapan' black and white slide film from among about ten or twelve identically boxed films kept in a lightproof attaché case along with a selection of other types of Polaroid films, all similarly sealed in their manufacturers' packaging.

3   I selected one package or carton, without prompting, and closely examined the outer container before unsealing one end. I was satisfied that the sealed ends had not been tampered with. The carton was sealed in the normal fashion with several spots of adhesive, obviously machine-applied. Inside the outer box was the instruction leaflet, the cassette containing the chemicals and emulsions required to develop the film,

and a black plastic cylindrical container with a grey-coloured pop-off lid inside which was a typical 35mm roll of film in its metal sheathing case. I am quite familiar with the original type of Polaroid film in its flat-pack form which is developed inside the 'luncheon-box'-sized camera, but I was unaware that 35mm slide film was also available for near-instantaneous development.

4   After examining this roll, which looked identical to any other roll of film, Robin Foy asked me to return it to its protective plastic cylinder, reseal the pop-off lid and make an identifiable mark on a sticky address label, which I then used to seal the cylinder containing the roll of film. Once this was completed I returned the developing cassette to the outer box together with the instruction leaflet and placed it in the attaché case for safe keeping until after the end of the experimental session. Robin asked me to retain the sealed film in its container in my possession. At no stage did he or anyone else handle the material.

5   I placed the film container in my trouser pocket and descended to the cellar room with the others. Round the perimeter of the room were 14 chairs. Robin asked us to arrange ourselves so that we were seated alternately man/woman. Our four hosts were located at one end of the rectangular room; the rest of us occupied the remaining seats. Also in the room was a circular table between 4 and 5 feet in diameter, about 2 feet high. Little more than a 6-inch gap separated the edge of the table and the knees of those sitters who were on the narrower side of the room. On Robin Foy's left was a small table carrying a cassette player housing the music tapes, and a tape recorder used to record the experimental sitting. On the central table stood a glass dome which, with its wooden plinth and acrylic plastic stand, measured about 18 to 20 inches in height. Also on the table was a beautiful crystal, a plastic bowl containing a ping-pong ball and a plastic bag which (we were told) related to another ongoing experiment. Before the central light was switched off, the bowl and ball were placed on the floor on the side of the table opposite our hosts.

6   Once everyone was seated, and our hosts had wrapped Velcro bands with luminous strips round their wrists, I was asked to place the sealed container wherever I wanted on the central table. I selected a place behind the glass dome and near the edge furthest away from the positions occupied by our hosts such that, in my opinion, it would have been impossible for any of them to have either reached across or walked round the table to retrieve the film or even to have been able to see it in the dark. The luminous wristbands allowed every movement of our hosts to be monitored. Apart from the time Robin Foy left his chair to switch the light on at the end of the session neither he nor his co-hosts moved from their allotted positions during the time the room was in darkness.

7   Towards the end of the session a spirit communicator called Joseph said there had been some success with the experimental photographic film and added, perhaps jocularly, that, when the light was restored, I should give the container a little shake to make sure the film roll had not disappeared. Despite his jocularity I did shake the container. It was still there.

8   The sealed roll had been in its place on the table throughout the session, which lasted about two-and-a-quarter hours. Having shaken the tub I put it back in my pocket, and all fourteen of us returned upstairs for refreshments. Immediately thereafter we were invited round a worktop in the kitchen area of the refreshment room where there was a black rectangular box-like object which was plugged into a mains socket. Alan, one of the Scole team, lifted the lid of the machine and removed the developing cassette from its outer box, placing it into the machine. I then took the film tub from my pocket and removed the roll of film from its sealed container, enabling him to load this into the machine too. This was the first time anyone else had touched the film since the box was first opened before the session. Having loaded the film into the machine, and before closing the lid, Alan explained that there would follow a simple chemical development process inside the machine lasting a couple of minutes – a process similar to that which takes place inside a photographic booth.

9   A buzzer indicated that the development process had finished. Alan removed the film and put the developing cassette into a waste bin. The film was carefully unwound and drawn slowly through a magnified viewer. The stretch occupied by the first few frames was blank. Then there appeared a picture occupying a full frame. Initially it looked like an outline diagram resembling a Christmas tree on its side; the background area was light grey in colour. The roll of film was unwound a little further to reveal another frame in the form of a mirror-image of the first frame, save that the lighter background areas in each film were different shapes. Sandra Foy, who was also viewing the pictures, suddenly realised that the lines composing the pattern were in fact themselves made up from tiny writing. We scrutinised the remainder of the film, but no further images were apparent. Alan then prepared two slides from the two developed frames so that they could both be projected onto a screen which was being set up in the library room. When projected it was obvious that writing made up the pattern in each frame, and that not simply was the pattern mirrored but the written message in each frame was also mirror-imaged.

10 I must emphasise that no camera was involved, that the film was rolled onto a spool inside a plastic container which had not been handled by anyone else from the time I removed it from its manufacturer's outer packaging until it was handed to Alan for insertion in the developing

machine, and that pictures appeared only in positions roughly where frames three and four would normally have been located on the roll. The text of the writing was:–

Reflexionis, Lucis in Terra, et in Planetis

None of the fourteen people who witnessed this was familiar with Latin. I understand the words translate as:–

Reflecting clearly into the Earth and into the Planets

but at the time the nature of the message was unrecognisable to those present.

11 All the above is based on extensive notes made by me, Denzil James Fairbairn, at my home at 94 Windmill Road, Raunds, Northants, NN9 6SJ and embodied in a lengthy faxed communication to Robin Foy dated May 27. I testify to the truth of the above.

APPENDIX D: DOUBTS OVER THE DRAGON FILM

The strip of 35mm film which emerged from the Polaroid developer at Scole in the presence of Walter and Karin Schnittger (WS & KS) on 17th January 1997, and described in Chapter VI, had more than one significant feature. None of the three principal investigators was present. We have the testimony signed by the Schnittgers the following day, and on which this account is based. The film, a PolaChrome colour slide, was bought by them direct from Jessops of Leicester and, together with their own padlock, it remained throughout in their possession. WS opened the package, placed the film in its plastic container into the Alan box, locked it and locked the keys in his car while KS guarded the box. WS then placed the box in the middle of the table on a sheet of paper round which he drew an outline, including the position of the padlock where it rested on the paper, and then with KS checked the room. They were then joined by the Group, wearing as usual their luminous wristbands. On the evidence of the wristbands, WS and KS were satisfied that no sitters left their positions during the sitting. The box and padlock were seen to be in their marked positions at the end of the sitting. WS then opened it, removed the tub, inspected the inside of the film processing unit, removed and marked both the film and the chemical processing cassette, placed both into the processor aided by Alan, and then watched the film developed, finally identifying the film by checking for the presence of his mark (see Plate 9).

Images found to have appeared on the film (the Dragon film) during the sitting possessed a number of characteristics which later aroused the suspicions briefly referred to earlier in Chaper VI and discussed in Appendix H. Rather more puzzling was the meaning the images were intended to convey. A number of hermetic authorities were consulted, and while most recognised the symbols, none could find a coherent message. It would take us beyond the limited scope of this Report to analyse the meanings attached to each of them – there appears not to be universal agreement even on this – but at least one of the diagrams was the subject of a slightly acerbic comment by Emily when MK, during a solo sitting on March 5th, suggested that the presence of such symbols appearing to convey messages might, however veridical, create the impression that we were being "dragged back to the occult mysteries of medievalism that enlightened science is trying to escape". He was going on to suggest that they might strike as strange those who were looking for messages of goodwill designed to elevate man's spiritual consciousness, etc., whereupon Emily in a rare display of impatience commented: "So a word meaning God on a message on a film isn't good enough for anyone then?" (One of the symbols is generally thought to be a kind of Hebrew acronym, as indicated by dots above the letters, of a word meaning the name of the Lord, which in Hebraic tradition may never be pronounced.) It was made clear that the Team, while aware of the contents, had no control over the individual or group responsible for exercising their right to place their own thought images on the films. A discussion about the mechanism by which the film was produced served merely to indicate the essentially interpretative functions of the Team. It also displayed their tendency to give undertakings to make further inquiries in the expectation that we would later be given clearer answers, but this often proved not to be the case, save where more clues were required for the solution of puzzles, some of them connected with the films, some not.

In addition to the Dragon film, the Schnittgers were also given the two German poem films (see Chapter V) at one of their private sittings with the Group. They played an important role in the sittings at Scole, as well as during the two sittings held in Ibiza (see Chapter XI). In the brief earlier reference to the precautions taken before and during the production of the German poem film, it was noted that the only possible criticism of the protocol was that the film used had been selected by WS from stock in the keeping of the Foys. This fault was corrected later for what proved to be the 'Wie der Staub' film [see Plate 6], the importance of which merits a more detailed statement. Accordingly we give below WS's account, in his own words, of the sitting which produced this film. We also reproduce the substance of two further statements signed by the Schnittgers and relating to subsequent sittings, but omitting repetition of previously described precautions. The statements are written by Walter Schnittger:–

The Wie der Staub Film

The week before our sitting on 22nd November 1996, Robin Foy telephoned to inform us that a film experiment was planned for the following week, when both of us, along with Hans Schaer, were due to attend. He asked me to buy a Polaroid Polachrome 35mm Colour Slide film and a padlock which could lock the film in a wooden container. He asked us not to handle the film more than was necessary. I bought a safety lock, packed in its original sealed container, in Norwich DIY market the same day, and ordered three such films, one with 12 and the other two with 36 exposures, from Jessop's in Norwich, from whose store they were picked up by Karin the following Thursday. All remained in our exclusive possession until our arrival with the films in a plastic bag, for the sitting on Friday, 22nd November.

At the Foys' home I carefully examined the very solid wooden container [the Alan box] placed on the coffee table of the living room, noting that it could just accommodate one film roll in its plastic tub. I removed the padlock and two keys from their package and placed them on the table in front of me. I selected the 12-exposure roll, removed the developing cassette and tub from their packaging and immediately placed the tub with the unopened film in the box, which I padlocked right away. I left the chemical cassette in the room. I took the locked box with me to my car where I deposited the two padlock keys, handing over my car keys to Hans, who remained with us throughout. All members of the Group witnessed this procedure.

From the moment of locking the box until the time the film was processed after the sitting, the box was solely in my hands. It was never allowed to stand alone and was not even touched by anyone else. In the cellar I held the box on my lap, with both hands until, having told him I was right-handed, I was asked by Edwin to place the box in my right hand in such a way that my forefinger was on the lid with the lower part of the finger feeling the locking mechanism. The padlock itself was in the palm of my hand, with the thumb holding the left side and the remaining three fingers the right side of the box.

With my hand in this position, Edwin asked me to place the box on the table so that the base rested on the table. My right arm, from hand to elbow, rested on the table while my left hand remained on my left knee. During the several minutes which followed, with my hand in this position, the table vibrated several times, sometimes so strongly that the crystals on the table started to rattle. I felt a light sensation in my arm and leg, like a low voltage, and experienced very frequent touches on my right hand, particularly around the finger tips but also passing over the back of my hand. On one occasion the pullover and shirt on my right arm were pulled up and a finger circled my wrist; then the clothes were pulled down again. It felt as though at least five hands were touching my right arm at the same time, some of them quite powerful, as if they were seeking to pull fingers away from the container (which I did not allow) or to apply force to the container, so that some effort was needed to keep it in place. I once experienced a sensation of coldness as though a piece of ice had been placed on the back of my hand.

Throughout this period I maintained a commentary on my experiences or exchanged information with Edwin, who repeatedly wanted to know how I felt. On one occasion when I said I felt well, I received a 'good boy' pat on my left shoulder. I also received several touches on my knees. After several minutes I was allowed to replace the box on my lap and relax my grip, but the experiment was then repeated, although this time there were fewer touches and no real 'battling' for control of the container, as before. I was then asked to replace the box on my lap, and hold it in both hands until after the sitting, when I retrieved my car key from Hans, took the box to my car to pick up the padlock keys, and returned to make a close examination of the processing machine to ensure that it was empty. I then inserted the cartridge containing the chemical gel and finally unlocked the box, removed the plastic tub, extracted the film and inserted it into the processor. This I then closed and started the clearly audible processing mechanism, which took about two minutes. I removed the film, which we all inspected. This showed text, symbols and lines over the whole length of the film. together with some German words like Wie and Staub in handwriting and strange mirror-written text.

The 'X-ray' Film

Karin and I, this time without the presence of Hans Schaer, attended a further sitting on Friday, 6th December 1996, employing precisely the same protocol as described above, except that I locked the padlock keys in my car, locked the car and retained the car key. Again the box was held in my right hand on the table, when I was touched several times, although less force was applied to my hand than on the earlier occasion. What emerged from the processor (see Plate 7) had the appearance of a series of X-rays of my fingers and thumb.

The Dragon Film

This film was the outcome of a further sitting together with Karin on 17th January 1997. The preliminary procedure was similar to the foregoing, except that the box was under Karin's observation when I went to the car to lock up the padlock keys. It was not touched by anyone else during that brief period. This time the Group remained upstairs while I placed the box in the centre of the table in such a way that the opposite corners of the box were directed to the four cardinal points as indicated by the four luminous tabs. A plain sheet of A4 paper had already been placed in the centre to allow me to describe an inked outline round the box and hanging padlock. At Robin's request both of us carefully checked the room but found nothing suspicious.

During the sitting which followed none of the six participants moved from their seats, as judged from the positions of the luminous armbands worn by the Group. At the end of the session I checked to ensure that the outlines on the centre paper corresponded precisely with the position of the box and its lock. Upstairs, Karin again kept the box under close observation while I retrieved the padlock keys from my car. After ensuring that the processing unit was empty, I marked both the chemical processing spool and the film with my special shortened signature and, with Alan's assistance, placed both into the processor, after which I identified the signature on the film, which contained the hermetic symbols (see Plate 9).

APPENDIX E: BUGLE-PLAYING EVIDENCE:
A STATEMENT BY DR HANS SCHAER

The experience and testimony of Dr Hans Schaer, a member of the SPR and one of our co-investigators, is of sufficient importance to warrant fairly detailed treatment. Not only has Dr Schaer, a Swiss lawyer/businessman residing in Küsnacht, near Zürich, and the owner of a holiday home in the Mediterranean island of Ibiza, sat with the Scole Group on thirteen occasions, but his sittings have been in his two homes and in the premises of the Parapsychological Society of Zürich in Zürich, as well as at Scole itself.

All six members of the original group were his guests for sittings at his Ibiza residence in October 1995, and accordingly when the four persons then comprising the Group were invited back the following summer they felt at home in the farmhouse which their host has converted into the attractive, and geographically fairly remote, holiday retreat described in Chapter XI. The Group had two sittings, on 28th June and 1st July, 1996. The following account relates only to the first sitting, since control conditions applying to a film experiment during the second sitting were less than perfect. We reproduce below the substance of Dr Schaer's principal testimony as conveyed to us in signed statements, and to which he has sent us his written confirmation. It is based on a verbatim transcript of a taped interview conducted by RF, and on subsequent clarifying statements sent to us by Dr Schaer and supported by tape recordings of the two-and-a-half-hour sitting.

The room in which the two sittings took place, the main living room of the house, had all doors and windows very carefully covered with either black plastic or plasticised black cloth. The main door was locked in three different ways. None of the other doors leading into the room could have been opened without the removal of the attached material. I sat alone with the four members of the Group. No one else was in either the room or the house. We sat round a table of about one meter diameter on which were placed five crystals, the largest in the centre, and the others round the edge, pointing directly to north, south, east and west, as determined by Robin Foy's compass, which he had brought with him for the purpose of correct alignment. Robin sat at the west end; I sat on his left; his wife Sandra next to me, and then Alan and Diana to complete the circle. All the Group wore their illuminated armband strips. No light could be seen anywhere in the room.

I have a collection of trumpets at my home in Küsnacht, one of which I had with me in Ibiza. Before the sitting I had asked Robin whether he thought it would be possible to establish a musical contact with the spirit side, since we had already experienced our regular oral contact, both through the mediums and via 'direct voice'. My hope had been to get Louis Armstrong, or some other well-known jazz musician, to play a solo for me and make himself recognisable that way. Would the spirits be willing to go along with such an experiment? He replied: "You can always ask. I suggest you take the trumpet with you into the sitting room and place it beside your chair on the floor." That is precisely what I did. The trumpet was the only musical instrument in the whole house.

When I was asked during the sitting whether I had any questions, therefore, I asked about the possibility of the musical communication. The answer from the spirit side was that they were completely unprepared for such an experiment, since they had concentrated on the film experiments throughout recent sittings. Nevertheless they said they would see what they could do. The spirit voice told me to put the trumpet on the table. I lifted it up and laid it on the table in such a way that the mouthpiece was parallel with the edge of the table, lying directly in front of me. A spirit light approached the trumpet and hovered over it, distributing enough light to enable everyone to see that the instrument was lying on the table. After a while, again in total darkness, a few light trumpet sounds were heard, indicating that someone was operating the valves of the trumpet. At that stage I felt a breeze over my face, and it was apparent that the trumpet was being blown into. A full note was produced, followed by three or four other notes. These were followed by a number of sequences of various sounds, which sounded like military bugle notes, but no melody was played. When we put the light on at the end of the session, the trumpet had moved about 10 cm towards the centre of the table.

I must comment that the Scole Group, to say nothing of the spirit Team, could not have been prepared in advance for my request. Indeed this was one of the reasons I wished to have a sitting in Ibiza, where there was no possibility that the Group might install hidden microphones, loudspeakers, tape recorders, etc. I also knew that none of the Group could play a trumpet, and that there would have been no opportunity to make prior recordings of the trumpet noises. Moreover, the fact that the mouthpiece was placed on the table in the manner described ensured that not even the most experienced trumpet player could blow into it, even if he had been able to kneel down in front of it where I was sitting against the table. Even then, my right hand was placed next to the trumpet's mouthpiece. Thus it was surprising that they could not only get a few light sounds from it but later a real blast which almost threw us off our chairs.

As the tape recording of the sitting demonstrates, there were also drum-beats coming from the table, although there were no instruments or implements which could have produced these sounds normally. The sounds made were more typical of metal than wooden sticks, such was the strength of the drumming. I had expected to see marks on the table, which would have been normal for such hard drumming, but there was nothing to be seen. I must emphasise that the security was good: I could see the armbands of the Group, and felt in control of the whole sitting.

Note: A transcript of a tape-recorded interview between Robin Foy and Hans Schaer, together with supporting statements by Dr Schaer relating to this and other sittings, are among the documents proposed to be deposited for inspection at the offices of the Society.

APPENDIX F:
EVIDENCE FROM TWO CALIFORNIAN SITTINGS

The first occasion on which one of us (MK) had the opportunity to observe the Group's work outside Scole, was in March/April 1997 in California. The circumstances were such as to allow little opportunity for the installation of any secret equipment, and in the two sittings attended by MK, the first in a private home in Mill Valley, just north of San Francisco, and the second in a converted garage at the home of their host in Los Angeles, there were between 15 and 22 witnesses. This summary is based on MK's contemporaneous shorthand notes, and confirmation by the two hosts of the accuracy of the reports.

The sitting in the spacious Mill Valley home of Richard and Connie Adams was attended by 15 persons, among them Dr Bernard Haisch, astronomer, and Editor-in-Chief of the *Journal for Scientific Exploration*, his wife Marsha Sims, executive editor, Dr Russell Targ, a well-known physicist, and a long time research worker in the paranormal field, Dr Marilyn Schlitz of the Institute of Noetic Sciences, a well known parapsychologist, and a number of astrophysicists associated with their respective institutions. A large room, some 10 x 5m, normally used as a gymnasium, was blacked out for the sitting, and searched by two of the invited scientists after it had been visited briefly by the Group to attend to the placing and tab-marking of the central table, and checking the effectiveness of the blackout arrangements. The venue of the sitting had to be changed at the last minute to satisfy time and environmental requirements, so the Group knew nothing about the location beyond the travelling directions given them the previous day. They were not paid, reimbursed or accommodated for their visit, but remained for refreshments and informal discussion with the participants afterwards.

The experimental sitting which followed lasted about two hours. No tape record was made. Despite the unpropitious circumstances, MK adjudged it a success, as did everyone he spoke to afterwards, although the phenomena under the circumstances were neither as spectacular nor as readily forthcoming as they were to be the following week in Los Angeles. These circumstances included the fact that the Group were in a strange environment; they had no opportunity to become accustomed to the room and its 'vibes' (which they had done when sitting elsewhere outside Scole); they knew none of the sitters apart from MK, but assumed that most or all were fairly sceptical scientists, a fact which induced in them some nervousness and anxiety, since they felt themselves to be 'on trial' in an atmosphere likely to be psychologically more intimidating and less conducive to mental tranquillity than when sitting among people accustomed to and believers in mediumship phenomena, as in Los Angeles. Moreover there had recently been a few subnormal sittings with visiting scientists at Scole, and hence there was some concern lest the 'vibes' might not be harmonious enough, with a much larger number of perhaps less well-briefed scientific observers, to generate the requisite energies.

Seats or stools were arranged in a square around the large, slatted circular garden table, on which the Group had fixed luminous tabs at the cardinal compass points. Those on three sides of the square were seated against the walls. The rest, including the four Scole Group, were on the fourth side and were at least 1.10 or 1.30m distant from the edge of the table. As usual, the Group wore luminous wristbands and sat side by side, the men in cuffless shirtsleeves. The only things on the table were four crystals against each tab, and two larger crystals. Not all the sitters could see all the luminous tabs, notably the wristbands, but some of those sitting adjacent to the Group assured MK that the tabs were visible to them throughout, enabling them to see any untoward movement. Events which occurred during the sitting, which was held in complete darkness, included the following:–

1   *Lights.* A sharply identified light spot, which appeared several minutes into the sitting and, after the usual introduction from 'Manu', darted around all areas of the room at great speed, changing course rapidly, striking the table with an audible 'ping', illuminating patches on the ceiling, and hovering bright and still for several seconds. Sitters had earlier been invited by MK to test this phenomenon against the hypothesis of any normal physical explanation.

2   *Touches and Occlusions.* Several sitters reported frequent occlusions of one or more of the table tabs (attributed by RF to movement of solid spirit persons). Most of the sitters (not MK) reported experiencing touches. One sitter described in some detail the size and feel of a hand touching her, and which she was able to examine closely enough to describe its fingernails. Another sitter, Marsha Sims, who sat on MK's immediate left towards one corner, said she was stroked on the left side of her face and hair. Another had his spectacles removed from a breast pocket and placed on his lap.

3   *Noises.* The main noises appeared to be linked with the association of the locale with American Indians, who (we were told by our host, Richard Adams) regard the hill on which the house is built as sacred. We first heard the sound of heavy footsteps apparently walking round the room; and when we commented that the solid cement floor, with a slate surfacing, ought not to vibrate, the steps grew heavier and noisier, and the vibration more evident. After references had been made by sitters to a possible Indian influence or presence, a drumming proceeded from the

direction of the table, although it was not possible to establish a precise rhythm. This was followed by a performance on two parchment drums hanging some 1.7 to 2.1 metres high on the wall behind three or four of the sitters, and about 1.6m apart. The drums were 'played' by unseen hands or sticks to something approaching a regular beat, as background music proceeded quietly throughout the sitting. The conclusion of this performance, which seemed inconsistent with undetected human movement (physical performance would have necessitated standing immediately in front of or on top of three or four sitters and employing extended fingers or drumsticks) was greeted with applause. Above the hubbub of talk there emerged a humming, dirge-like lament, to which we listened carefully immediately the sitters became aware that it was not proceeding from one of them. Sitters familiar with the locality said it was typical Indian chant or song, associated with (possibly ritual) dances. What seemed to be footsteps appropriate to such a dance followed. A male voice, which Mr Adams considered to be characteristic of a male Indian, and which had the characteristics of a typical independent voice transmission, came through in strangulated form. (Mr Adams, an experienced student of native American affairs, has lived among indigenous tribes and studied their customs.)

4   *Table Movement.* The table tabs were seen by some sitters to move slightly, accompanied by a mild noise. Checked by compass reading after the sitting, the table was found to have swivelled by about 5° or 6 anticlockwise. It was not within touching distance of any of the sitters. The table was twice heard vibrating or shuddering, a feature which subsequent manual testing failed to replicate.

5   *Identification.*   Emily Bradshaw, the principal communicator (speaking through Diana, one of the two trance mediums), referred in passing to 'Marsha'. Marsha (Mrs Haisch) was talking at the time and failed to hear the reference, but her husband and most other sitters, MK included, did. No earlier reference to Marsha had been made either to the Team or the Scole Group, since there had been no time for introductions after their arrival.

Discussion at the Sitting

When communications began, and MK was 'recognised' and greeted, Emily Bradshaw correctly divined that the location was in an area where the fishing was good, while Edwin, the first male communicator, discerned the scent of pines. The bay area is famous for its fish, and the house is surrounded by pine trees. Edwin also commented that "we seem to be high up". The house is on a fairly steep hillside, several hundred feet above sea level. Emily suggested that there was a burial ground nearby because someone on her side was talking about it; but on this

234

there was no local information. (It should be noted that the Group were unlikely to be aware of these details, since the location of the sitting had been changed at the last minute, and they had been given driving directions only the previous evening.)

The lengthy discussion, in the form of a question-and-answer session, produced some interesting descriptions of the after-life experience.

The Los Angeles Sitting

This was the penultimate sitting, organised on 5th April 1997 in the home of Brian Hurst for the Scole Group. Mr Hurst, a well known professional medium living in a quiet residential area of north Los Angeles, said he had been inspired by a spirit message to help the Group, whom he had once visited when in England, and by whose activities he had been very impressed. As a result, he had invited them to California, where he had spent several weeks converting his large garage into a suitable, reasonably well sound-proofed room capable of holding some 25 people.

The meeting MK attended was typical of several that had been held for groups of 20 or so sitters, the maximum the room could hold (together with the Group and the host). Most but by no means all the sitters were connected with the Spiritualist movement or with healing groups, but some appeared to have no sort of prior affiliations or beliefs. They were there to satisfy their curiosity, and their scepticism in some cases. All sitters were treated beforehand to the sort of briefing which those attending Scole seminars, normally for no more than ten persons, experienced. Alan showed slides of some of the single-frame films which had been produced paranormally at Scole, followed by a comprehensive introduction from Robin Foy.

The converted garage was around 5m x 6m and accessed by a single door from a bedroom. Chairs were lined up against all four walls. In the centre was a small, low, circular table supported by a simple tubular steel frame. The four compass points were marked on the table with luminous tabs, and the four smaller crystals positioned alongside them, together with two larger ones. Above the table, suspended from a rafter, was a string of bells. Some 80 or 90cm away were chimes, similarly suspended, and likewise identified with a luminous tab. An ioniser had been humming away for some time, but to reduce background noise and possible interference Brian Hurst switched it off after the sitting started. Unlike the San Francisco sitting, this event was tape-recorded by our host, the microphone lying on the floor about a metre in front of him. MK's draft account was checked against the taped record. During the sitting the following physical occurrences were noted:–

a) *Occlusions.* Several (not MK) claimed to have noted masking of one or more of the four table tabs, from time to time.

b) *Lights.* The movement of a point of light, which performed elaborate gyrations in all parts of the room, was made more spectacular by three dive-bombing acts in which the light hit the top of the table audibly and then emerged from beneath it. MK was within a half a metre of the point at which it emerged, and at least 3m distant from the nearest member of the Group. This light 'switched' on and off arbitrarily and instantaneously. MK asked out loud whether it could visit him to enable him to see what he was writing. It responded immediately, although remaining next to his hand for so brief a moment that he still could not see his notebook.

c) *Touches.* Nearly everyone reported having been touched in some way. Shortly after we had been told that there were three spirit forms present and a cat, several sitters, MK included, reported feeling a characteristic tail-brush against both legs. Some sitters wore sandals, or were barefoot, and one declared that her toes were being tickled. MK asked any who had not been touched but wished to be to call out their names so the spirit visitor might be collectively invited to accord them a touch. Two did, Margaret and Sue. Both reported within the next few minutes that they felt touches. Another lady sitter said she had yet to be touched, but later reported that she subsequently had had the experience. One of the men, on whose chest the light was seen to settle, then disappear, said he felt something physical inside him, a movement around his chest. Emily said this was a healing operation: perhaps he had something amiss in his chest? The light emerged from him, and he confirmed that he had a heart condition. MK was touched on his (vascularly challenged) left leg four times. When one of the women said she had just been touched on her leg Patrick, one of the more jocular communicators, pleaded not guilty, albeit with some feigned regret.

d) *Bells and Chimes.* These were both rung noisily. The swirling movement of the luminous tab attached to the chimes (in particular) enabled everyone to see that the chimes were being swung round vigorously, making a musical din. The bell string was similarly treated, at times simultaneously.

e) *Table Levitation.* It was clear from viewing the table tabs that on more than one occasion the table was moving. First it took the form of a wobble; then it shifted about one metre to MK's right before returning to its position in the centre of the room, to the accompaniment of astonished comments and gasps from the sitters. The table then rose three quarters of a metre in the air. MK reports that he had somewhat underestimated its height above the ground, and was corrected by one of the spirit Team, who thought it was nearer two feet up – a fact which became more apparent when the table was gently lowered. Had it been possible for someone to have left his or her seat unobserved to lift the table, one or more of the luminous tabs would have been masked, unless the silent intruder had crawled under the table, in which event there would almost certainly have been noises of crystals rolling around or dropping off onto the floor. The table was seen to twist clockwise, and it also gave two or three characteristic vibratory shudders, during which we heard the crystals shaking around. An attempt was made to replicate this immediately after the sitting, but without success.

f) *Tape Recorder Interference.* The tape recorder, which was playing background music at low volume throughout the proceedings, was suddenly turned up. As Robin Foy raised his hands in the air to show from the armbands that he was not touching the machine, the volume altered. We were treated to a pleasant rendition of Swan Lake before the volume subsided.

g) *Clothing Interference.* One sitter reported that his jacket had been pulled off him, although it was unclear whether he was wearing or just holding it.

h) *Direct Voice.* We heard a strangulated voice, quite faint but sharp, which Robin identified as Reginald. The conversation with him was brief and unenlightening, but audible, and appeared not to proceed from or have anything to do with the medium (Alan). Amid some hilarity another spirit communicator urged Reginald to "come up here with the rest of us" and stop hiding under the carpet.

i) *Sparking Crystals.* A wholly novel feature occurred when sharp flashes of mini-lightning were produced from two levitated crystals being struck against each other. This occurred several times, and in different parts of the room and at different heights above our heads. The flashes were quite bright, and the 'click' noise of the strikes unmistakable.

The atmosphere was lively, even hilarious on occasions. Some of the phenomena generated great enthusiasm and excitement. Patrick in particular kept the sitters entertained by a series of progressively more outrageous puns. When Robin Foy said that an unexpected touch made him jump, Patrick commented that it was only a medium jump – one of his wittier remarks, which was well received.

During the course of a lengthy discussion, EB identified a Bobbie who had hoped to be present. The sitter to whom she had been giving advice said she did know a Bobbie, a close friend. Involved in an auto-accident? Yes. He was driving? Yes – he played the guitar. (This brought an instant rebuke from Edwin, who said one should never volunteer information to the spirits: it simply gave ammunition to critics.) He was always joyful and smiling? Yes. He was driving a blue car? Yes. The deceased driver was anxious to reassure his mother and friends that he was fine. He used to smoke a little pot? Yes. And doodle? Yes.

A new spirit visitor was then described by Emily. He was (a) short, (b) dark-haired, (c) thinnish, (d) olive-skinned; he (e) died very young and unexpectedly, just going about his business, (f) was an adopted son whose foster-mother was still grieving for him, (g) lived not far from the location of the sitting, and (h) died in the evening. All the statements were recognised by Brian Hurst as applying to someone he had known.

MK comments that, in theory, Brian Hurst might have taken the opportunity to speak to the Group, who were lodging with him during the visit, in order to brief them about the people due to attend the sitting. In practice this does not seem likely, in view of the fact that applicants gave no details about themselves, let alone any recently deceased relatives or friends, so it was unlikely that he could have been aware of some of the above-mentioned information in advance of the sitting. It should be noted that three sittings were held each week – save for the week when the Group drove 400 miles north to Mill Valley to Mr Adams's home – and each was attended by about 22 persons.

APPENDIX G: INGRID SLACK'S TESTIMONY

Ingrid Slack, a psychologist with the Open University, an SPR member, and a very experienced investigator of mediumship, gives the following account of her 11th November 1996 sitting (No 17, referred to in Chapter VII):–

On 11th November 1996, at the Foys' home at Street Farmhouse, Scole, Diss, and in the company of David Fontana (DF), I entered a brightly-lit lounge where I met the members of the Scole Group, Robin and Sandra Foy and the two mediums, Alan and Diana. After introductions, DF and I were taken to the cellar where the sitting was to take place, and invited to examine the room and its environs for as long as we needed. We then returned to the lounge for a short briefing, since it was my first visit, and then returned to the cellar. Robin and Sandra Foy and the two mediums put on their luminous wristbands and took their places around the small table. Clockwise around the table the seating arrangements were: DF on my left, Sandra, Alan, Diana, Robin and myself.

As customary, the session began with music and singing from the Group in which DF and I joined. First Manu, the principal spirit guide, addressed us through Diana, then subsequently a female voice, who I was told was Emily Bradshaw, addressed us through Diana, while a male voice known as Joseph addressed us through Alan.

Dancing Lights

The first phenomena that I saw were small points of golden light dancing in the corner of the room diagonally opposite to me and to my left. They danced animatedly upwards and downwards for several moments.

Glowing Orb

Shortly following this, there appeared a ball of diffused light, which I estimated to have a diameter of about 20cm, close to the ceiling in the same corner to my left as the previous dancing lights. The ball had no physical boundary: it was simply a three-dimensional orb of diffused golden light. It hung suspended for a moment in the corner about 30cm beneath the ceiling. Slowly the orb moved towards the centre of the room, pausing above the centre of the table round which we were all sitting. It lowered itself by about 17cm, remained still, then retreated slowly upwards and backwards into the corner from which it came. There were no beams of light to the orb, and the light was not reflected onto a surface; it moved independently in space. This occurred twice in succession, and I became aware of an overwhelming feeling of gentleness and love which seemed to accompany this particular phenomenon or, more accurately, which this phenomenon seemed to embody.

Quartz Crystal

A large quartz crystal, about 9cm long and 3cm wide, which was on the table to my left between DF and myself, gradually illuminated itself from within until the complete shape glowed brightly. It then rose steadily, passed in front of DF at eye level, then moved slowly in my direction until it was directly in front of me, where it paused for a few moments. Then, just as smoothly and slowly, it returned silently to its place on the table. The movement was very smooth and steady throughout, and the shape was complete and without obscuration. (As soon as the sitting ended I picked up the crystal to re-examine it. As before the sitting, there was nothing extraordinary or untoward about it.) After the shape returned to the table the silhouette of the middle three fingers of a hand was seen to move gently in front of the crystal, fingertips touching the table, the hand upright and in front of the crystal so that the still-glowing crystal provided the light which enabled the hand to be visible.

Growth of a Lighted Object

Immediately to my left and in front of DF and slightly in from the edge of the table I saw a very small self-illuminated but indeterminate shape begin to grow. It seemed gradually to form itself into a rock-like shape until it was about 9cm in height with a base of about 11cm, narrowing asymmetrically to a peak at the top. When the shape was complete it rose to my eye level, moved steadily in front of DF and then across to me until it was directly in front of me. It then returned noiselessly to its place on the table where it gradually disappeared. While it was in front of me I put out my hand to touch it. As my hand brushed against the form I felt a texture akin to that of muslin. At the end of the sitting there was nothing where it had been on the table.

Small Figures

Three figure-like objects appeared in front of us. They were about 30cm in length and quite narrow, about 4cm wide. A drape hung from the head of each figure to its full length, so no body-shape was discernible. The whole shape was illuminated, and at the top there was what could be described as a form of face. There was some specific movement where a mouth might be. These forms moved in front of me, and as I touched the drape I again felt a texture akin to muslin as the form moved away out of my reach towards DF on my left.

Soft Breezes

On two separate occasions I was aware of a soft breeze blowing directly onto my face. I would remind the reader that there are no windows in the cellar and only one door, which was tightly closed, relatively far away and in any case behind me.

Touches

On three occasions I was aware of what felt like a firm touch on my left thigh. DF was sitting only about 30cm to my left, making it impossible for a human hand and arm to intrude between us without our both being aware of the fact.

The Film

A film had been placed in its tub in the middle of the table throughout this sitting. At one point during the proceedings the film was lifted from the table at DF's request, and again at his request placed unerringly and without fumbling into my hands. As this occurred I felt the side of a large, cool, masculine hand touching mine from the left. As DF was sitting close to me on this side (see above) it is difficult to credit that anyone could have reached across in front of him to touch me. In any case Sandra Foy rather than Robin or Alan was sitting on DF's left.

A Direct Spirit Voice

Later in the sitting a form of voice seemed to emanate from a point over the table to my left and some way in front of me. It would have been between Sandra and Alan but about 60cm in front of them; and DF, the Foys and I reported having to lean forward to hear it. There was clearly a sound which could be interpreted as a voice, though the words were indistinct.

My Reactions

Throughout the sitting I tried to remain vigilant and attentive to all the phenomena and the details surrounding them. I cannot see any way in which the things I saw could have been manipulated by any of the members of the Group or by other mechanical or electrical means. I cannot explain why I should have experienced such an intense emotional reaction to the glowing orb.

241

APPENDIX H: DOUBTS ABOUT THE FILMS

The first doubts were raised immediately after the production on 19th November 1996 of the Ruth 2 film (see Chapter VII). This, it will be recalled, was the first-ever transparency on Kodachrome 200 film of a 1.3-metre-long roll which Kodak had developed in their Wimbledon processing unit. MK had taken the strip to Ralph Noyes to get an enlargement made before sending the original to Scole. As a matter of routine inquiry, Noyes asked the photographer whether he could see any way in which such a message could be imprinted on an unexposed reel of film, horizontally crossing several frames, leaving the reel fully wound up in its canister to await development. After a little trouble, the photographer was able to describe how he had used a strip of acetate trimmed to fit the emulsified area. On this he had written an appropriate message or drawing with a fine felt-tipped pen. In the darkroom he laid the acetate strip over the necessary length of film which he pulled from its cassette, and used a flashgun to imprint the message. He then wound the film back into its cassette and made it ready for normal development. The possibility that this was the process employed by the Group seemed to be reinforced by the appearance on the film of a faint boundary between the end of the message and the rest of the film.

Some months later Dr Alan Gauld independently reported that the Dragon film described in Chapter VI, which had been produced under the supervision of the Schnittgers, could have been made by a similar process. So it was inevitable that suspicion would attach to these films when they were publicly presented.

At a very early stage in our meetings at Scole, we had frankly discussed with the Group mechanisms for faking the Polaroid films – the only type of film which was then being used. This was pursued in part by a direct contact via AE to Polaroid with the full knowledge and consent of the Group, and partly by the Group themselves, on their own initiative, in discussion with the company responsible for making copies of their films. Although at that stage the use of acetate strips was not suggested, it was acknowledged that, given the right specialist equipment and skill, it would indeed be possible to make any sort of film.

These facts merit close examination, even considering the contextual obstacles to the films' production by normal means. The obvious question arises: why if the images are simply the thought-impressions created by spirit forces should there be signs on the films akin to those yielded by the methods likely to have been used by fakers? We stated Chapter XIV that doubts about all these films are made more acute in that they appear to be intended to point to a discarnate origin, and that this creates a credibility hurdle even more intimidating – at least to the Western mind – than that posed by the acceptance of psychic photography, or other phenomena which might be ascribed to the living.

The Ruth 2 film, alike with the Schnittger Dragon film, has been described as showing clear signs of human execution. It cannot be argued, however, that there is anything *inherently* paranormal in any film images. Anything which by itself was paranormal could not be a film. A film is something made by one or more of a number of known, established processes. In other words, a film is a normal object. The only factor which could endow it with supernormality is – and can only be – the circumstances in which the images on it are created. The images themselves cannot but bear similarities to man-made images, otherwise they would simply not be recognisable as images. This may even apply to those rare published cases in which still films show ghostlike figures, whose lack of opacity or size or perspective are all anomalous. Only when it is demonstrated that the exposure was normal, not double, and the film was pristine, and correctly developed, etc., does the image acquire the possibility of paranormality.

It may be objected that, while this is true, it does not follow that we should disregard all manner of marks which appear to point to a possible human intervention. But if there were no such tell-tale indications, and the film was exactly what a good camera shot should be, we would still be left with nothing to indicate paranormality. Indeed, we might well meet a no less determined criticism for that very reason. What it would indicate, we would be told, is an altogether suspicious degree of perfection, quite at odds with the trial-and-error progress characteristic of both the film and the direct taped voice experiments we deal with in the next Appendix. Botching therefore does not prove fraud, any more than perfection proves its absence.

The Ruth 2 film was the first to be obtained on Kodachrome. The chemical substances and processes involved in the development of Kodachrome film are quite different from those relating to Polaroid film. That is why we had not been expecting anything to come of this first experimental trial. Its novel qualities may be the reason why the transparency was streaked with wash like a painter's excessive dilution of his water colouring, whereas the succeeding Kodachrome films were not. Nor are the marks of possible human intervention which have been suggested by one acute critic of the Dragon film found on all the other films. However, although this fact somewhat weakens the doubts about authenticity, it is nevertheless natural to ask what explanation the Team gave for their techniques.

We do not know. The point was, of course, raised with them. But we appeared to be dealing with intermediaries who were not always in immediate touch with the (apparent) sub-team responsible for the photographic work, and who sometimes said they were not in a position to explain, either because they simply didn't know, or because it would involve explanations meaningless in our earth-bound terminology, or (perhaps) because they might not do so. The impression was created of an eager group competing for the chance to employ their skills in what for them might have been as unique and adventurous an experiment as was its reception for those in our world. We were certainly told that there was a fair measure of entrepreneurial freedom on the 'other side'. The diversity of the material transmitted seemed to support that. But as far as explanation is concerned, we got little farther than the statement, made during the several discussions about the Ruth poem, that these were the impress of images formed in the minds of those invited to participate. We had been promised a further explanation, albeit coupled with doubts about our capacity to comprehend it, but this was fated never to be fulfilled.

A fraud assumption among colleagues has been prompted to a large extent by the discovery that all the symbols on the Dragon film appeared to have been copied or slightly adapted from an illustrated book by Maurice Bessy (Bessy, 1963), and that it was a fairly simple matter to show how the images on the film might have been generated by copying or tracing them with some adaptations to enable them to be fitted into a 24-mm height, and then employing a normal procedure to transfer them onto film, presumably in the manner that had been demonstrated by a photographic expert to Ralph Noyes after the production of the Ruth 2 film four months earlier. Dr Gauld pointed to evidence that this could have been the manner in which the films had been produced, since he discerned marks consistent with a tracing on acetate paper, and had noted that the fairly coarse lines were precisely the kind made by pens used for acetate tracing, with slight over- and under-shootings and irregularities characteristic of hasty tracings. The crude fudging over the feet of the figure standing on the dragon, and the general simplification of figures, were also consistent in his view with the limitations of the kind of pens that might be used for detailed drawing on acetate for reproduction.

It would be misleading to conceal the unease which this lack of explanation generated. If, as the Team told us, the films were thought-images, why should they, or at least the Dragon film, have borne features typical of a somewhat clumsily traced reproduction? It is no less pertinent to ask why, when the avowed object is to provide evidence of survival, should the origin of so little of the film material be inaccessible. Why were all the verses in the two Ruth films reproduced entirely from one page which, albeit in rarified conditions, was in the public domain, and none of it derived from elsewhere in the poem? And if the Dragon film was not made from tracings made with the aid of strips of acetate, why should they give every appearance of having been thus manufactured?

While such doubts are entirely reasonable, it could be contended that they are based on challengeable assumptions. One is that there is something inherently suspicious about reproductions from an existing book. Whether one considers the book to be a work of scholarship or a concession to coffee table decoration is irrelevant: it is akin to questioning the existence of spirit communicators because one disapproves of the tawdry tunes they apparently require to bestir them. Nor is it easy to discover what is so objectionable in the concept of reproductions of existing drawings or photographs when there had never been any claim or pretence to novelty. Indeed, most of the early still photographs we had been shown before commencing our investigation were of existing pictures, a fact positively proclaimed by the Team, not grudgingly admitted. It was in any event obvious that this was the case. If the pictures had been entirely original they could just as logically be denounced as frauds as if they were copies. But if the Dragon film artist was intent on conveying a message comprising alchemical symbols, then it obviously would have to have been copied from somewhere. Interestingly, in the case of one of the cityscape pictures, that depicting a photograph of St Paul's Cathedral during the London blitz, a comparison between it and the original photograph from which it appears to have been taken reveals distinct differences, especially in the fact that the width of the dome in the former is relatively wider than the height. That is, it shows a non-uniform distortion.

The fact that all the Dragon drawings, as mentioned earlier, have been found in a single book by Bessy neither supports nor undermines the fraud hypothesis. The book is simply a convenient annotated collection of previously published drawings. Indeed at an early stage WS was excited to find one or two of these drawings in a 17th Century German manual. Considering the huge number of books on alchemy, the cabbala and hermeticism published in two periods before around 1610, and the many copies made of these in subsequent years (e.g. McLean, 1997), there is no way to be certain whether the pictures in the Dragon film were copies of the originals, or of one of the many reproductions made over the past four or five hundred years; but it does seem almost certain that they were copied from various parts of Bessy's book, bearing all the signs of having been traced from entire or small sections of the contents, and hence arousing understandable suspicions.

We do not pretend to know the answers to the various questions about the creation of these pictures, but we think some relevant factors must be remembered. One is that, were these pictures created by entities existing as pure thought, and operating perhaps from vivid memories possessed by their disembodied personalities, it would be surprising if the products were as perfect as some critics expect. But they were never claimed to be. They show great variations in artistry, detail and draughtsmanship. Assuming paranormality, perhaps this is due to the learning curve of the Team, or to changes in the energy patterns during the sittings, or because different spiritual artists with different ideas and levels of competence are involved . . . we do not know, and we ought not to rely on our assumptions. The recollections which appeared to be responsible for the Ruth films were a strange and astonishing mixture of the very precise with the muddled: precise handwriting but confused thoughts, as we saw in Chapter VII. Other films fail to exhibit the aesthetic defects which have been discerned in the Dragon film. We reiterate that the paranormality of this and the other films rests in the circumstances in which they have been produced, not in the films themselves.

Were there no other circumstantial evidence pointing to authenticity, we would consider such criticisms, allied to acknowledged procedural weaknesses in the production of at least some of the pictures, to be such as would disqualify the material from serious consideration in what purports to be a balanced and comprehensive report. But here is the difficulty: uphold a fraud hypothesis, and one cannot escape the conclusion that all else is spurious. We have been at pains to show that this simply flies in the face of so much apparently impressive evidence.

The plain fact is that we have no concept of the mechanism that would or could be employed if assumed discarnate entities from another dimension composed of pure thought seek to impress images of a widely varying type onto film. Once a suspicion matures into a conviction that signs characteristic of human activity point inescapably towards fraud, then every feature, however innocent, assumes a sinister complexion. To the natural, but absurd, question: well, how would you set about the task if you were a disembodied spirit? the sceptic must presume the existence of various faculties, and the non-existence of various constraints, of which neither he nor we have any knowledge. All that can be said is that readers must judge for themselves, on the strength or weakness of the evidence we have reported, where the balance of probabilities in the present instance appears to be.

APPENDIX I: DOUBTS ABOUT THE TAPES

Many of the considerations discussed in the immediately preceding Appendix apply also to the tape recording experiments, although here we have at least been given some attempts at an explanation by the Team, as recounted in the report of the Ibiza discussion in Chapter XI. If there is indeed some process by which spirit thought is converted into physical impressions on magnetic tape, then it probably follows that the mental impress of thought-recollections or images, howsoever derived, involve physical interference with the emulsion, as the tape revolves from one spool to the other. It will be seen that the initial attempts at communicating directly on tape had some limited success (see Chapter VIII), but that with practice the transmissions became clearer, although still attended by billows of white noise. For both the films and the tape recordings, it would be surprising, and certainly inconsistent with the claimed process of experimental efforts to surmount difficulties of incomprehensible dimensions, were either of these different manifestations perfect. But they are not perfect, and the imperfections have aroused suspicion.

By the time the last tests had been conducted, two in Ibiza and the later one in England, the stage had been reached where the only proffered alternative explanation to paranormality was that a pre-recorded radio signal had been secretly beamed from either outside or inside the room, probably via a micro-transmitter, and received directly onto a tape in a recorder from which the microphone had been removed. In consequence we were obliged to review the evidence to see what assumptions would be required to make this radio-transmission theory sustainable. We had hoped to settle this more conclusively by having a further sitting at which a message could be recorded in direct response to a question or request from one of us, thus countering the claim that a pre-recorded message could be responsible, but the Group's timetable in the early autumn of 1997, together with the fulfilment of their prior commitments in Germany and Holland, and their need to get the video experiment in operation, required them to go into closed session. However, during the Group's brief visits to the Continent and Dublin in September 1997 and in the presence of the Schnittgers and several sitters, voices were reported to have emanated from the same tape recorder, minus its microphone, in response to questions. But we have no direct experience of this.

A review of all the evidence does in fact make the radio-signal suggestion look improbable. First is the fact that the earliest transmissions at the beginning of 1997 were heard by several of us, including Professor Carr and Ingrid Slack, over a number of sittings in what had every appearance of being a trial-and-error groping towards

247

establishing a distant link. This process was accompanied by sounds of much apparent internal tinkering from the tape recorder, including noises similar to those associated with tuning a primitive radio to a distant foreign station, and messages of encouragement or advice from the Team between supposed entities. If this involved a series of pre-recorded transmissions, it was astonishingly accomplished. Not only that: we were ourselves participants in some of the operations. Our rôles must therefore have had to be presumed upon, and the timing associated with them to be in consequence of accurate advance guesses, in order that the noises could emerge at the right moments.

The theory of pre-recorded transmissions beamed into the room has to overcome at least three further objections. MK reports that, during the two transmissions in Ibiza, the taped messages were inaudible during the sitting, and equally were not on the general recording tape. Only when the tape from the doctored recorder was played back were the attempted communications audible. An accomplice acting as radio operator (whose existence would need to be established, since there were no other people associated with the Group in or near the house or as far as we know even on the Island) would have had to control a suppression button to prevent the transmission from being heard, and again to have acted at exactly the appropriate times.

In addition, many of the ingredients which the Group would have needed to know in advance in order to fake the tapes at the Ibiza sittings were only decided by participants on the spot. They were not predetermined. No one could have accurately predicted how long MK would take discussing proposed procedures before the sittings proper began, or indeed how long it would take before other preparations had been completed. So only those present would know when to operate an illicit radio transmission. This means that the radio transmitter would have to have been held and controlled by one of the Group, even though on a warm midsummer's evening everyone was attired in the lightest of garments, rendering its safe and successful concealment and operation improbable. MK, who was responsible for the conduct of these experiments, points out that at the subsequent 16th August meeting at Scole, where the recording obtained on the microphoneless tape was clearly heard by all participants, the orchestral music specifically intended for him had emotionally charged associations with his early boyhood which were not known to any other living person. Furthermore, the rendition was based on his recollections of old 78s in which the soloist was Rachmaninoff himself. (The suggestion, which has been put to him, that he might have forgotten having mentioned this piece of music and its significance to one of the Group, none of whom shows any interest in classical music, he confidently dismisses.)

However, when the tape of the 16th August sitting was examined by an SPR member with specialist knowledge of the acoustic properties of tape recordings, Frank Franklyn, a senior electronics engineer who was also a mature Ph.D. student under AE's supervision, he expressed the view that it was "almost certainly a fake". What he found on the tape, and more particularly the deductions he drew from it, bear striking similarity to the conclusions drawn from the appearance of human handiwork in the Dragon film. For example, Franklyn records an increase in background noise level half a minute into the recording, as though the volume control had been increased. He discerns a 'breathing rate' of a breath every four seconds. The inference is that this is all part of the human fabrication process. What would spirits be breathing? Then there is a noise akin to something nearby being accidentally knocked, sounds typical of those made close to a microphone, background changes as though a gramophone record was being switched on, and wow and flutter characteristic of the use of a poor-quality sound source. The increase in speech level suggested to him that the microphone was turned towards a speaker located some distance from the microphone. The reverberating room noise suggested recording at a distance from the microphone; an increase in the voice level coincided with a typical reduction in background noise.

This analysis strikes us as wholly reasonable if one has no knowledge of the build-up to the experiment, and is unaware of the objections listed above to the theory that this and similar or comparable tape recordings might have been beamed in by radio from a pre-recorded message, or of the contradictions inherent in the presupposition on which it is based. As we have shown in the context of the Dragon film issue, the presupposition is that, for paranormality to be suggested, there must be some aspect of the content of the tape recording which clearly could not be man-made. Since that is impossible, the Team or their supposed collaborators would seem to have no alternative but to produce a tape which has on it noises characteristic of one that is man-made. The idea that there could be noises characteristic only of a spirit tape seems untenable. How could such noises be recognised as 'spirit' noises?

If this argument is accepted, then the attributes to which Franklyn has attached such sinister implications may now be seen in a more innocent light. The assumption that a spirit, if such there be, can create the sound of a human voice without making a noise like human breath ill accords with the literature of psychical research, with its numerous references to 'spirits' speaking through mediums or by supposed direct voice. In our experience, such direct voices are invariably associated with breathing sounds, at least initially. It might be observed, too, that if the idea is to produce an impressive fake, one would hardly imagine that allegedly highly professional operators would produce a version replete with clues pointing to its fabrication when it would have been a simple matter to create a more polished version.

The fact is that, if the possibility of paranormality can be accepted, the evidence seems fairly consistent with trial and error in the use of some unfamiliar psychic energy. Just as the early film strip impressions were limited and fragmentary, so too with the attempts at what might be described as electronic voice phenomena, but which both the Team and the Group preferred to call Trans-Dimensional Communications (TDC), using a microphone-less recorder with a battery-powered tape. If paranormality is assumed, it is reasonable to suppose that phenomena of this kind can be created only by employing means which produce noises similar to those which would be created were the recording man-made, however maladroitly.

APPENDIX J:
DOUBTS ABOUT THE IBIZA POLAROID FILMS

[MK was the only one of the three principal investigators present at the two Ibiza sittings, and therefore has sole responsibility for this Appendix.]

Perhaps the most testing alternative scenario to a paranormal explanation for the results obtained at Ibiza relates to the square 75 mm x 75 mm Polaroid automatic plates produced at the two sittings of 29th June and 1st July, 1997 (see Chapter XI and Plates 17 and 19). Since we have already pointed out that there can be nothing inherently paranormal in any films, it behoves us to attempt to falsify the hypothesis that the images on them could have been made fraudulently. Similar pictures can be produced, and have been, by focusing an LED at very close range onto unexposed plates in the dark. Tony Cornell has shown that this simple mechanism can produce images which, like those at Ibiza, become apparent only after being processed through a lens-blanked Polaroid camera. This demonstration is not only ingenious, but appears to overcome what MK and his associates in Ibiza had considered to be an insurmountable control, namely that secret identifying marks made by him in complete darkness on each of the six frames to be treated would preclude substitution.

The fraudulent method hypothesised by Tony Cornell overcomes the need to postulate the secretion of previously fabricated films, since it presupposes the direct abstraction of the plates from the table, their fraudulent exposure there and then, and their replacement in their original positions a few centimetres from MK and WS. It assumes that the forger could lean over or get up from his or her seat, remove the six films from the central table in the first experiment, and from the small table on MK's right in the second, return to his seat (let us assume a male culprit for convenience), create the images with an LED, and then replace them closely enough in their original positions not to arouse suspicion before returning once more to his seat: all this to be done noiselessly in total darkness. To establish whether this method, or something akin to it, could have been employed, MK outlines the steps which a fraudster would have been obliged to take in the circumstances prevailing in Ibiza (since Tony Cornell has not sought to replicate the Ibiza milieu), and examine these in relation to members of the Group.

In preparation for the operations described below, one of the Group, wearing luminous wristbands (which remained visible to the six non-Group participants throughout the two relatively short sittings), must have chosen one of two options to avoid being observable when undertaking this deception: either equipped himself with pieces of masking material to cover his wristbands (taking the risk that the investigators would notice this absence over a relatively long period of time), or risked the consequences of making an audible rasping sound when removing them and getting his neighbours to hold the wristbands for him to mask his temporary employment in the faking operation.

However, MK points out that:–

a) either step would require detectable movement, whether during the process of covering or when stripping the wristbands. In both cases both arms would have to be employed. There would in consequence be a risk of detection from any of the six observers;

b) the wristband covers would require to be concealed before and after this process – difficult given the flimsy garments worn;

c) there would be an additional high level of risk because the culprit must operate for several minutes without the identifying wriststrips.

These reservations apply to each of the Group.

If the option of using the help of neighbours is chosen (there being no arms on the chairs on which to place or hang the wristbands), the gap between members of the Group would make it impossible for a neighbour to hold an armband in anywhere near the correct position. Even ignoring this objection, MK considers the demands on each Group member would be as follows:–

Robin Foy had only one neighbour, the medium Diana, as a possible helper, since on his left, and at too great a distance, was one of the observers, and he was constantly engaged in altering music volume, changing tapes on both the recorders, and talking a good deal of the time, all of which would have made it difficult and risky to cover the bands on his arms – which, unlike those of the other three, needed and were constantly seen to be in motion. He was, moreover, on the opposite side of the table from MK and hence furthest away from the scene of action.

Diana would be dependent on using Robin's right arm on one side, and Alan's left arm on the other, to hold her wristbands. These would have to be held motionless for the entire period of the faking operation. That would have been difficult for Robin when his hands were so often in motion.

Alan. Precisely the same considerations apply, except that his wristbands would have to be held by Diana and Sandra. Both he and Diana, being apparently in trance, would run greater risks if seen to move their arms. Both would also have to silence their supposed spirit communicators during periods of movement.

Sandra would have been dependent on the collaboration of MK on her right to cope with one of her wristbands, in addition to the likelihood that MK might hear sounds of movement.

General. The hypothesis of fraud presupposes a lack of observation by each one of the observers and a readiness by one or more of the Group to run a great risk of challenge and exposure. Even extensible arms, or the production from a secret hiding place of a telescopic rod, could only have complicated matters and added to detection risks. Had there been any way in which the attention of observers could have been diverted while these essential manoeuvres were performed, the danger of discovery might have been thought an acceptable risk; but one of the positive merits of darkness (this experiment could have been undertaken only in darkness) is that it limits the scope for such diversion. And there were virtually no other visual displays to distract attention on either evening.

Making certain not to scrape chair legs on the stone floor, the culprit would then have to rise and abstract from the central table top each of the six films which at the first sitting MK had placed in front of him. Our deceiver would have to manage this and return noiselessly and unnoticed to his seat a metre or so away. Holding the six films in one hand, taking great care not to allow the slippery plates to slide onto the stone floor and alert the watchers, he would then have to produce his masked three-volt LED pen to make his abstract drawings.

In addition, it should be noted that Alan was wearing shorts and a short-sleeved shirt, Diana and Sandra wore light summer frocks, and Robin Foy a T-shirt or light pullover, all short of pockets suitable for concealing even a small LED pencil. Furthermore, since the faker would have no idea where on the table MK had placed the films, abstracting them would inevitably involve a deal of groping around within inches of MK's face, his being the only chair placed close to the table. There would equally be no way of knowing where on the table MK had placed the tape recorder for the first experiment. Knocking into this, or brushing against the equally invisible crystal located very close to where the films had been placed during the first experiment, or coming into contact with one of MK's hands or arms which were or might have been hovering over the table, would not merely have led to discovery: it would have spelled the end of the Scole Group as a credible operation.

To make matters more difficult for the potential faker, Edwin predicted towards the end of the first sitting that film no.6 was likely to contain something somewhat different from the rest. But there was no way by which the faker could know which film was marked as No.6 in MK's secret code. He would therefore have had to take on a 1:6 chance of getting it right. Not significant odds, perhaps, but certainly an additional and apparently unnecessary risk if, as a fraud hypothesis must imply, 'Edwin' is in reality only one of the mediums.

The problems listed above would have been still more serious for possible fakers during the second sitting, because MK stacked all the films in an irregular heap on the corner of the side table between himself and Walter Schnittger, placing the half-emptied cassette alongside them. The faker would then have to:–

a) manoeuvre round the back of MK's chair and grope about the top of a table he could not see;

b) make certain that he did not knock over the pile of invisible films or the cassette, or risk touching WS's left hand in order to abstract all of the films without detection, and then to reverse the process when replacing them some minutes later. The disposition of the chairs would have made these movements awkward even in daylight.

Robin Foy would be the least likely candidate to carry out this manoeuvre because:–

a) he was farthest away, and had more hazards to negotiate over a longer distance than the other Group members, since he would have had to move one or both the side tables in order to grope his way behind the mediums' chairs to gain access to the main table during the first sitting and the side table during the second;

b) he is a heavily-built man, ill-fitted for such delicate physical manoeuvres;

c) he was doing a good deal of the commenting and conversational exchanges throughout, and it was obvious to all where his voice was coming from.

Diana and *Alan* were better placed, but both for much of the time were delivering comments from the male and female communicators, a function difficult to reconcile with a subtle and dangerous abstraction operation and the furtive artwork which the hypothesis requires.

Sandra was best placed for the task, although she was taking a lively part in the conversation during the sitting, as the tape recording shows.

In the first sitting one of the Group would have had to remove the candle from the candlestick (seen on the left of Plate 19) and return to place it upright on or near the centre of the table, where it was duly knocked over later by MK when feeling round for a suspected spare film.

To rise undetected from his chair and walk between two and four metres to the doorway entrance where the candlestick was located, the deceiver would have had to remove armbands, a process fraught with the hazards previously listed. The candle would have had to be balanced on its end on the table (a difficult manoeuvre in itself), and a warning to MK transmitted through Alan to be particularly careful when moving his hands around the table. Even if the deceiver was equipped with image intensifiers, the gratuitous trick with the candle, which was not part of the scheduled programme, would hardly justify the almost certain risk of detection.

Towards the end of the sitting, when both male and female communicators appeared to be speaking through the mediums, and before the films had been collected for re-insertion, there were flashes of light in the far corner of the room, the illumination (commented on by everyone save the mediums), being enough to prompt fears that the blank negatives might have been affected, although there was an assurance from the communicators that we need not worry. The lights, like miniature sheet lightning flashes, were at a distance of three metres or more from the nearest member of the Group.

In retrospect these lightning-type flashes might seem to be the least explicable of all the phenomena, because they were unlike any ordinary illumination, were silent, and flickered like marsh gas. None of the Group appeared to possess any instrument which could produce this effect at a distance.

Tony Cornell's experiment, which was intended to demonstrate how the films could have been faked, was conducted on assumptions that were seriously incorrect, perhaps inevitably in view of the fact that none of the participants at Ibiza was consulted with the aim of making conditions as close to the original as possible. It has been necessary to describe these fairly elaborate procedural details, which must be read in conjunction with the account of the two sittings given in Chapter XI, to enable readers to form a balanced judgement of the fraud hypothesis as it applies to the two Ibiza experiments. Although in retrospect access to the films was theoretically possible, the precautions employed must be taken into account. However well-rehearsed and skilled a fraudster may have been, he or she was not in control of events and could not have determined just where films were placed or how he or she could have been sure of avoiding brushing into either WS or MK in the second sitting during the abstraction and replacement processes. In sum, MK and his co-investigators in Ibiza unanimously consider that the Cornell criticisms have failed to expose any practical defects, and are based either on inadequate appreciation of the conditions of the Ibiza tests, or on wholly unrealistic assumptions about the aural, tactile and visual deficiencies of all the observers.

It is fair to add that an alternative scenario has been seriously advanced in which, instead of removing films from the table, the faker undertakes this operation *in situ*, in full view of six observers watching for any movement of the luminous wristbands, and under the nose of the experimenter. However, it will be remembered that, in the second experiment, all six marked plates were piled up on a small side table wedged between MK and WS, a few inches away from the wall – although for all the faker knew the films might have been placed anywhere. There is no way in which the plates could have been worked on by a member of the Group squeezing himself or herself between the two of them, and bent over the side table within an inch or two of either man, without detection.

APPENDIX K: DOUBTS ABOUT THE 'ALAN' BOX

There has been much controversy over the box constructed at the behest of the Team by Alan or his son, as described in Chapter VI, since it was from this that there emerged some of the most spectacularly impressive films, notably the final one (the Daguerre strip). We therefore have to examine every possibility of deception. In more than one case, including that of the Daguerre film, the weakness turned on the fact that the box had been made by those who were under examination, whereas no successful film emerged in the later sittings from the box made by MK's carpenter.

The hypothesis that faking might have taken place initially centred on the possibility of a secret panel in the Alan box, but this was superseded when the box was examined at the University of Nottingham, and it was found that, by squeezing the hasp which carries the padlock securing the lid, it was possible to push its right-hand arm further into the right-hand socket, thereby enabling the left arm to be released from its socket by swivelling the hasp (after which the right-hand arm could also be removed). This allowed the box lid to be opened without interfering with the padlock and hence permitted any contents to be removed and/or replaced.

It has not, however, been demonstrated that this could be done undetected. The base of the screws holding the socket had been hammered into the underside of the lid during construction in order to ensure that the socket was firmly secured. As investigators we made a point of examining the box after each sitting, and consistently found the seals to be fully intact. Had there been a fracture of the seals it would have been noted immediately by us as well as by one or other of the invited sitters. These included Dr Gauld, who, with Professor West, had opportunities to examine both the Alan and Keen boxes before and after the sitting at which the Daguerre film strip was produced, as described in Chapter IX. Dr Gauld assures us that the seal did not fracture during testing experiments at the University of Nottingham, but did so only during subsequent handling. We have no wish to quarrel with such an experienced and careful investigator. Because the seal has since fractured, by whatever cause, there is no merit in pursuing a hypothesis which is now incapable of demonstration. That the seal was broken when the box was returned to us is the only fact we can report on the strength of our own experience. However, it is relevant to point out that Dr Gauld agrees that initially the process of squeezing the hasp to release one of the arms from its socket, thereby enabling the opposite arm also to be released, required considerable pressure. This pressure reduced each time the experiment was repeated, but MK, who later tested the resistance of the hasp, still found that he had to exert considerable finger pressure, holding the box firmly to detach one of the arms and – what was more tricky – to get both arms back into their sockets again, even in daylight.

If this had indeed been the method used at sittings, one would have expected the hasp, well before it was subjected to testing in Nottingham, to have already revealed the consequences of regular squeezing and to have been relatively easy to open, with the retaining screw effectively loosened. It should be remembered that the box was handed over to us after each sitting so that it could be externally examined. Indeed, not only did the Group give us every opportunity to do this when we attended sittings: they invited us to take it away for expert examination. That is not a normal feature of magicians' tricks.

The fraud hypothesis also presupposes on the part of the faker the ability to conceal his wristbands effectively enough to render unauthorised movement safe from detection by experienced and critical investigators. We have already argued, in the context of the Ibiza Polaroid experiments (Chapter XI and Appendix J), how difficult this would seem to have been. He would then need to remove the box in darkness from its position (precisely defined by an inked contour line drawn on an A4 sheet) in the centre of the table. Then, after swivelling the hasp without breaking the seal, he must free the lid. The next step would be to open the lid and remove and hide the tub while making certain that the dangling padlock did not attract attention. While performing this delicate operation, he must extract a substitute tub, with film, from his pocket, trusting that the original had not been secretly marked by the investigators, place it in the box, close the lid and (a manoeuvre which practical testing has shown to be very tricky) get the detached hasp back into its socket. Finally, he would face the challenge of replacing the box so exactly in its former position on the marked paper that subsequent inspection of the outline of the base of the box and of its pendulous padlock would reveal no evidence that they had been moved. The alternative scenario, in which the film is switched for a prepared fake, and replaced in the original tub, would involve opening and replacing the snap-off lid of the tub. And all this to be effected swiftly and precisely in darkness. The fraudster must also rely on good luck or some diversionary operation to ensure that the movement or absence of his or her wristbands was not observed by any of the three investigators, a risky business when those sitting with MK during the production of the Daguerre film in this case were the current President of the Society, Donald West, an emeritus professor of clinical criminology, and a past President, Dr Alan Gauld, one of the country's leading experts on mediumship and séance room phenomena.

Still on the subject of the Alan box, it must be remembered that the first two of the last three film strips reported by the Schnittgers were made when this box could not be either touched, substituted or opened by anyone other than the investigators. The precise positioning of WS's fingers clasping the box was in accord with directions from the Team, and apparently designed to protect the hasp and all five exposed surfaces from interference. The fraud hypothesis can therefore be upheld only if both the Schnittgers, and probably Dr Schaer too, were parties to the deception. It could hardly be contended that WS, an experienced senior engineer whose meticulously recorded observations show a high level of methodical diligence, could have been so negligent and sloppy as to have allowed the box to be moved from his grip, the lid opened and the tub switched, while all the time believing himself to be grasping every accessible side.

If there were any doubts about the Alan box, it may be asked, why was it not taken away for expert examination? After one sitting, we asked to have the box for precisely this purpose, and it was unhesitatingly handed to MK. However, one of us pointed out that critics might contend that we had been handed a substitute box. There might have been one identical in appearance but not in reality, or else virtually the same but for the introduction of a secret panel. A clean bill of health would therefore have meant nothing to the seriously sceptical. Accordingly the box, after careful examination by the investigators, was returned to the Group. But after the sitting on 9th November 1996, DF on the instructions of the Team took the box away with him and retained it until the 11th November sitting. He was therefore able to examine it at his leisure although, in accordance with his promise at the sitting, he did not open it. In addition, there was never anything to stop any of the experimenters from identifying the box with a secret mark had it not already been readily identifiable from the painted seals and the distinctive graining of the wood (a consideration which renders the box-substitution theory open to further objection). Since we were never asked not to make such marks, there was no way by which the Group could be sure than we had not done so.

APPENDIX L: DOUBTS ABOUT LIGHTS AND TOUCHES

By concentrating on the merits of issues concerning the minutiae of physical controls, it would be easy to overlook the value of what is frequently dismissed as unreliable subjective testimony. Indeed, in recognising this attitude towards subjective testimony, we have deliberately concentrated in this Report on evidence susceptible to objective investigation. However, it would be inappropriate to dismiss or ignore the consistency of testimony from many others apart from ourselves as to the range and impressiveness of light phenomena and touches. One feature of the touches experienced by all of us, as well as by others introduced at our request (or, in the cases of Professor Robert Morris and Dr Sheldrake, at the unprompted suggestion of the Team) was that they were often felt in places apparently inaccessible to any members of the Group had they contrived to move undetected from their chairs. Nor, unless they had furnished themselves with night-vision equipment and crawled round the table in order to touch our legs on sides away from any of them (or on occasions on sides of our legs that were in close proximity to those of a fellow-investigator), did it seem feasible for them to have created these sensations by manipulation. Even this would have involved the prior movement of arms to remove or conceal luminous wristbands, the displacement of chairs, and engaging in some fairly agile foot and knee work while maintaining conversations apparently originating from the direction of their abandoned seats. Any such movements would have risked detection, exposure and all its consequences. At Scole in particular, the problem of producing touches or manipulating lights on the side of the table opposite the Group's seats was made all the more difficult by the barriers formed by the ogee-shaped quadrant supports. As far as RF is concerned, apart from his preoccupation with tape recorders and commentaries, he is too well built for any such nimble manoeuvrings.

Even gymnastics on the part of a hypothetical fraudster could not satisfactorily account for the low-level touches experienced by the 18 sitters who participated in a session attended by MK in the converted garage at Brian Hurst's home in north Los Angeles in early April 1997, where the Group had been invited for a series of sittings for which they seemingly brought only the minimum equipment: crystals, tape recorders and music tapes (see Appendix F). Here there were cries of delight when successive sitters reported the distinctive sensation of what seemed to be a cat's upraised tail brushing against their legs. Sitting against the middle wall opposite the Group, at a distance of three or four metres, MK experienced this readily recognisable sensation too, while noting that the wristbands of the Group remained in their proper

259

places – and ascertained immediately after the sitting that no cat could be seen in the room.

Somewhat more audible was an episode the previous week when MK and the Group visited the home of Richard and Connie Adams in Mill Valley, north of San Francisco, for a sitting to which a number of scientists had been invited, including some well-known names in the paranormal field (details in Appendix F). The noise in the Mill Valley sitting, like those reported by Hans Schaer in his signed testimony of sittings in 1996 in Ibiza, took a rhythmic or musical form. Located at or near a place said to be sacred to the local Indian tribe, the floor of the large room – a domestic gymnasium – where some 20 people were assembled began to vibrate with a heavy rhythmic beat, shortly followed by an impressive drumming which appeared to come from one or both of two skin drums suspended well above the heads of those seated against one wall. Here, too, sitters reported touches, and in one case hair stroking, in another, removal of spectacles, but in no particular order or sequence. At an untranscribed sitting with the Schnittgers, MK described a caressing hand grasping his, with the fingers and even the nail of one of them clearly visible.

There was ample indication, too, that lights and touches were capable of adapting immediately in response to what was said by sitters. When during the seventh sitting (13th April 1996; R6), AE having been granted permission by Emily to rest his fingers on the edge of the table, it shifted round marginally to the left and then to the right, vibrating, this immediately stopped when DF said it was behaving like a dog shuddering. When MK light-heartedly suggested that we ought not to say this, and Emily commented that it didn't like being compared with a dog, the shaking at once resumed. At the same sitting MK was asked by an energy voice whether he was having trouble with his left leg. MK confirmed this: he had been hit by a falling limb of a tree. He then described how he was first touched between his knuckles, and then there followed a "strong feeling . . . [on the] inner side of my left knee and slightly on top of it. Just like a gentle finger, exploring ... touching my knee where I damaged it, where the bruising is." Bearing in mind that his left knee was just below the table, and he was sitting between the other two investigators, it would have been difficult to discover a less readily accessible position for normal touching.

Attention must also be drawn to the hands we saw silhouetted in the light of the crystals as they picked them up. The position of these hands could be accounted for only if a fraudster were crouching on the table. The same position would have had to be adopted on other occasions, e.g. when DF had his sweater pulled forward over the table by an unseen hand, and DF and BC had their arms raised simultaneously above their heads by an unseen force contacting them from above the table.

Not only did we fail to observe any sign of movement by any of the Group or hear any associated suspicious noise, but we have to take into account the absence of experience of such things by any of the scores of persons not associated with our inquiry, many of whom have readily offered their unqualified supporting testimony, having sat with the Group before and during the period of our investigation. All of them, and hundreds of readers of *The Spiritual Scientist*, would have been well aware of our interest and involvement, and would hardly have been slow to voice their suspicions if they felt they might have been victims of a deception. Only one person known to have sat with the Group during a seminar at Scole expressed doubts to one of us. Throughout our sittings we bore in mind that our principal objective was to establish whether a fraud hypothesis could be falsified, and indeed the participants in the Mill Valley sitting were specifically briefed in advance by MK to watch the light phenomena with a view to establishing by what means they might have been created normally. No one offered any theories.

If we look again at the list of over 30 different well-attested features of the light display listed in Chapter III, even in the absence of the associated phenomena just described, and ignoring the later evidence, it challenges explanation in terms of conjuring tricks. Even were one or more of the Group to have smuggled in items of equipment about their person undetected, no apparatus known to us or the experts consulted has been devised which could convincingly perform more than a few of the feats so extensively witnessed. The most obvious apparatus is an extensible rod through which is threaded a thin wire with an LED at its extremity, and a hand-held mechanism for increasing or diminishing luminosity, a slight variation on the theory which had been considered and rejected by James Webster, an ex-magician, in October 1994 (Webster, 1994). But even had this necessarily cumbersome piece of flexible equipment been capable of being imported concealed about the person of one of the Group, and even had he been able to manipulate it without appearing to move his arms, this would not begin to explain most of the phenomena we have listed above.

APPENDIX M: DOUBTS ABOUT THE RUTH FILMS

In Chapter VII we have given a detailed account of the circumstances which gave birth to two films bearing, in writing very similar to that of Dorothy Wordsworth, excerpts from three stanzas which amend the first edition of a *Lyrical Ballads* poem, *Ruth*. Inevitably, the extraordinary nature of this evidence obliges us to examine the likelihood that there may be a normal explanation, that is, that both films were fakes.

We have pointed out that copies of the relevant page from the Yale MS have been in the public domain, however obscurely, ever since the page was reproduced in Christies' catalogue for their auction of rare books and manuscripts on 9th December 1965. For the sake of the fraud hypothesis we must suppose that a member of the Group, or perhaps some unknown co-conspirator with a taste for the arcane and a competence in sophisticated forgery, either possessed or had seen a copy of the catalogue, or had come across one in a second-hand bookshop, noted that lot 149 might prove valuable raw material for an intricate deception, discovered that it had been sold by a member of the family to the Yale Library, undertook some research to find out more about the poem and its several editions, copied the handwriting (introducing a few subtle textual meanderings to give verisimilitude to support Joseph's statement that "it's as if he'd lost touch with his thoughts"), faked the films and perfected any related conjuring tricks required to deceive the investigators. This possibility has been forcefully put to us by a colleague, on the orthodox principle that any doubting critic would expect that all possible normal explanations should first be falsified.

Thus a good many assumptions are required to sustain the fraud hypothesis, or indeed any variant of it. In addition, if the entire operation were a fraud, it would be difficult to resist the conclusion that all the rest of the phenomena described in this Report were equally fraudulent. If this conclusion is not accepted, one would be obliged to sustain the fraud hypothesis by contending that, although in some cases the Group's phenomena were genuine, others were faked (in other words, that we had on our hands what is known as a 'mixed mediumship'), and that the Group would therefore be risking everything simply in order to add a spurious effect to those accepted as genuine.

Let us first deal with assumptions about the Christies' catalogue. It is not to be found where expected in the main Christies' archives, but in a separate catalogue of special book sales. According to the 1999 edition of *Sheppard's Book Dealers in the British Isles*, the standard reference work, there are not many antiquarian booksellers specialising in such catalogues, and none in East Anglia. Few of them handle old book-sale catalogues. Inquiries as to its present availability produced from one such specialist the description 'extremely rare'. Christies themselves have only one pressroom and one bound archival copy, neither of which is on display or carries any indication of the identity of the purchaser. Nevertheless, some 500 copies of this substantial catalogue are estimated to have been printed, and while inquiries of antiquarian booksellers reveal that there appears to be no commercial market for such ephemera, it is contended that a book browser may have found one in a second-hand bookshop, or at a car boot or jumble sale, or even in a dustbin on auctioneers' premises. It is noteworthy that all the material on both Ruth films is contained in the single sheet which Dorothy pasted into her copy, and that the catalogue did contain a fairly detailed account of the copy's provenance, together with a reference to the date 1800, the year the original poem was first published.

A parsimonious presumption, therefore, is that, unless the Group already possessed a copy or had come across one on the bookshelves of a friend, one of them, or an associated agent, had chanced on the catalogue and found on page 40 the raw material for a fraud. The descriptive material, moreover, would have provided virtually all the information required for intelligent hints to be given to the investigators, with added authority attaching to responses to questions.

The plausibility of this scenario, however, depends entirely on the assumption that the mediums had studied the evidence, and perhaps undertaken or been fed the results of further Wordsworthian research in order to dispense (admittedly well-known) quotations from, for example, the *Immortality Ode* or from the subtitle of *The Prelude*. It is hardly possible to entertain the notion that all this was a product of cryptomnesia, having been unconsciously stored in the mediums' subliminal consciousness, since it must have been associated with the very wide-awake faking of the films. We must also note the point that there is nothing in the reproduction of the verses or in the information accompanying it which indicates any particular significant difference from the original version; yet statements via the medium refer to its emotional resonance. Was this a wild guess or the product of much original research? At the end of the day we are forced back to the old dilemma: that while individual phenomena bear signs that some critics would strongly contend indicate fraud, other evidence, quite independent of the Wordsworth material, points in the opposite direction. Like us, the reader has the choice of opposites.

Even had our hypothetical faker chanced on a copy, it would have been no simple matter to conclude from catalogue annotations the identity of the real purchaser. Libraries normally buy through agents, not wishing to advertise their interest in a lot, and hence risk over-bidding.

It is clear from statements made through the medium, Alan, that the Team (or Alan himself, on the fraud hypothesis) were aware of the chequered and complex history of the verses and that the changes made to the original text of the 1800 edition from the third to the first person had a special personal significance for Wordsworth. Yet, as we have shown, no expert appears to have picked this up. We have therefore to assume that this was no more than a wild, and lucky, guess on the part of Alan, or the *eminence grise* briefing him.

Before that choice is made, however, some elaboration is needed on our earlier observation (see footnote in Chapter VII) that authorities on Wordsworth have failed to draw attention to any particular significance in the change from the third to the first person in the second edition, a change which might account for the emotional or autobiographical reference. Had they done so, what evidential value attaches to the Team's reference to emotions associated with the composition of these changes would be considerably reduced. Only a close examination of the alterations made in the *sequence* of verses in the 1802 edition yields an explanation of this apparent oversight. What appears in the 1802 edition as Stanza 28 reads:–

> Sometimes most earnestly he said,
> "Oh Ruth! I have been worse than dead:
> False thoughts, thoughts bold and vain
> Encompass'd me on every side
> When I, in thoughtlessness and pride,
> Had cross'd the Spanish Main."

For unknown reasons, however, this stanza cannot be found in the Yale MS. It may well have been sent independently to the printers, but its inclusion is essential in order to make sense of the next stanza which appears in the Ruth 1 film ("Whatever in those climes I found . . ."). As printed in the 1802 edition, there are no closing quotation marks, so that all the first person sentiments which follow can be ascribed to the youth. The quotation marks are never actually closed. This omission is corrected in the 1805 and subsequent editions, in which the author reverts to the third person. So whereas the 1800 version gives the youth sentiments not of remorse and self-criticism but of love, prospect and promise, the changes to the first person introduced by the poet for the 1802 edition appear to associate him with the temptations of voluptuous thoughts rather than with pure hopes of high intent.

There was therefore no reason why any expert commentator should ascribe autobiographical significance to the changes and hence draw attention to them. We speculate later why Wordsworth altered the sequence and personified the sentiments of the protagonist by the incorporation of new stanzas, and why he subsequently withdrew them. What we are at present concerned to explain is that, so far as can be seen, even the most dedicated and learned hoaxer would have had no reason to suspect any emotional or autobiographical significance in these extracts: and yet the Team's statements seem to show that they themselves were in fact aware of the existence of this subtle and minor set of changes in the ephemeral second edition of a volume containing a little-remarked poem among the hundreds written by Wordsworth over a period of more than sixty years. Unless we subscribe to the fraud hypothesis, it may be felt that the discovery and use of this extract, without that prior knowledge, would equate to a search for hidden treasure by digging desultorily here and there in the hope of unearthing a concealed hoard whose existence no one had any reason to suspect.

It will be recalled that during the 18th November 1996 sitting Edwin appeared to support the notion that the changes into the first person singular might have an autobiographical significance. A closer look at the situation at Dove Cottage in the spring of 1802 may show why there may well have been "a lot of emotion involved", in Edwin's words.

By the end of the previous year the revolutionary war with France was coming to a temporary halt. The Peace of Amiens was signed on 27th March 1802, the very month during which Wordsworth was struggling with the amendments to *Ruth*. Dorothy dreaded the emotional turmoil her beloved brother experienced so often when revising his poems. We may reasonably hazard that here was no exception. The advent of the peace would have turned Wordsworth's thoughts once more to the possibility of visiting France and renewing contact with the woman whom circumstances had obliged him not merely to abandon but, along with their illegitimate daughter, to leave entirely dependent on her family. (Wordsworth had been in no position to marry Annette. He was almost penniless, a Protestant and a supporter of the Revolution – and an Englishman living temporarily in a dangerous country. The Vallons by contrast were comfortable, bourgeois, Catholic and Monarchist.) Annette's devotion to Wordsworth, as we know from letters unearthed shortly before the last war, was deep and durable. As for Wordsworth himself, his youthful love had long since been enveloped in a sense of moral responsibility admixed with guilt, for in the previous month he appeared to have at last determined on marrying Mary. Stephen Gill (1990) records that Wordsworth, having met Mary on 14th February at Penrith, and again at Middleham in early April, 1802, "must have told Mary that he was determined to see Annette before their marriage", and this he duly did at Calais in August of that year, together with Dorothy.

We know little of what occurred when Wordsworth saw Annette, and his nine-year-old daughter for the first time, since Dorothy was unusually reticent of comment in her *Journal*. But it is surely not too fanciful to assume that the prospect of the meeting and the planning of it may have been in the poet's mind as he found himself identifying with the love-torn protagonist of *Ruth*. Why else would he have sought to place into the first person these expiational confessions? The autobiographical content of some of Wordsworth's verses has more often been associated with passages in his more celebrated works, notably the Lucy poems and in *The Prelude*. This might well be a further illustration. Perhaps W. J. B. Owen, in his analysis of *Wordsworth as Critic* (Owen, 1969) came close to the answer when he refers to removal of passages of text which might be considered "painful in the passion" for the purpose of giving pleasure. Whatever the truth, something prompted Wordsworth to change his mind, and in subsequent editions to restore to the emotional detachment of the third person some of the sentiments which he had temporarily converted to the first. Professor Harper's studies (Harper, op. cit.) of Dorothy's *Journal* convinced him that "his nature had received while in France a blow from which he never fully recovered, and whose causes could not have been made known to the world".

The fraud hypothesis must also be extended to account for the date of 1880, which we have discussed in Chapter VII. True, our own explanation can be accounted little more than surmise, and would have to be based on what most would consider the inherently improbable assumption of post-mortem collusion between the two poets. For what it is worth, it does link closely with the final quoted statement from Edwin when the accuracy of the date was challenged. The fraud hypothesis must presuppose either that this was a meaningless number or a mistake for 1800, the date appearing on the Christies' catalogue above the descriptive introduction to the lot. This explanation gains merit from Dr Gauld's contention that the strength of any supposed close emotional relationship between Myers and Wordsworth in Chapter VII is weaker than suggested. We acknowledge that there is much unsupported speculation in both views but, as always, present them for the reader's own judgement.

In presenting this Appendix we must make clear that, although DF does not diverge from MK and AE on the discussion of the fraud hypothesis, he considers the examination of the possible authorship of the Ruth films takes us too far into matters of literary speculation. He prefers not to hazard suggestions as to the authorship, but considers that those who wish to do so might prefer to attribute to Myers the paranormal origin of the film verses. Myers had already been identified (by Emily Bradshaw) as a communicator – "that great man" – and was closely linked with the Diotima film message (see Chapter V). One of his own poems had already been transmitted; he shared with Wordsworth, whom he admired, a love of the Lake District as well as poetry. His biography of Wordsworth was first published in 1880. DF speculates that Joseph's reference to someone fond of words was not untypical of the clues in which the Team chose to indulge (e.g. the strewth/truth puns on 'Ruth' given shortly afterwards in the same sitting), and he considers it noteworthy that no direct reference was made to Wordsworth himself during the 11th November sitting. When, during the subsequent 18th November discussions, MK queried the "degree of autobiographical evidentiality" behind the poem, and "whether the significance related to Wordsworth or more indirectly to Myers", he received the answer "I can't answer that; I can't help you". Joseph's subsequent remark, "it was the gentleman himself, his own feelings when he added those particular verses changed prior to publication" is clearly confusing, as Wordsworth published both versions of the poem in different editions. Likewise MK's subsequent comment that the verses "appear to be inspired by [Wordsworth's] recollection of Miss Vallon", and his suggestion that they "had been indirectly inspired by Annie Marshall" evoked the same response: "I can't help you with that". Such non-committal responses, and the absence of further evidence, has led DF to argue that it is unnecessary to postulate any direct paranormal involvement by Wordsworth himself, although his argument is not fully accepted by AE and MK.

ACKNOWLEDGEMENTS

Our principal acknowledgements must be to the members of the Scole Group themselves, whose hospitality and friendship we have enjoyed and whose trust we believe we gained and retained. They were always conscious of our rôle as detached investigators in search of the truth. It would not simply have been a betrayal of that trust had any of us tried to act in a fashion inconsistent with the rules under which we had agreed to work together: such unethical behaviour would have ensured the speedy ending of our relationship. Similarly, any unethical conduct on the part of the Group would have forfeited our trust. (It is important to stress that at no time did any of the Group even ask us to discuss any suspicion of fraud with them before making it public. They therefore knew – and appeared happy to accept – that we were professionally bound to reveal immediately any evidence of deception.) It must also be stressed that neither individually nor collectively did the Group ever seek financial help from us or make any direct or implied monetary demands on us, although their circumstances have been such as would have made this neither unreasonable nor unexpected, since, by devoting so much time and effort to our investigation, they have in fact sacrificed the prospects of augmenting their income. As we have mentioned earlier, this was particularly apparent during the Group's visit to the USA. Anonymous donations and a vote-in-aid to the investigators from the Tate funds of the SPR (which are gratefully acknowledged) have helped us to defray only the Group's costs in transcribing the tapes of our sittings, without which the preparation of this report would not have been possible, and in reproducing and enlarging the photographs for our benefit.

In addition we are greatly indebted to the Group, or more accurately the New Spiritual Science Foundation, for their permission to reproduce the illustrations contained in this Report, whose copyright they possess.

We also pay grateful and affectionate tribute to the important contribution made by our former colleague and dear friend Ralph Noyes, who died in May 1998. He played a leading rôle in the preliminaries which resulted in the original invitation to investigate the Scole Group's claims and activities, and attended the first two sittings. Thereafter he remained as a special consultant, the only other person beyond the three present signatories to have been privileged to read the transcripts and annotations of all the sittings. His wise, detached and cautious appraisals, and his gentle encouragement, were of enormous value to us.

We must in addition express our thanks to several of our colleagues who have attended sittings and provided us with written accounts of their experiences and reactions. Particular thanks are due to Alan Gauld for his rôle of rigorously objective critic and for his encyclopaedic familiarity with the personalities and early history of the Society, to Tony Cornell for his and Alan Gauld's experiments in seeking to re-create by normal means some of the film material, and to explore means by which some of the phenomena might be susceptible to a non-paranormal explanation. Our gratitude is also due to our co-investigators, Walter and Karin Schnittger, whose own sittings with the Group, sometimes in the company of one or more of us, have resulted in some highly valuable and carefully documented material evidence, a good deal of it discussed herein. Likewise Dr Hans Schaer, another co-investigator, whose thirteen sittings with the group over a period of more than two years in three countries has been accompanied by fully documented and signed accounts readily provided at our request. His very generous support of the group's activities, including the purchase of a video camera for their use, and his hosting of sittings in Ibiza and Switzerland, have greatly augmented the volume and quality of evidence, some of which forms an important part of this Report. We must also thank Ingrid Slack for her assistance at three sittings, and her advice and support throughout, and Prof. Bernard Carr, Dr John Beloff, Prof. Donald West, Prof. Grattan-Guinness, Prof. Robert Morris, Prof. Archie Roy and Dr Rupert Sheldrake, all of whom joined us at some point for sittings.

In addition we must thank Denzil Fairbairn and a group of co-sitters at a seminar held on 25th May 1996, for their signed account of the circumstances in which a Polaroid film was produced; Beverley Dear for her successful research into the source of the Golden Chain film, and her valuable personal references affording us insight into the background and probity of the two mediums; Douglas Tarr of the Edison National Memorial Site for a wealth of valuable material on Edison; our SPR colleague Rosemary Dinnage for her constructive comments on the draft of our report and, with Mary Rose Barrington, help in grappling with the Ruth poem; Dr Hubert Larcher in Paris for his efforts, albeit unavailing, to identify the mysterious 'RS' associated with his compatriot Louis Daguerre; Prof. Harold Shurmer for providing a slice of germanium; Frank Franklyn for his analysis of the 'Rachmaninoff' tape recording, and Michael Green and David and Julie Rousseau for their efforts to interpret some of the pictogrammic or hieroglyphic material contained in two or three of the films, even though we have not thought it appropriate to depart from our principal objectives by attempting to analyse their meanings.

We also acknowledge with thanks the help of the Curator of Rare Books and MSS at the Beinecke Library in Yale, and his kind permission to reproduce without fee one page of the script of Wordsworth's corrections to the second edition of the *Lyrical Ballads* embodying textual changes in *Ruth*.

School Barn Farm
Pentlow, Sudbury   CO10 7JN

MONTAGUE KEEN

10 Foxgrove Avenue
Beckenham   BR3 5BA

ARTHUR ELLISON

6 Larch Grove
Lisvane, Cardiff   CF14 0TH

DAVID FONTANA

REFERENCES

Allan, R. (1997) Crystal powers. Electronic switches made from silicon carbide will be able to operate in conditions that would destroy silicon chips. *New Scientist (14th June).*

Atkins, R. (1933) *The Clubs of Augustan London.* Harvard University Press.

Balfour, Countess of (1960) The Palm Sunday Case. *ProcSPR 52 (189),* 83.

Barrington, M. R. (1996) *JSPR 61 (845),* 268–270.

Beard, P. (1966) *Survival of Death,* 51. London: Psychic Press.

Beloff, J. (1993) *Parapsychology: A Concise History.* London: Athlone Press.

Bessy, M. (1963) *A Pictorial History of Magic and the Supernatural.* London: Spring Books.

Braude, S. (1998) *Postmortem survival: the state of the deba*te. (Lecture to Society for Psychical Research, 23rd March).

Brett and Jones (1963) *Lyrical Ballads.* Methuen.

Butler and Green (1992) *Lyrical Ballads and Other Poems, 1797–1800.* Cornell University Press.

Carlotto, M. (1997) Evidence that objects on Mars are artificial. *Journal of Scientific Exploration 11,* 2.

Curtis, J. (1971) *Wordsworth's Experiments with Tradition: the Lyrical poems of 1802 with Texts of the Poems based on early MSS.* Cornell University Press.

Darwin, B. (1903) *British Clubs.* William Collins.

Edison, T. A. (1921/1926) Interviews in *New York Times,* 23rd January 1921 and 15th October 1926.

Edwards, H. (1962) *The Mediumship of Jack Webber.* Surrey: Healer Publishing.

Fodor, N. (1933) *Encyclopaedia of Psychic Science,* 331.

Foy, Robin P. (1996) *In Pursuit of Physical Mediumship.* London: Janus.

Escott, T. H. S. (1914) *Club Makers and Club Members.* Fisher Unwin.

Garrod, H. W. (1922, 1927) *Wordsworth's Lectures and Essays.* Oxford University Press.

Gauld, A. (1982) *Mediumship and Survival.* Paladin.

Geley, G. (1927) *Clairvoyance and Materialisation.* London.

Gill, S. (1990) *Wordsworth: An Autobiography,* 205. Oxford University Press.

Goodman, F. (1989) *Magic Symbols.* London: Brian Trodd Publishing House.

Green, C. (1963) *London Clubs.* Chivas Royal Regal Production, Cassell.

Gregory, A. (1985) *The Strange Case of Rudi Schneider.* Scarecrow Press.

Haisch, B. (ed.) et al. (1996) Reports on Government-sponsored remote viewing programs. *Journal of Scientific Exploration 10,* 1.

Harper, G. McL. (1921) *Wordsworth's French Daughter.*

Hart, H. (1959) *The Enigma of Survival.* London: Rider.

Heinzerling, J. (1997) All about EVP. *Fortean Times No 104.*

Inglis, B. (1984) *Science and Parascience: A History of the Paranormal, 1914–1939,* 156 et seq. (Crandon); 66 et seq. London: Hodder and Stoughton.

Jacobus, M. (1976) *Tradition and Experiment in Wordsworth's Lyrical Ballads.* Clarenden Press.

Johnson, A. (1908) *ProcSPR 21* (55).

Lejeune, A. (1979) *The Gentlemen's Clubs of London.* MacDonald & Jane.

Lewis, Malcolm (1995) Is the Ark losing direction? *Noah's Ark Society 4* (60) (July).

Lodge, Sir O. (1909) *The Survival of Man,* 287. Methuen.

Lodge, Sir O. et al. (1901) *ProcSPR 17* (42).

McClean, A. (1997) Alchemy in the age of Rudolf II. (Paper read at the September 1997 Conference on Prague, Alchemy and the Hermetic Tradition).

Murphy, G. and Ballou, O. (1960) *William James on Psychical Research.* New York: The Viking Press [re-issued by Augustus M. Kelley, Clifton, New Jersey, 1973].

Myers, F. W. H. (1961) *Fragments of Inner Life.* Society for Psychical Research.

Myers, F. W. H. (1903) *Human Personality and its Survival of Bodily Death, Vol. II,* 282.

Myers, F. W. H. (1880) *Wordsworth.* Macmillan.

Myers, F. W. H. (1881) *Wordsworth.* English Men of Letters Series, ed. J. Morley.

Nevill, R. (1911) *London Clubs.* Chatto & Windus.

Nicol, F. (1972) The founders of the S.P.R. *ProcSPR 55* (205), 341–367.

Oppenheim, J. (1985) *The Other World: Spiritualism and Psychical Research in England, 1850–1914.* Cambridge University Press.

Owen, A. (1989) *Spiritualism and the Subversion and Feminine,* 210–211. Virago Press,.

Owen, W. J. B. (1969) *Wordsworth as Critic,* 63. University of Toronto Press.

Podmore, F. (1902) *Modern Spiritualism (2 vols).* Methuen.

Polidoro, M. and Rinaldi, G. M. (1998) Eusapia's sapient foot: a new consideration of the Feilding Report. *JSPR 62* (850), 242–257.

Pottle, F. A. (1966) *Yale University Library Gazette 41* (2), quoting Hale White's *Description of Wordsworth and Coleridge Manuscripts in the Possession of T. Norton.* London: Longman, 1897.

Robert, J. (1983) Notre Metro. Published by the Paris Metro.

Salter, W. H. (1958) *ProcSPR 52* (187), 1.

Spiritual Scientist (1994) *No.1.*

Sturrock, P. (1994) Applied statistical inference. *Journal of Scientific Exploration 8* (4).

Tappan, C. (1878) *Discourses through the Mediumship of Mrs Cora L. V. Tappan.*

Targ, R. and Puthoff H. (1977) *Mind-Reach.* London: Jonathan Cape.

Thomas, C. D. (1922) *Some New Evidence for Human Survival.*

Thomas, C. D. (1928–9) The modus operandi of trance communication according to descriptions received through Mrs Osborne Leonard. *ProcSPR 38,* 49–100.

Thomas, C. D. (1935) A proxy case extending over 11 sittings with Mrs Osborne Leonard. *ProcSPR 43,* 439–519.

Timbs, J. (1872) *Clubs and Clublife in London from the 17th Century to 1872.* Savill.

Tyrrell, G. N. M. (1953) *Apparitions.* Society for Psychical Research [originally published in 1943; reprinted 1973].

Verrall, M. de G. (Mrs A. W.) (1894) *ProcSPR 8,* 473 et seq.

Verrall, M. de G. (1906) On a series of automatic writings. *ProcSPR 20 (53).*

Verrall, M. de G. (1910) Classical and literary allusions in Mrs Piper's trance. *ProcSPR 24,* 39–85.

Webster, J. B. (1994) Witness report of an early visitor to the Scole Group. *The Spiritual Scientist (Issue 1).* New Spiritual Science Foundation, Scole, Diss, Norfolk, IP21 4DR

Wiseman, R. (1992) The Feilding Report: a reconsideration. *JSPR 58 (826),* 129–153.

Wiseman, R. and Schlitz, M. (1998) Further report on the remote detection of staring and the experimenter effect. (Paper presented at the 22nd SPR Conference).

White, H. (1897) *Description of Wordsworth and Coleridge Manuscripts in the Possession of T. Norton.* London: Longman.

THE SCOLE INVESTIGATION: COMMENTARY ON STRATEGY AND OUTCOME

by D. J. West

Investigation of the physical phenomena of the séance room has virtually ceased, perhaps because modern observational instruments have made fraud too difficult, perhaps because the reputation the SPR has acquired for assuming everything fraudulent has rendered genuine psychics uncooperative. On learning that the Scole Group were regularly producing phenomena and that leading SPR members had obtained their agreement to an investigation, I hoped that at last this branch of research might take a giant step forward, but in the event I found this report sadly unconvincing.

Spiritualist tradition provokes scepticism by imposing conditions that impede investigation, such as darkness, rules that cast the investigators in the role of 'sitters' who must not move or touch without permission, and the supposed necessity for music and chatter which distracts attention and further limits observation of varied happenings that occur without prior warning. Magicians and illusionists could hardly devise better circumstances for their tricks. What excited my interest in Scole was a report of images being psychically impressed onto undeveloped film enclosed in a secure box. Unlike strange movements and touches, this seemed readily testable without requiring light. All one needs is a pristine film inserted in full view with precautions against subsequent surreptitious substitution of a previously prepared film, or replacement of the box with a similar one containing a doctored film.

In the event, meaningful images, which would have required much preparation were they produced normally, appeared on a number of films, but only when a box made by the son of one of the group was used, a box which was subsequently shown by Dr Gauld to be far from secure. When the films were enclosed in secure envelopes provided by Dr Wiseman nothing of the sort appeared, and when a secure padlocked box was provided by the investigators the films remained blank. Doubts would have been dispelled if only an image could have been obtained using a secure locked box and a film on which the investigators had made a prior identifying mark to forestall substitution. (In previous experiments only the film's container was marked.) Although film phenomena continued for some time, this simple, non-intrusive protocol was never achieved. The authors suggest (p.108) that "these doubts are not relevant . . . when a sealed security bag was used or when the film tubs were hand-held". However, of the two occasions when odd specks of light and other marks appeared when the Wiseman bags were used, one result was described as "a disappointment" (p.89) and the other, subsequently lost, was "a poor quality film" making copying difficult. When the film tubs were held by the Schnittgers they were using films from stock that had been stored at Scole out of the control of the investigators.

The spirits' declared aim (p.52) was "to perfect our experiments to the point where we produce repeatable, successful results". This would certainly have been endorsed by the SPR pioneers, Myers and Rayleigh. If, as alleged, their spirits were helping, it is strange that they did not seem to appreciate the impact just one more image obtained under proper control would have made. Straightforward, repeatable tests, which would have been much more convincing than ephemeral effects under cover of darkness, were not forthcoming. The investigators failed to interest the spirits in simple ESP tests or in operating a device produced by Maurice Grosse for registering movements of objects shielded from normal intervention (p.53).

Floating lights, mysterious luminous appearances, movements of objects and touches by seemingly disembodied hands would all have been more impressive had the effects been directly viewable, but requests for the use of thermal imaging devices or infra-red cameras were refused or put off with hints that eventually something of the sort would be allowed. Since sources of heat already present were giving off infra-red without harm to the mediums, the resistance to making use of it to view the phenomena appears unreasonable and suspicious.

The Scole group, supposedly under directions from spirits, determined the nature and timing of the phenomena. The investigators acted much like the audience at an orchestrated performance. Had they been given greater freedom to design appropriate tests, validation of the occurrence of gross physical effects would have been more straightforward. Strip searches and physical restraints with ropes, handcuffs and the like are clumsy, inefficient and deeply embarrassing, and unnecessary if other tests are allowed. For instance, could not the many apports allegedly passing through the cellar walls have been directed into a securely closed box? Palpable force was involved in the many touches, movements, ringing of bells and vibrations of the table described in the report. One recordable tug on a measuring instrument shielded from normal interference would have been worth more than any number of such manifestations.

At an interim presentation of the progress of the research to members of the SPR Council, it was suggested that the Scole group should be asked to agree to further trials with protocols precisely followed. This proved impracticable when the spirits announced that the investigatory sittings must cease. The reason given does not appear in the report, but was set out in the Scole magazine *The Spiritual Scientist,* for March

1999. It was due to interference from "an interdimensional time wave pattern that was coming from the future in our own world, and was being generated by a crystalline time probe." . . . "It is only when our four energies are reaching out that this interference from the future takes place." . . . "Since the probing of time . . . was a violation of the cosmic and interdimensional laws of time and space, it must not be allowed to continue."

The investigators cannot be blamed for restrictions imposed by others. Indeed they are to be congratulated for successfully negotiating permission for themselves and selected visitors to attend Scole sessions, to try some limited experiments and to publish their observations freely. However, when investigators agree to imperfect protocols not of their own design, the outcome, as historical examples have shown repeatedly, is generally inconclusive and a great waste of effort, serving only to generate sterile controversy about the possibility or probability of hoaxing, as has happened here. Ideally, agreement with psychic claimants should be reached at the outset about what phenomena are under scrutiny and what tests are needed to establish with reasonable certainty that they could not be produced by normal means. It is tempting for investigators to consent to work under less ideal circumstances for the sake of seeing something, but this can be self-defeating.

The merits of different aspects of the Scole output are argued elsewhere. I was present at one session only (although invited a second time when I was not free) and most of what was seen on that occasion I believe could have been produced normally. The report comments in several places (e.g. p.64) that objects and touches were "delivered with a precision which seemed inconsistent with the absence of light". That would not apply were an infra-red viewer, denied the investigators, in use by others. The gyrations of small spot lights resembled what Cornell demonstrated to me with his LED lights. The interrupted patterns traced by the lights could have been created by the partial interposition of small screens or obstructing fingers and the apparent disappearance through the table could have been engineered by strategic switching on and off of different bulbs. I was unconvinced that the luminous spots on wrist bands were a secure method of control. It was impossible for sitters to monitor them all continuously and in the dark they could be covered and others substituted. It is said that lack of space would have prevented a trickster moving behind sitters to ring bells or perform other tricks, but that was not my impression. It is also said that moving and replacing the box with the film inside it, when its exact position was marked with a pencil, would have been impractical in the dark. This assumes that some more robust marker, a set square for example, was not put in place before removal. The authors' counter arguments would have been more impressive had they in each instance tried for themselves whether the suggested manoeuvres were possible.

The report is frank about many details calculated to arouse suspicion. However, despite the carefully worded conclusion, which reviews some of the weaknesses in the evidence, the body of the report leaves no doubt about the authors' belief in the genuineness of the phenomena, which may account for a certain lack of enthusiasm for exploring alternative hypotheses. It was others who located the originals from which some of the mysterious photographic images were taken and who discovered that the image of the Ruth poem was as reproduced in the Christie's catalogue, that many of the references to the Cross-Correspondences and matters concerning SPR history were contained in one accessible book and that some of the lights and photographic effects were reproducible normally. The authors emphasise the qualifications and gravitas of many witnesses of the Scole phenomena, but this is far less relevant than the often limited opportunity for witnesses to observe or the investigators to experiment. Little mention is made of the views of persons like myself and Professor Robert Morris, who expressed reservations on the basis of what they experienced. It is pointed out that direct evidence of deception is absent, that some of the phenomena are very difficult to explain normally and that the Scole production should be viewed as a whole. However, the absence of any one conclusive test, the fact that supposedly paranormal images on film were seemingly obtained by mundane methods of reproduction from identifiable sources and the implausible, if not nonsensical, quality of some of the Scole communications cited in this report and in *The Spiritual Scientist* amount in total to substantial reason for doubt.

The authors were given reason to hope that the Scole group would eventually repeat one or other of their effects under conditions virtually precluding a normal explanation. Accordingly, they accepted the spirit team as collaborators in devising protocols. That the goal was never quite reached is no reflection on their commendable patience and diligence in its pursuit. They have put on record an instructive account which will be helpful to anyone researching séance room effects in the future.

32 Fen Road
Milton, Cambridge   CB4 6AD

SOME COMMENTS ON THE SCOLE REPORT

by A. D. Cornell

When first hearing early reports about the mental and physical effects experienced by those involved in the investigation of the Scole group, the immediate reaction was that some greater advance in the understanding of the subject would be the inevitable result. The apparent degree of cooperation between the mediums and investigators, the content of the mental communication and the type of physical effects reported by those attending the séances – all appeared to be different from the pattern of past investigations. However, as more details came to light, the claim of a 'breakthrough' in the presentation of the effects, the evidence for their paranormal nature and the conditions in which they occurred raised considerable doubts in the minds of other investigators with equal if not more experience in the field.

Having now read the report there can be no doubt in my mind about the sincerity of all those involved and they must be congratulated for their patience and the considerable amount of work entailed in the actual investigation and preparation of the report. One must also admire the investigators' perseverance in the face of their repeatedly being unable to introduce better control conditions. However, on the basis of the conditions that prevailed throughout one cannot agree with their insistence that most if not all the phenomena could be shown to be paranormal. The protocol was mainly if not entirely dictated by the Spirit team, thus severely restricting the greater degree of control that the investigators should have insisted upon. Although I did not attend any of the Scole séances myself, the descriptions of the circumstances and phenomena given to me by six Council members who did indicated that the pattern of the Scole group séances, with the possible exception of new forms of various light phenomena, was in essence no different from the usual spiritualist séance room proceedings. The playing of music to raise the vibrations, the trance addresses through the mediums by various communicators, the production of physical effects of the most mundane and banal nature – in near if not complete darkness – are certainly no 'breakthrough' and nothing new.

I have sat with more than a dozen physical mediums in well over a hundred séances in varying conditions of darkness. I can consequently fully understand the mixed reactions of doubt by some and complete acceptance of the paranormal nature of the effects by others investigating such proceedings. The authors make it plain that by and large they are of the view that the physical phenomena they experienced at Scole were produced by paranormal means. They also intimate that they were all far from inexperienced in the investigation of such phenomena. However, the claim that various séance room phenomena are paranormally produced by discarnate spirits is in one sense an insult to both the intellect of the alleged discarnates (if indeed such exist) and the living who accept them as evidence. One should be entitled to expect some-thing of a more sophisticated evidential nature than touches, vibrating tables, the ringing of bells and odd lights flitting here and there as proof of survival. Such a momentous claim of immortality ought to be matched with an equally outstanding effect, impossible to have been normally produced by human means.

It might well be that the apparently inexplicable cause of the behaviour of the lights (which also puzzled many other visitors to Scole), and the 'foolproof' means by which the films and Polaroids were produced, were all sufficiently inexplicable in normal terms for the authors to express the views they do. One must nevertheless take into account the possibility that they were so enthralled by the dramatic performance of it all in the dark that they accepted without questioning enough whether it could have other than a paranormal explanation. Alan Gauld has shown how in the dark the padlocked Alan box could be opened and closed in a matter of seconds. The Dragon film images were all taken from an easily available book and displayed clear signs of how they could have been produced by normal means. The same applies to the Ruth film hand-writing, which has all the appearance of a photographed hand-traced copy of the reproduction, slightly reduced in size, of the original page corrections in Christie's Catalogue. In view of the normal explanation that could be given for many of the phenomena, one is bound to ask whether a high proportion if not all were wrongly interpreted. This might particularly apply to the light effects, occurring as they did in conditions that did not allow an overall view of their source. One must also question to what extent some of the experiences might have been subjective. For example, in the numbered list of light effects in Chapter III, one investigator claimed that a light (13) that first touched his chest could then be felt moving around inside his body.

Some of the light effects can be produced by the use of an LED (Light-Emitting Diode) on the end of an extensible reaching rod or dangling on the end of a thin electric wire. Also one should note that an LED powered with a small watch battery suspended by magicians' invisible string will miraculously remain alight if dropped into a glass of water. Such effects may appear inexplicable in normal terms and can easily lead one to assume a paranormal cause.

Without question the value of human testimony in such matters can not and should not be ignored, but claims for the paranormal nature of any events, particularly those experienced in the séance room, may be driven by a 'strong desire to believe'. Just because one cannot explain something immediately in normal terms it does not follow that it must be paranormal. It is almost obligatory for any investigator, if he wishes to be taken seriously in the contentious field of psychical research, to at least attempt to replicate by normal means any witnessed paranormal effect. In this regard, there is little if any indication that the authors of the report have ever tried to undertake this important requirement.

Conditions in which Phenomena Occurred

Doubts about the authenticity of the trance communication content, purporting to provide evidence of Cross-Correspondences of the type reported by SPR pioneers, and the possibility of a normal explanation of the physical effects have already been raised by Dr Alan Gauld and others. As already indicated I too have considerable doubts about the paranormal origin of the lights, and the verbal and written photographic communications, particularly those of the Dragon and Ruth films (and the Ibiza Polaroids, which I will touch on later). In addition to the major weakness of the whole investigation represented by these and the absence of any infra-red viewing or recording, I am equally concerned with the fact that the authors are prepared to accept the paranormal nature of the physical effects under the uncontrolled conditions in which they occurred. For example:–

1 At no time were the mediums ever searched before or after any of the sittings.

2 All the sittings were held in total or near total darkness.

3 The mediums were never restrained in any way and were allowed to sit beside one another. In a properly controlled investigation they would have been controlled by investigators sitting on either side, and in this case also sitting between the mediums. The investigators, seated on the other side of the table, were in the position of visitors or observers rather than researchers.

4 Continuous music was allowed to be played which could be used to cover up the noise of any normal human movement around the table (as felt moving behind him by one SPR Council member during the séance he attended at Scole with another group).

5 The Velcro-attached luminous armbands used to indicate everyone's position around the table were never replaced with more difficult to remove luminous fittings.

6 The four luminous table-top tabs were never removed to ensure that they were not being used as reference points by anyone producing any physical phenomena by normal means.

7 Most equipment used was provided by the Scole group and not the investigators.

8   The photographic phenomena were always confined to the Scole box, never that of MK.

9   The 35mm film metal co ntainers put in the boxes were never identity marked – only the tubs.

10   The Ibiza Polaroids were not placed in light-tight sealed envelopes as an extra control.

Although most of these points have been dealt with in the report, they remain valid criticisms of specific shortcomings that cannot be ignored. The authors of the report express the view that one must judge the paranormal nature of the phenomena both verbal and physical as a whole. Nevertheless, the lack of control conditions that the above list represents (however difficult they might have been to change at the risk of offending members of the Scole group) tends to reduce almost to zero the evidential value of the physical effects as indicators of paranormal action.

The Lights, Ibiza and Cambridge Polaroids

As already mentioned above, some of the behaviour patterns of the lights at Scole resemble effects that can be obtained from LEDs. Experiments undertaken in Cambridge in early 1996 with different configurations of these lights strongly supported this idea. Three SPR members who had been to Scole thought they appeared to be the same and felt similar to the touch in the dark. However, without any actual comparison of like with like no definite conclusions were possible. It was only much later, in 1997, when attempts to replicate the Ibiza Polaroids were made by Alan Gauld and myself in Cambridge, that it became apparent that LEDs can also be used to produce effects resembling some of the other alleged paranormal effects.

While replicating exactly the same procedure that MK said he had been instructed by the Spirit team to follow at Ibiza, a number of polaroids were exposed by me to different lights. The use of various tungsten and halogen bulbs with different coloured filters failed to produce similar diffused patterns to those obtained at Ibiza. Repeated attempts in two further three-hour experiments with various strengths of light and exposure to infra-red and low-level radioactive sources produced no better results. Following the thought that perhaps the use of LEDs could produce more than one type of paranormal light effect, their use was incorporated in the procedure, and only then were the almost identical colour-matching compositions of the Ibiza Polaroids obtained. With the help of another SPR member, Mr Tony Percy, further experiments produced positive results. When a modified 2 x 2-inch car-key light and pen light, both with a 3-volt green LED, were pressed onto the Polaroid film surface or held 1–2 inches above it for between 1 and 5 seconds, white, green and yellow patterns of varying composition similar to the Ibiza Polaroids were created. The black patches that are evident in the Ibiza films were replicated by placing a small cut-out patch of cardboard on the surface of the film and subjecting it to a 3-second green LED exposure.

MK's reaction to the Cambridge Polaroids (as discussed in Appendix J of the report) was, and continues to be, that they were of no consequence, having not been reproduced under conditions absolutely identical to those that existed at Ibiza. Neither could they, he argues, be held as evidence for the Ibiza polaroids having been produced by normal means, as none of the others present around the gate-legged table could have done this without detection by MK. In fact the whole object of the Cambridge experiment was not to attempt to replicate the polaroid images in exactly the same circumstances that prevailed at Ibiza (which would be difficult if not impossible anyway), but to see how, if at all, such images could be produced by normal means, and having done so then try (with some success) to create them undetected in a totally dark room – a question which the authors never attempted to address. Reproduction of the Polaroids in the report is confined to only two examples from the first Ibiza set (Plate 17). The reader is consequently denied the chance to compare side by side the first Ibiza six with the Cambridge set of six. If the authors are so confident about the paranormal nature of the Ibiza polaroids, they should surely allow more comparisons to be made than they have done. The inclusion of two examples of each of the Cambridge and Ibiza polaroids side by side in Plate 18 does however to some extent provide that facility. The suggestion that no one could have used an LED to produce the effects in the one hour of dark conditions, during which music was played, and people doubtless talked, coughed and moved about in their chairs, while the Polaroids lay on the table in front of MK, is not entirely convincing. An hour of darkness is a long time in which to be so sure that one's attention might not be diverted sufficiently to allow for the theoretical possibility of the Polaroids being handled by someone else. Why the simple expedient of making the whole experiment more foolproof and evidential, by placing each of the films in a light-proof sealed and signed envelope, was not undertaken defies comprehension. It conforms to a pattern in which a rigorous need for strict controls to validate such inexplicable occurrences was never respected.

The Daily Mail Apport

The credence the authors place upon the paranormal nature of the 1st April 1944 *Daily Mail* apport mentioned in Chapter I (p.35) could well be unwarranted. Despite the evidence of the chemical analysis MK obtained, which he considers to confirm the genuineness of the wartime letterpress-printed apport, there remain details that suggest otherwise. In a letter to me on the subject dated 12th April 1999 in which he described his findings (as outlined in the footnote on page 35), he ended his letter with the comment – "So you appear to be mistaken about the genuineness claim, But Alan [Gauld] was right when he said that newspapers during the war carried a red banner or masthead of some sort. This one is black! Is this the nearest we can get to a permanent paranormal object or do you have an alternative theory? It really is very puzzling, no?"

Like everything else connected with the Scole phenomena, complications cloud any attempt to get a clear answer regarding their true value. Either the chemical analysis and or the red logo would appear to be the key to the genuineness of the wartime claim. The importance of it having been printed by the letterpress method becomes less evidential in view of the fact that it is likely that many, if not all, of the thousands of replica wartime copies of various national newspapers reprinted in 1973 and early 80s were also printed by the letterpress method. The replica copy of the 1st April 1944 with a black "LATE WAR NEWS" logo which I bought in July 1997 for £15 from "Remember Then" appears, according to two senior newspaper print managers, also to have been printed by letterpress. I have not had it chemically analysed but as far as I know, neither did MK although I gave him a sample of it in October '97, to compare like with like. Dr Skelton Foord of the National Newspaper Library checked for me the six month January to June 1944 editions of the *Daily Mail* and confirmed that they all had red "LATE WAR NEWS" logos. The managing director of John Frost Newspapers (who hold large stocks of old and new newspaper editions which they supply to the media), states that in his opinion any wartime copy of the *Daily Mail* with a black "Late War News" logo can only be a replica. It was his firm that provided the original wartime 1st April 1944 edition to the publishers Marshall Cavendish to copy and reprint.

It is interesting to note that of all the different wartime national newspaper editions selected for reprinting, only two *Daily Mail* dates were chosen. One was the 1st April 1944 principally reporting Russian advances on Odessa and the death of Orde Wingate. But reporting also as it did on its front page the trial of Helen Duncan, it might well have been bought by quite a few spiritualists even if it did not have a red logo. Further investigation of the contradictions that are involved in the evidence for the paranormality of the Scole *Daily Mail* apport is certainly required.

While acknowledging that it is always easy to criticise and the fact that no amount of evidence will ever satisfy the out and out non-believing critic, the lack of proper control conditions and of any attempts by the investigators to replicate the effects by normal means are the greatest weaknesses of the report, which any critic will unfortunately but justifiably single out. As a result the report is less evidential than the authors claim it to be. This applies in particular to the fact that all the phenomena acclaimed as most difficult to explain were produced in near if not total darkness. The insistence by the Spirit team that no infra-red or thermal image camera recording could be taken of any part of the proceedings, represents the ultimate Achilles heel of the investigation. The investigators certainly cannot be blamed for this, as they tried several times to introduce the idea and emphasised that it could do no bodily harm to anyone. This fact was demonstrated as long ago as April 1930, when Eugène Osty obtained some very positive and interesting laboratory experimental results using a camera with a quartz lens, infra-red beams and ultra-violet light in sittings with Rudi Schneider at the Paris Institut Métapsychique International. Osty's findings were more indicative of a PK human faculty than any manipulation by spirits. This is another consideration the investigators should have made more allowance for than they do, instead of accepting that everything was the result of discarnate activity.

What better way could the claims of the Scole Group be verifiably presented (and those of any other physical séance circle) than to have a replayable continuous infra-red video record verifying some of the physical effects for the whole world to see? The fact that such promises are repeatedly made by physical mediums but never come about, or are side-stepped at the last minute (as has been my experience several times), may well indicate that no such record is likely to be made. Such reluctance to allow what is really going on in the dark to be seen in every detail may well indicate a recognition that it would reveal too much and could sound the death knell of its practice.

In conclusion, I have said that much of the phenomena reported can be produced by normal means. That is not to say that they were so produced or that paranormal effects do not ever occur in séance rooms. But it is enough to undermine any claim that the major effects *must* have been paranormal, which is the sort of evidence that psychical research looks for.

22 Victoria Street
Cambridge   CB1 1JP

COMMENTS ON THE SCOLE REPORT

by Alan Gauld

Introduction

There are five preliminary points which I would wish readers to bear in mind throughout what follows. The first is that, however critical I may be of the contents of the Scole Report, I greatly admire the huge amount of work put in by the authors, particularly the senior author, and the dedication of the Scole Group. The second, equally important, is that I am not levelling accusations of hoaxing or fraud against any of those involved – I have known the leader of the Scole group for well over thirty years without finding any reason to regard him as anything other than totally sincere. My comments here are entirely concerned with the acceptability or otherwise of the evidence presented in the Scole Report. The third is that I am not by any means a total disbeliever in the paranormal phenomena associated with physical mediumship. The fourth is that I do not myself have any overall explanation that I regard as completely satisfactory of the various happenings reported from Scole. The phenomena that I witnessed on my own visit ranged from some that would not have been too difficult to explain normally (little floating 'figurines' that looked exactly like crumpled pieces of gauze or tulle illuminated from within, whirling lights with dark gaps in the circle such as an interposed black object might have produced), to some that were not altogether easy to explain (a small hard light that several times quite firmly tapped first one of my upturned palms and then the other without presenting any sign of an attachment such as one might have expected to see or feel). And the fifth is that my comments presuppose that the reader is adequately familiar with the contents of the Scole Report.

Some particular issues

Under this heading I shall discuss a selection of the matters that occupy a chapter and/or an appendix of the Scole Report, or substantial parts of a chapter or appendix. I have selected them because each is in various ways of central importance; and also because through facilities available to me, and/or through the courtesy of MK, I was well placed to look into them.

The 'Alan' Box (Appendix K)

The 'Alan' Box was involved in several of the cases in which ostensibly paranormal markings appeared on 35mm films. The fact, therefore, that it could quickly and readily be opened (and conversely closed again) by slightly rotating one of the arms that held the hasp, squeezing and freeing the hasp and flipping back the lid, is of some importance. Since there seems to be a certain hesitation in admitting that this could have been done without breaking the red enamel that covered the screw-head on the arm (something which I did at least a dozen times), I will quote from a statement kindly supplied by a colleague and fellow SPR member to whom I showed the box on the same day that a technician and I discovered the above method of opening it:–

> I recall some time ago Dr A. Gauld demonstrating how the Scole box could be opened without breaking the seal.

> H. P. Wilkinson 16th April 1999

The arm was stiffish (it loosened somewhat with repetitive openings) but was never difficult to push the small distance necessary to free the hasp. A coin pressed against it moved it readily enough – the shortest measured time taken to open and close it again was about ten seconds (this did not include putting in or removing a film).

I would not myself want to assert for a moment that all this has to be read as proof of tampering. The box appeared to have been run up out of workshop odds and ends, and the very ingenuousness of its construction could be taken as an argument against fraud, as could the readiness with which it was passed over for examination. What it does mean, how-ever, is that no findings the genuineness of which depends just on the security of the 'Alan' box can be regarded as satisfactory or as suitable for presentation as evidence of paranormality. In some cases where the 'Alan' box was used there were additional safeguards – the box was to some extent illuminated by a red LED, or was held by a sitter – and on these occasions substitution of a prepared film during a sitting would obviously have been considerably more difficult and more hazardous, though I would hesitate to claim that a skilled operator could not have managed it.

The 'Dragon' Film (Chapter VI; Appendix H)

Among the marked films of which the claim to paranormality rests on the 'Alan' box is the so-called 'Dragon' film. This film was sent to me in the hope that I might help to make sense of the pictorial symbolism, but when I discovered that the images on it had all been taken from one book, and that they bore strong indications of having been traced on (or in two cases copied freehand onto) acetate paper before being transferred to film – a supposition which I confirmed by having an artistic friend, who did not see the original film, produce an independent version on acetate paper (see Figures 1 to 4b) – I cannot pretend that I did not develop certain reservations. Others of the films have similar characteristics.

Figure 1. Above: Detail from the Dragon film. Centre: Source picture (reduced to 60%). Below: The source picture copied on acetate paper by an artist who had not seen the Scole film.

Figure 2. *Above: Details from the Dragon film. Centre: Source pictures. Below: Source pictures copied on acetate paper by artist who had not seen the Scole film.*

282

287

QVADRANS MVRALIS

Figure 3. Above: Details from the Dragon film. Centre: Source pictures (left-hand one reduced to 60%). Below: Source pictures copied on acetate paper by artist who had not seen the Scole film.

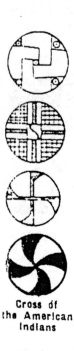

Cross of
the American
Indians

QVADRANS MVRALIS

644

622

528

Figure 4a. Details from Dragon film (top) with source pictures. Note that the symbol under the word 'Cassiel' in the middle picture came from the top of the circular diagram above. The drawings corresponding to some of these pictures are shown overleaf.

Figure 4b. Details from the source pictures on the preceding page copied onto acetate paper by an artist who had not seen the Scole film.

The authors of the Report (if I understand them correctly) reply that the film images cannot but bear similarities to man-made images, otherwise they would not be recognisable as images. It is the circumstances in which the images are produced that constitute the evidence for paranormality. But this argument skirts round the real point, which is this. All the images on these films were ostensibly anomalous in that they should not, under the circumstances supposed to have obtained, have been there at all. Now some anomalous images do not (so to speak) carry a particular method of manufacture on their faces (the Serios films, for example, and no doubt also the cogwheel-like mark, now lost, that appeared on the film in Dr Wiseman's Security bag). But others do, and among them is the Dragon film – the authors do not deny the close resemblance to a tracing on acetate paper. (Another example is the polaroid films discussed in Appendix J to the Report. In these the central bright spot, with a surround of yellow and a further surround of green, are exactly like the effects which Mr Cornell obtained by briefly flashing a small green LED above similar polaroid plates; and the dark unexposed areas, with slightly fogged edges, are exactly like the ones he obtained by laying irregularly shaped pieces of cardboard on the sensitive surface. No other methods produced anything remotely like the required results.) Now where we have images that rather obviously suggest a fairly straightforward method of normal production, and which (like the Dragon film and most of its *confrères*) were not obtained under conditions of the most stringent control (the authors believe that the Ibiza polaroids are beyond reproach in that respect, though I would not entirely agree), there really is no choice but to set aside the supposed evidence for paranormality as not having reaching admissible standards.

A supplementary consideration is this. What are reproduced in the Dragon film are not whole illustrations from the Bessy volume, but parts, often quite small parts, of those illustrations; so small, indeed, and so inconspicuous that many of them took a fair while to locate even after Mr Cornell and I had instituted a systematic search. To reproduce those small parts minus their surroundings by ordinary photographic procedures would have required some quite protracted work. Tracing the selected parts onto acetate paper and flashing the result onto the film strip would have been a far simpler procedure (and, *nota bene*, the picture of the Dragon itself has been partially redrawn to fit it within the 24mm available height of the film strip). Thus these images bear all the signs of having been made by the simplest method that could have produced them.

The authors go on to remark that the fact that all the drawings on the Dragon film come from a single book neither supports nor undermines the fraud hypothesis. But this is surely not altogether true. If one asks oneself how it would be most convenient for an intending hoaxer to proceed in such a matter, one surely has to agree that his most economical policy would be to take some not too excessively common book with suitable illustrations and trace parts of those illustrations in such a way that a casual reader of the book would be unlikely to spot the source of the derived film images. In other words the hoax hypothesis would predict pretty much the kind of features that the Dragon film possesses.

Finally the authors observe that since we have no idea of the mechanism by which discarnate entities might impress images on to film, we are prone to interpret in terms of hoax every feature of those images that could be supposed due to human activity. And it is indeed perfectly true that we have no idea of the constraints under which discarnate entities, if such there are, might operate. We cannot say, for instance, that they do not have an acetate-paper-tracing cast of mind, so that any internal images they may have tend to externalize themselves as or be translated into forms that resemble acetate paper tracings. But it should be noted that the evidence that spirit entities may have intervened in the Scole circle depends in part on the evidence from ostensibly paranormal film images. If the evidence for the genuineness of the film images is assailed, it cannot be rescued by accepting as true a hypothesis (discarnate spirits) the validity of which depends in part on the genuineness of the film images.

As I remarked above some parts of the film evidence seem rather more resistant to the substitution hypothesis than is the Dragon film, notably the occasions on which the 'Alan' box was held in a sitter's hand (placing the fingers strictly in accordance with instructions from the spirits), and the occasion on which it was illuminated by a red LED. Readers must study for themselves the accounts of these occasions in the Scole Report, and decide in each instance how far the possibility of substitution of a pre-prepared film was ruled out. Against this they must set the evidence, just outlined, which many would regard as rather strongly indicative of substitution. If, after examining and thinking about all this material, any reader can reach an absolutely definite conclusion, I can only say he has a much clearer mind than I can lay claim to.

The 'SPR Communications' (Chapters IV and V)

By these I mean the various communications and items of information, most spoken by the mediums, but some imprinted on 35mm film, that relate to, and by implication emanate from, individuals prominent in the early days of the SPR. Most of these communications were originally verified from passages in early volumes of the *Proceedings of the Society for Psychical Research*, but instead of dismissing the evidence as having too obvious a possible normal source, the authors seem to regard early volumes of *Proceedings* as so obscure that knowledge of them by the Scole communicators (I use this term neutrally) might indicate the operation of paranormal powers. Thus we have the curious spectacle of an article being published in the current *Proceedings* that takes knowledge of the contents of past *Proceedings* as evidence for paranormality and indeed survival. But more was to come. For between the first and the second drafts of the Scole Report it was discovered that some eighty per cent of the material in question is to be found in a single semi-popular book, Sir Oliver Lodge's *The Survival of Man* (1909), which went through at least thirteen editions in its unabridged form. The principal missing case ('No 5 Selwyn Gardens') is to be found in a number of other semi-popular sources. *The Survival of Man* contains not just outlines of the cases concerned, but details – dates, page references, forms of words and quotations (including one in Greek) – derived from the original *Proceedings* articles and reproduced in the Scole communications.

The authors agree that "it would be stretching credulity to attribute all this to coincidence", and that the discoveries "undermine" the evidence, but in reply, though they toy with the possibility of cryptomnesia (it would have to have been cryptomnesia involving both mediums), and also with the thought that discarnate entities might suffer from a restriction of memory to especially familiar items, such as particular books or articles, they end by in effect leaving readers to make up their own minds. But surely there is only one safe and reasonable conclusion that a reader can come to, and it is that whatever the ins and outs of the matter there is nothing in any of these cases that can possibly be put forward as serious evidence for paranormal processes, let alone for survival. There are easily located normal sources for all the information given, and there is no satisfactory way of demonstrating that these sources were not in some way tapped by normal means. Had communications been received which could only be verified from the quite numerous unpublished documents relating to the SPR's early history and personnel which are stored away in various large libraries, matters might have been entirely different. But of such communications there was not an inkling.

It should be noted also that in one case ("The Myers encomium and the Diotima clue") the information given (which, including as it did twelve lines of verse and a Greek quotation, might have been too copious for ready retention in memory) was imprinted on a 35mm film. The safeguards against film substitution in this case were among the least impressive (the film remained at Scole in its tub, which had been sealed with gummed paper signed by DF, for a week). Thus the problems raised by the 'SPR communications' merge with the problems raised by the evidential status of the images on the cassette films, and difficulties that arise in connection with the one become also difficulties for the other.

The same is true of the next and last case that I shall single out for special discussion, for it too is a 'film' case, and it too is, in the minds of at least two of the authors, an important part of the presumed evidence for an SPR connection.

The 'Ruth' Films (Chapter VII; Appendix M)

There are two 'Ruth' films, that is to say films on which there appear in longhand stanzas from the 1802 revision of Wordsworth's poem of that name. It should be noted at the outset that neither of the two 'Ruth' films, as the authors themselves state, was produced in wholly fraud-proof conditions, and it was in connection with the second of them that the late Ralph Noyes detected what could be interpreted as signs of tracing on acetate paper. The handwriting on the films is a close approximation to Dorothy Wordsworth's handwriting when she transcribed the stanzas in question onto a leaf inserted into a copy of the 1800 edition of Wordsworth's *Lyrical Ballads*. This copy of the *Lyrical Ballads* is now in the Beinecke Library of Yale University. The stanzas imprinted on the films were supplemented by various statements by the communicators about the authorship, date and edition of the verses concerned. The statements showed an apparent knowledge of some fairly obscure points in Wordsworthian scholarship.

Two questions therefore arise. The first is whether or not there exists a normal source from which the written stanzas on the 'Ruth' films could have been derived. No one has seriously suggested that a member of the Scole group visited the Beinecke Library and there saw the original manuscript. The only remaining possibility, for reasons to be mentioned shortly, is that the film versions derive from an illustration in the Christie's catalogue of the 1965 sale at which Yale University purchased the item in question. That they do so derive is strongly suggested by the following considerations: (i) The films contain between them in whole or part (though sometimes muddled and sometimes with duplications) four of the seven stanzas added to '*Ruth*' in 1802. The four stanzas concerned are the four reproduced in the catalogue. (ii) The lengths of the lines on the 'Ruth' films, and also the gaps between lines where these can be assessed, coincide closely (to within the nearest millimetre in most instances) with the corresponding measurements in the Christie's catalogue. These line-lengths are slightly shorter (approximately one millimetre in ten) than their equivalents in the Yale original, because the catalogue illustrations are slightly reduced in size. It is extremely unlikely that there is anywhere another reproduction of the stanzas with precisely the dimensions of the catalogue one, and of course a microfilm copy, such as the British Library possesses, could project any line length from a range of possibilities. The 'Ruth' films bear a marked resemblance to somewhat slipshod tracings of the Christie's catalogue.

The second question is that of whether or not there is an obvious normal source for the information purveyed by the communicators about the background to the insertion of the extra stanzas. And there is indeed one very obvious source, namely the Christie's catalogue which we have just been discussing. This catalogue contains on pp.40–41 a fairly detailed entry about the item concerned, and if one disregards information given, or strongly hinted at, to the communicators by MK in the course of conversation (e.g. the year 1799), it can readily be seen that all the Wordsworth material transmitted at the sittings could have been derived from it. We can tabulate the facts as follows:–

Communicated Information	Christie's Catalogue
It comes from a gentleman who is very fond of words	Wordsworth
Name 'Ruth'	Yes
Written in 1800 (information from RF)	First edition of poem dated 1800; alterations 1802
There was a first and a second edition	Implied
A lot of change	"Eight new verses"
It [the changed version] does exist	Implied by catalogue entry
It was in the family until some years ago	"The property of M.C. Wordsworth"
It is somewhere unusual	A fair inference from fact of sale by Christie's
1802, the final edition	1802 is the last edition mentioned
It didn't contain all that you have	[Too ambiguous to assess]

It is obvious that the simplest hypothesis we can apply to the two 'Ruth' films is that the stanzas, the handwriting and the background information all derive from the Christie's sale catalogue of 9th December 1965. Of course copies of this catalogue (Christie's informed Mr A. D. Cornell that at least one block of 500 would have been printed, possibly more than one block) are not easy to locate; but as the authors themselves say it is not fanciful to suppose that people tend to keep Christie's catalogues, and there is no saying when or where one might come across one (a fact I can vouch for in general terms myself).

Two further aspects of the 'Ruth' films and their interpretation require comment. One is the hypothesis put forward especially by MK that the new stanzas, and the change from third-person to first-person, had a specially poignant meaning for Wordsworth because at the time he wrote them (probably 1802) circumstances had once again stirred into life memories of his much earlier affair with Annette Vallon, the implication being that this strengthens the case for his own, no doubt indirect, involvement in the production of the films. Of this proposal one might say (a) that since there is so little to preclude the possibility that the 'Ruth' films and everything to do with them may simply derive from the Christie's catalogue it is from a parapsychological point of view absolutely pointless to devise subtle interpretations of their content, and (b) that even if one neglects the preceding point the fact remains that nowhere in the communications is an Annette Vallon connection so much as implied. It was MK himself who introduced Annette Vallon's name into the séance room conversation, and the only unprompted otherworldly support for his idea appears to be Edwin's remark that there was "a lot of emotion" involved, which anyone could discover just by reading the stanzas (after all Wordsworth's view of poetry was that it is "emotion recollected in tranquillity").

The other has to do with the date 1880, which appears rather oddly at the left hand end of the second film underneath some squiggles which the authors interpret as "To Ruth". Because F. W. H. Myers published a book on Wordsworth in 1880, the authors take '1880' as a sign of his involvement (an idea perhaps congenial to them because of their belief that he might be behind the 'SPR communications'). They go on to draw parallels between Myers's relationship with Annie Marshall and Wordsworth's with Annette Vallon, parallels which they think would have made it particularly appropriate for Myers to indicate his presence 'behind' the reproduction of the 'Ruth' stanzas. Again one might make two comments: (a) Why should one not regard the date 1880 as merely a commonplace mistake for 1800 – this was the authors' first supposition, and the date 1800 is prominent in the catalogue entry? There is nothing apart from the date 1880 which presents even the slightest impediment to the view that the stanzas were simply reproduced because they were *there*, in a copy of the Christie's catalogue. (b) The supposed parallel between Ruth and her lover on the one hand and Annie Marshall and Myers on the other will not stand examination. It is quite clear that the real parallel would have been, as John Beer implies in his very informative *Providence and Love* (1998), between Annie Marshall and the heroine of Wordsworth's 'Lucy' poems. Indeed to see this one has only to look at Myers's rather emotional remarks about 'Lucy' (Myers, 1935, p.38) and at the comparison he draws between Ruth and Lucy (p.139). To the living Myers Ruth as a person had no special significance. Lucy had.

To summarize now about the 'SPR communications' and the 'Ruth' case. If by 'evidence for survival' one means evidence for the post-mortem survival of particular individuals with their own, perhaps diminished, constellations of memories, and their own emotions, plans, and personal characteristics, there is no evidence of survival in the Scole Report. It has become clear that the whole of what purported to be such evidence had possible normal sources, either sources so readily available that they cannot be ruled out, or sources that are rather strongly indicated by features of the evidence in question. The mere existence of these sources, whether in fact tapped or not, completely undermines (as I shall try to demonstrate in the next section) the putative evidence for survival, and indeed any evidence for any kind of paranormality based on the same materials.

It should be emphasized further that we are not talking here of one or two cases, specially selected for their weakness. We are talking of a whole swathe of cases with repercussions through much of the Scole Report. I need mention only the fact that the communicators who delivered the 'SPR communications', and who comment on the 'Ruth' and 'Myers encomium' films, also acted as compères for various of the other types of phenomena.

Some General Issues to do with Evidence

I have talked of the evidence in certain selected cases being 'satisfactory', 'admissible', etc., or not (mostly not), and I will now touch briefly on some issues relating to the assessment and acceptability of evidence in the Scole case and other cases resembling it. A good deal of what I shall say will be obvious to the verge of triteness, perhaps beyond. But it seems to me that some of these obvious points have been somewhat overlooked by the authors of the Scole Report.

The Primacy of Normal Explanation

Almost everyone would agree that in this area explanations involving putative paranormal factors should not be advanced until explanations invoking only normal ones (that is, factors accepted by or derivable from current scientific knowledge) have been exhausted. This explanatory principle leads to a methodological one. One cannot, of course, move to a paranormal explanation just because one is unable to think of a normal one (though unfortunately many people do just this). There are lots of phenomena that are mysterious, in the sense that no one has thought of a generally convincing explanation of them, but which very few would suppose to be paranormal (in his numerous volumes William R. Corliss has catalogued hundreds of such). If a phenomenon is to be regarded as paranormal there must be compelling reasons for ruling out any sort of normal explanation. Or, to put it another way, normal explanations must be presumed to hold, even if one can't work out their details, unless one can obtain and present findings that actively preclude all received normal explanations however ingeniously developed. The principle of the primacy of normal explanation thus leads to a methodological assumption which has to be adopted in all attempts to demonstrate that paranormal phenomena really occur.

The normal explanation that most readily obtrudes itself in cases such as the present is that of hoaxing, and the above methodological assumption then becomes what we may for short call the methodological hypothesis of hoaxing (this, rather than 'fraud', being the appropriate term in the particular case of the Scole investigation, since money did not change hands). In order to demonstrate that the phenomena under scrutiny are indeed paranormal, you have to find ways of defeating the hoax hypothesis by producing evidence that defies explanation in terms of currently accepted scientific and technological principles. We might call such evidence 'ostensibly infrangible' evidence, meaning that as yet no one has found a way of cracking it. 'Infrangibility' in this sense is impossible to define in detail. One cannot lay down a list of criteria of infrangibility that will be applicable in all instances, and there is always likely to be scope for argument. In the present context one might reasonably claim that infrangibility has been attained when the best efforts of relevant experts – including, for preference, their best practical efforts – have not unearthed a method of replicating the phenomena by normal means (failure to seek out normal methods of replication has been one of the major shortcomings of the present investigation). A sign that the evidence is getting near infrangibility is likely to be that hostile critics start to allege that the investigators themselves must be part of the plot. (The suggestion of investigator complicity raises a further and somewhat different layer of problems, which I shall not discuss because the claim has not been raised in the present case.)

It should be emphasized that the methodological assumption of production by normal means is just that – an impartial principle which tells the investigator what sort of evidence he has to strive to obtain. It does not *per se* involve actual accusations of hoaxing, or any unpleasant feelings towards the persons under investigation, a point which intelligent mediums will readily grasp.

The present case has some overall features which make it exceptionally difficult to get ostensibly infrangible evidence or anything approaching it. The choice of venue was usually up to the Scole Group and never to the investigators; the phenomena took place in darkness or near-darkness; there was no control of the mediums apart from the armbands (which they had designed and manufactured themselves and of which the security was never subjected to independent testing and experimentation); what is more, the members of the Scole group sat next to each other, and there was no hand control. Certain particularly desirable and seemingly innocuous controls (the use of infra-red cameras, thermal imaging cameras, or image intensifiers, the marking of the 35mm films or their cassettes) were actually refused (the ban on infra-red cameras, etc., appears almost absurd when one remembers that at one sitting the 'Alan' box was sufficiently illuminated by a red LED for the investigators to claim that no one could have touched it); the mediums (or the spirits) had a considerable hand in designing or vetting the experimental protocols (some of which were markedly defective); and important items of apparatus were provided, manufactured or tinkered with by members of the Scole Group or their relatives. When conditions like these prevail, one can never be absolutely sure that there was not something surreptitiously going on, or some hidden feature of the situation, that would have nullified any paranormal interpretation. The history of physical mediumship contains numerous salutary examples of dark sittings in which the investigators or witnesses were convinced to the extent of giving signed statements that they had witnessed inexplicable phenomena; yet we know exactly how the effects were achieved. In some cases the séances concerned were staged especially to demonstrate the unreliability of such testimony (for examples see Hodgson, 1892, pp.296–307; Besterman, 1968, pp.152–155). Nor should it be supposed that a knowledge of the literature of conjuring and mediumistic fraud together with experience as a sitter will necessarily prevent one from being deceived. The main lesson to be learned from such knowledge and experience is that one should beware of making claims as to the genuineness of any darkened séance room phenomenon on the sole grounds that one cannot understand how it could have been achieved by normal means. Even professional conjurers may have little idea how the tricks are accomplished (cf. Price & Dingwall, 1922, pp.16–17), though they would almost certainly be prudent enough not to conclude that the phenomena must therefore have been genuine. The only answer to the uncertainties of dark sittings (indeed of many light sittings) is to have in place control conditions which will sufficiently defeat the methodological hypothesis of production by normal means, should the phenomena occur under them. The essence of such control conditions has to be to limit the features of the situation that have a direct bearing on the genuineness or otherwise of the phenomena to a small and manageable number for which the investigators themselves (and none others) can completely answer. Only that way is any agreement likely among relevant experts that the phenomena cannot be replicated by normal means. Acceptable control conditions for the Scole phenomena would not (as I shall try to illustrate) have been too difficult to devise, and in fact, though perhaps almost fortuitously, were not far from being achieved on a few occasions.

Kinds of Evidence

In science, as in more ordinary commonsense activities and problems, there is often the possibility of both direct and indirect evidence. Consider the craters on the moon, the existence of which has been known since the seventeenth century. For a long time a favoured supposition was that they are the craters of extinct volcanoes, but now it is generally held that they are impact craters, caused by collisions with large meteorites, or with small to middling comets or asteroids. With the doubtful exception of some mediaeval monks of Canterbury, no one has ever directly observed either a volcanic eruption or an unmistakable meteorite impact on the moon, although of course such an observation could quite conceivably be made. All the evidence concerning the two hypotheses is actually indirect and comes from observation of matters predicted by one or other of the hypotheses. It relates, for instance, to the profiles of terrestrial and lunar volcanoes and to the fact that impact craters would have the characteristics of explosion craters rather than of mere indentations. In some branches of science (e.g. forensic science) almost all the evidence under consideration is indirect.

A similar distinction can be made in the present instance in connection both with the hoax hypothesis and with the hypothesis that the phenomena are genuine. There is no direct evidence of hoaxing, in the sense of it having been directly observed, but there is a great deal of indirect evidence, in the sense of observation of things that a proponent of the hoax hypothesis could plausibly claim to be predicted by his theory and would regard himself as vindicated by finding. Examples might be the 'overall features' of the case mentioned two paragraphs ago, plus not a few other and more specific findings, for instance the clear resemblance of some of the marks on films to marks made by simple and obvious normal processes; the fact that the 'Alan' box which had held these films could be quickly and easily opened without undoing the padlock; the fact that images were not obtained when films were placed in a properly made box supplied by the investigators; on the mental side, the fact that so much of the correct information given or 'veridical' material conveyed could be obtained from single convenient sources; and finally and above all the fact that the 'spirits' refused to go back and produce any of the phenomena under acceptable conditions. Individually these examples, or many of them, could perhaps be dismissed as whims or oddities or as evidence that hoaxing was possible in the case of such and such a phenomenon but not that it took place. Put together they form a pattern on the basis of which hostile critics could, and probably will, mount a powerful indictment. The pattern is exactly the sort of thing they would predict if hoaxing were at work.

The distinction between direct and indirect evidence is harder to draw in connection with the hypothesis that the phenomena are genuine. To have direct evidence of genuineness it is not enough just to witness the phenomenon in question, e.g. a light travelling through the dark séance room performing various evolutions. All relevant background circumstances must be observable, known, or accessible to you. For instance one of the lights might move into a tightly glued wooden box with a perspex side (made and brought, of course, by the investigators, and never let out of their hands) and move around therein to command, preferably while the mediums were watched with image intensifiers. Bearing in mind that the lights could apparently pass unhindered through the table top and out from beneath it, there seems no reason why this should not have been achieved. Such an observation would have been a strong candidate for constituting the infrangible evidence discussed earlier.

As for indirect evidence of genuineness, that the phenomena are genuine (unlike the hypothesis of hoaxing) is not a specific kind of hypothesis about the phenomena that itself leads to any special predictions except that phenomena will occur which are demonstrably not normal. We might, however, reasonably say that indirect evidence for genuineness would have been obtained if, for instance, the investigators carefully marked a film and placed it in their own glued or adequately padlocked box, brought it to the sitting, took the box away still unopened, opened it elsewhere, removed the film, sent it at once for independent developing, and then found that images had been imprinted on it. Here an abnormal something is not observed happening, but is afterwards found to have happened under conditions for which the investigators could wholly answer. Evidence of this quality would likewise be a candidate for being deemed infrangible and hence for being held to defeat the methodological hypothesis of production by normal means.

There could also be what might be termed 'circumstantial' evidence of genuineness. This will usually consist of evidence (such as the authors of the present Report bring forward) of the good characters of the mediums and of their apparent lack of motives for deception. Obviously there could also be circumstantial evidence for hoaxing.

Overview

The central problem with Scole is that though there is no direct evidence for hoaxing, there is quite a lot of indirect evidence for it, while on the other hand, though there is a fair amount of possible direct or indirect evidence for genuineness, very little of it seems good enough to defeat the methodological hypothesis of production by normal means.

There are in addition some firm claims that there is satisfactory circumstantial evidence of the sort just mentioned (i.e. evidence for the honesty and good character of the members of the Scole group). Now with regard to this last, the evidence might certainly and justifiably make one claim that the phenomena are worth investigating, but it is by definition not itself evidence about the phenomena, and it is never going to be a substitute for direct or indirect evidence for genuineness. It will always be vulnerable to the accusation of investigator ignorance – we can never know enough about people's motives, character, etc., to rule out the hoax hypothesis on this basis. There are on record not a few cases of 'disinterested deception' in which persons of apparent good character have been detected carrying out hoaxes for which they had no obvious motives such as fame or money. Podmore (1902, vol. 2, pp.272–273, 287–288, 292; cf. *JSPR 6*, 1894, pp.274–278) cites a number of examples from the SPR's early days and I have come across some more recent ones myself. One may note also that disinterested deception seems to have become rife in the world of crop circles.

A single bit of really good direct or indirect evidence for genuineness or hoax would outweigh all circumstantial evidence. Without such direct or indirect evidence the arguments will inevitably degenerate into endlessly repeated assertions of 'those who know them say they're quite honest'; 'but the phenomena are obviously hoaxes'; 'they have no motives for hoaxing'; 'of course they have – they might have made money, achieved fame, etc.'; 'they have no expertise in conjuring'; 'how can you be sure?' And so on and so forth. Of course one might try to persuade oneself that one's psychological insight into people's characters is such that one would *know* if persons of whom one had seen a good deal were attempting to deceive one. But this is just as fatal, and as often falsified, an assumption as the belief that one's knowledge of the literature of mediumistic fraud and one's experience as a sitter would prevent one from being taken in in one's turn.

This leaves us to apply the methodological hypothesis of hoaxing in the light of on the one hand the purported bits of direct and indirect evidence for genuineness and on the other the purported indirect evidence for hoaxing. I have already given a good many examples of what might be regarded as indirect evidence of hoaxing. But there are also examples of phenomena which (assuming that they occurred exactly as described – the accounts are often quite inadequate) seem rather difficult to explain away in normal terms, and which might be thought – which are thought by the authors – to constitute direct or indirect evidence for genuineness of a standard at any rate approaching what I called infrangibility. These phenomena are mainly physical ones. For instance we have the mark that was produced on the film in Dr Wiseman's secure bag; a light that was seen to enter and move about in a glass tank the sides and top of which were glued up, though, regrettably, the bottom wasn't glued to the base; we have an occasion on which the 'Alan' box was illuminated by a red LED and none the less the film inside it was marked; we have occasions in which the same box was held in a sitter's hand with similar results; we have a table-tennis ball which became illuminated from within and was then propelled across a segment of the underneath of the séance table, a segment inaccessible from where the members of the Scole Group were sitting; and so on.

Now I am far from saying that such things do not happen or that the indirect evidence for hoaxing *proves* the whole thing was a hoax. It simply seems to me that the positive evidence, such as it is, has not the clout to defeat the methodological hypothesis of hoaxing. There are several reasons for saying this.

The most fundamental is the one remarked on earlier, that although the conditions of the sittings – darkness, lack of proper controls of the mediums, inadequate experimental protocols, refusal of infra-red surveillance, etc. – were almost always such as to prevent the investigators from having a full knowledge of, let alone full control over, all the possibly relevant circumstances and happenings, the authors of the Report in effect rely for their defence of the possible genuineness of the phenomena on the fact that they are themselves unable to explain in normal terms certain of the happenings which took place in their presence. That the whole history of physical mediumship and its investigation shows this defence to be quite insufficient has already been pointed out. And the insufficiency is compounded by the fact that the authors totally failed to carry out their own investigations into possible normal methods for reproducing the phenomena. It was left to outsiders to make the principal discoveries in that area.

A second reason is that the shortcomings of the positive evidence have to be taken in conjunction with (indeed they merge with) the indirect evidence for hoaxing. In a field where so much is obscure or unknown, and things are so often not what they seem, such evidence cannot be held to prove that a hoax was perpetrated. But it can be held to add enormously to the difficulty of defeating the methodological hypothesis of hoaxing. For from the point of view of that hypothesis any evidence that points to the possibility of hoaxing has to have a worse rather than a better construction put upon it, and can only be overcome by absolutely infrangible counter-evidence of the strongest kind. Readers can make up their own minds how far the Scole Report has provided such counter-evidence.

My own opinion is, as I said, that the methodological hypothesis of hoaxing has not been satisfactorily overcome. To defeat that hypothesis much of the work would need to be done again under acceptable conditions of control. One can only hope that this may happen, and

I would emphasize once more that such conditions are by no means difficult to specify. In fact they could (one would have thought) easily have been developed out of such observations as the appearance of a moving light inside the glass fish tank, or the table-tennis ball that lit up and moved, or better still both in combination. But nothing spectacular would have been needed. A tiny effect under tight control would have been far more impressive than any amount of more dramatic displays in loose conditions. It is probable that the work will not be done again and, while there are a few additional things that might be undertaken without further sittings – for example a detailed analysis of the séance transcripts to discover whether or not someone was silent at critical periods and so could have been out of his seat, and whether momentary distractions could have covered up key manoeuvres – it seems to me that they would probably not be worth the effort.

Of course another point of view altogether might be adopted with regard to these phenomena. It is that of certain (not all) spiritualists and involves accepting as a matter of faith that a certain favoured medium regarded as worthy by all who know him is entirely honest, so that the phenomena that go on in his presence may be accepted with total confidence. People who wish to make this leap may do so without remark from me. But no scientist *qua* scientist (or any other rigorous inquirer) would dream of claiming that evidence obtained with no other safeguard than that was suitable for public presentation, and when psychical researchers sit as investigators in a spiritualist circle tensions between these two very different attitudes can often be detected. It is to the credit of the Scole group, and/or those who communicate through them, that they have set out to bridge this gap to the mutual benefit of both parties. But the results for them have been mixed indeed. Let us assume that the entities who have communicated to and through the group are what they purport to be, discarnate intelligences, some of them even 'spirit scientists'. The knowledge and perspectives of these spirits are supposedly to varying degrees in advance of our own. Yet through following their dictates and transmitting their statements the group has regularly frustrated the investigators' attempts to secure wholly satisfactory controls and experimental protocols, and has produced evidence even the best of which must be regarded as inconclusive and a good deal more of which constitutes apparent indirect evidence of hoaxing. Furthermore members of the group have been subjected to gratuitously unkind press comments. One cannot but think of William James's postulated 'Cosmic Joker' (mentioned by the authors in chapter XV), or that Joker's more parochial representatives, though whether the 'joke' (which may have been salutary but is not exactly side-splitting) could have been intended against the group or against the investigators is not apparent.

School of Psychology
University of Nottingham
Nottingham NG7 2RD

Acknowledgement

I am indebted to Ms Susan Brady of the Beinecke Library of Yale University for information about the size of the handwritten stanzas (referred to above) pasted into a copy in the Library's possession of the 1800 edition of Wordsworth's *Lyrical Ballads*.

REFERENCES

Beer, J. (1998) *Providence and Love: Studies in Wordsworth, Channing, Myers, George Eliot, and Ruskin.* Oxford: Clarendon Press.

Besterman, T. (1968) *Collected Papers on the Paranormal.* New York: Garrett Publications.

Hodgson, R. (1892) Mr Davey's imitations by conjuring of phenomena sometimes attributed to spirit agency. *ProcSPR 8,* 253–310.

Myers, F. W. H. (1935) *Wordsworth.* Pocket edition. London: Macmillan.

Podmore, F. (1902) *Modern Spiritualism: A History and a Criticism.* (2 vols.) London: Methuen.

Price, H. and Dingwall, E. J. (eds.) (1922) *Revelations of a Spirit Medium.* London: Kegan Paul, Trench, Trubner & Co.

SCOLE: A RESPONSE TO CRITICS

by Montague Keen and Arthur Ellison

The main criticism of the Report is that the evidence nowhere provides compelling reasons to rule out any sort of normal explanation. It is not enough (the argument goes) to say you cannot think of a normal explanation: it may perhaps turn up later. Put by David Hume in its most quoted and intimidating form, "no testimony is sufficient to establish a miracle unless the testimony be of such a kind that its falsehood would be more miraculous than the fact which it endeavours to establish". One must present findings that in some way or other "actively preclude all received normal explanations," as Alan Gauld has put it.

However, all such received explanations are simply those we have been able to think of. This still leaves those we have not been able to think of. By employing this argument, therefore, our critics have ensured that no evidence can be considered watertight. We are not, of course, in the business of providing proof. That is the province of the distiller or the mathematician. We are dealing only with degrees of probability. What is probable to one person may be highly improbable to his neighbour. All depends on the accumulation of prejudices which compose his belief system, but of whose existence and strength he may be wholly unaware.

That judgement of facts is not simply influenced but positively distorted by such prejudices is common experience. It is especially noteworthy in the present case. The failure of the apparent spirit communicators to speak and act in a manner conforming to the expectations and obedient to the presumptions of the critic is a potent encouragement to dismissal or ridicule. If the showering of small apported gifts on participants in a séance, the presence and behaviour of strange lights or the gossamer caresses of unearthly forms strike one public critic as "madness", and all the utterances of the communicators as banal, vapid and dull (Appleyard, 1999), then it is difficult to conceive of any evidence, however weighty, likely to overcome this entrenched hostility. Others may find the same events impressive and the identical messages coherent, sensible and even wise, although it is worth noting that no one other than the three principal investigators and members of the Scole Group has actually read the verbatim transcripts of sittings, which alone would enable a worthwhile verdict to be given on the quality and precision of the communicators' speech. The judgement, that is to say, is essentially subjective. Much that masquerades as argument is no more than a rationalisation of a strongly felt, although perhaps unconscious, revulsion. The issue is no longer one for science but for psychologists. That is why we have chosen to let readers judge for themselves.

Before they do so, however, let them beware of emulating the enthusiasm with which our critics jettison themselves into pitfalls of their own making. The first such pitfall is in the oft-repeated dictum that we must reject a paranormal explanation unless and until all normal possibilities have been eliminated. This may sound reasonable, but in practice, as is apparent from the foregoing criticisms, it means that any theoretical weakness in the protocol, related to any of the wide range of phenomena examined, must warrant the elimination of that phenomenon from serious consideration. The primacy of the normal explanation, as Dr Gauld has put it, requires as much.

One consequence of this approach is to acknowledge the importance and welcome the principle of considering the cumulative impact of all the relevant evidence while proceeding to do the opposite. Another is to select what are perceived to be the individual weaknesses in the circumstances within which specific phenomena occur, while ignoring the more solid evidence. Where it cannot be ignored, as in parts of Gauld's fairly expressed criticisms, it is consigned to the safe repository of phenomena for which no immediately available explanation is at hand, but for which one might turn up later, like meteorites from a supposedly empty firmament. What should distinguish phenomena eligible for admission to this repository from those which ought to be redirected to the paranormal department is the conclusion of sober observers that what was experienced was not merely difficult to square with any man-made process of which we could conceive, but positively at variance with the operation of accepted physical laws. Much of the phenomena connected with lights, and some of the tactile and audible manifestations, conform quite safely to this requirement.

The extent to which the critic, or the reader, finds the evidence persuasive depends to an alarming degree on how we expect spirit entities to behave. If we find the rattling of tables, the dancing of light forms, or the apporting of a half-crown in settlement of a non-existent debt as absurd, trivial, unspiritual or frivolous (as Cornell apparently does), because it offends our assumptions about how we would go about proving an after-life if *we* were transported to the next world, then we will be inclined to reject evidence which might otherwise be considered very convincing. This is a very common error; and it is an error because it taints objective experience with subjective expectation. Especially is this true when considering reactions to the content of communications. In our opinion these were usually characterised by intelligent, sometimes mildly witty and often precisely phrased observations and sensible discussions on a wide range of practical and ontological issues. Others, disappointed that no blinding revelation or apocalyptic pronouncement has been made, will conclude that what emerges is no more than the product of the mediums' subconscious if it is not all consciously invented. Our contention is that all criticisms thus founded are misdirected.

We must also accept that any assessment of paranormality must be influenced by the prior experience of the sitter. If he has no familiarity with the literature, but arrives equipped with all the presuppositions which a life-long induction into a materialist philosophy creates, his boggle threshold will be low: the mere suggestion of telepathy will outrage his common sense. If the sitter is well versed in the literature of psychical research, and considers the case for extra-sensory perception to have long since been well established, he is less likely to find his belief system affronted by evidence much of which has been amply precedented. We are clearly in the latter category, but we have had constantly to bear in mind the great majority who fall into the former category. It cannot be said of our SPR critics that they are ignorant of the literature. On the contrary, they have made important contributions to it over many years. But most of their reservations are intended to anticipate criticisms from sceptics who have little knowledge of the subject and profound prejudices against it. We think this has forced them into postures which are an affront to common sense.

None of our critics has been able to point to a single example of fraud or deception. This in itself is quite remarkable, because for four years members of the Group had been under scrutiny from a large number of visitors, by no means all of them gullible believers. From scores of sittings in several different venues in six different countries (Ireland, USA, Spain, Switzerland, Germany and the Netherlands) outside their home base, we have neither experienced nor received reports of a single false move, inflexion or slip of the tongue. Yet we are invited to believe that, while providing the astonishing array of light phenomena we have listed on pages 54–57, members of the Group can keep up an intelligent conversation with sitters on a wide range of subjects with their voices appearing to come from the positions in which they are seated, while simultaneously contriving to crawl round chairs, tap sitters' knuckles and fabricate semi-luminous floating bodies which trail gossamer-like substances across the hands. Typical of what was experienced is evident from this extract of a comprehensive account provided by a highly experienced sitter:–

> . . . there came a series of unmistakable light taps on the right side of the lower part of my right leg moving about a little between knee and ankle. There were perhaps a dozen taps in all which I felt through the trouser leg . . . No member of the Scole Group could have made these taps without leaving their seat and making their way round to kneel behind the back of my chair. There was not the slightest indication that anyone had left or could have left their seat, or any sound of anyone creeping around behind the sitters, unless you

count the fact that we once heard a clunk apparently from one of the chairs
standing against the end wall.   [Gauld, 1997]

No one has been able to suggest the powerful but thus far undiscovered motive of six (later four) people sitting in a home circle to conceive and execute a deception unparalleled in its duration, variety, skill and secrecy. There is nothing in our critics' appraisals which would begin to account for the fact that a single false move, inflexion or remark at any time by any member of the Group over an extended period and before scores of watchful witnesses would have resulted in public exposure. In the course of his temperate and reasoned analysis, Dr Gauld candidly acknowledges that his personal acquaintance with Robin Foy for more than 30 years makes it difficult to conceive that Foy could have been capable of such skilled deception. Perhaps, then, the Foys were innocent dupes of the others. Apart from ignoring the equally persuasive testimony of SPR member Beverley Dear, a friend and neighbour of 20 years, in favour of the integrity of the two mediums, any such theory presupposes a situation so contrary to the evidence as hardly to merit serious consideration. It is inherent in the production of lights, raps, touches and films that all the Group must have been parties to deception, even if only one or two were responsible for its execution at any one time.

Dr Gauld has argued, in the context of the so-called 'SPR Communications', that "there is no satisfactory way of demonstrating that these sources [of Lodge's *Survival of Man,* and volumes of early *SPR Proceedings*] were not in some way tapped by normal means". "Normal means" equals either deliberate fraud or subliminal recollection by the two mediums when in the trance state. Neither presupposes anything paranormal. But subliminal recollection (even though it must defy the mediums' assertion that they had never read the sources in question) is wholly incompatible with their responses to questions which reveal considerable knowledge of the background, circumstances and sometimes persons involved. As Professor West points out in dismissing the notion of unconscious operation, the fabrication of the films would have required careful advance planning. Many of the messages purporting to come from the communicators gave advance information about the films, thereby underlining the premeditated nature of the presumed conspiracy. The information would have to have been very thoroughly conned. And since we are forced by the fraud hypothesis to assume that the mediums were playing a rôle, active or passive, in the multitude of physical effects occurring when performing their apparent function as instruments of discarnate communicators, the notion that cryptomnesia, joint or individual, might be the answer becomes untenable.

So it is either fraud or it is paranormal. It really will not do for Gauld to import euphemisms such as "hoaxing" to make it sound less distasteful and more innocuous. Hoaxing is to "deceive by a mischievous fabrication or fiction . . . in which the credulity of the victim is imposed on", to paraphrase the *Oxford English Dictionary*. No serious student of the Scole investigation can reasonably conclude that their four years' work and some 500 sittings, most of them closed to outsiders, warrants the assumptions implicit in such a practice. Nor is there the slightest evidence that any of them would gain anything save the vilification of friends and admirers were hoaxing to be claimed. Fraud need not always be practised for monetary or other gain. Paranormality does not necessarily imply survival, but reluctance to accept survival as an explanation does force one back on some extended form of extrasensory perception by the mediums. We have not opted for either alternative. The reader can make up his own mind; but before doing so he might be well advised to consider the cogent reasons why this alternative, an aspect of the so-called super-psi hypothesis, failed to impress Gauld as author of that authoritative work, *Mediumship and Survival*.

We do not think it profitable to go further into the details relating to the circumstances of each piece of evidence, but we must comment on Gauld's odd reasoning over the much-disputed Dragon film and the fact that the several alchemical drawings appear to have been taken from Bessy's popular coffee-table book. It is not in the least clear why this should of itself be a subject for surprise, let alone suspicion; nor does it make sense to argue that "films should not carry a particular method of manufacture". That suggests that if one can see how something could have been made manually, i.e. normally, then its authenticity must be rejected. This argues that there is a premium on making a film which could not be produced normally. We have pointed out that no such film can exist, otherwise it would not be a film. One wonders what type of image could survive this criterion. Obviously, only one that is clearly paranormal! But since none can be, we are thrown back on examining the circumstances in which the film is created. Gauld is quite right to point to defects in the protocol relating to several of the films, but he glosses over others where the security was stricter, especially those for which the Schnittgers were responsible.

Gauld believes that the images on the Dragon film "bear all the signs of having been made by the simplest method that could have achieved the purpose in hand." However, it would be equally logical to argue against a more complex method, on the grounds that no spirit entity would seek to employ a more elaborate or difficult method when a simpler one was available. By what process of reason does one assume that a paranormal mechanism *has* to differ from that employed normally? What method, apart from the circumstances leading to their development, would satisfy Gauld and others that the pictures were paranormal? The assumption that a fraudster responsible for this and all the other films would select images in a form such that the casual reader of the [Bessy] book would be unlikely to spot its source is quite inconsistent with the fact that most of the films with which we were concerned – with the notable exception of the electrical diagram – appeared to be deliberately intended for the purpose of providing puzzles for the investigators rather than information for the general public, e.g. the Ruth and Diotima films. Even the fact that the Dragon's tail in the film strip has been swivelled round to fit into the height of a 35mm film is regarded as evidence of fraud. To others it may be self-evident that, if the communicators wished for whatever reason to convey some message or other by means of reproducing a number of hermetic symbols, of which the Dragon was one, some tail realignment would clearly have been necessary. We do not argue that this is what happened, merely that as a deduction it is equally reasonable or unreasonable. Similarly, Gauld appears to consider it self-evident that a fraudster would choose the easiest, most convenient, illustrations to reproduce, but this is not the least apparent in some of the films. Rather the contrary: the elaborate totem-pole-like glyphs on the Daguerre film or the mysterious inscriptions in two sections of the Wie und Staub film, for example.

The disputes about the authenticity of the two Ruth films have been well rehearsed in Chapter VII and Appendix M, and it must be left to the reader to say whether the accumulation of necessary assumptions upon which Gauld's speculations are based are more or less improbable than the deductions made from established sources in a piece of literary detection. But at the end of the day both theories are speculative.

It is not suggested that accounts of this kind provide definitive proof of anything. Taken in conjunction with much other evidence, however, they constitute formidable obstacles to the view that everything was faked. West has rightly drawn attention to the limitations to which observers like himself were subject, but he seems to have overlooked the fact that we and others, including in small part himself, were active participants in some of the arrangements which gave birth to films. The Daguerre film was developed by Kodak from a roll which had been concealed in an unopened tub placed in one of the two locked boxes on marked paper in the centre of the séance room table by West and Gauld. The circumstances are detailed in Appendix K, which examines how a fraud was theoretically possible. Gauld has restated his explanation, and opined that even when on other occasions the box was being firmly held by Schnittger, or made visible on the table by the proximity of an LED, he would "hesitate to claim that a skilled operator could not have managed it." We cordially invite such operators to try, and we must challenge some of Gauld's assumptions. In addition to the difficulties we have earlier listed, it must be pointed out that any tampering with the hasp to enable the box lid to be lifted and the film tub to be switched when the box was positioned on the peripherally marked paper would not only oblige one of the Group to employ one hand to hold the box firmly, so that its position remained unchanged, but to use the other to squeeze open the hasp and eventually to replace the horizontal ends into their sockets. Such a feat we have considered improbable in total darkness even for an expert, but virtually impossible if the front of the box were not facing the fraudster. Yet there was no restriction on the manner in which the visitors orientated each of the boxes, and equally no evidence that the 'Alan' box was placed with the front facing the suspected cheats. Nor was there any way in which any of the Group could have known whether the Kodachrome spools were 36 or 24 frames in length. A wrong guess would have been fatal.

Whatever experiments have been performed on the box by our critics, none would be considered relevant unless conducted before witnesses in darkness and in physical circumstances as near as possible identical to those prevailing at Scole, and with the illusionist wearing luminous wristbands. One wonders what professional or amateur magician would take such risks, even were he able to encumber himself with the intimidating range of equipment, from infra-red or image-intensifying viewers, LEDs with their infinitely versatile thread attachments, to set-square templates and other means to deceive the wary.

Several examples of the tendency to push improbable hypotheses well beyond the boundary of plausibility are illustrated in Tony Cornell's comments. Like West, he has stated that coherent images were produced only when the 'Alan' box was used. Not only is this untrue, but it can readily be seen to be so by anyone reading the Report, or even the summary of film developments listed in the first Appendix. The Alan box was not even made until almost a year after the start of our sittings. By that time at least seven films had been produced.

Two of Cornell's criticisms are particularly detailed. Neither withstands examination. The first states that the Polaroid film plates at Ibiza lay on the table in front of MK for at least an hour, during which time it might have been possible for one of the Group, operating the 2" x 2" green LED light as he (Cornell) had done, to have held the films in their hand and reproduced the effects seen. But it has been made quite clear to Cornell that on the second occasion, when images were produced on two films, the communicators had asked MK to place them in whatever fashion he chose, not on the central table – which was required for a separate experiment not involving film – but on a small side table wedged on his right between his chair and that occupied by fellow-investigator Schnittger. We are therefore asked to believe that one of the Group, risking the detection which would seem likely to have followed the removal or concealment of identifying luminous armbands, would have been able to creep between the wall and the rear of MK's chair in pitch darkness, aided perhaps by hitherto undiscerned infra-red binoculars, and, avoiding a low-level table abutting the rear wall, to bend or kneel down in order to grope successfully for films stacked haphazardly on the table within inches of the arms of the two investigators. Thus positioned they would have to ensure that they were able to avoid knocking over or displacing any of the randomly deposited films while ensuring that no noise, hint or smell of breath would be detected. Equally hazardous would be the journey back to their seats and the restoration of the presumably missing wristbands, all while under the scrutiny of six observers.

There is a further practical difficulty which Cornell has overlooked: the hypothetical fraudster would have been obliged to select the third and fourth films from the middle of the stacked pack to work on, since these (during the second experiment) were the only ones to contain images! They are reproduced in Plate 17.

The complaint that we have somehow sought to suppress contrary evidence by failing to reproduce in this Report the images which Cornell and Gauld managed to create on Polaroid films used in the Ibiza experiments is absurd. We clearly recognised (in Appendix J) Cornell's success. Our point throughout has never been that these or other images cannot be created manually: only that it did not appear to us that all of them could have been man-made in the conditions which prevailed when they were created. Reproduction for reasons of comparison would therefore be pointless.

Cornell has allowed his quite reasonable argument, that his artificial creations and those made at Scole are very similar, to predicate a scenario which must presume on a remarkable degree of ineptitude, poor vision and defective hearing on the part of all the observers, one matched in probability only by the foolhardy risk-taking and nocturnal skills of the theoretical fraudster.

Still less productive are his efforts to extricate himself from the *Daily Mail* entanglement (see footnote on p.35). He does so by combining misquotation with misunderstanding, from which basis he generalises about our allegedly unclear answers and too many outstanding questions.

MK had confirmed to Cornell (Keen, 1999) that the tests carried out in March 1999 at the laboratories of the Print Industry Research Association had clearly established that the copy of the *Daily Mail* dated 1st April 1944, and said by the Group to have been apported into the séance chamber, was not only on wartime newsprint, but had also been printed by letterpress, a system long since superseded, although we accept Cornell's statement that some of the post-war facsimiles may have been printed by this means.

Cornell first incorrectly attributes to MK a statement that the 'apport' newsprint had been compared with a later facsimile of the same issue. But that would have been pointless when the aim was to establish whether the 'apport' was of wartime origin. In fact it was compared with a broadly contemporary, wartime, newspaper. He then ignores the crucial finding that it was produced by letterpress. Even had necessary reels (or webs) of wartime newsprint been still extant half a century after they were superseded by those of higher quality, it would still cost a small fortune to employ the obsolete machinery necessary to use hot metal technology, the use of which creates visible indentations in the paper.

These facts demolish Cornell's suspicions. But worse is to come. MK had mistakenly accepted as true the assertion that all editions of daily wartime newspapers carried a red logo on the front page, and he had observed to Cornell how odd it was that the supposedly apported *Daily Mail* had a logo in black. Cornell now makes a meal of this, but subsequent investigation at the British Library's newspaper library shows that some daily papers, the *Daily Telegraph* and the *Daily Sketch* for example, had nothing at all in red on the front page for that period, while the archivist of *The Times* informs us that no red logo has been carried by the paper since the 18th Century. It is in any case quite nonsensical to suggest, and very easy to demonstrate as untrue, that all morning newspapers invariably carried a "Late War News" banner, whether in red or black, regardless of which edition was printed. Most morning newspapers published an early version for provincial distribution and a later one for London and the Home Counties, sometimes banner-marked as a 4a.m. edition. The British Library retained only the latter edition of each newspaper. That for the *Daily Mail* has "Late War News" in red on the banner, and can readily be seen to differ from the apported copy, in that the account of Mrs Duncan's sentencing has been removed from the front page, and a far more extensive report of the trial appears on an inside page. We do not know whether the original earlier edition, which is presumably the apport, carried a red logo: no copies appear to be extant. Dr Skelton Foord of the British Library was certainly correct in telling Cornell that all the copies of the *Daily Mail* in the British Library archives for that period had a red logo on the front page, but that's as far as it goes and, according to him, as far as he went. The upshot is that there is no possible substitution mystery other than that manufactured by a reluctance to accept independent expert findings plus the evidence of ten minutes' research at the newspaper record office. There are no contradictions involved, save those based on misunderstandings and inadequate investigation.

A further major criticism we have faced is the failure of the investigators to experiment themselves with the suggested normal means by which the phenomena could have been produced. But we have already made it clear that we could see no way in which the light phenomena we list on pages 54–57 *could* have been produced by normal means; and it therefore follows that we would not know where to start. We had no suggestions from any who sat with us. Cornell made a brave attempt at showing how an LED suspended on an all but invisible thread might have been employed, but it bore no relation to what we experienced. Indeed it was like an attempt to replicate sheet lightning by producing flint sparks from a cigarette lighter. We would require his device to change shape, alter its visible appearance, increase and decrease in intensity in response to concerted hand-pressure on investigators' knees, switch itself on and off instantaneously, respond to investigators' requests, accurately locate parts of apparently invisible sitters, create lightning-type flashes three metres or more away from seats occupied by the Group, invade solid objects, describe geometrical shapes at very high speed, and hit glass surfaces and wooden objects with a clearly heard noise. We question whether Cornell's experiment was able to meet any of these preliminary specifications, and we are content to await proper demonstration of these feats before some of the seemingly harder tasks are set. The only remarkable feature of Cornell's demonstration appears to be its success in persuading West, and apparently Gauld too, that it could have created the visual effects they witnessed as visitors.

Cornell has claimed to have had more experience of physical mediumship phenomena than has anyone else in the last fifty years, but the phenomena have always been in control conditions he considers inadequate to provide proof that anything paranormal happened. But by the same token these conditions equally fail to provide evidence that it did not. He did not have the benefit of a sitting at Scole and has not attempted to respond to the several challenges posed in our conclusions. Nor, regrettably, did he make any attempt to seek or respond to our proffered help in testing any of his hypotheses under something approaching the conditions in which they were demonstrated to us in our sittings. We have pointed out that there can be nothing inherently paranormal in any film. That makes it all the more important to seek to replicate not just the results but the circumstances attaching to the appearance of the phenomena.

The fact that equipment was provided by the Group rather than the experimenters has been cited as constituting a significant weakening of proper experimental procedure. This may be so in theory, although we were asked to provide the original amplifier to attach to the germanium gadget, and did so; but in practice there was very little equipment involved. The principal items were the electrically operated machine for developing 35mm Polaroid film donated by Polaroid and examined carefully by the investigators; a Panasonic tape recorder which was not only examined and tested by the investigators before the highly successful experiment in the transmission of music and voice-over, but which we were urged (at the 16th August 1997 sitting) to take away and get expertly examined with the aid of the manufacturer's wiring code. Such items as a ping-pong ball, a translucent kitchen bowl or a glued-up glass tank were standard items whose origin and ownership must surely be accepted as irrelevant.

Both West and Gauld have complained that the investigators failed to examine all normal possibilities when describing apparently paranormal phenomena; others have protested that we have spent far too much time in detailed examination of a fraud hypothesis for the benefit of those unwilling to accept any evidence they have not personally experienced. We are not aware that we have somehow traded on the authoritative qualities of those present. It is not unreasonable to point to the qualifications and experience of observers and investigators.

We have already made clear that, contrary to West's understanding, several films *were* successfully produced before the Scole box was made, and we have also noted elsewhere the occasions when much laxer controls failed to produce a successful film. We must agree, in the light of events, that it would certainly have been desirable to mark the rolls of films themselves, rather than just their containers, even when the latter had some form of seal over their cap and were under the control of an investigator throughout. This was certainly discussed informally with the Group, on a belt-and-braces policy, but we understood that there was some concern, whether by them or by the Team we cannot be certain, that handling the film itself might impart something of the handler's own energies, presumably on the same basis that the 'vibes' of owners of personal objects are said to be susceptible to psychometry by mediums, a phenomenon first recorded nearly 160 years ago. Because other security measures appeared adequate, we therefore believed that this additional safeguard was not essential, although Walter Schnittger did mark the film itself (albeit only after its removal from the locked box: he had concluded that substitution was a greater risk during the development process than during a period when the box containing the film and tub was under his physical control throughout the evening). It was not the case that we were positively forbidden by the Team to open and tamper with the films before they were sealed in bags or boxes.

Magicians and illusionists, West argues, could hardly devise better circumstances for their tricks. That may well be a commonly held opinion, but it is scarcely consistent with the prior and post examination of the séance room and of the limited range of equipment employed; with the construction and subsequent adaptation of the germanium gadget by or under the direction of both a professor of electrical engineering and

315

Walter Schnittger, an automotive engineer; with requests by the purported illusionists that those investigating them use only films bought and handled entirely by the investigators themselves; with a willingness to use security bags sealed and opened by the investigators; or with the readiness of all members of the Group to wear luminous wristbands, any perceived movement of which would be inconsistent with the relative immobility of a trance condition by both mediums.

The fact is that working in the dark can be as great a handicap to an illusionist as it undoubtedly is to the investigators, unless he can not only equip himself with an infra-red viewing device or thermal image enhancer but use them undetected. There is no evidence that any such device was ever used, and we have been at pains to point to cases where it could hardly have been possible without the almost certain peril of discovery, especially during sittings in flimsy summer dresses or shirt-sleeves and shorts. An adequately compact thermal imaging device capable of enabling the operator to see clearly for a metre or two in total darkness would, we have been told, cost anywhere between £3,000 and £10,000.

Nor is it the case that "simple procedures that would have served to provide sound evidence were repeatedly and consistently refused." At the outset the investigators introduced the concept of security bags for films likely to remain at Scole between sittings, and this was welcomed by the communicating Team. It was a communicator who said that we should buy our own films and not use the stock left by Polaroid with the Foys. The Team raised no objection to the use of an entirely different type of film which we bought. There was no objection to DF's four-point protocol. There were no restrictions placed on the manner in which two boxes, when they were used together for film work, were to be juxtaposed. In the second of the two Ibiza sittings MK was allowed to put the extracted blank films anywhere and anyhow. He could have placed them on his lap had he wished. Indeed a study of the transcripts of our early sittings does little to bear out West's impression. Regrettable though the ban on infra-red equipment was, it followed precedent of most such circles, as Cornell's experience shows.

Gauld has reasonably spelled out the sort of minimum requirements compliance with which would appear to defeat the theory of deception. However, when something begins to approach that standard, a loophole is detected. Take the fish-tank. A light was seen to enter it and later disappear from it. There was no conceivable method of getting into it save by lifting the glued-up sides and top from its moulded base, a task which would have required both hands, not a little effort and the risk amounting to certainty that the observers would notice changes in the position or level of the plate glass enclosure as the lighting device was inserted and subsequently removed, although no device was visible during illumination. It is not adequate to retreat behind the airy assumption that, difficult though it may seem, a skilled illusionist could do it. Please produce the illusionist, and we shall see!

Then we have criticism of the procedure relating to some of the early films, but the fact that one poor-quality film was considered unlikely to reproduce satisfactorily, and appears to have been lost or mislaid by the Foys, who are now lumbered with four years' accumulation of films and tapes and may well have attached little importance to it, does not outweigh the fact that "although the result did not match our qualitative expectations we could find no way in which this procedure could be faulted". Nor has West provided one, unless it is suggested that we invented or imagined what we carefully examined on a large screen. A dog is still a dog though it be in the last stages of emaciating mange.

Rather more serious is the mistaken assertion that when the film tubs were held by the Schnittgers they were using Scole film stock. As we make clear in Appendix D, the 17th January 1997 film in Plate 9 (Dragon) came from Polachrome bought directly from Jessops of Leicester by the Schnittgers. Likewise with the Wie der Staub film (Plate 6).

After quite fairly disparaging the suitability and efficacy of body searches of members of the Group, West makes a sound point when he suggests that an invitation to produce apports inside a sealed container would have been impressive. We agree. We ourselves experienced very few apports, and only one (two small pieces of metal provided for AE to measure for an unspecified purpose) was found inside a container, the glass dome, which would probably have required two hands to lift safely. All we can confidently say of the large number reported to have appeared before our investigation started is that the *Daily Mail,* if fraudulent, must have been securely wrapped in a light-proof and substantially airtight package for almost exactly 50 years.

Some of our own reservations about the conduct or preferences of the Team are endorsed in West's comments: their methods did not reflect what we could reasonably have expected of former SPR luminaries, but we must point out that we had every expectation that the experiments would continue, and that attempts at new and the replication of old experiments would be possible. But, disappointing and confusing though such shortcomings were, they do not show that the entire range of phenomena were fraudulent. All they do is to provide new ontological puzzles in the debate between the survival and the super-psi explanations. The final terminated messages reported to have been conveyed to the Group, not by the regular Team, with whom they had lost contact, was not material to our investigation and ought not to be imported as a retrospective slur on it.

There is a further complaint: that we made little mention of the views of people like West or Professor Robert Morris, "who expressed reservations on the basis of their experiences." That is partly because no such reservations were expressed to us at the time, although there were some useful suggestions made for modifying the protocol, and partly because there were a number of sitters who have conveyed more positive impressions. Their reports will be among the supplementary papers to be deposited with the Society. We were looking for evidence of deception or suggestions from fellow sitters as to how various phenomena might have been created normally. We looked in vain.

Finally, West considers that the "ready accessibility" of information on the film images renders the long chapters devoted to them largely worthless as evidence. But by no means all of the contents of the films were readily accessible; some appear not to have been accessible at all. Examples are the initials on the technical sketch film which proved to be recognisably similar to the initialled signature of Thomas Edison; and the German poem (see footnote at the end of Chapter V).

In any event, the argument that ready accessibility for much of the material presupposes fraud, implies that the same must go for the considerable weight of oral evidence which shows every sign of having been a spontaneous response to questions raised by investigators, some of it requiring not a little technical knowledge. If the totality of the evidence rules out fraud as a universal explanation for all the phenomena and all the oral messages, which we believe most detached readers will find themselves forced to conclude, then there can be no legitimate complaint about the space we have devoted to this material.

Finally we must deplore the manner in which some of our critics have steadfastly ignored some of the most impressive evidence where it comes from the testimony of the Schnittgers or Hans Schaer; backed up for the main part by contemporaneous tape recordings. This implies that their testimony is false, since much of it simply cannot be written off with the usual evasive dismissals wearisomely employed by sceptics: misperception, inattention, misdirection, etc. The fraud hypothesis must rest firmly on the assumption that these collaborating investigators have falsified their evidence. There is a point beyond which honest doubt becomes obstinate rejection. We feel our critics may have passed it.

Professor Ellison wishes to make two additional points, both of them supported by his co-authors, as a footnote to the above:–

Dr Gauld's view that the method of production of the various physical items was just as expected if they had been 'normally' produced, i.e. fraudulent, has been substantially answered, but the same applies in even more detail to the acoustic productions. These show all the characteristics of having been produced in a normal room by a sound engineer, including the various adjustments which would have to have been made. This puzzled me until I realised that this is just what might have been expected for a physical production. Putative discarnate sound engineers would not be expected to have powers of immediately getting the volume right, etc., without adjustment. Why should they? The communicators did not at any time appear to be infallible and their experiments were often not successful. It is important to realise that we really had little idea of what was going on to produce the results we experienced. But it certainly does appear, at least to me, to be genuinely paranormal, for all the reasons already emphasised.

May I add a final point? I have given considerable thought to why we three, rather than others also having considerable experience, were selected and invited to attend (as observers, it must be remembered). I think that the reason may be because we had particular psychological characteristics likely to make us catalysts rather then inhibitors. (The 'Experimenter Effect' is surely sufficiently well established to be taken into account.) All three of us knew from experience that paranormal phenomena did sometimes take place, i.e. they were not beyond our 'boggle threshold'. I think also that we would all be considered open-minded and objective 'scientists', and also warm and friendly individuals. As the Scole Group were also warm and friendly, the proceedings took place in an atmosphere likely, in my experience at least, to produce success.

The communicators, it should be remembered, selected us, and they did appear to have a pretty good idea what conditions were likely to lead to success. And they presumably felt that our reputations were such that we should not be considered naïve. I cannot imagine any such group inviting to regular sessions well-known sceptics, valuable though their suggestions often are and certainly were to us.

REFERENCES

Appleyard, B. (1999) Life after death. *The Sunday Times, 27th June.*

Gauld, A. (1997) Report on a sitting with the Scole Group on 24th January 1997. (Unpublished).

Keen, M. (1999) Letter (unpublished) dated 21st May 1999 to A. Cornell.

SCOLE: ADDITIONAL RESPONSE

by David Fontana

Monty Keen and Arthur Ellison have responded appropriately to each of the criticisms levelled at the Report, and I have no intention of exhausting the reader's patience by going over the same ground. My concern is simply to supplement what they have said by emphasizing a few additional points which counter these criticisms (although we had supposed that many of these points were already adequately argued in the text). Mindful of the fact that Professor West, Dr Gauld and Tony Cornell do not have an opportunity to reply to me, I must in fairness confine myself to remarks which I trust are not unduly contentious.

Professor West

Professor West's thoughtful critique is welcome. He re-emphasizes the weaknesses in our protocols detailed in the Report, and shows a due understanding of the difficulties that we – in common with many of those before us – have faced when investigating physical phenomena. The crux of the difficulty is that those who produce the phenomena, whether mediums or their supposed spirit helpers, often dictate the conditions under which they can or cannot work. Understandably this is anathema to the scientist, who likes to control all the variables in an experiment, leaving him or her to concentrate solely upon those under direct investigation. However, past history indicates that, except in relatively rare circumstances (which it must be said have still failed to impress the sceptics), such rigour is unobtainable in what we might for convenience call the séance room. Those responsible for producing séance room phenomena, whether we attribute these phenomena to mediums or to the spirits they claim work through them, insist that they know the conditions under which they can and cannot work.

In many other areas of human endeavour, such insistence is accepted as a matter of course. No one supposes that writers, poets, musicians and others who practise the creative arts could produce their best work if they were told by outsiders the precise conditions under which they must labour. And if we have learnt anything from the century and more of investigation undertaken by this Society, it is that mediumship is much closer to an art than to a science. Thus investigators are confronted by a dilemma. Generally they are present in the séance room as invited guests rather than as major-domos. Should they then insist upon their protocols, at the cost of blank sittings or even exclusion from the séance room, or should they accept the status quo and study what is on offer?

Opinions must be divided on this. I respect the views of those who consider that if all variables cannot be controlled, and all natural explanations for phenomena ruled out, then psychical researchers must ignore the séance room. I also respect the views of those who argue that we must, whatever the shortcomings, continue to explore psi wherever it is said to occur. If I may draw an analogy from my own subject, psychology, the former views are comparable to those of experimental psychologists who confine their endeavours to the psychology laboratory, while the latter are more akin to those of counselling, occupational, educational and other applied psychologists, who work with real people in the real world. Both approaches have in their different ways been vitally important to the development of the subject, and when antagonisms and suspicions are set aside, psychologists in both camps learn a great deal from each other. Similarly, parapsychologists working in the laboratory can learn from those working in the field and vice versa. No subject that studies human behaviour can properly advance if it refuses to observe people in the context in which they live and work.

However, it is obviously important that those who conduct research in the field control those variables that are susceptible to control, and observe and record those variables that are not. Provided they are meticulous in presenting their data, avoid unsupported conclusions, draw attention to shortcomings where they exist and provide the detail needed for others to identify any additional shortcomings, their work is worth attention, both for the information it contains and, as Professor West rightly points out, for the help this information can provide to those attempting similar research in the future.

The investigation of physical phenomena, once a major concern of this Society, has always been, and is likely to remain, a difficult area for the investigator. The common-sense view that such things as the paranormal levitation of objects, spirit lights, materializations, direct voices etc. cannot happen means that securing conviction in those without first-hand experience of the phenomena concerned is particularly difficult. For many such people, physical phenomena cannot be other than the result of fraud. But much of science – and particularly of parapsychology – works upon the basis of probabilities. Put simply, science asks "what is the probability that an effect is due to the variable under investigation rather than to other variables?".

Ideally, the scientist seeks to control as many of these other variables as possible, but even when comprehensive control proves impractical as in the case of physical phenomena, the question of probability still remains central – in the present instance the probability that the observed effects were due to paranormality rather than to fraud. The results cannot be subjected to statistical analysis as in laboratory work, and more is left to individual judgement (and perhaps consensus) than to scientific appraisal, but this does not alter the fact that we must still assess the balance of probabilities.

To help such assessment the concluding chapter of the Report contains a summary of the various skills, subterfuges, equipment and physical gymnastics in which the Scole Group would have had to engage if fraud were present. If the reader is already convinced that physical phenomena are impossible, then the conclusion will always be that in spite of all counter indications the balance tips against a paranormal explanation, but to enter the debate with such prior conviction prevents an unbiased weighing of the evidence. Lack of bias demands a degree of openness towards the evidence for paranormality, wherever that evidence may occur.

In the present instance, the reader must decide whether or not the shortcomings in protocol – which as Professor West acknowledges were not of our choosing (and which the Scole group insisted were not of theirs) – are sufficient to invalidate over 200 man-hours of careful observation and the many safeguards that did in fact operate.

Dr Gauld

Dr Gauld's critique commences with the assurance that he is concerned only "with the acceptability or otherwise of the evidence presented in the Scole Report", and is not levelling accusations of hoaxing or fraud against any of those involved. By 'acceptable' one assumes he means acceptable as evidence for the occurrence of para-normal phenomena, and it follows from this that if the evidence is unacceptable the alternative hypothesis of hoaxing must follow, since – as Dr Gauld himself appears to accept – hoaxing is the only possible alternative. By refraining from accusations of hoaxing he therefore appears to come down on the side of acceptability or at least in a position of neutrality, with the case undecided either way.

After reading through the rest of his carefully reasoned critique it seems to me that the arguments in favour of the hoaxing hypothesis indeed fail to amount to a convincing case. In essence these arguments, as summarised by Dr Gauld, rest upon five main pieces of what he describes as indirect evidence, and it is worth looking at each of these in turn and offering some relevant comment.

1 *The vulnerability of the Alan box in which some of the films were placed.* As indicated in the Report, we did not witness Dr Gauld opening the lid of the locked box without fracturing the security seals, but assuming that this feat was possible, we must bear in mind (as Dr Gauld rightly and fairly does and as Monty Keen and Arthur Ellison argue in more detail) that the security of the box was protected during the sitting by safeguards other than the integrity of the lid. Before the evidence obtained in connection with the box can be discounted, it must therefore

be demonstrated that the lid could be opened and closed, undetected, while these various safeguards operate. As this has not been done, the fact that the box proved vulnerable in conditions bearing no resemblance to those of the sittings carries little real weight.

2 *Some of the images on the films "reveal a particular method of manufacture".* Having sought to argue that some (a few) images bore signs of "a particular method of manufacture", Dr Gauld goes on to say that the counter argument offered in our Report that "It is the circumstances in which the images are produced that constitute the evidence for paranormality" skirts round the real point. With respect it does nothing of the kind. Any evidence for the paranormality of the film images resides far more in the circumstances of production than in the actual images themselves. Good circumstances of production and poor images are immeasurably more convincing than poor circumstances and good images.

3 *Some of the images are taken from recognizable sources.* Dr Gauld regards this as suspicious, but I disagree. The Scole Group made clear to us from the outset that their communicators specifically stated that many of the images appearing on the films were from existing sources. The Group themselves were indefatigable in hunting down these sources, seeing them in effect as examples of the 'puzzles' that their communicators seemed to enjoy setting. Thus there is nothing particularly suspicious *per se* in Dr Gauld's discovery that the images in the Dragon film came from a book known to him. Dr Gauld nevertheless attempts to justify his position by proposing that:–

> If one asks oneself how it would be most convenient for an intending hoaxer to proceed in such a matter, one surely has to agree that his most economical policy would be to take some not too excessively common book with suitable illustrations and trace parts of those illustrations in such a way that a casual reader of the book would be unlikely to spot the source of the derived film images. In other words the hoax hypothesis would predict pretty much the kind of features that the Dragon film possesses.

In advancing this proposal Dr Gauld seems to depart from the admirably objective approach that characterizes the rest of his critique by advancing conjecture as established fact (" . . . one surely has to agree . . . "). I would counter that the most economical policy would simply be to supply freehand drawings of one's own invention (or of recognizable symbols if one wished to imply gravitas). Why go to the trouble of tracings when the merest squiggles, if surrounded by all the other elaborate deceptions which the fraud hypothesis has to presume, would do perfectly well?

4 *A major part of the supposed communications from deceased SPR members contain material reasonably accessible in the public domain.* This is an important criticism, and we draw attention in our concluding

chapter to our own disappointment that the communicators did not supply more obscure information. There is no way in which this criticism can be turned aside, as it is a simple statement of fact. However, Dr Gauld's contention that "The knowledge and perspective of these spirits are supposedly to varying degrees in advance of our own" (and therefore by implication that they should, if genuine, have known better than to give familiar material) can be disputed. Assuming that survival is possible, we have no sure way of knowing how much of earth memories are retained, and what problems may present themselves when communicating these memories. The inadequacy of human memory is all too evident within our own lives. I have written well over 100 scientific papers and articles and produced more than 20 books, and in spite of reasonably good powers of recall I would be hard pressed to remember details of more than a small proportion of this material. If called upon when in the next world to give references to something I have written many years ago, I fear I would fall back on one of my better known books, since it would contain the writings with which I am currently, and therefore likely to remain, most familiar.

Of course, we cannot argue that these supposed communications from former SPR worthies prove the continuing existence of the gentlemen concerned, and then hide behind the defence that the inadequacy of these communications simply tells us that the communicators have faulty memories. But at the very least we should perhaps pause before we assume (as Dr Gauld may be implying) that any sign of fallibility on the part of the communicators *automatically* casts doubt on their reality.

5 *The inadequate controls operated by the investigators.* We make clear in the Report where our controls fell short of those we requested, and there no need for me to add to this information or to the points emphasized by Monty Keen and Arthur Ellison in their response. Ultimately, the question is whether or not those controls and the circumstances that obtained were sufficient to suggest that the balance of probabilities weighs against hoaxing.

However, it is important to respond to Dr Gauld's assertion that "you have to find ways of defeating the hoax hypothesis by producing evidence that defies explanation in terms of currently accepted scientific and technological principles. We might call such evidence 'ostensibly infrangible' ". I doubt if at any time in the history of this Society 'infrangible' evidence for physical phenomena has been obtained (if it were obtained it might well, in any case, challenge 'currently accepted scientific and technological principles'). Nevertheless, this has not prevented respected investigators from publishing evidence which is worthy of serious consideration and from reaching personal conviction. Dr Gauld himself tells us elsewhere in his critique that he is "not by any means a total disbeliever in the paranormal phenomena associated with physical mediumship", and we must assume he regards this position as tenable even in the absence of infrangible evidence. In fact he wrote nearly 30 years ago that certain brief experiences of physical phenomena which he had obtained at the time and which he carefully detailed (Gauld, 1971), although insufficient to be presented to others "as providing evidence for the reality of physical phenomena", had nevertheless "for ever cured me of any tendencies I may once have possessed or might otherwise have developed towards a merely armchair scepticism with regard to such matters".

In view of this openness I am unclear why Dr Gauld should write in his critique that the authors of the Report "in effect rely for their defence of the possible genuineness of the phenomena on the fact that they are themselves unable to explain in normal terms certain of the happenings which took place in their presence . . . the whole history of physical mediumship and its investigation shows this to be an insufficient defence . . . " In the absence of what Dr Gauld would consider infrangible evidence our main concern was not to defend or attack any particular point of view but to present the evidence as we found it. However, there is nothing amiss with a defence based upon the fact that investigators are unable to offer alternative explanations for their findings. Much of scientific discovery depends upon just such a defence. It is then for others to test this defence by attempting to demonstrate, using the same experimental conditions, that such alternatives do in fact exist. In the absence of such an attempt there is a risk that alternative explanations amount to little more than the 'armchair scepticism' which Dr Gauld rightly rejects.

Tony Cornell

Many of the above observations apply also to Tony Cornell's critique. As a highly experienced investigator his views deserve attention, and although (as he concedes) many of his criticisms are already dealt with in the Report, re-emphasising them helps indicate the difficulties facing researchers in this field, and provides further guidance for the future. However he could have mentioned another difficulty, one that is in fact made apparent by his own critique, namely that what may appear satisfactory to observers of physical phenomena seems much less so to those who merely read about it. The immediate and understandable reaction of the reader is to think up normal explanations. Discussing Scole recently with a good friend and colleague who is also an accomplished magician I was asked to consider such possibilities as hidden threads attached to crystals, and accomplices dark of clothes and motives creeping unseen and unheard around and under the table. My friend had not at that point had an opportunity to read the Report, and his reaction was perfectly understandable. But had we not considered these and many other possibilities both at the time and subsequently, we would have had no right to put together this Report.

Speaking personally, in addition to practical experience of physical phenomena in various settings, I have been an attentive reader of the literature on possible séance room fraud, from Houdini's *A Magician Among the Spirits* (strangely unsatisfactory at every level) and Carrington's *The Physical Phenomena of Spiritualism* (still an excellent introduction) to the recent debate on Palladino in our own *Journal*. I am also well aware of what can be done with LEDs, with fibre optics, with lasers, with extending rods, with inflatable artifacts, with hidden threads, with pseudopods, with trapdoors, with accomplices, with secret panels, with misdirection, with obfuscation and with the various other devices and subterfuges that could in theory be introduced into the séance room in order to mislead the archetypal gullible scientist. Professor Ellison and Monty Keen are equally if not more experienced and knowledgeable. Thus the least that can be said is that the Scole investigation started from a base of séance room literacy rather than illiteracy.

Our level of relative sophistication weighs against Tony's suggestion that "we were so enthralled by the dramatic performance of it all in the dark" that we accepted everything without sufficient question. I must also take issue with him on his statement that "The authors make it plain that by and large they are of the view that the physical phenomena they experienced at Scole were produced by paranormal means". Whatever our private views, the thing we in fact make plain in the Report is that as scientists it is our job to present the evidence and to leave others to draw their own conclusions from it.

Tony is also in error in many important points of detail, but these have been addressed by Monty Keen, and repetition is unnecessary. Some of these errors of detail are largely understandable in that through no fault of his own Tony was unable to attend any of the sittings. The fact that he has shown such a keen interest throughout the investigation in spite of this inability deserves particular thanks, and by identifying the kind of misgivings that others who were not at the sittings may have – and thus allowing us to offer comprehensive answers to them – he has performed a valuable service.

General Comments

Overall, I am a little disappointed that none of the three critiques addresses the conditions, summarised in the conclusion to our Report, that would have had to be satisfied were hoaxing the explanation for the Scole phenomena. In effect, the authors of the critiques put a question mark against the honesty of members of the Scole Group without direct evidence that dishonesty took place and without discussion of how, given the conditions of the sittings, such dishonesty could have been perpetrated regularly and without detection during the four years in which the Group operated. Dr Gauld reports that he has known the leader of the Group, Robin Foy, for 30 years "without finding any reason to regard him as anything other than totally sincere", which suggests that if hoaxing took place Dr Gauld may prefer to attribute it to Diana and Alan, the two mediums. This being so, he must assume that not only would they have had to deceive the investigators and the many others who had sittings with the Group at home and abroad, they would have had to deceive the highly experienced Foys twice a week for the four years, importing clandestinely on each occasion into the séance room the various pieces of (probably expensive and perhaps bulky) equipment needed to carry out their subterfuge. They would also have had to conceal the presence of an accomplice (ideally elsewhere in the building) to assist with the radio transmissions.

On the question of motive, Dr Gauld writes that "we can never know enough about people's motives, character, etc. to rule out the hoax hypothesis on this basis". In theory this is true, but in practice social and professional life, to say nothing of our legal system, depends upon sifting the evidence for motive and character, and making judgements accordingly. As we make clear in our Report, in the present instance we can rule out financial gain (the mediums indignantly rejected the offer of financial assistance from the SPR, and along with the Foys were considerably out-of-pocket as a result of their work) and publicity-seeking (they sought to remain anonymous). To this we can add the fact that throughout our investigation we never at any time had cause to doubt the complete integrity of any member of the Scole group. Thus against our knowledge of the absence of apparent motive and our knowledge of the presence of good character, Dr Gauld sets his 'disinterested deception'. Again on the balance of possibilities, the reader must decide on which side of the debate he prefers to place himself.

Dr Gauld ends his critique with a reference to the "gratuitously unkind press comments" to which the Scole Group has been subjected. I presume he is referring to the article in *The Sunday Times* of 27th June, and if so he might have added that such comments were not only unkind but for the most part either incorrect or misleadingly incomplete (as I make clear in Issue 12 of *The Paranormal Review*). He might also have added that the article demonstrates graphically how criticisms such as those he himself voices can be misrepresented by the media in order to discredit serious psychical research of the kind detailed in our Report.

REFERENCE

Gauld, A. (1971) A series of 'drop in' communicators. *ProcSPR* 55, 204 (whole issue).

COMMENTS ON AN EXAMPLE OF
TRADITIONAL RESEARCH

by Maurice Grosse

I was involved in the original discussions and decision to investigate the claims of the Scole Group. This arose because of my position as a Council member of the SPR and a founder member of the PRISM Council.

I attended the first presentation of the Scole photographic material to members of PRISM at the headquarters of the National Spiritualists' Union, Stansted. Following this presentation, I suggested that what I had heard and seen from the Scole members might relate to poltergeist-type phenomena. This remark angered the group to such an extent that I was barred from any participation in Scole activity. However, I took a great interest in the progress my colleagues were making at the Scole sittings, and from time to time I made suggestions regarding the protocol that I thought should be carried out by the authors of the report.

In order to make it quite clear that I was not hostile to the Scole group or the investigation because I had been barred from séances, I did at one time offer financial help to the group to enable them to continue their sittings. This offer was conveyed to them by Montague Keen, but was refused. During the whole of this investigation I was kept up to date with the activity the authors were experiencing. I was very much aware, as were the authors, of the weaknesses surrounding some of the control conditions. These weaknesses were the subject of long discussion both during and outside PRISM meetings. We knew that criticisms would be aimed at the investigators, especially regarding the lack of adequate illumination, but we all agreed that we should press on with the investigation regardless of the restrictions placed on the investigators.

To suggest that the three authors of this report, who incidentally are among the most experienced and knowledgeable investigators in psychical research, are naïve and unaware of the possibilities for deceit is frankly absurd. The critics are using the well-worn tactic of taking individual episodes, examining them for deception, and then assuming they are tricks because it is possible that they could be. This shows a basic misunderstanding of the whole process of paranormal activity. This type of criticism is invariably aimed at well-authenticated poltergeist-type activity, much to the chagrin of the unfortunate victims. It is imperative that a balanced view is taken of all the reported activity as a whole. If in consequence the consensus of opinion is that it is impossible to explain all of the experiences in a logical manner, then by definition some of the activity is illogical. There is no doubt in my mind that in some of the séances, especially those that took place away from Scole's own territory, the chance for deliberate deceit was very slim. When assessing the evidence, critics should be mindful of the fact that nobody was ever caught cheating. That in itself is significant, considering the number of séances that took place and the remarks of critical observers who claimed that some of the antics of the phenomena were physically impossible to reproduce.

Alan Gauld's critique of the Scole investigation gives a detailed personal analysis of the contents, and is sometimes dismissive of the protocol and conclusions drawn. However, many of his criticisms are as much a product of conjecture as the contents of the report he criticises. Originally the protocol certainly gave me some concern, but it became clear that, if the investigation was to continue, the rules were largely in the hands of the 'communicators'. The investigators accepted this, and consequently were even more alert to deception. I believe they were correct in doing so, considering the quantity and quality of the anomalous phenomena experienced.

This report is of great importance to the cause of psychical research. It follows the best tradition of the Society in presenting a particular branch of research that has been sadly neglected by investigators for many years. In the annals of the history of our Society, and particularly with early members who were distinguished scientists, investigators never shrank from publishing reports on various aspects of investigations and procedures. Under difficult circumstances the authors are carrying on that tradition.

25 Woodberry Crescent
Muswell Hill, London   N10 1PJ

REFEREE'S REPORT AND
SOME SUBSEQUENT COMMENTS

by Crawford Knox

I first became aware of the Scole Report when, in his letter of 1st March 1999, Dr Beloff wrote to me to ask if I would act as referee for its suitability for publication in the *SPR Proceedings*. I had to phone the SPR office to enquire as to its nature. My reply as referee dated 16th March follows. I omit only a final paragraph making some detailed points that are no longer relevant and some personal words to Dr Beloff.

You asked me to act as referee for the Scole Report. I have read it with some care but I have not attempted to scrutinise critically every statement or claim in the report or all the evidence offered for each of the many phenomena reported: nor would I wish to be taken as endorsing everything the authors say. This said, however, I offer the following conclusions:–

1 The report is long, detailed and clearly presented and demands, I believe, to be taken very seriously.

2 If it is read as a *whole*, I think it is likely that it will mark an important step in attempts to place on a firm footing evidence for the existence of a spirit world and its impact on our everyday world and for survival of death.

3 The phenomena reported over the 36–7 sessions are very diverse in character and in large measure free-standing in the sense that doubts cast on one particular session or phenomenon or class of phenomena do not necessarily cast doubt on the wide range of others. The significant number of observers of integrity also adds to its credibility.

4 When the report is considered as a whole, as it needs to be,this very diversity, of itself, makes it very difficult to dismiss it as a product of fraud or hoaxing, and when to this is added the highly technical character of the many processes involved, the difficulty of imagining any way in which fraud could have been perpetrated over this wide range of phenomena, the lack of any obvious motive, the safeguards that were in place, and the personal integrity of the investigators and, I have no reason to doubt, the group, I believe that we have no sensible choice but to receive this report at face value (within the limits of human fallibility) and subject it to close scrutiny to discern what we can about the communicators and processes involved and its wider implications.

5 In the very nature of the range of phenomena concerned, I consider that this is not the kind of report whose strength is dependent

on the strength of the weakest link. As the report recognises, some phenomena were more firmly based than others and some, taken in isolation, might have had a natural explanation: but a natural explanation does not preclude a supernatural explanation, and the phenomena all need to be seen in the context of the circumstances of that particular occasion and of the sequence as a whole. It is the evidence as a whole and its *strongest* evidence that should be given most weight, as this should allow us to view less sceptically other evidence that just might have a natural explanation.

6 As the report recognises, further safeguards against fraud or hoaxing would have been desirable. The absence of light is the most obvious, and, as is clear from the appendices, potential critics would, no doubt, have wished to add further safeguards, probably to the point of being counterproductive. But those options are not, and mostly were not, open and what is before us is a report of what occurred.

Following this I was given copies of the correspondence which had by then taken place and wrote to Montague Keen on 19th April. The essence of the letter was in the following two paragraphs:–

I believe that your report is very important, but it does (of course) give rise to further questions, in particular about the identity of the communicators and 'the team' behind them. You said that you hoped to publish more on this in due course and I look forward to this. When we spoke, I referred to a letter that I wrote to the editor of the *JSPR* of October 1982 which raised the problem of the spectrum of communicators, ranging at the one extreme from the 'quasi-personalities' such as Hodgson's 'Sir Walter Scott' and 'Philip' to seemingly authentic communicators like Mrs Willett in *Swan on a Black Sea* and Myers himself in *The Road to Immortality*. But the latter itself raises puzzles as the second volume, *Beyond Human Personality*, raises greater doubts. The same issue arises on the recent purported communications from Raynor Johnson through Sheila Gwillam. . . .

The other issue that I keep meeting is the way in which work in all fields that brings into question current ways of looking at the world is seen, even by those who might be expected to welcome it, as so threatening that it has to be opposed by all means, rational and irrational. On this, you may recall the review by Theodore Rockwell of the *Spindrift Papers* in the *JASPR* (October 1993) which shows the problems that its authors met and discusses this problem of communication with reference, in particular, to work by Deborah Tannen. There was further correspondence on the *Spindrift Papers* in the *JASPR* of January 1996.

I received further copies of correspondence and wrote to Dr Beloff on 17th June as follows:–

It appears that what is at issue here goes far beyond the Scole Report itself and goes to the very nature of parapsychology. I believe the issues raised by Alan's criticisms are therefore of importance and deserve, and will I hope receive, wide discussion in their own right.

Broadly, since the 1930s parapsychology has modelled itself on the hard sciences and has increasingly tightened and elaborated its experimental protocols. The results have been important, but in the absence of any wider explanatory paradigm within which the results can find a home, they have had little wider impact. The result, however, has been that parapsychology has tended to concentrate on those phenomena to which the rigorous protocols can be applied, and a wide range of other phenomena, which do not lend themselves to such treatment, have tended to be regarded as of peripheral interest. More importantly, when reports of such wider phenomena have forced themselves to attention, they have tended to be viewed by some critics, not on their own merits, but by the standards of experimental protocols inappropriate to them.

In my view, Alan's approach, while valid in some cases, is not appropriate to the Scole report. In contrast, I believe a new approach is emerging which is no less rigorous but less restrictive. It is to be found, for example, in Robert Almeder's book *Death and Personal Survival* where he takes issue with critics of investigations of such wider phenomena as Ian Stevenson's work on reincarnation. In your own review of that book, you describe it as a very good book indeed which should be compulsory reading for anyone wishing to argue the case for or against survival, and you note that in the strongest cases, nothing less than a widespread conspiracy to tell lies for no apparent reason would have to be assumed if we want to retain a normal explanation. This seems to me to apply to the Scole report.

In these circumstances there emerges clearly this much wider issue about the future of parapsychology and the entire way in which it is to be viewed. I believe that it is only by looking very widely that a new explanatory paradigm is likely to emerge. This is an issue of concern to people literally worldwide and the Scole report is only one, though an important, example to which this issue applies. In my view, such a wider discussion would warrant a separate volume of the *Proceedings* to which many might wish to contribute.

To this I would add only that because the 36–7 sessions and the very diverse phenomena are not closely linked, one could eliminate a significant proportion of them and still be left with virtually the same problem of explaining them. I found, and still find, no evidence of cheating or hoaxing, but, in this context, whether or not there was marginal cheating or hoaxing does not really matter.

Lightning Source UK Ltd.
Milton Keynes UK
UKOW030739211011

180674UK00001B/31/P